Prince of the Press

The cities and towns of Oppenheim's network, 1664–1736 (Bill Nelson)

Prince of the Press

How One Collector Built History's
Most Enduring and Remarkable
Jewish Library

Joshua Teplitsky

Yale

UNIVERSITY PRESS
New Haven & London

Published with assistance from the Annie Burr Lewis Fund and from the foundation established in memory of James Wesley Cooper of the Class of 1865, Yale College.

Yale University Press books may be purchased in quantity for educational, business, or promotional use. For information, please e-mail sales.press@yale.edu (U.S. office) or sales@yaleup.co.uk (U.K. office).

Set in Bulmer type by Tseng Information Systems, Inc.
Printed in the United States of America.

Library of Congress Control Number: 2018944524
ISBN 978-0-300-23490-9 (hardcover : alk. paper)

A catalogue record for this book is available from the British Library.

This paper meets the requirements of ANSI/NISO z39.48-1992 (Permanence of Paper).

10 9 8 7 6 5 4 3 2 1

For my parents, with love

. . . of making many books there is no end.
—Ecclesiastes 12:12

Contents

Acknowledgments

PERHAPS THE GREATEST LESSON I have learned from a study of the many worlds of books is the great number of people who contribute to any finished, published work. Behind every printed book stands colleagues and confidants, astute and generous critics, gracious funders, and friends whose impact on a finished project is palpable to the author at every page, even when it is not readily apparent to readers. It is my pleasure to take this opportunity to thank some of the colleagues and friends who lent their intellectual and moral support to this work, without which it could not have been written.

This project began as a doctoral thesis at New York University under the supervision of David Engel, who agreed to guide a project far from his own area of specialization, with the promise to prod my thinking and challenge my responses. He never wavered in that commitment, and I have learned much from his incisive questions and the "lifetime service contract" that comes with being his student. Elisheva Carlebach has been a constant source of wisdom and mentorship from long before the dissertation began, through the many stages of the writing of this book, and beyond. I am grateful for her unflagging support and the care and kindness that she perennially extends. My thanks to the Department of Hebrew and Judaic Studies and the Department of History at NYU, and to the faculty and staff there who contributed to the intellectual climate that first shaped this project. Hasia Diner, who has been supportive of my scholarship and the progress of this book, has my particular appreciation as well.

Although this book is based on a dissertation, it was significantly rewritten in large part during my time at the University of Oxford as the Albert and Rachel Lehmann Junior Research Fellow in Jewish History and Culture at the Oxford Centre for Hebrew and Jewish Studies and St. Peter's College, Oxford. My thanks to the members of the Lehmann family who made this position, and my time at Oxford, possible to begin with and to my colleagues at Oxford, who welcomed me and provided a rich intellectual home to expand my horizons and think this project into its current form, including then president of the OCHJS Martin Goodman, Abigail Green, John-Paul Ghobrial, David Parrott, Lyndal Roper, and Giora Sternberg. My special thanks to Derek Penslar, David Rechter, Piet van Boxel, Joanna Weinberg, Miri Freud-Kandel, Adrianna X. Jacobs, Sara Hirschhorn, Shane Macgiollabhui, and Constantinos Repapis, and to Anna Remington and Gabriel Citron, all of whom helped me find a home in the city of dreaming spires. During my tenure there, I had the good fortune to be adopted by the Oxford Seminar in Advanced Jewish Studies, "On the Word of a Jew," convened by Nina Caputo and Mitchell Hart. I am grateful to the members of the seminar for their conviviality.

My enduring appreciation to the staff of the Special Collections Reading Room of the Bodleian Library, which has been home, since 1829, to Oppenheim's entire collection. I particularly thank Cesar Merchan-Hamann and the OCHJS for the invitation to present my findings in the form of the Catherine Lewis Lectures, which shaped much of the structure of this book. Special thanks to Rahel Fronda, who was instrumental in securing the rights for and reproduction of the images that populate the pages of this book.

In the process of researching this book I consulted material from the Jewish Museum in Prague, the Národni Archiv (National Archives), and the Národni Muzeum (National Museum), in Prague; the National Library of Israel and the Central Archives for the History of the Jewish People, Jerusalem; the Library of the Jewish Theological Seminary of America; and the rare book collection of Yeshiva University in New York. My thanks to the staff of all of these institutions who made this precious material available to me.

I thank my colleagues in the History Department at Stony Brook University for welcoming me into their ranks and supporting my work, especially Sara Lipton, who has been both friend and mentor; Gary Marker; Paul Gootenberg; and colleagues in the world of early modern book history Erika Honisch and Douglas Pfeiffer. Travel for researching this book and sharing my work in conferences and workshops was supported by awards from the Research Initiative Grant of the Faculty in the Fine Arts, Humanities, and Lettered Social Sciences; the President's Distinguished Travel Grants; and the UUP Individual Development Awards.

Along the road to completing this book, I have been the beneficiary of kind invitations to share my work and to receive valuable feedback. My thinking about this project was shaped by conversations with Anne Oravetz Albert, Elisheva Baumgarten, Avriel Bar-Levav, Shlomo Berger *z"l*, Jay Berkovitz, Francesca Bregoli, Robert Chazan, Joseph Davis, Yaakov Deutsch, Arye Edrei, Aya Elyada, Shmuel Feiner, Sharon Flatto, Rachel Furst, Yehuda Galinsky, Debra Glasberg Gail, Rachel Greenblatt, Francois Guesnet, Elliot Horowitz *z"l*, Maoz Kahana, Arthur Kiron, Howard Louthan, Verena Kasper Marienberg, Michael Miller, Tamara Morsel-Eisenberg, David Myers, Alexandr Putík, Lucia Raspe, Claudia Rosenzweig, Jacob J. Schacter, Andrea Schatz, Emile Schrijver, David Sclar, Michael Silber, Avi Siluk, Pavel Sládek, Ephraim Shoham-Steiner, Adam Teller, Mirjam Thulin, Chava Turniansky, and Rebekka Voß. Working with three partners on a Digital Humanities project about books-in-motion called "Footprints: Jewish Books Through Time and Place" brought many of the questions of this work into sharp relief, and I thank Michelle Chesner, Marjorie Lehman, and Adam Shear for their ongoing collaborative energies.

This book was completed during a sabbatical leave from teaching thanks to fellowships from the Katz Center for Advanced Judaic Studies at the University of Pennsylvania and the National Library of Israel in Jerusalem. My thanks to Steven Weitzman, Natalie Dohrmann, and the staff of the Katz Center in Philadelphia, as well as to the members of the fellowship year for their feedback to my work. My thanks to the National Library of Israel, particularly Elchanan Reiner, Aviad Stollman, Yoel Finkelman, Amir Schwarz Eisler, and the staff of the reading rooms there. Special thanks to Ted Fram for his official mentorship during this year and his unofficial guidance for several years now. My thanks also to Scott Ury for making a home for me at the Stephen Roth Institute for the Study of Contemporary Antisemitism and Racism at Tel Aviv University.

My thanks to Heather Gold and the staff at Yale University Press for shepherding this book along with care and attention, to Bill Nelson for his creation of a map of Oppenheim's Europe, and to Jessie Dolch for her skillful copyediting of the text.

Sections from Chapter 2 have appeared in *Jewish History* 29 (2015): 245–271, and from Chapter 5 in *Jewish Social Studies* 19, no. 3 (2013): 109–138. I acknowledge the permission of the editors and publishers to use these materials in this book.

Every portion of this book has been read by colleagues and friends, without whom it could not have been written. While I accept full responsibility for its shortcomings, I am proud to thank Rachel Bergstein, Julie Yanofsky-Goldstein, Devi Mays, Lara Rabinovitch, and David Weinfeld. Shira Kohn and Alexander Kaye have been friends, compatriots, and trusted critics of my writing for a long time, and I hope for an even longer time to come. Magda Teter and Debra Kaplan—mentors, colleagues, and friends—have seen this project through many stages and many line-edits. I am fortunate for all of their support.

During my time in Israel, I found a home thanks to the boundless hospitality of Irv and Lynn Shapiro, whom I have come to think of as a second family. They exhibit the purest form of *hachnasat orchim* and were instrumental in creating a space in which the final stages of this book unfolded.

My stay in Israel completing this work was made particularly sweet by the time I spent with family and friends there. I thank my siblings, Aliza, Rachel and Michael Porcelain, and Naomi, for their years as fellow travelers, and my amazing nephew and niece, Kobe and Noa Porcelain, for bringing such joy to my life. My parents, Rosanne and Steven Teplitsky, instilled a love of books and reading in me to rival that of even David Oppenheim's and have indulged that passion ever since. I dedicate this book to them.

Prince of the Press

Introduction

Collecting a library, besides being the unusual thing and far from trivial or vulgar, may turn out to be one of those happy tokens . . . since, being extraordinary, difficult, and of great expense, it cannot but cause everyone to speak well, and with admiration, of him who puts it into effect.
—Gabriel Naudé, *Advice on Establishing a Library,* 1627

IN THE CEMETERY OF THE Prague Jewish community, clear of the cluttered interior of overlaid monuments, a tombstone stands adorned with a Shield of David to invoke the namesake of the man buried beneath: David Oppenheim (1664-1736), Prague's chief rabbi from 1703 until his death. Tourists and visitors to the crowded burial ground can take photos of the monument or pay their respects, but for students of the Jewish past, a second edifice far from Prague memorializes in a more fitting manner the story of this man in history and memory: his formidable library. In the Bodleian Library of the University of Oxford some forty-five hundred books and one thousand manuscripts bear testimony to the insatiable collecting activities of this man in search of a library that would include every Jewish book.[1] Over the course of his lifetime, Oppenheim bought, found, published, and received books and manuscripts from across Europe and the Middle East, many of which carried traces of previous owners and prior journeys of these objects before they found their final resting place upon his shelves.

Oppenheim's library has served scholars of the Jewish past in decisive ways. Medieval manuscripts drawn from its shelves provide the bases for histories of Jewish law and liturgy; small paperback pamphlets fuel research into early modern Yiddish and the genres of popular culture;

historical treatises provide material for inquiries into collective memory; Sabbatean treatises in printed and manuscript form offer insights into mysticism and messianism; works of grammar and lexicology challenge scholars to consider the linguistic dimensions of Jews in ages past; and scientific and mathematical manuals inspire debates over Jews' embrace of the sciences. Attention to the physical material that fills these volumes enthralls as well. Oppenheim idiosyncratically owned books printed on vellum, others bound in rich leather or velvet, and still more printed on colored paper, in hues of blue, orange, yellow, and grey. The illuminations in his books and manuscripts offer ever enticing reasons for this collection's continued draw for scholars. And yet the rich history of their accumulation—an artifact of a particular moment in Jewish history, culture, and politics—has not been told.

David Oppenheim built his library and used its contents from his unique position in Jewish society. He stood at the meeting point of overlapping networks of influential figures from different but connected aspects of early modern Jewish governance, including the noble court, the *kehillah* (Jewish community), and the rabbinate. Oppenheim lived at the high point of the age of the Court Jews (*Hofjuden;* also called *Hoffakotren* or *Hofagenten*), a Jewish elite of wealth and power who dominated the material and social life of Central European Jewry between the Thirty Years War (1618-1648) and the Napoleonic Wars (1803-1815).[2] The members of this class financed the projects of German absolutist princes and their consolidation of centralizing states. As provisioners of war material, securers of loans, and financiers of major building projects, the members of these wealthy Jewish families played a significant role in the formation of modern German politics. But their activities had important implications for Jewish life as well. Their positions at royal and noble courts often made them the unofficial spokesmen for the Jewish communities of the Holy Roman Empire and Habsburg monarchy, advocates for the physical security and material sustenance of their fellow Jews. On account of their personal wealth and political influence, they also shaped the dimensions of Jewish communal leadership and sponsored Jewish communal buildings, charities, and book publication. And Oppenheim was related to the most powerful and wealthy of them. His uncle Samuel Oppenheimer (1630–1703) was the most important, famous, and best-positioned of all of Europe's Jews in his service to the Habsburg court in Vienna. He used his connections to Jews across the Holy Roman Empire to finance the Habsburg monarchy's wars with both the French in the west and the Ottomans in the east, notably against the siege of Vienna in 1683.[3] David Oppenheim's other paternal and maternal uncles included Moses Oppenheimer, the Court Jew of Heidelberg, and members of the wealthy Wohl family, who dominated the leadership and economics of the city of Frankfurt. Oppenheim's own marriage furthered new and important alliances. His first wife, Gnendel, was daughter of the Court Jew of Hanover, Leffman Behrens (1643–1714; in Hebrew he was referred to as Eliezer Lippman Kohen), and his second wife, Shifra, was a member of the influential Wedeles clan that occupied central roles in the governance of Jewish Prague. He in turn secured marriages for his son to the daughter of Samson Wertheimer (successor to Samuel Oppenheimer in Vienna) and for his daughters to rabbis and financiers in Cleves, Friedberg, and Hanover.[4] The resources of Oppenheim's powerful family furnished him with immeasurable wealth and access to the inner circles of local and imperial power.

Oppenheim's family stature was matched by his credentials as a man of learning. His education brought him into the tutelage of the most creative and highly recognized Jewish scholars of the age. During his childhood in the 1670s in the Rhineland city of Worms, he was taught by the illustrious scholar Yair Hayyim Bachrach, and as he traveled during the 1670s and 1680s he studied in the major centers of Jewish learning: under Gerson Ulif Ashkenazi in Metz, Benjamin Wolf Epstein in Friedberg, and Isaac Benjamin Wolff of Landsberg.[5] The training they offered and the pedigree they conferred by ordaining him as a rabbi in 1684 established his standing as a man of rabbinic letters of the highest order.

Social class and intellectual pedigree combined to secure Oppenheim's occupation of premier leadership positions, first with his appointment to the rabbinate of Nikolsburg (in Moravia) in 1691, and then with his arrival in Prague, the largest urban Jewish settlement in Christian Europe, in 1703. Additionally, in 1713 he was named rabbi of half of the Jewish regions of Bohemia, and in 1718 his dominion was confirmed over the second half, allowing him to implement a reorganization of its rabbinic structure. These official posts were matched by honorific titles of rabbinic leadership for the communities of Slutzk and Brisk in the Polish-Lithuanian Commonwealth. He was named the "Prince," or *Nasi,* of the Land of Israel by the Jews of Jerusalem, which enhanced his standing in the world of Jewish letters but occasioned suspicion in the courts of the Habsburg monarchy.

In his role as rabbi in these various locations, Oppenheim was expected to play a part in the apparatus of communal administration, as interpreter of the written statutes of the *kehillah* and chief justice of its highest court. The position conferred authority in less institutionally formal ways as well: in addition to acting as a local court of appeals, Oppenheim decided upon matters of Jewish practice in response to queries from rabbis of cities, towns, and villages and acted on behalf of people who wrote him in the hopes that he would advance their professional and personal interests. Letters crossed his desk from his local Moravian and Bohemian jurisdictions as well as from correspondents farther afield in Italy, the Netherlands, and Poland.

At the core of Oppenheim's identity and activity as a rabbi, intellectual, and communal leader stood his library. His library gained renown among Jewish colleagues and Christian contemporaries, many of whom took pains to visit it in Hanover—where it was housed from 1703—and use the contents of the collection. It thus informed the decisions of local courts and distant decisors. He possessed highbrow scholarly material alongside popular pamphlets and broadsides, and he preserved diplomatic exchanges and communal ordinances in manuscript—an archive of contemporary Jewish life. His collection of manuscripts furnished the printing market with classic texts for wider dissemination. Oppenheim's intellectual authority made him a much-sought-after source for endorsements for newly written books. Remarkably, although Oppenheim was esteemed and famous across European learned circles as an intimate of the world of letters, virtually none of his own writings were published during his lifetime, or for more than two centuries after his death. The restriction of his writings to manuscript form (even in multiple manuscript copies) consigned his intellectual oeuvre to the margins of Jewish study, when they garnered any attention at all. He has thus receded into history, disappearing behind the library that survived him.

An Age of Collecting: Libraries in Early
Modern European Politics and Culture

Prince of the Press tells the story of premodern Jewish life, politics, and intellectual culture through an exploration of a book collection, the man who assembled it, and the circles of individuals who brought it into being and made use of it. Collecting may at first seem a strange point of entry into a discussion of politics, but scholars have long recognized the meeting of social and political worlds in even the most personal of collections. In his 1931 essay "Unpacking My Library," Walter Benjamin plumbed the meaning of collecting as a "relationship to objects which does not emphasize their functional, utilitarian value," but rather their social meaning. Benjamin noted that

> the most profound enchantment for the collector is the locking
> of individual items within a magic circle in which they are fixed
> as the final thrill, the thrill of acquisition, passes over them.
> Everything remembered and thought, everything conscious,
> becomes the pedestal, the frame, the base, the lock of his prop-
> erty. The period, the region, the craftsmanship, the former
> ownership—for a true collector the whole background of an
> item adds up to a magic encyclopedia whose quintessence is
> the fate of his object.[6]

Benjamin's consideration of the collector captures the dynamic of a whole that is greater than the sum of its parts but that nonetheless preserves the unique character and history of each object within it. Lingering behind the collector's final acquisition and assimilation of each book into the total collection lies the tantalizing notion that the individual histories of books-in-motion reveal more than the idiosyncratic stories of former owners—which they assuredly and invitingly do—but also offer coordinates for the spheres of activity of the collector and as representative of arteries of power and influence. When taken together, the books of a collection do not simply provide an aggregate of individual items; rather, the whole advances a map that traces economies of exchange and communities of regard as books traveled along various pathways to reach the shelves of the collector.

Whereas Benjamin's collector acts on his or her own personal initiative, in the cosmos of early modern Europe in which David Oppenheim operated, collecting was an important act linked to the overlapping worlds of knowledge and politics, and their material bases.[7] Early modern theorists expressed an acute awareness of the potential of collections of books to serve people of power and influence, and especially as a means of garnering prestige. In 1627, the French intellectual Gabriel Naudé penned a consideration of the function of a library while in the service of Henri de Mesme, president of the Paris *parlement*. Naudé's text *Advis pour dresser une bibliothèque* (*Advice on Establishing a Library*) represented a sort of early modern conduct literature that belonged alongside other books of tutelage and training for courtiers. The book led a nobleman who wished to build a library through the essential components of a collection: it must contain both ancient and modern texts, both books and manuscripts; it must speak to a variety of disciplines; and it must be carefully catalogued and accessible to a scholarly public. A library of this sort, Naudé averred, saved ancient texts from oblivion and furnished scholars with the materials to produce new knowledge. A library's chief function was to serve as a scholarly resource, but Naudé framed every stage of its construction in terms of a subtler (and no less significant) outcome: since it was "extraordinary, difficult, and of great expense" it would "cause everyone to speak well, and with admiration, of him who puts it into effect."[8] Much as they were a service to the world of intellectuals, libraries were bound up with the reputation and position of the people who assembled them, and could accrue significant political capital to their owners.

Naudé's treatise expressed a set of principles then current in cultural imaginings of the early modern library. In their pursuit of the "extraordinary, difficult, and expensive," Naudé, Oppenheim, and numerous others were participating in an early modern drive to collect. Over the course of two centuries, European collections moved from the curious to the extensive, a means first of expressing marvel and then of bringing order to nature, matter, and knowledge.[9] This was the world made by Renaissance materialism, the discovery of the New World, and the invention of the printing press; it was the age of the English cabinets of curiosities, the Italian studios, and the German *Wunderkammer,* of materialism driven by an epistemological shift that was concerned with experience as arbiter of truth, rather than received wisdom from tradition. An essential component of this process was access to the stuff of knowledge via the direct possession of those objects that bore such truths.[10] Central to this endeavor were two assumptions: first, that the human mind was up to this task, and second, that the task had to be accomplished not merely through contemplation, but through encounter.[11] Ownership of an increasing number of objects meant bringing disparate parts into a single whole; it was a way of shaping a narrative and making the surrounding world—of nature, of politics, of religion—intelligible. This thirst for objects was not limited to natural or technological materials; the earliest forms of Renaissance collecting were of manuscripts, which were quickly followed by luxury items, like the objects featured in works of Renaissance painting, as well as the exquisite paints and sculptural materials used to represent this lavish new world.[12]

This was a deeply material way of knowing. Collecting entailed the accumulation of material, which in turn required significant material resources. Early modern libraries were thus seldom the province of scholarly solitude. The seventeenth century witnessed the rise of libraries in the service of state aggrandizement, and scholarly knowledge was intertwined with political activity.[13] Whether in the ducal courts of Italy or the Habsburg *Hofbibliothek* owned by the dynasty in Vienna; the French Bibliothèque Mazarine and Bibliothèque du Roy; the Bibliotheca Augustana at Wolfenbüttel; or the electoral libraries in Berlin and Dresden, the accumulation of literary material accompanied the efforts of rulers to incorporate learning into the mission of the regime as both a product of its beneficence and a prop to its legitimacy.[14] In Central Europe, the age of collecting manifested a larger process of state consolidation, made all the more urgent by

the ravaging effects of the Thirty Years War. Possession of a collection be-
spoke power, and its despoliation symbolized an opponent's defeat. In the
midst of the Thirty Years War the Catholic allies of the Habsburgs led by
Duke Maximilian of Bavaria occupied Protestant Heidelberg in retribution
for its ruler's part in rebellion; to fully signify victory, the army expropriated
Heidelberg's library, packing its contents into 196 boxes and bequeathing it
to Rome as a gift.[15] Independent towns and nobles assembled libraries and
archives as counterballasts to state efforts to undermine local prerogative
and ancient tradition.[16]

Collecting, wealth, status, and scholarship were closely intertwined.
Cultures of antiquarian research, legal reasoning, and record-keeping furnished statesmen with the necessary expertise for governance and the symbolic authority such knowledge conferred.[17] Conversely, the power held by
economic and social elites supported scholars and artists in the pursuit of
knowledge, and their patronage directed the contours and development of
new knowledge. The very circumstances under which Naudé composed his
treatise reflected these conditions. Like other books of conduct common to
the courts of Renaissance and Baroque Europe, Naudé's intellectual production took place in the service of a patron, whose material support enabled his client to think and write. Naudé's advice was offered to elevate his
patron's standing, and that standing in turn shaped the circumstances of
Naudé's intellectual production.[18]

Learning and politics were mutually reinforcing in power centers
across Europe, but this trend was particularly acute for Jews on account
of the fact that Jews were not sovereign anywhere in Europe. In the case of
Jewish self-governance, a more tendentious relationship obtained between
the coercive power of a community's leadership and its authority to act.
The institutions that guided Jewish communal, ritual, and daily life were
always contingent, at least in part, upon forces external to Jews themselves,
usually in the form of charters and other negotiated terms of settlement,
rights of residence, and collective taxation. Instead, in legitimating the policies directed by Jewish communal elites toward governing their own constituents, Jewish intellectuals generated a vision of leadership that derived
not primarily from might, wealth, or even welfare, but from creating a "holy

community," a *kehillah kedoshah*, which was characterized by its fidelity to Jewish law, Torah, and its study.[19] Whereas communal leadership *in practice* was rooted in economic wealth, the theoretical garb for the *kehillah*'s standing was woven out of the primacy of study and scholarship. Piety thrummed through the lives of Europe's Jews (much as it did for Europe's Christians) as an expectation, but the idealized form of that piety was filtered through the authority of the text, literacy, and study.[20] Study was represented as the highest ideal for the Jewish male—a form of valor and nobility.[21] The intellectual energies rabbis poured into interpreting law to cohere with practice—and not only the reverse—demonstrate the importance of the self-image of fidelity to law and study as a basis for other aspects of Jewish life.[22] Learning conferred authority on the exercise of power.[23]

If the authority of study was an abstract ideal, Oppenheim's genius lay in his ability to give that abstraction a physical manifestation in the symbols and apparatus of study itself: books. In turn, he identified himself with his collection and its ongoing expansion, merging the authority of texts with his position as a leader, effectively creating a personal source of status at once independent of communal institutions and at the same time decisive for their functioning. Even as the items that populated his library came from his personal ties, independent of the boundaries of the *kehillah*, his books provided him with expertise, authority, and elevated institutional standing. *Prince of the Press* is therefore a book about *both* a man and a library, about Oppenheim's political activities and the library as a means for their achievement.

A Universal Jewish Library?

Oppenheim's eighteenth-century library of Jewish books represents an ideal vehicle for thinking about book cultures across borders and the ways in which Jewish life both intersected with its larger ambience and differed from it. Oppenheim assembled his collection with the aid of contributors and sellers from across Europe and the Mediterranean basin, through contacts with scribes, scholars, supplicants, and widows. His collection testifies to the myriad connections Jews maintained with each other across political frontiers as he maintained ties not simply with the Jews of the Holy Roman Empire and their presses, but also with Amsterdam, Venice, and Constantinople. He labored to obtain manuscripts from the Mediterranean worlds of the Iberian diaspora in the Ottoman Empire, especially Jerusalem, and relied on scribes and scriptoria in Italy. In Poland-Lithuania, where the difficult conditions of Jewish life in the mid-seventeenth century had brought a halt to the productivity of the printing presses that had been so active only a century before (and would continue to hum once more half a century after Oppenheim's death), Oppenheim relied on used book dealers and copyists to ensure his collection's completion and, when necessary, provided books from presses in return. His collection inspired not only the movement of objects, but the transit of people as well, as Jewish and Christian intellectuals traveled to visit the collection and consult its holdings.

Prince of the Press shows how books and libraries are important sites of political and cultural authority and contest, even in the absence of the formal mechanisms of the state—and are perhaps even more significant on that very account. Through Oppenheim's library we can arrive at a political life of books and explore the ways in which his holdings wove together various strands of early modern Jewish society. His library operated as an agent of symbolic power and practical knowledge-authority, akin to the great libraries being constructed in the capitals of European sovereigns, yet with the important distinction that neither he nor his Jewish contemporaries were sovereign in any place in Europe or the world. Learning and leadership, commerce and culture were intertwined both in the forces that brought his library into being and in the culture that this library reflects. Oppenheim was the lynchpin between spheres of Jewish commercial life and Jewish cultural life. His story reveals the dynamic impact of one upon the other as revealed through this Jewish library.

The term "Jewish library" requires some explanation. To call any premodern book "Jewish" is not such a simple matter. Books in Hebrew characters in the age of print were the product of cooperative endeavors between Jews and Christians. The labor of book production was accomplished by a variety of individuals: the owner of the press, the typesetter, various editors, and, in many cases, a censor, not to mention the actual authors of books as well as their heirs, who might posthumously publish their writings. Moreover, technologies of book production, decoration, and illumination traveled between presses and shops, with the woodcuts and copper plates that created the decorations and print that adorned the title pages and contents of books sometimes quite literally traveling between print shops of Christians and Jews.[24] The early print history of two books fundamental to Jewish culture—the Talmud and the rabbinic Bible—are both stories of intensive collaboration between Jewish and Christian actors and interests.[25]

An aggregate of such books into a Jewish library similarly poses a challenge to definition. Oppenheim self-consciously styled himself as a man in the ceaseless pursuit of books. From almost the inception of his collecting activity he expressed an inchoate plan to absorb books into his collection "without end," an intention toward great comprehensiveness. But this comprehensiveness bore a particular Jewish hue, generally marked by the Hebrew alphabet. The overwhelming majority of his books, with so few exceptions that they might be counted on two hands, were written with Hebrew characters, and it may not be inaccurate to say "Jewish" characters instead; the riches of his Yiddish collection point to the relevance of Jewish languages beyond rabbinic Hebrew yet within Hebrew characters. Oppenheim owned all of the classics of rabbinic literature necessary for a career as judge and teacher: multiple editions of the Bible and Talmud with the generations of commentary that had accreted to them. But his collection did not stop there. He kept an up-to-date collection of rabbinic writings on law and philosophy. His library ranged across fiction and poetry and prayer and song, composed not only by Jews, but by non-Jews as well. On the other hand, works composed by non-Jewish scholars on non-Jewish themes entered Oppenheim's collection only once they had been "judaized"—that is, translated, either in his own time or centuries before they arrived in his care. His multiple copies of the *Canon* of Avicenna—rendered into Hebrew by translators before his time—represent one such example from among many.[26] It is hard to imagine Avicenna in Arabic being included in the collection; it is impossible to imagine Avicenna in Hebrew being left out of it. The French and German romances of King Arthur's court would matter very little to this collector, but the Yiddish tales of *Kenig Artur's Hof* were, of course, included.[27] Aids to study and scholarship by Christian Hebraists were not beyond the scope of the collection, as the inclusion of Johannes Buxtorf's *Concordantiae Bibliorum Hebraicae* and the dictionary of Philippus Aquinas make clear.[28] Conversely, as long as books were produced by and for Jews, no matter the vernacular or the audience, they were eligible for inclusion on Oppenheim's shelves. A Spanish *Vara de Iuda* (a translation of Ibn Verga's *Shevet Yehuda*) belonged in the collection, as did a compilation of sermons delivered in Portuguese to the Amsterdam community by Saul Levi Morteira and Solomon Oliveyra b. David.[29] He owned prayer books for the rites of Central and Eastern European Jews alongside songs to be sung on Purim according to the Italian custom and decisions of Ottoman rabbis with rulings from London.[30]

Both the extent and the limitation of this library make clear that Oppenheim's conception of it was one that included material from as far across the Jewish world as he could reach. What made these works "Jewish" in their eighteenth-century context was that their collector and owner pressed them, during his lifetime, into the service of Jewish communal, legal, and literary uses, which all relied on access to the collection granted by Oppenheim himself. Moreover, the fact that his collection included administrative documents alongside literary manuscripts and printed books meant that his library came to function as an archive for communal records, a repository of legal precedents to be consulted by rabbinic courts, and a treasure trove of unpublished manuscripts for enterprising printers to introduce to a Jewish reading public.

As a functional collection, Oppenheim's library exposes the nature of early modern Jewish communal decision making and power brokerage as dependent upon personal contacts. This view not just of intellectual life but of political power comes to light via the two-pronged character of a study of objects in motion. The anthropologist Arjun Appadurai succinctly captures this dynamic as follows: "From a *theoretical* point of view human actors encode things with significance, from a *methodological* point of view it is the things-in-motion that illuminate their human and social context."[31] When we follow the movement of books into Oppenheim's collection and think not only about their cultural and intellectual significance but also about the motivations by which contemporaries supported his drive to collect, we come to see beyond the collection into Oppenheim's own unique social standing. The pieces of his library linked *people* to each other through Oppenheim's mediation: Court Jews to impoverished widows, rabbis to domestic servants, intellectuals to tradespeople, Jewish scribes and scholars to Christian Hebraists, Ashkenazim to Sephardim, and Europeans to the Land of Israel. Oppenheim used his family wealth, the circulation of extant books and manuscripts, and the production of new books both to cultivate scholarly expertise and to broadcast the authority that such expertise conferred upon him.

Kinship, Capital, and Communal Leadership: Early Modern Politics in Practice

Oppenheim's library and personal papers are valuable for a reconstruction of early modern Jewish culture precisely because they were not commissioned by official institutions, but rather were owned by, composed for, and preserved on behalf of an individual acting in his own capacity, not by communal order. The remnants of his personal papers were preserved by collectors who wished to emulate him, not by state-based institutions. His life — and not just his library — therefore offers a vantage point from which to consider Jewish politics in practice. Historians of the Jews acknowledge the great importance of studying the dynamics of Jewish politics with regard to the policies directed toward them both by the states in which they lived and by their own practices of self-governance. When working to produce a political history with texts produced by Jews in the early modern period, however, scholars of Jewish life have often had to satisfy themselves with documents belonging to one of two categories: either the prescriptive texts of communal statute or the rulings of Jewish legal courts and rabbinic decisors.[32] In *Prince of the Press* I offer a different approach to Jewish political history by uncovering a lateral "archive" for the study of the Jewish political past: a library rich with previous owners' inscriptions and volumes of handwritten letters, and the politics of favor that they represent. In this way I invite scholars to direct their attention to the material object of the book as a means of arriving at a richer portrait of Jewish political culture as reflected by extrainstitutional activity. In Oppenheim's circles, books became a form of currency that could be converted into material well-being, employment, political sponsorship, and intellectual patronage.

An inquiry of this nature calls for an expansive definition of political culture in general, and Jewish political culture in particular. Political culture, as a study of a set of practices, reorients our focus away from watershed episodes in political history and toward a study of the ways in which politics were conducted.[33] Events and episodes are undeniably important, but the dynamics by which those episodes take place are instructive for understanding how power relations were constituted, often most decisively through informal means. In making this book's focus political culture rather than politics itself or political theory, I aim to explore Jewish political life not primarily as it was explicitly theorized, but as it was *practiced*. I look to the wider set of negotiations, persuasions, and competitions that constituted the frames for action.[34]

Oppenheim's library opens a window into Jewish political culture of the early modern period as it was practiced, rather than as it was prescribed. Oppenheim stood at the meeting places of various forms of exchange: of people, ideas, esteem, favors, money, and books. Fellow Jews often approached him in the hopes of engaging him as a power broker who might intervene with his relatives to secure favorable outcomes for political hopefuls. And the means to cultivate Oppenheim's political favor was provided by the gift (or promise) of a book to augment his collection. His library was both a vehicle for promoting an image of prestige and a point of access for supplicants who hoped to benefit from their proximity to this power broker. Using manuscript letters and published prefaces to books alongside state records and communal statutes, I follow the exchange of literary artifacts to plumb issues of persona, power, and reputation in the Jewish communities of Central Europe during the early modern period.

Much of that power structure was based on a unique set of circumstances in the political structure of Central Europe. By the close of the

Thirty Years War, debt and fighting had ravaged the traditional alliances between state activity and private capital, yet the destruction wrought by war made the need for capital ever more urgent. To accommodate the needs of both older and emergent state apparatuses, electors, dukes, and kings sought alternate routes of credit outside of the traditional political order to finance the affairs of state and the trappings of the court.[35] Gone were the traditional houses of credit of the sixteenth and seventeenth centuries; the militarizing state was so unwieldy and the wreckage of war and inflation so encompassing that past creditors had ceased to function or to offer their services.[36]

A process of building a state that was bigger, stronger, and more encompassing than ever before began from a meeting of weaknesses. On one hand, the Habsburgs and other German princes were in dire need of financial aid; one the other, Jews, who had not fared as poorly as many of their neighbors during the thirty years of religious and political conflict, settled where they did and obtained privileges to trade and administer their own affairs by the grace of emperors and estates. Jews, as outsiders of the political order—rather than the noble diets and landed estates that could refuse revenue through recourse to historic "liberties"—were particularly attractive as creditors for the gradually emerging project of state centralization and absolutism. A high-risk investment thus found its risk-taking investors, who had little to lose and much to gain. Out of this alliance rose the interwoven families of the Court Jews of Central Europe, the family structure in which Oppenheim's activities took place.[37]

Hardly a single ascendant territory could be found without a Court Jew to privately finance the developments of states that, in an age before citizenship, had not yet developed the massive bureaucratic mechanisms to effectively tax their inhabitants. Court Jews furnished regimes with armaments, uniforms, and food but also supported refurbishment of the physical structures of fortresses. In the domestic affairs of the court they provided furniture and linens, ornaments and jewels, fine wines and spices. The fragmentary structure of the Holy Roman Empire produced a need for hundreds of Court Jews. Although some combatants of the Thirty Years War aspired to create a unified German polity in the heart of the continent,

the Peace of Westphalia that concluded the conflict enshrined a principle
of fragmentation, destining the Holy Roman Empire to remain a polity of
competing semisovereign jurisdictions until its dissolution at the dawn of
the nineteenth century.[38] The Westphalian arrangement preserved the existence of weak territories against the aspirations of the strong and secured
the integrity of the empire's constituent territories. Even as each polity
within the empire enjoyed a nominal internal sovereignty, it could not sustain itself without recourse to commerce beyond its limited borders. This
federated system of economic cooperation and political fragmentation nur-
tured Jewish economic opportunity. Courts emerged in the seventeenth-
century as important engines of economic growth, stimuli to employment
in building, crafts, and administration.[39] The needs of individual polities
were small enough that they could be satisfied by individuals acting in con-
cert (in this case Jews), but that satisfaction required the coordinated effort
of networked individuals with access to resources beyond the limited frontiers of each individual territory. By some estimates twelve hundred Court
Jews were active in various capacities over the span of one hundred years,
some at the highest echelons of state power.[40]

Jonathan Israel has suggested that "the close collaboration and interdependence between them [Court Jews], interlocking with the correspondence between *kehillot* in different countries, made their activity more
thoroughly international and specifically Jewish than the banking and con-
tracting of later times."[41] It was this interdependence — created by the economic need of the polities they served — that made the Court Jews important for the constitutions of Jewish political and cultural life as well, and
made David Oppenheim so important to Jews of the empire. Court Jews
intervened to forestall expulsions and defend Jewish physical and cultural
interests.[42] Increasingly, the activities of the Court Jews of Europe came
to resemble that of the courts in which they served. The yawning income
gap between these wealthy families and the bulk of the Jewish population
in towns and villages across the German countryside effected a shift in the
structure of local communal politics. Whereas earlier a semblance of democratic procedure had reigned in theory, over the course of the seventeenth
and eighteenth centuries electoral arrangements were replaced with per-

manent oligarchies.[43] In evolving into oligarchy, German Jews were participating in a larger trend regnant across medium-sized towns in which permanent ruling groups became the order of the day, a "regime of uncles" in the phrasing of the German towns' influential historian Mack Walker.[44] And much as the towns were governed by familial oligarchies, the marriage strategies of Jewish elites consolidated power in the hands of relatives.

Court Jews participated in the inner circles of governance on account of their financial utility to the state. This utility, in turn, positioned them to serve as the unofficial representatives of Jewish collective material concerns to the ears of a sovereign. In this regard they were markedly different from the communally appointed *shtadlanim* (intercessors) retained by the Jews of the Polish-Lithuanian Commonwealth and even in some German areas; they were also more effective.[45] The inclusion of Jews in the world of the court by virtue of their services to the state created a de facto point of access through which the concerns of their communities might be conveyed. Samuel Oppenheimer's critical financing of Habsburg military campaigns established a small niche for Jewish settlement in the city of Vienna after 1674 and, more importantly for Jews across Central Europe, positioned him as a voice to intercede on behalf of Jews under Habsburg rule.[46] Oppenheimer's successor, Samson Wertheimer, was a member of the imperial retinue who similarly intervened at moments of Jewish collective concern. In 1700, Wertheimer aided the Jews of Frankfurt in obstructing the publication of a book of slander against Jews by Andreas Eisenmenger titled *Entdecktes Judenthum* (Judaism Exposed).[47] And Vienna was not the only site for court-Jewish activity. In 1704, Leffman Behrens, Oppenheim's father-in-law in Hanover, decisively shaped the impact of a religious disputation by recruiting a Jewish participant from Stadthagen (some forty-five kilometers away), sending a carriage and taking care of all the necessary accommodations to bring him to Hanover.[48]

This Jewish "regime of uncles" was marked both by its wealth and by the influence it exercised over the spaces and practices of Jewish communal life. The Court Jews established synagogues and study houses, funded tuition in centers of advanced Talmud study, sponsored the production of printed books and manuscript Torah scrolls, and accessorized ritual spaces with covers for the ark, candelabra, and goblets.[49] The lessons of the court also furnished the Court Jews with the tools for political administration. In the noble and royal courts, politics were conducted through a complex system of patronage, clientage, and credit.

Oppenheim's authority was based in study and scholarship, but his power derived from the worldly domains of courts and commerce. When communities and individual Jews sought security or opportunity, they recognized that the surest avenue to success was through the support of Court Jews. But such avenues were not open to all, and Jews of peripheral locations needed personal points of contact in order to gain access to these essential power brokers. So they turned to Oppenheim's mediation. Individual supplicants sought his aid and intervention in acquiring travel documents, yeshiva placements, marriage arrangements, and the edge over rivals for competitive rabbinic posts. And the means by which individuals reached out to Oppenheim was through their shared love of books. Students seeking permissions to reside in a town began with a discussion of newly published works. Rabbis hoping for support for their candidacy for rabbinic promotion wrote with information about scholarship. And the Jews of Jerusalem, seeking a philanthropic patron, sent manuscripts the likes of which could be found nowhere else. Oppenheim's library became a virtual space for Jews who had no access to the world of the Court Jews to come into contact with them, and Oppenheim was the key.

The patronage networks in which Oppenheim participated were not, moreover, limited to politics alone. Intellectual influence was similarly a product of the patronage system at work in scientific and artistic production across Europe and in the worlds of the Court Jews.[50] On account of his well-established reputation and his access to wealth to support the publication of new books, Oppenheim was sought out by publishers and printers and maintained a careful involvement in the financing of Jewish texts. But books required more than material support: in order to gain intellectual currency, Jewish books were printed with prefatory material in the form of approbata (*haskamot*), short letters of commendation that precede a book's central text. Caught between a form of censorship and proto-copyright, perhaps best understood as endorsements, approbata were produced at the nexus between authors, publishers, printers, readers, and the commercial and rabbinic elites of premodern Jewry. This relationship between economic (and political) influence and the production of books did not just facilitate knowledge-making; it set the terms by which new ideas were disseminated, and how they were received. Denizens of early modern Europe knew to evaluate the authority of knowledge on the basis of the character of the people who produced it, and readers learned to establish a book's credibility upon the reputational credit of the people involved in its publication—author, printer, patron, and approbator.[51] In a system of knowledge-making that rested on personal contact and the credibility of reputation, patronage established the social identity of scholars and marked them as reliable.[52] Of all of the writing that emerged from Oppenheim's pen, only his approbata were regularly printed; upward of seventy such letters accompanied books out of the print shop. In lending the weight of his reputation to newly printed books, Oppenheim played an important role in how books were perceived, and therefore bought, sold, and read. In the process, he took advantage of these moments of endorsement to craft his own reputation among a wider Jewish "republic of letters," reinforcing and enhancing his standing as a unique arbiter of literary quality on account of his unique collection.

If Oppenheim's courtly networks allowed him to emerge victorious against some rivals, associations at times brought troubles of their own. If approbata cemented ties between authors and endorsers, an accidental approbation to a book of Sabbatean leanings could entrench Oppenheim in accusations of heresy. And while patronage of the book trade could bring Oppenheim fame when it resulted in his invitation to become *Nasi Eretz Yisrael* (Prince of the Land of Israel), that same title invited litigation and charges of international sedition.

Self-Fashioning and Reputation

Oppenheim's authority and influence in the world of Jewish books stemmed from a carefully cultivated persona that he took pains to craft. He identified deeply with his library and fashioned a sense of selfhood that was in essence characterized by his bibliophilia. In 1696, on a visit to Vienna, home of his uncle Samuel Oppenheimer, Oppenheim received a question from a fellow scholar soliciting his opinion on a matter of Jewish law. Before he launched into an excursus in direct response to the query, he gave a half-hearted apology for the partial response he was about to provide:

> Behold at this time I am like a craftsman without his tools, the house of gum and dripping balm[53] is in Nikolsburg, for there is my home, a great place of gathering for sages,[54] and at the time I am here, in Vienna, I am not found in front of a single book of responsa. And a man like me, whose greatest delight is in books (*nahat yenahet be-sefarim*) and the details that emerge from them so that I may distinguish between them and according to them cut to the truth of the law, and assuredly the rabbis had before them a house full of books and responsa, and I have only those that I have memorized, which rise and fall from the Talmud which is familiar to me, a small vessel that holds greatness.[55]

Oppenheim's use of the refrain "whose greatest delight is in books"—though also used by others among his contemporaries to describe themselves—served him to perpetuate an image of a man whose name was synonymous with his library. Describing himself as such a man cast his personhood in terms of his affection for books. This trope provided a point of access for supplicants who would seek his favor: a man who delighted in books could be delighted by receiving them, and such delight might be handsomely rewarded. The emotions of joy and delight translated into scholarly credentials for Oppenheim and political currency for those who sought his counsel and patronage.[56]

Bibliophilia became ever more deeply associated with the public persona of this man. In a short time, students and fellow scholars learned that the way to his heart and his sponsorship was through the exchange of books. They sought him out, offered flattery and respect, and often sent him gifts he might not have had the chance to acquire himself, because

Oppenheim was not a cloistered book collector; he was a powerful man with powerful contacts. His training under the leading rabbinic luminaries of his generation translated into significant rabbinic appointments, and his family relations meant that he was an important intercessor — not directly to state authorities, but with courtly relations who had access to sovereigns. He exerted authority and influence not only over his immediate jurisdiction but over the wider exchange of Jewish law between scholars, the decisions of Jewish courts, and the politics of Jewish communal administration. Oppenheim's library and the ways that he used it reveal the many moving parts of early modern Jewry in Central Europe, and the individuals at work who brought it into being. Oppenheim lived between and within these different worlds, and his library provided a vantage point from which he could exert an effect on the exercise of power. Both his library and his position within Jewish politics were shaped by family ties and educational experience, allowing him to achieve the stature that was, in turn, decisive for others. Collecting and power shaped the career of this man, and in turn shaped the times in which he lived.

ONE

Creating a Collector

Nothing can be done in imitation of other libraries unless, by means of their
catalogues which have been compiled, one knows what they contain.
—Gabriel Naudé, *Advice on Establishing a Library,* 1627

IN 1686, AT THE AGE OF TWENTY-TWO, David Oppenheim
surveyed the books in his possession. His library already comprised an
impressive assemblage of more than four hundred Jewish titles in a time
when no more than two thousand such titles existed.[1] With great care and
appreciation for books as both carriers of knowledge and material commodities, Oppenheim recorded each item in a small notebook, listing them
first alphabetically and then according to the circumstances of their acquisition, including former owners and prices paid.[2] In many cases these were
secondhand books, whose pages preserved the touch and tastes of owners
and readers who had come before him. His catalogue chronicles the meeting place of two energies: the personal biography of an aspiring collector,
and the wider economy of books to which he had access.

Oppenheim's decision to accumulate a library and establish his identity as a preeminent collector began in earnest in his late teens, by which
time he had graduated from the rabbinic training that was expected of
young men of his social class. Following almost a decade of study among
some of the most influential rabbinic scholars of his age in Worms, Metz,
Friedberg, and Landsberg, Oppenheim had earned a name for himself as
an emerging thinker and authority. His entry into adulthood also meant
marriage, and the strategic union of families of fortune and influence that
matrimony brought with it, as well as the beginnings of economic indepen-

dence and the accumulation of personal property, which for Oppenheim was first and foremost his books.

During his early years of collecting, Oppenheim's library did not have the luxury of being tailored to his personal tastes. His acquisitions followed the conventional path of a growing library: Gabriel Naudé's advice manual instructed its readers in 1627 that "the promptest, the easiest, and the most advantageous" means of building a library was in "the acquisition of some other entire and undissipated library."[3] Oppenheim's library absorbed many smaller collections, sometimes only individual volumes, sometimes the entire holdings of an insolvent family. In incorporating these previously owned books in this secondhand economy, Oppenheim's library was often shaped by the choices made by previous owners and by market supply and came to reflect a distinct heritage of the medieval and early modern Rhineland, especially his native city of Worms. His collection therefore opens vistas beyond his personal practices and into the culture of book ownership by a wider swath of the Jewish population than just Oppenheim himself. Lingering within the margins and flyleaves of Oppenheim's collection are fragments of evidence of the ways that Jewish men and women related to books as objects of inquiry, stores of material value, and keepers of sentimental secrets.

In itemizing the pieces of his collection in his earliest catalogue, Oppenheim recorded the sites of their acquisition, the people he transacted with, and the travelers who made up the world of book exchange for Jews in the seventeenth century. His personal catalogue reveals the manifold ties Oppenheim had with family wealth, local vendors, and skilled scribes. Tracing the elements of the catalogue permits a reconstruction of the domains of book acquisition in Oppenheim's world, which involved education, exchange, family, and travel.

Oppenheim's catalogue and collection thus offer two parallel insights into the world of early modern Jewish book culture. On one hand, his careful record of his acquisitions reveals the specific patterns that brought this formidable library into being. On the other hand, the "acquisition of undissipated libraries" permits reflection on the culture of book ownership and usage far beyond the preferences of this individual man. By exploring the collection not simply as the preserve of a single man but rather as a collection of other collections, we can discover a culture of book ownership and readership in the early modern period. Books mattered to individuals not just as objects of study but as powerful registers of identity and sentimentality. This approach to books was an important basis of the economy that put those objects into motion and the ability of those objects to purchase the favors that made premodern Jewish politics work in Oppenheim's time.

Early Years in the Rhineland

Oppenheim was raised in Worms, in the Rhineland-Palatinate, a Jewish community that boasted of a long Jewish heritage. Although the earliest documentation of Jewish privileges in Worms dates to the twelfth century, and the city's first synagogue was inaugurated in 1034, in some versions of the city's founding myths its Jewish community predated even the destruction of the Second Temple in Jerusalem.[4] According to the seventeenth-century chronicler Juspe Schammes of Worms in his *Mayse nissim,* the earliest Jewish settlers had arrived after the biblical exile from the Holy Land following the destruction of the First Temple (ca. 586 BCE). The Jews of Worms became too comfortable though, Schammes reports, and refused the call to return to Judaea during the construction of the Second Temple. On account of that reluctance, they were fated to atone for their sins with greater suffering than other Jewish settlements.[5] Although this ancient pedigree was exaggerated, Jews in Worms did have a sense of the uniqueness of their centuries-long continuity.[6] Worms—alongside its neighbors Speyer and Mainz—situated on the river Rhine, was the cradle of Ashkenazic culture, home to such medieval luminaries as Rabbeinu Gershom b. Judah, "Me'or haGolah" (960–1040), and Rabbi Shlomo Yitzhaki (Rashi, 1040–1105) as well as the Rhineland Pietists Judah Hasid and Eleazar of Worms.[7] During the Middle Ages, these three cities formed something of a regional unit called *SHuM* (an acronym for the Hebrew names of Speyer, Worms, Mainz). Of the large Jewish settlements of Central Europe that could date their origins to the Middle Ages, Worms was one of only four— along with Frankfurt, Friedberg, and Prague—that survived the rash of expulsions in the sixteenth century.[8]

Seventeenth-century Worms, free city of the Holy Roman Empire within the territory of the Rheinpfalz, or Rhineland-Palatinate, was home to a proud community of Jews, whose Jewish quarter placed them within a larger Christian (in this case predominantly Lutheran) milieu.[9] Worms had a population of more than seven thousand at the start of the seventeenth century, but thirty years of war, economic hardship, and an outbreak of the plague in the 1660s meant that around the time of Oppenheim's birth the city had scarcely more than three thousand inhabitants.[10] Its Jewish population, although it had numbered as many as twenty-five hundred in the sixteenth century, held firm in the seventeenth century at approximately one hundred families, and probably did not exceed seven hundred individuals, or just under a quarter of the city's total population.[11]

Jews and Christians interacted in various ways in this city. Despite official charters proscribing excessive interactions between people of the two faiths, such as curfews, the demands of commerce and the curiosities of daily life often undermined these legal pretensions. Jews and Christians could be found mingling in the marketplace, in each other's homes, and even as tourists in each other's places of worship.[12] Christian municipal authorities and Jewish leaders reluctantly made their peace with these interactions: a 1684 statute of the Worms Jewish community threatened excessive discussion between Jews and gentiles in the synagogue with a hefty fine but could not stop interaction entirely. Rather, the *kehillah* had to content itself with a demand that "no one shall speak excessively in the synagogue with an uncircumcised man or woman [*sic*] but rather shall go outside and speak with them."[13] Just as contacts between Jews and Christians were a norm of everyday life, relations among Jews were never unequivocally harmonious. One piece of folk wisdom in legends about the city expressed the following dilemma between the costs and benefits of Jewish life in Worms: "One can hear no *kaddish* or *barekhu* [ritual prayers that require a minimum of ten adult Jewish males to recite] in a small community, but in a small community one will experience no jealousy and hatred as he does in a community full of Jews."[14] The spiritual benefits of living with a quorum of men for prayer was easily offset by the internecine strife that accompanied a larger population.

Having originated in the town of Oppenheim, not far from Worms, by the seventeenth century the family (called Oppenheim in Hebrew and Yiddish but Oppenheimer in German) was a pillar of the Worms *kehillah*. David Oppenheim's grandfather, Simon Wolf, a *parnas* (warden) of the community, lived there, and it was there that he raised three sons, Moses, Samuel, and Abraham, and two daughters, Sara and Hendel.[15] Simon Wolf's three sons extended the family's dealings beyond the city of Worms to nearby Heidelberg, the capital of the Rhineland-Palatinate, and from that base achieved a financial reputation that they eventually parlayed into imperial preeminence.[16] While Samuel rose through the ranks to the service of the emperor in Vienna, and Moses established an estate in Heidelberg, Abraham, the youngest of Simon Wolf's three sons, preferred a more local course of action; in 1657 he relinquished all rights to settle in Heidelberg, selling them to his brother Samuel.[17] In Worms Abraham achieved considerable wealth as a trader and investor and owned six houses within the city's walls and an estate outside of the city.[18] The *Wormser Memorbuch* singled him out for his generous donations, naming him as *he-aluf* (the chief), *ha-parnas* (the warden), and *ha-yashish* (the elder)—all titles of considerable weight in the *kehillah*.[19] In 1656 Abraham further expressed his largesse when he committed himself as a financial guarantor for the construction of a new synagogue in Worms. Over the course of his lifetime in the city he often held leadership posts that were decisive both for internal Jewish affairs and for Jews' relationships with the city's rulers.[20]

Abraham was married to Blümele, the daughter of David Wohl, leader of the Frankfurt Jewish community.[21] Memorials to Blümele identify her as a woman of valor, charity, and piety—typical encomia for an upstanding Jewish woman of this period, although perhaps all memorials are favorable.[22] Blümele's family was not only one of commercial influence, but of scholarly activity as well, and the merging of these families served to link their fortunes. It was through this union that, in 1664, David Oppenheim was born in Worms. He had three sisters and a brother, and possibly more who died young, as was common at the time. Beyond a reference in the *Wormser Memorbuch* to Abraham Oppenheim having "raised his sons in the study of Torah," very little information is available about Oppenheim's early family life.[23] The young David began his education around the age of four.[24] Jewish education in the early modern period was stratified according to wealth. Although every autonomous community took upon itself the creation of schools that would educate their young boys, families of means often eschewed these in favor of private tutors of greater skill who could pay exclusive attention to their sons. Unlike other boys his age, whose education came from the communally supported school, David had a personal tutor, Yair Hayyim Bachrach (1638–1702), because of his family's wealth. Bachrach's life was marked by dislocation and wandering but also by intellectual ferment and creativity that scholars of the Jewish past have often juxtaposed with a more quiescent rabbinics in the eighteenth century.[25] Bachrach's tutelage socialized Oppenheim into the three major aspects of the world of the rabbinate and Oppenheim's future scholarly persona: curriculum, epistolary communication, and bibliophilia.[26] Bachrach must have been an exacting master. He took his cue from rabbinic dicta which reassured that it was "permitted for a teacher to reprimand a student sternly" if such reprimand would inspire more rigorous study.[27] And yet, the master and student appear to have developed a warm relationship, and exchanges in letters compensated for the physical distance that soon separated them. In reflecting on his time with Bachrach, Oppenheim specifically recalled a lesson in the importance of correspondence that Bachrach had imparted: "I remember what my master and teacher entrusted me with when I parted from him: that he will forgive his honor and that I should write him letters of tidings among the items of a student's inquiries from his teacher."[28] Bachrach expected his student to keep him abreast of the events in his life, and not to limit his writing to matters of scholarly discourse alone.

Bachrach may have continued to exercise an influence over Oppenheim's ongoing education, as the young man moved on, in his teen years, to study with Bachrach's close colleagues in some of the greatest centers of study of western Ashkenaz.[29] Oppenheim spent several years of study in Metz, in the yeshiva of Gerson Ulif Ashkenazi, who had started his career in Moravia and Vienna but moved westward following the expulsion of the Jews from the city in 1670.[30] Ashkenazi left his impact on Oppenheim, both intellectually and in his professional conduct. Nearly two decades after his time in Metz, Oppenheim incorporated lessons he had learned from observing Ashkenazi's conduct in deciding matters of law.[31] In the winter of 1680–1681, after his studies in Metz, Oppenheim relocated to study with Benjamin Wolf Epstein in Friedberg, somewhat closer to his familiar cities of Worms, Heidelberg, and Frankfurt.[32] Oppenheim's studies moved him one final time, to Landsberg, to the yeshiva of R. Isaac Benjamin Wolff.[33]

Through these educational travels, Oppenheim was engaging in an activity akin to those of Christian contemporaries. Young men of his time and place traveled about in a "Grand Tour" to prepare for careers in state bureaucracies, which required training in diverse and specialized understandings of law and politics and became essential for attaining rank within the administration of a well-ordered state.[34] Extended periods away from home in a variety of new settings cultivated this new sensibility in young men from noble and elite families. Travels of this sort were a means of becoming acquainted with and weaving one's self into the fabric of the world of letters and learning, as in the experiences of the Huguenot Charles-Étienne Jordan (1700–1745), who kept a literary diary as he traveled in search of diverse book collections.[35] A Jewish youth did not have to be a son of nobility or even extreme wealth to study. Jewish communities made provisions for local and foreign youths to be supported as they arrived to a town or city to study there.[36] And it was during this time of adolescent study that young Jewish men, too, began small library collections and to leave their mark on individual copies of books.

Impersonal Printing and Personal Stories: Births and Deaths in Books

Many early modern books preserve a sense of the individuality of book usage, despite their mass production. The invention of the printing press introduced a revolution into the shape of knowledge. For the first time, readers could be assured that the texts they held before them were identical to those in the hands of readers in countless other locations.[37] But even if typesetting guaranteed the standardization of the mise-en-page, the same layout could be produced in larger and smaller versions, could be printed on paper of different quality, and could be bound in very different ways. Upon leaving the floor of the print shop, books were subject to a further form of individuation and personalization, as readers filled the blank spaces in margins and flyleaves with material of their own.[38] From pasting broadside posters into folio volumes to inscribing records of major milestones, readers ensured that their copies of books gained their own distinguishing marks.

Perhaps the most common form of personalization was the inscription of an owner's signature, an act that established proprietorship over an object against the claims of others. One space in which such inscriptions were necessary was the study hall, in which students who were studying the same text might seek to distinguish their copy from those of their peers. Jewish students signaled an awareness of the virtues of ownership by inscribing their names in the fronts of their books with warnings to unlicensed users. One book that made its way into Oppenheim's collection includes a short rhymed verse inscribed into the flyleaf of a book on Jewish ethics:

> Me-ahar she-ra'iti anshei ra'ot
> she-konim sefarim bli ma'ot
> lokhim be-heh etzba'ot,
> kedei she-lo u-ve-lo ba-zo ha-ta'ut
> hatamti 'alav shemi,
> ve-zehu sheli.

> Since I have seen wicked men
> who purchase books without a cent
> acquiring with five fingers (of the hand)
> in order to avoid such an error,
> I have signed my name,
> and this is my claim.[39]

The student's poem acknowledged the importance of staking a claim to owning a book alongside, perhaps, some anxiety about the act of writing in a book.[40] Some Jewish textual traditions had discouraged students from writing directly in their books as a kind of violation, yet numerous students overcame this inhibition and found ways to express their exclusive ownership of objects, whether by composing rhyming verse of this sort or by resorting to the thrice-repetition of their names in accordance with a tradition that three times produced a *hazakah,* a substantive claim, on an object. The claims of ownership were especially relevant for students, who conducted most of their study away from the homes of their families and the possession such spaces entailed. Instead, early modern students — Jewish and non-Jewish alike — experienced education as a form of travel, and travel as a risk to personal property.

Beyond the fear of theft, Jewish students wrote in their personal book copies with souvenirs of their study. The inscriptions that populate the volumes in Oppenheim's collection reveal that there was a near-mystical connection between a book, its owner, and the transmission of content from the pages of the first to the mind of the second.[41] The former owner of a manuscript copy of a commentary on the Mishnah tractate Avot used the blank pages at the end of the volume to similarly state his credentials when he wrote in 1691, "I studied from this book, Meir b. Barukh of Krakow the capital, who encamps upon its flag in Wischnitz near Brisk of Lithuania, and now I am a teacher in Mirtitz in Bohemia."[42] Jewish students sometimes made the mystical bond between study and study-object even more explicit, by inscribing their books with verses of kabbalistic resonance. One, for instance, was taken from Exod 21:1, "And these are the rules which you shall place before them," and another, "*Pitum ha-ketoret,*" was an excerpt from the liturgy describing the rituals of temple incense offerings. Recitation of the latter phrase was associated with health (especially in times of plague) and fortune.[43]

Some students, especially of professional training in ritual slaughter, used ownership of a book as a form of certification and material attestation of personal expertise, as in the case of an owner of a *Sefer tikkunei zevah* (Prague, 1604) who added his name on the final page with an inscription reading, "I studied the laws of ritual slaughter in this book," and then added a doodle of animals ready for the butcher's knife (fig. 1.1).[44] A simi

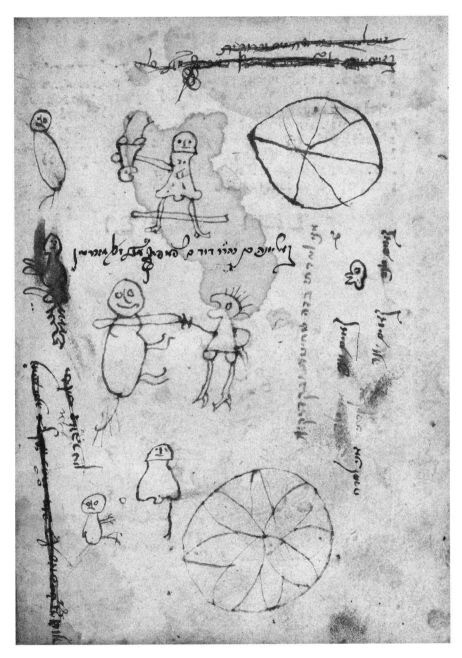

Fig. 1.1. Owner's inscription on back page of Opp. 4° 605 (1): *Sefer tikkunei zevah* (Prague, 1604), showing doodles related to ritual slaughter, which the owner learned from reading the book. Courtesy of the Bodleian Libraries, University of Oxford.

lar work carried inscriptions within its blank pages written by a student's teachers, who gave their certification that the student had fully completed his training and was fit for the task of producing kosher meat.[45]

Even as some inscriptions in books represented an ethos of owner-ship and personal qualifications, their claims to exclusion reveal that books often circulated outside of the hands of their owners. Caveats in the flyleaves of books cautioning away those who would make use of a book "without permission" tacitly acknowledged that books *could* be borrowed and lent when proper consent was given. The female author Rivke b. Meir of Tiktin reminded her readers as much in her manual for women's conduct, *Sefer meneket Rivkah* (Prague, 1609), in citing a Talmudic passage (Ketubbot 50a) regarding proper behavior: "How is it possible for people to act righ-teously at all times? Rather, this refers to people who purchase religious books and lend them to people to learn from them — thus many may bene-fit from them."[46] And some rare instances of inscription do indeed reveal occasions when readers borrowed books from each other.[47]

Students and readers of the contents of a text were not the only ones who left their marks on books. In an age in which paper was not always readily available and was the most expensive part of the printing process, and loose leaves could easily be lost or destroyed, the blank pages of bound volumes offered a space on which to record personal and familial memories for posterity.[48] It was common during the early modern period for literate men and women to note family milestones — such as births and deaths or a miraculous deliverance from danger — in the flyleaves of books.[49] The blank pages at the end of a manuscript copy of *Hesed le-Avraham* from Oppen-heim's collection recounts the trauma that befell the Worms preacher Aaron Teomim and his wife Esther during their travels on horseback to Neustadt in 1686. Upon their approach to the town gates, a rogue horse attacked the couple, spooking their horses and threatening injury. Although no one was within earshot, their cries to heaven found divine favor, and the owner of the wild horse miraculously appeared and saved the lives of the couple. The record on the blank pages of the manuscript served as a memorial for future generations, a reminder of God's providence. A similar tale occupied the blank pages of a Haggadah from the collection (Venice, 1641), which preserved the story of Raphael, a Jew in Nikolsburg in 1690 who on the eve of the Sabbath was on the way to the market to buy fish when he was suddenly and unexpectedly paralyzed, only to be swiftly restored to health. The event prompted the observance of an annual commemoration of the miracle in the form of a "Purim," and the inscription furnished its celebrants with a record of the past.[50]

Even the life and death of entire communities could be recorded on the blank pages of books. In 1689, Worms was besieged by the occupying forces of the French Army. On the blank leaves of one of his copies of Solomon Ibn Verga's *Shevet Yehuda* — a historical accounting of the expulsion of Spanish Jewry — Oppenheim added the end of Jewish life in Worms to the story of Jewish wandering.[51] Oppenheim specifically selected a book that was dedicated to preserving the past and appended a tale of local trauma to a longer history of Jewish suffering at the hands of others, a single manuscript leaf to accompany the printed book. He recorded the end of the city as beginning in fire. Ignited around midday, within a short time flames had engulfed the main synagogue and the Rashi Synagogue. The Oppenheim families' holdings were destroyed, forcing them into exile "like a bird to the next branch." The city was ultimately rebuilt and its Jewish community reconstituted, a task to which the Oppenheim family contributed mightily.[52]

Oppenheim's library thus reveals a variety of ways in which users interacted with their books beyond reading and actively shaped their contents long after the printing process was completed. That the origins of his library lay in the purchasing choices and tastes of others carried a challenge with it as well. His earliest acquisitions were decisively shaped by the thrift of previous owners. This thrift particularly manifested itself in the binding of multiple titles within a single volume, a practice quite typical of the early modern period. Publishers were in the business of printing books, not *binding* books; they often remitted a title to a bookseller as a collection of loose leaves, to be bound by buyers according to their individual specifications. The sheer expense of binding often motivated buyers to press multiple titles into a single codex. This was not always the case, but it was just as common to have anthological volumes as it was to have individuated ones.[53]

The volumes of the collection often represented the idiosyncrasies of pre-vious owners and resist simple storage by title. Where would the modern librarian place a volume that houses both Jacob Weil's book of instruc-tion for kosher butchering (*Tikkunei zevah;* Prague, 1604) and a Yiddish translation of the pseudo-history of Josephus, *Yosippon* (Krakow, 1589)? Or what to do with twenty-one manuscripts bound within a single volume (Ms. Opp. 134)? Binding and unbinding represents only one example of the potential welter of disorder that prevailed at the time in the world of books.[54] One solution to this challenge came with the production of guide-books to the maze of titles in a library collection: the catalogue.

Bibliographies and Book Lists

Cataloguing is a necessary act of bringing order to a multiplicity of objects. But listing books can also represent an owner's symbolic assertion of mas-tery over a subject. This impulse can be discerned in small collections as much as in large ones. Owners of some books would use the convenience of the empty page to itemize the rest of their library holdings. Thus Jacob of Berlin listed the three other books in his modest collection in the flyleaf of his small octavo edition of *Iggeret ha-Ramban* (Amsterdam, 1652).[55] And it was precisely in the same spirit that David Oppenheim converted the empty pages of a student's notebook into a guide to a library of 480 items.

Oppenheim compiled his catalogue in a once-blank notebook that had been given to him nearly a decade before in 1675, which he had first used to copy a manual of calendrical calculation, a *Sefer evronot,* at the age of eleven (fig. 1.2).[56] Empty notebooks such as these were a valuable gift for students, who often copied selections from printed books onto bound blank sheets to equip themselves with the bare necessities for study, a prac-tice of commonplacing that scholars had used for centuries.[57] Whether as amanuensis to a master, to compensate for a scarcity of titles, or simply to produce a concise and portable anthology of key texts, yeshiva students began to produce their own manuscript copies of books (even of books that circulated in print), accumulating a functional library of essential texts.

As the young man accumulated more and more books, the notebook

Fig. 1.2. Oppenheim's *Sefer evronot* (Ms. Opp. 699), title page with inscription, "Belongs to the clever youth called David, son of the chief warden and leader Abraham, man of Oppenheim, today Wednesday the 27th of Elul 5435 [September 18, 1675]." Courtesy of the Bodleian Libraries, University of Oxford.

of a student became the accounting log of the collector. On the sixty-third page of this bound paper volume, Oppenheim lyrically introduced his catalogue and his charge (fig. 1.3):

Be-Mazal Tov
BM"T [be-Mazal Tov] sefarim she-kaniti me-honi
li-khvod elokai tzuri ve-koni
ve-sidarti al otiyot be-seder
kol ot kiton ve-heder
le-ma'an himatzeh yimatzeh be-kal ve-nimratz
eizeh sefer haser asher ba-aretz
ve-H[ashem] yizakeni le-kanes u-lekabetz
ve-lihyot torat kel be-yisrael mefuzar u-merubatz
ve-le-asot sefarim ad ein ketz
ve-yihayenu ve-yimaher yeme ha-ketz
amen amen amen

With Good Fortune:
With good fortune the books that I have bought with my
    wealth
to honor my God who formed and acquired me
and I have organized them by letter in order
each letter in its vessel[58] and quarter
so that the finder may find with facility at hand
any book which is missing from the land
and may God grant me to collect and accrue them
that God's Torah in Israel may spread far and wide
and to make books without end
and to sustain us and speedily bring the days of the end
Amen Amen Amen.[59]

The introductory poem gives a sense of both Oppenheim's collecting mission and his literary prowess; an enduring component of Oppenheim's mature writing was his delight in allusion.[60] This earliest piece of Oppen-

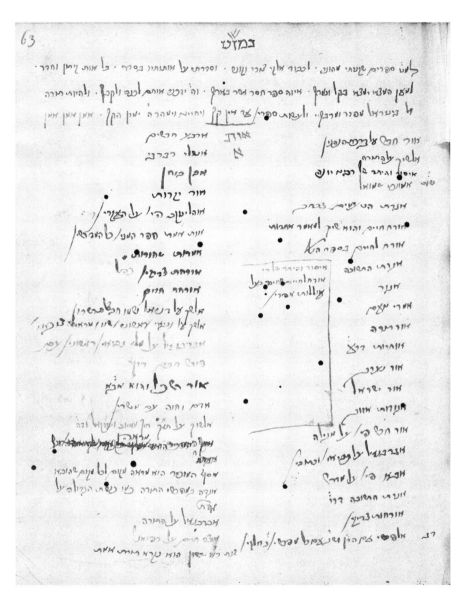

Fig. 1.3. First page of Oppenheim's manuscript list of books (Ms. Opp. 699, f. 63r).
Courtesy of the Bodleian Libraries, University of Oxford.

heim's original writing included an example of this playfulness, which re-
versed the meaning of an ancient aphorism. In this introduction, Oppenheim underscored his intention "to make books without end," an allusion
to Eccl 12:12. In its initial context, the verse condemns the proliferation of
knowledge as hopelessly unmanageable, as it warns that "of making many
books there is no end; and much study is a weariness of the flesh."[61] But
Oppenheim's youthful prose and collector's energy inverted that despera-
tion into aspiration and took it instead as instruction for a program of acquisition in action.[62]

In preparing this notebook, Oppenheim was participating in a mode
of knowledge-organization that was at once ancient and novel. Books about
books—including library catalogues, bibliographies, sales catalogues, and
other related genres—found their origins in antiquity and were in use
throughout the Middle Ages. But the advent of print produced a new impetus for the production of "meta-books" whose function was the organization of extant copies, on the one hand, and the expression of universal
aspirations, on the other.

Library catalogues and bibliographies differ fundamentally from each
other in this regard: the former reflect the realities of a collection's holdings,
and the latter offer the expanse of possibilities for acquisition and reading.
Although bibliographies appeared in varying forms from at least as early as
the fourth century, a watershed moment in bibliography arrived with the
work of Conrad Gesner (1516–1665), whose *Bibliotheca universalis* (Zurich,
1545) undertook a listing of all known works in Latin, Greek, and Hebrew.
Gesner's principle of comprehensiveness—which refused to exclude even
those books that the compiler held in low esteem—served as a model for
vernacular compendia. Gabriel Naudé introduced the term *bibliographia*
in 1633, and by the mid-seventeenth century the term "bibliography" had
achieved linguistic coinage.[63]

The first bibliography created by and for Jews did not emerge until
more than a century after Gesner. Barely five years before Oppenheim
began his personal catalogue, the Hebrew printer Shabbetai Bass (1641–
1718) published his *Sefer siftei yeshenim* (Amsterdam, 1680), the first complete bibliography of Jewish works directed toward a Jewish audience.[64]

Bass's guide dramatically eased the process of collecting books by establishing a roster of Jewish literature, creating a list against which contemporary collections could be checked and desiderata easily identified. *Siftei yeshenim* represented more than just an aspirational inventory; in enumerating all extant Jewish books, it mapped the horizons of Jewish literary culture and expressed an emergent ideal of what a library could be. Like Gesner before him, Bass's vision of bibliographic comprehensiveness was the bedrock of the collector's quest.[65]

But the boundaries between an inventory of a collection and an idealized bibliography were not absolute. In his 1627 *Advice on Establishing a Library,* Gabriel Naudé identified the consultation of catalogues as a vital preparatory task. He enjoined his readers to transcribe the catalogues of libraries great and small in order to gain the insight of models not only of titles but also of size. Such catalogues, Naudé argued, would also serve to point readers toward the location of books that the collector might not have the fortune to add to his collection—at the very least, they could be accessed elsewhere.[66]

The importance of access was present in Oppenheim's personal catalogue as well. In producing an inventory of his own possessions, Oppenheim was sensitive to both the contents of the library and the social contacts that enabled their acquisition. His catalogue first organized all of the titles in alphabetical order; he designated a blank page for each letter and added items to the list over time. He then created a second list to record the provenance of the books, paying attention to the previous owner and the price he paid for each (fig. 1.4). This duplicate listing reflected a careful reckoning with both the intellectual and material worth of his holdings—a combined sensitivity to the quality of the objects and the human agents who moved them.

Secondhand Books: The Impact of Place and Personal Ties

Where and how did Oppenheim acquire his books? In early modern Europe, shops dedicated specifically to the sale of books—and especially carrying Judaica—were hardly a common sight. Books were sold directly

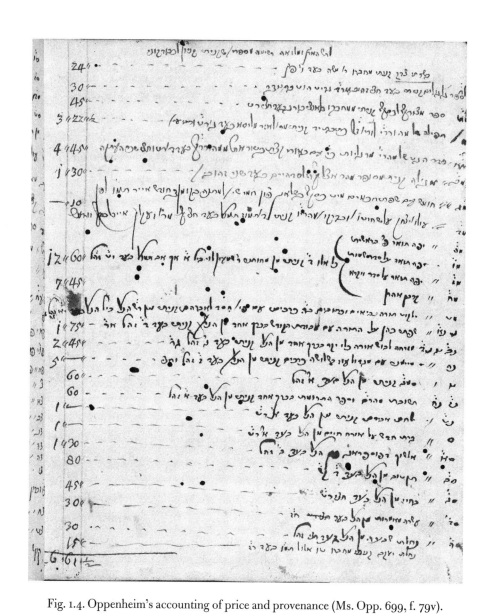

Fig. 1.4. Oppenheim's accounting of price and provenance (Ms. Opp. 699, f. 79v).
Courtesy of the Bodleian Libraries, University of Oxford.

by printers or publishers, and Oppenheim's catalogue reveals the occasional purchase directly from the printer's shop, as in an instance in which he purchased five books printed in Sulzbach in 1685, which were then all bound together into a single volume.[67] But far more often people came to own books through a secondary book economy, which resold and recycled books that had been printed long before and was an even more common form of book circulation. Oppenheim acquired books through a number of secondhand means: from vendors, as gifts, and by purchasing entire collections from insolvent individuals.

With the wealth of his extended family at his disposal, Oppenheim expanded his collection to encompass an array of materials from the heritage of his hometown. Most of his acquisitions came from local sellers, some of whom may have been members of his larger network of relatives. These included purchases from sellers named Seklin Euchel, Josman, and Samuel, of the Worms community, as well as a book written by the city's chief rabbi Aaron Teomim. Two weeks before the Jewish New Year in the autumn of 1686 Oppenheim purchased almost one hundred items from Zanwill (of Mannheim), scribe in Worms. As a scribe, Zanwill was in the business of producing and disseminating literary material in both printed and manuscript forms, and his familiarity with the market for manuscripts made for an easy transition to the commerce in books. In Worms Oppenheim also drew upon the inventories of several book vendors. In 1686 he spent 2.2 reichsthalers on a purchase of ten volumes from a vendor in Worms that included items from Riva di Trento, Mantua, Venice, and Prague.[68] Twenty-five other books came from Shimon ha-Levi of Fürth in the late summer of that same year; these included books of practical law (an *Olot Yitzhak* offered commentary on the manual for ritual slaughter, *Shehitot u-bedikot*), commentaries on the Bible (*Alsheikh, Kli Yakar, Siftei kohen,* and others), commentaries to the great codes of Jewish law (*Semag, Meimuni, Bayit hadash* on *Orah hayyim*), and responsa (*Teshuvo Maharam*).[69]

Although the authorship, genre, and provenance of these books varied, a significant proportion of Oppenheim's early acquisitions reflected local conditions. The preponderance of particular books in a location might indicate the strength of a local culture, or of the necessity of particular resources for daily, communal, and ritual life. This was certainly the case in Worms, the starting ground of Oppenheim's collection. These books reflected both the circumstantiality of which books were available to Oppenheim and his more deliberate investment in collecting works that reflected the culture of his native territory. Oppenheim collected items relating to the mythic past of Jews in the city, its historical texts, and the customs of its Jewish residents, constructing something of an archive of the cultural heritage of the Jews of Worms and the medieval Rhineland.[70] Given the fact of the continuous presence of Jews in Worms since the Middle Ages, the city was a rich source for Jewish books and manuscripts whose provenance dated back centuries. A manuscript of the Pentateuch and Megillat Esther, for example, included inscriptions dating their ownership to fifteenth- and sixteenth-century holders in the city.[71]

Oppenheim's collection of material relating to the city of Worms included texts by authors from Worms, texts chronicling the history of Jewish Worms, and texts reflective of the practices of the city's Jews. His manuscript collection included items from the Rhineland Pietists, especially Judah Hasid b. Samuel (d. 1217) and his student, Eleazar of Worms (1176–1238),[72] as well as later works by the kabbalist Elijah Loans (1555–1636).[73] His books also covered the religious life of the Jews of Worms, their prayers,[74] customs,[75] and Talmudic commentaries,[76] and included even the *Worms Memorbuch,*[77] an important list of all of the city's Jewish deceased that was likely used for synagogue memorial rituals. Any number of the books in Oppenheim's collection came from former owners in Worms as well. He also captured the wider history of Central European Jewry in the chronicle of Josel of Rosheim (1478–1554),[78] the autobiography of Yom Tov Lipmann Heller (1579–1654),[79] and martyrologies of Jews from as far east as Ofen (modern Budapest).[80]

The pages of his catalogue reveal his contacts with book agents in the city and the circumstances by which books flowed into his collection. The origins of his library were in local identification with a city in which his family wielded great wealth and influence, and whose dominance was palpable to all of the Jews of the city. But vendors were not the only way that Oppenheim acquired books. In fact, his earliest transactions were not purchases at all: they were gifts. Some of the very earliest books that entered his collection arrived as presents to commemorate his marriage in 1681.[81]

Oppenheim married Gnendel, daughter of Leffman Behrens, the Court Jew of Hanover.[82] Like Oppenheim's uncles, Behrens rose to prominence on account of his commercial services, among them his large cloth manufactory and tobacco factory. Behrens' service to his patron, Duke Ernst August, brought prestige to Hanover on the imperial and even international scenes: in 1692 the duke was elevated to the rank of electoral prince with the help of Behrens' contribution of 1.1 million reichsthalers to the imperial treasury.[83] The Oppenheim and Behrens families were not strangers to each other. On several occasions Behrens lent support to and did business with Samuel Oppenheimer, David's uncle, the Court Jew of Vienna.[84] The marriage of their children, however, further solidified a bond between them that was typical of German Jewry during this period—a Jewry that was dominated by an upper class that practiced tactical endogamy.[85]

The careful practice of marriage alliance as a strategy for consolidating power and ensuring the commercial and professional successes of its kinship group had a complementary measure for Jews outside of the network of kin. These nonrelations could express their affiliation through gifts. Gifts were an important act for establishing relationships, made more important in relating to the union of these two influential families; mingling sentimentality with solidarity, gifts helped to forge affective bonds and establish patterns of reciprocal relationships.[86]

Gifts came to Oppenheim from local well-wishers, relatives, and teachers in the places where he traveled. He received a *Pentateuch with Three Commentaries* (Hanau, 1611-1614) from a widow in Worms, the *Sha'arei orah* from a relative named Zanwill, and the *Amudei shiv'a* from a Worms resident named Hayyim. His teacher, Isaac Benjamin Wolff, *Av Beit Din* (chief judge) of Landsberg and rabbi of the Mark (or Margraviate) of Brandenburg, presented him with a commentary to the Talmudic tractate *Bava Kama.* Oppenheim's tutor from his childhood years in Worms, Yair Hayyim Bachrach, presented him with two books as gifts, one of which was Bachrach's own recently printed collection of responsa (Frankfurt am Main, 1679). Relatives continued this commemorative tradition: his uncle

Samuel Oppenheimer gave him a copy of the *Ein Yaakov,* and his father-in-law gave him the gift of a Pentateuch "with a silver covering" a few years later in 1686.[87] Oppenheim's catalogue indicates the gift of two books from the same man, Toch, bound together in a single volume.[88]

Widows, Women, and the Gender of Early Modern Books

Disparities between rich and poor were also important in another way for this collection's early growth. While Oppenheim's family assets provided him with near-unlimited resources, the financial need of *others* also significantly drove the collection forward. Oppenheim bought portions of libraries, or perhaps libraries in their entirety, from the estates of former users, often from the widows who survived the male original owners. Likely the executors of the estates of their husbands, these women had a greater need of liquid cash than the scholarly contents of books that belonged to a world of rabbinic scholarship from which they were formally excluded. On April 6, 1688, Oppenheim gained thirty-seven volumes for his collection by purchasing them from the widow of one Joseph ha-Levi. In September 1691 he procured nineteen books from the widow of Abraham (Avrum) Stern of Worms, for a sum of 20 reichsthalers and 12.5 batzen.[89] These small-scale book collectors tended to be far more modest in their holdings—virtually all of their books were printed between the late sixteenth century and middle of the seventeenth century and were items that were relatively available and did not require substantial access to rare book vendors and collectors.

These acquisitions were only a minor expenditure for Oppenheim, who had the great wealth of his family at his disposal, but they could represent quite a significant transaction for the people from whom he purchased them. In the mid-eighteenth century, some German-Jewish households reported assets of approximately 3,000–6,000 reichsthalers, but many others had between 500 and 2,000 reichsthalers as their net worth. The memoirist Glikl of Hameln gives a sense of the range of family assets when she discusses the variety of wealth in Hamburg at approximately the same period as Oppenheim's life:

> And at that time, there were only about forty households in
> Altona, including those who had come from Hamburg, and
> even though there were not greatly wealthy ones, everyone sus-
> tained themselves with honor. The greatly wealthy at that time
> were Hayyim Furst, may he rest in peace, who was a man of
> tens of thousands of reichsthalers, my father, of blessed mem-
> ory, who had 8,000 reichsthalers, others had 6,000, and some
> had 2,000, but all treated each other well and lived together in
> love and great affection.[90]

In Worms during Oppenheim's youth, a doctor rented a home from a local
Jewish woman, paying 10 reichsthalers annually for the use of the entire
house minus a few rooms, even as Oppenheim's own family was conducting trade deals in the thousands and tens of thousands.[91]

A widow's search for solvency by liquidating her husband's book
collection was a common strategy; it could also create moments of conflict
as books formed a fault line between gendered approaches to property. In
1694 — when he was already serving as chief rabbi of Moravia — Oppenheim
received a letter from a yeshiva student who was distressed that despite a
promise by his teacher that upon his death he would bequeath his books
to his pupil, the deceased's widow was putting them up for sale instead.[92]
Although the widow was desperately in need of material sustenance and
treated the books like any other commodity, the male student pointed to the
special — perhaps inalienable — bond that persisted in the master-student relationship and the bequest of books. The student appealed to Oppenheim,
believing that a scholar and bibliophile would see things his way. We do not
know how Oppenheim replied, but the question reveals the gendered tensions that inhered in the uses of the book, and the difficulty in ascribing a
single type of usage for these commodities. In a similar distinction, Oppenheim's contemporary, Pinhas Katzenellinbogen, stipulated in his will that
upon his death his books would go to his son, "with the explicit provision"
that the son would provide an annual stipend of 25 Rhenish gold pieces for
his mother, the man's widow.[93] Books were never free of their status as a store
of value, nor were they empty of sentimental and even metaphysical power.[94]

The dimensions of early modern Jewish domestic economics manifested in other domains of book exchange as well, often in gendered ways. In another book owned by Oppenheim, an inscription given on the title page reveals that the book's previous owner had come by it as part of the terms of her divorce settlement, as stipulated by her *ketubah*. The book was later owned, however, by the brother of this woman's ex-husband. The new (male) owner justified his holding of this book, which ought to have been included in the *ketubah* payment of his brother's ex-wife, by explicitly noting in the volume that he had redeemed the book from the divorcee for cash.[95]

It was not uncommon for books to serve as stores of monetary value. An inscription in Oppenheim's printed copy of *Sefer rosh amanah,* by Don Isaac Abarbanel, reveals that a former owner "used this book as a guarantee of a loan of 3 gold pieces."[96] And, of course, not all books women owned were simply for commodification. An entire market of Yiddish books was produced during the early modern period for "women and men who are like women," and Oppenheim did not shy away from including these materials in his collection.[97] His formidable resources did not prejudice him against the cheap pamphlets on low-quality paper that were designed for public consumption and entertainment. They populated his shelves in abundance. This, too, was consonant with Naudé's admonition to the builder of a great library not to overvalue books of "price and bulk" to the detriment of gathering "little books."[98]

The books in Oppenheim's collection comprised not only stories, but also twenty-eight volumes of prayers designed predominantly for women (*tkhines*), books of instruction for women's religious practices (the *Sefer mitzvot nashim,* or Book of Women's Commandments), and twenty editions of the Yiddish Bible translation, the *Tsene-urene.*[99] His collection included instructions for women for the washing and salting of meat in the home to ensure its kosher preparation, and Yiddish manuals of rudimentary science to treat such illnesses as vertigo.[100] Evidence of female ownership survives in some volumes of Oppenheim's collection, such as a Yiddish edition of the historical work *Yosippon,* owned by Hinde, daughter of Zanwill (perhaps the same Zanwill who sold so many other books to

Oppenheim).[101] He also owned a manuscript of a German translation of the
Pentateuch that was made in the sixteenth century on behalf of a woman.[102]

New Books

The secondhand economy of recycled books formed the bedrock of Oppenheim's earliest collection, but the acquisition of newly produced books was
important to him as well. In the years following his marriage, Oppenheim
continued to travel between various centers of study in the western Holy
Roman Empire in order to continue his rabbinical training.[103] Travel in person and by proxy allowed Oppenheim to reach wider book markets than
those in his immediate vicinity and to extend his reach to encompass the
print matter that rolled off of presses across Europe, a practice he continued
throughout his adulthood. One of the few opportunities to buy new books
came at the annual trade fairs in Frankfurt and Leipzig.[104] These fairs were
often a site of interaction between sellers and readers of Hebrew books,
both Jewish and Christian, from across much of the continent.[105] In 1687
Oppenheim dispatched a rabbi by the name of Leizer to the Frankfurt fair
to buy books on his behalf.[106] Later, when the book trade's center of gravity
shifted eastward to Leipzig, Oppenheim occasionally traveled there in person from his rabbinic post in Prague to jostle among the hundreds of sellers
and thousands of buyers—Jewish and non-Jewish—who participated in
this annual affair.[107]

At other times books came to him from the hands of the very men
who had written them—new authors who presented fresh copies of their
work to the budding collector.[108] In the absence of bookstores, individual
authors might double as vendors of their own literary products, taking to
the roads to peddle the books they had written and published. As Oppenheim's reputation grew, some individuals even made copies of their manuscripts before publication to give to Oppenheim.[109] Perhaps those peddlers
took the trouble to bind newly printed books themselves. Oppenheim accounted for the cost of binding only once in his catalogue, in which he recorded a cost of 9 batzen in order to bind books together.[110]

A parallel form of making "new" books was also available to Oppenheim through the labor of scribes and copyists. These skilled workers did not simply sell old titles; they copied and transcribed them into new forms, renewing their circulation, usually by commission. In Europe of the early modern period, no sharp categorical distinction obtained between the printed book and the manuscript. Indeed, for centuries after the advent of printing technology students and scholars continued to use manuscripts alongside printed matter — in their function there was little need to distinguish between the two.[111] One might read the text of the Pentateuch or the Talmud from a handwritten copy just as easily as from any of the printed editions, and often with more ready availability. Manuscripts and printed texts could be considered as so interchangeable that they could even be bound together in a single volume. And when Oppenheim built his first library catalogue, he made no categorical distinction between manuscript and book — the only order to his inventory was alphabetical. As in numerous other library catalogues of the seventeenth century, the separation between manuscript and printed word was far from complete.[112]

A copied manuscript was both ancient text and newly produced matter. Much as a printed book continued to be glossed with marginalia, the manuscript might be considered a "published" text as well. Over the course of his career and collecting, Oppenheim worked with scribes to record communal decisions, transcribe diplomatic documents, and copy entire manuscripts of Jewish learning. In some cases these scribes were scholars in their own right, such as Zevi Hirsch Kaidenover, author of the *Kav ha-yashar,* a book of morals. Oppenheim added an *evronot* handwritten by Kaidenover to his growing collection.[113] At other times they were professional scribes who worked either in the employ of the *kehillah* administration or by private commission.

Oppenheim was intimately familiar with the demands involved in the labor of copying. In his personal catalogue of his books, he noted an expenditure of 4.5 reichsthalers for a scribe to copy a manuscript of the *Seder ha-get* (instructions for writs of divorce) and a further 1.3 reichsthalers in order to purchase a megillah from a "fast scribe" in Hildesheim.[114] In 1689, only a few weeks after his hometown of Worms had been ravaged by French forces, Oppenheim wrote a lengthy responsum from his new base in Han-

over. In the context of arranging for a reply, Oppenheim requested a copy of
a responsum in return but noted that "should the young men not be capable
and comfortable with writing, and they do not wish to copy it, surely there
must be a scribe, and I will pay the fee for copying."[115] The young collector, with his vast familial resources, evinced little concern over the price of
copying. Long literary works—those approximating two hundred folios—
could seldom be written in fewer than two and a half months—a costly
labor period.[116]

Oppenheim's knowledge about scribal culture could also shade into
the highly unusual. In one of his responsa, he was called upon to rule on
a dispute between scribes. The incident that prompted this inquiry came
from a curious case in which a disabled scribe who was lame in both of his
arms managed to write by holding a quill in his mouth.[117] The other scribes
in the community had raised hackles over this scribe's activity, citing legal
sources that sacred texts written in such a manner by a lame scribe would
not be fit for ritual use. Oppenheim ultimately ruled that even the sacred
writings produced by holding a pen in one's mouth were not ritually dis-
qualified, but only if no other qualified scribes were able to produce the
work.

Through the pages of Oppenheim's manuscripts we can glimpse the
experiences of scribes as well. In one instance, a copyist offered personal
reflections on the scribe's life as a vocation. In the opening pages of Oppenheim's copy of *Haze ha-tenufah,* copied in Vienna in 1716, the scribe offered
his life story in brief, as a form of defense against errors in the text. "Therefore I, too," wrote the scribe, "will place my apology before the eyes of all
who read this book; that they should not blame me nor find me culpable
for sins that are not before me should they find any stammering in any
place of reason and wisdom—this stumbling block is not from my hands."
The scribe could place such confidence in his ability on account of a long
career, begun early in his youth: "At the age of six and seven . . . I began to
accustom myself to writing." At age eleven he studied in Przemysl under the
tutelage of Joseph ha-Levi Horowitz, and at thirteen he studied in Lissa. In
both, he served to write "several hundred texts of different sorts" (*ketavim
mi-mikhtavim shonim,* a play on Esth 1:7). He next moved to work as Rabbi

Leib Zunz's scribe, and by age twenty-three he was the regional scribe in the community of Ludmir. Finally, he entered the service of David Oppenheim: "I was his scribe and faithful member of his household and I copied his compositions and books in Nikolsburg and in Prague and in Vienna and in Hanover" (the scribe had to be as mobile as the rabbi in whose retinue he served).[118]

Oppenheim's reliance on various scribes suggests that copyists specialized in particular genres. Some worked with mystical material, others as translators, and others with texts of scientific value. As he continued to grow his collection during his tenure in Prague, Oppenheim relied on one Azriel of Kortoszyn to reproduce multiple mystical texts.[119] Azriel's career offered an important transalpine link to an effervescence of editing and publishing activity in the Italian peninsula, specifically in Venice and Mantua. Before going to Prague to work for Oppenheim, Azriel had lived in Constantinople and Mantua. There, in the Italian city, he studied under the renowned kabbalist Moses Zacuto (ca. 1620–1698), who operated a scriptorium that facilitated the transmission of Lurianic kabbalah throughout Europe. Students would write to Zacuto with requests for inaccessible material, and he would instruct his students in their exact copy. Zacuto's students Benjamin Kohen of Reggio (d. 1730) and Abraham Rovigo (1650–1713)—both influential kabbalists in their own right who sympathized with the teachings of Sabbatean doctrine—continued the work of the diffusion of kabbalah in their own study houses.[120] Azriel even may have procured originals for Oppenheim, as some of the latter's manuscripts bear autograph glosses by Zacuto himself.[121]

David Oppenheim's upbringing in Worms, the center of Ashkenazic culture, had another important effect on his manuscript collection: it shaped the way he preferred to read. Azriel, a native of central Poland, gained familiarity with the Spanish script as a student in Mantua. He was therefore tasked by Oppenheim not strictly with reproduction, but more specifically to *transcribe* texts from one scribal hand into another.[122] Thanks to Azriel's labors, Oppenheim's library came to own duplicate copies of at least fifteen pairs of manuscripts transcribed from a Sephardic to an Ashkenazic script by Azriel's hand (fig. 1.5).

Such transcriptions were quite important: Oppenheim appears to have strongly preferred the Ashkenazic over the Spanish cursive. Thus a 1706 letter from Jerusalem written to Oppenheim told of a newly acquired book that would "take some time to copy" as it was written in the Sephardic hand.[123] The implications of this transcription were significant: a world of Jewish books can often seem boundless and fluid, as if the Jewish language of Hebrew might function to link educated Jews of disparate geographic locations across borders and without limitation. But language is mediated through its representative paleography, and by the early modern period Jews of different geographic regions had accustomed themselves to particular orthographies. Thus, even as books could be put into motion by Jewish diasporas of multiple centers, the products of those centers were not necessarily received seamlessly. Although certain bonds of solidarity may have obtained between Jews of different locations, they were also intimate familiars of their particular geography. Oppenheim's preference for the Ashkenazic cursive script reveals that his library, even when it aspired to assemble all extant Jewish books, had a Central European tint to it.

The transcription from Sephardic to Ashkenazic cursive was not limited to kabbalistic works alone. Multiple copies of books remain in the library of works in duplicate: once in Sephardic and a second time in Ashkenazic cursive, many of which bear inscriptions that report that the book's contents have been "copied letter-for-letter from a Sephardic hand."[124] One copyist gives us a sense of the labor demanded in the endeavor, as well as the involvement of the commissioner. A commentary on the astronomical work of al-Farghani called *Sefer Abualbar* was undertaken by a scribe in Vienna in 1717, to transcribe it from *"ketivat ha-sefaradi"* (the Sephardic hand) to *"ktav ashurit"* (i.e., Ashkenazic cursive) on Oppenheim's behalf. The work began on the first of the winter month of Shevat (roughly February) and continued until the twentieth of the same month and was checked periodically (presumably by Oppenheim) over the course of the process.[125]

Questions of language and representation kept at least one other scribe busy as well. Oppenheim employed a man named Meir b. Judah Leib Neumark of Hanau not solely as a scribe, but also as a translator. Meir's father, Judah Leib b. David Neumark, was the manager of the Hebrew

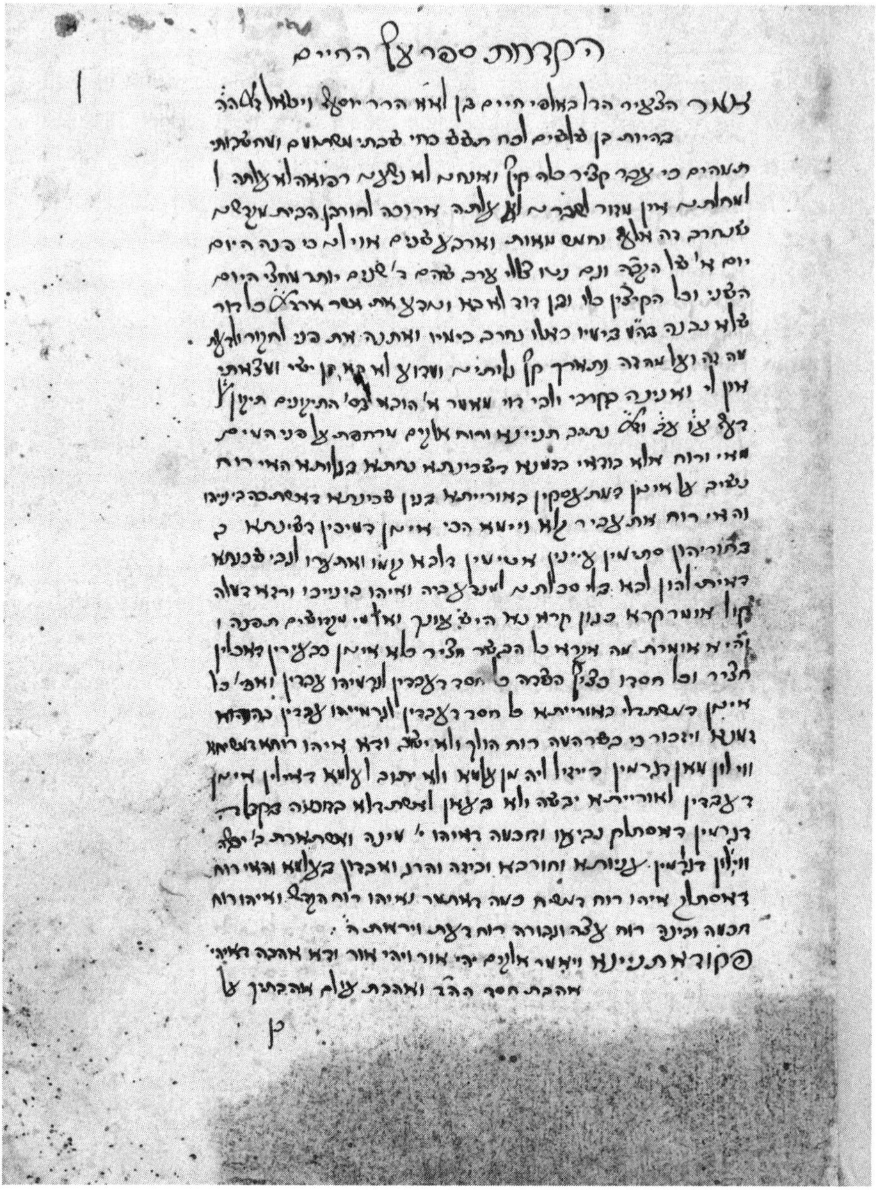

הקדמת ספר עץ החיים

Fig. 1.5. Examples of Oppenheim's employment of copyists to transcribe material from the Sephardic to the Ashkenazic hand, which he found more legible. Ms. Opp. 480, f. 1r (left, in Ashkenazic script) and Ms. Opp. 481, f. 1r (right, in a Sephardic hand). Courtesy of the Bodleian Libraries, University of Oxford.

אבוֹר הצעיר הדל כ׳חלפי חיים בן לאא הרר יוסף ויראל זלהה בהיותי בן
שלשים לכח התעשעבתי שבתי משתלמא וחחשבותי רעהים כי עבר קציר
כלה קיץ ואנחנו לא נשענו רפואה לא עלתה לחולייננו אין מחור לשברנו לא על יצ͏ר
אדוכה לחורבן הבית מקדשנו שבחר בו זה אלף וחמש מאות וחרבל שנים אוי לנו כי
פנה היום יוה הל׳ של הקבה וגם נטו צללי ערב שהם ד׳ שנים יותר מחצי היום הש׳ני ובל
הקיצין כל׳ וכן דור לא בא ונוד על את חשר אמרו רז׳׳ל כל דור שלא נבנה ב׳חמ בימיו
כאלו נחרב ב׳ מיו ואחרנה את פני לחקור ולה עת׳ מה זה ועל מה זה נתאחרן קן גלותינו
ומדועל לא בא בן ישי ולקחתי און לי ואניגה בקרבי ולבי ד׳׳ל אחמר א הובא בכל התיקונים
תיקוק ל דף של עב ועל נתב ב תנייא ורוח אלקים מרחפת על פני המים מאי ורוח אלא
בורחי בזמנא דשכינתא נחתא בגלוהה האי רוח נשיב על אינון דמתעסקן בואורייתא
בגין שכינתא דאשתכח בינייהו והאי רוח אקשעביר אלא וייאא הכי אינון דמוכין
דשינקא בחוריהון פתייקן עינין אטוימין דלבב קומו ואתערו לגבי שכינתא דאיל
וקין לכא בל ככלתני לטוכיה ביה ואיהו בינייבו ורוח דמלה קול אוימר קרא כאן קרא וא
היע עוינ ואל מי חיקרושוים רפנה והיא אוימר תלה אקרף כל הבער חצ׳ר כל אינ
כבעלדין דאכלין חצ׳ר וכל חפדו בצ׳ץ השדה כל חפר דעבדין לדרמייהו עבדין בהל
חטטא ויזבור כי בשר רוח הולך ולא ישוב ורא איהו רוח דמשיחא לו מאחן דרמין
בעייל ליה מן עלמא ולא יתוב לעלמא דאילן אינון דלבדין לאוריייתא יתבא ולא בעלתן
לשתגלא בחכיה בקבלה דבר מן דאפתליך נכיתו וחכמה דקיבהו מינה ואשתלוךת ב
יכטה וו לון דבר מן עווהה וחור בל ובי זב והרב ועבדין בעלמא והא רוח דאפתל
איהו רוח דמושיא בלה דאתמר ויהו רוח הקדט ויהו רוח חכמא וביה רוח עצר
אבורה רוח דעת ויראת ה

פקורא תניינא ואאהד אלקים יהי אור ויהי אור ורא אהבה דלייהי אהבן חפר
הרד ואהבת עולה להבתך על כן משכתיך חפד ועלב אמר
אם קלירו ואם קצבורו את האהבה עד שתחפן יראה אתלק יקת מאערק דשחאלא
ואהבה אלתקף יקת מפעורק דימימא ליית ירלה ולית יראה אית אהבה אית אהבה
יראק דרחיל בר עש להקבה כגין דלא נעיק מנכפוי או בגין דלא ימותן בני בחייוי
אשתכח דהא היה נחיית מככפוי או אם ימותן בני בחיייי דלא הוה דחיל לה ובלד זח
רחיע ליב א הן׳ו ירלה ואהבה לששוי לריאתא דילא להבה דילא לעיקרא אבל רתיחו ורהילא
בין עב ובין ב׳ש וכל גד אמר קבה שבעתי אתרכם בנט ירושלא בצבאות א׳ בתלאר
הסדרא אם קלירו ואם קצבורו את האהבה עד שתחפן דאיבו רתימו ופי עד רהיהו
 יחפן ולא על לכל פרח וירהא ואהבה עה לקבל פרח איהי שפחה ופהת שלא ירצה אחף ו
תחת עבר כי ימלך ושפחה כי תירש גביררה עכל ׳
ורנך

printing house in Berlin and author of a book of Hebrew grammar, *Shoresh David*.[126] Meir began his work as a bookseller at the age of fifteen.[127] He had translated a history book into Hebrew, labeled *Tirat melakhim,* at the age of sixteen, in Frankfurt am Main.[128] Oppenheim learned of this book and established contact with the young man, encouraging him to continue the translating endeavor. Oppenheim regularly enlisted Meir's services as an agent of cross-cultural mediation, especially to translate manuscripts from German and Latin into Hebrew. In 1703, after Oppenheim had officially been appointed to the Prague rabbinate, Meir Neumark completed a translation for the chief rabbi of a cosmographical work, which he titled *Tokhen ha-kadur* in Hebrew.[129] His efforts for Oppenheim appear to have been related to his familiarity with scientific treatises. He translated at least one other manuscript for Oppenheim that dealt with natural phenomena, called *Tekhunat ha-havayah*.[130] Neumark's activities demonstrate the scope of Oppenheim's interests beyond traditional studies of religious law or mysticism into the natural sciences, however rudimentary, as well.[131]

Oppenheim's scribal collaborators may not have been only male. Oppenheim's daughter, Sara (d. 1713), received such an education as well. Sara, who was married to Hayyim Yonah Teomim Fränkel, has the distinction of being one of the few known women who made her own copy of a Megillat Esther, a parchment scroll of the biblical book of Esther, which gained her a measure of fame during her lifetime. In a commentary to the book of Esther published in 1710, the Prague rabbi Moses Meir Perles considered whether or not a text such as this, written by a woman, might be admissible for ritual purpose.[132] Perles concluded in the negative and even considered it imperative that the work be immediately buried lest someone come to use it accidentally. And yet, it cannot be ignored that word had spread that the chief rabbi, who was involved with the intricacies of book collecting, had a female member of his household who could match the abilities of the men in his retinue, perhaps, in following the intricate laws for producing a legitimate megillah, even surpassing them.

Conclusion

As Oppenheim's social circles expanded, the contours of his collection grew to encompass an ever wider scope. As his fame spread and motivation grew for book producers to make special gifts of their wares, Oppenheim's collection gained an individuated tint that expressed elements of his own aesthetic. But that aesthetic was colored by the sense of place and belonging in which his collection began. His youth and education in the Rhineland appears to have anchored the collection in the heritage of Worms, rather than it being merely a reflection of conveniently accessible resources. Through the inscriptions in many of the collection's pages, the biographies of people who otherwise left no traces to historical posterity begin to come into the light. Their possessions, and their life stories, intersected with Oppenheim's through the exchange of books and reflect the ways in which rich and poor, widows and students regularly crossed paths with one another. But Oppenheim gathered books "without end" not simply to hoard them, but to use them in particular ways that would enhance his standing as a rabbi, scholar, and communal leader. It is to those ends that we now turn.

Politics, Patronage, and Paper

Books and Broadsides as Political Objects

It is certain that if he who is pursuing this project has sufficient influence and authority to do favors for his friends, there will not be one among them but will hold it an honor to present him the rarest books that come to hand, who will not admit him freely into his library or into those of his friends, or, in brief, who will not strive to aid this project and contribute to it all that he possibly can.

—Gabriel Naudé, *Advice on Establishing a Library,* 1627

UNLIKE THE USERS OF BOOKS WE encountered in the previous chapter, Oppenheim seldom wrote his own name directly into his books. Instead, he adopted a more elevated means of making sure that he marked ownership of his prized possessions. Into the front of numerous manuscripts, Oppenheim included a title page, a sort of ex libris to signal his unique possession. The page consisted of a central blank space for a title and brief description of the work, under which was another blank space for the insertion of a copy date. Framing this space on the right and left, respectively, were images of the biblical Moses and his brother Aaron, the high priest. Above both Moses the lawgiver and Aaron the high priest, atop the title of the book, was an image of King David, holding a lyre, suspended by two angels (fig. 2.1). The intention was clear: users of this object were in the presence of nobility, if not royalty, a man who followed in the footsteps of Israel's archetypical monarch. Like early modern rulers, who enlisted antiquarian research to cloak contemporary power in the authority of a bygone era, Oppenheim adopted ancient Israel's greatest political figure as his symbolic presence on the page to unite books, learning, and power.[1]

ספר
פלה הרמוז על
חמשים אופנים
במלואו

ש·941

Fig. 2.1. Ms. Opp. 242, title page: The prophet Moses and the priest Aaron frame the title on either side, and King David is above both. Courtesy of the Bodleian Libraries, University of Oxford.

Oppenheim's identification with his biblical namesake gained increasing attention. In a manuscript copied in Dessau in 1714, one artful scribe indulged a flair for decoration and drew up his own title page that paid tribute to the manuscript's commissioner.[2] This manuscript illumination made the association between Oppenheim and the biblical ruler explicit by citing a pseudo-biblical phrase "and David sat on his royal throne." But the David of the image sits not with scepter and throne but with book and inkwell before him (fig. 2.2).

The association between biblical monarchy and the eighteenth-century rabbi and collector reveals Oppenheim's use of an image to project power and authority. Other Jews responded to his self-fashioning. Letters to Oppenheim from colleagues and clients similarly adopted phrases about the biblical king to craft paeans to their contemporary. Jewish supplicants sought to ingratiate themselves within the world of the Court Jews by approaching Oppenheim as a point of access into the ranks of these wealthy figures. Oppenheim built his library through the resources of his family wealth, but those riches had greater meaning than mere cash value. Their influence at court translated into a decisive place over Jewish life in Central Europe, and Oppenheim and his library were, for some, the means to access that influence. These hopefuls expressed their requests and appreciation by offering tribute to Oppenheim in the form of a book. Books traveled into Oppenheim's collection as a kind of currency that could be exchanged for favor, financing, and political appointment. His acceptance of books as gifts exposes a world beyond the arrangements legislated on paper and committed to print—a system of politics that relied almost as much on personal ties as official legislation. The agents of this system were the Court Jews of Central Europe, whose influence was decisive not merely for lower-ranking scholars, students, and supplicants, but for Oppenheim's own career trajectories as well. In time, Oppenheim's significance to the world not solely of Jewish books but to Jewish philanthropy resulted in the allusions of royalty that adorned the title pages of books to find a concrete expression: with his appointment as a "prince" of the Jews of the Land of Israel.

Fig. 2.2. Ms. Opp. 258, title page: Jacob b. Asher's *Tur* with title page. At the bottom center sits David, with one finger keeping his place in a book, another book closed on the table, and an inkwell nearby. Courtesy of the Bodleian Libraries, University of Oxford.

The Politics of the Rabbinate

Oppenheim took up his first rabbinic position in Moravia, the eastern part of the Bohemian lands, around 1690, after a decade of training and travel in the western lands of the Holy Roman Empire.[3] His teacher, Yair Hayyim Bachrach, remarked on the impressive achievement of receiving such an appointment before the age of thirty—an achievement that was the result of both superior training and the right amount of familial heft.[4]

Oppenheim's arrival in Moravia introduced him to a Jewish world that was markedly different from that of the Rhineland in which he had been born and raised. He described the range of duties that fell to him in Moravia in a letter to Bachrach in the summer of 1694, listing three major obligations that sapped his time and strength, in which "the people stand upon me from morning until evening": "the business of the *yeshiva*," "matters of the *kehillah*," and "the business of the *medinah*."[5] These distinct functions were united in one man, but they each required different skills and different operations. His appointment entailed the intellectual leadership of the yeshiva, or study house, of Nikolsburg and oversight over the ritual affairs of the *kehillah*, such as certifying kosher butchers and managing the staff of preachers and teachers of the community. However, it was the latter of the three tasks—the business of the *medinah*—that was unique to Moravia and called for the greatest amount of negotiation between the rabbi, the state, and a host of intermediaries.

Moravian Jewry had weathered a series of expulsions during the fifteenth and sixteenth centuries that had concentrated a majority of its number in small and midsized noble towns. Unlike the Jewish settlements of neighboring Bohemia and much of the Holy Roman Empire—some of which could not achieve a quorum for prayers or sustain the basic institutions of Jewish daily life without recourse to larger regional associations— the Jewish communities of Moravia were significant self-sustaining entities that were home to yeshivot, ritual baths, kosher butchers, and rabbinic establishments.[6] Despite their individual self-sufficiency, however, the Jews of Moravia had forged a supracommunal association in the years after the

Thirty Years War that coordinated the activities of all of the individual Jewish settlements within the province.

This association, called the *Va'ad medinat Mehrin* (Council of the Province of Moravia), assembled every three years to deal with a variety of concerns for Moravian Jewry, including taxation, administration, and religious matters.[7] The provincial association was further subdivided into three districts: upper, middle, and lower Moravia. Each district appointed two leaders to oversee its internal administration and to serve as members of a six-person governing council for the entire province. The Va'ad convened every three years from its first meeting in 1650 until 1748. Like many individual Jewish communities of the early modern period, the governing council of the Va'ad preserved its decisions in writing under the title *Shai Takkanot* ("311 Statutes" — in Hebrew 311 equals the letters *shin-yud-alef* — after the 311 statutes established at the first meeting of the council) and continued to add records of later sessions.[8] The statutes codified practices that were likely already in force and lent the fixity of written law to the weight of custom's authority. In his capacity of chief rabbi of Moravian Jewry, Oppenheim presided over the general assembly of the regional association, lending symbolic weight to its proceedings, and asserted governing supremacy over every rabbi in the province by insisting on the revival of a custom that had fallen into disuse: the right to approve each and every rabbi appointed by their local communities in Moravia.[9] He was also responsible for the wider upkeep of religious education, in particular with the provision of books for study. In the absence of Jewish printing houses in Moravia between 1605 and 1750, the regional association tasked the chief rabbi with the procurement of enough volumes of the Talmud to furnish the students of the study houses of the province.[10]

Although Oppenheim formally took up the rabbinate of Moravia in 1690, his position was not uncontested. His appointment was complicated by the fact that he was not the only rabbi who claimed the mantle of Moravian chief rabbi. Another rabbi, in Kremsier, named Isaachar Baer Frankfurter also laid claim to the title.[11] The tensions between Oppenheim and his rival first emerged in 1692, when the location of the upcoming synod of the regional council was disputed.[12] Rabbi Frankfurter had lodged a bid to host the meeting in his home jurisdiction of Kremsier in contravention of the custom to hold the meeting on a rotating basis between the three districts of the province. And since the position of chief rabbi was as much a political appointment as it was an outcome of rabbinic expertise, both Oppenheim and his competitor took recourse not to scholarship to resolve this conflict, but rather to political alliances.

Frankfurter appears to have acted first, by lobbying the prince-bishop of Olmütz to support the relocation of the synod to Kremsier. But Oppenheim did not take this challenge lightly. With weeks to spare before the convening of the synod, Oppenheim urgently attempted to enlist the support of the powerful Ferdinand Josef von Dietrichstein, prince of Nikolsburg, to come to his aid, purporting to represent not only himself, but "all the local elders and inhabitants," who implored the prince for his aid.[13] Dietrichstein replied on May 18, 1692, calling for the meeting to be held in Butschowitz instead. His favorable ruling brought Oppenheim's grateful reply.[14] Oppenheim had carefully chosen his ally. The Dietrichstein clan was one of a handful of Moravian families intimately bound up with Austrian Habsburg politics, and Dietrichstein was of particular importance for his proximity to the court in Vienna; he served as majordomo to Emperor Leopold from 1683 to 1698.[15] That Dietrichstein was favorably disposed toward Oppenheim must have been a result of his relationship with Oppenheim's uncle, Samuel, in Vienna.

The contest between the rabbis and their noble proxies delayed the meeting of the *Va'ad* for a full two years, until 1694. The synod ultimately convened in Frankfurter's native Kremsier, despite Oppenheim and Dietrichstein's objections, but the records of its proceedings suggest both a compromise between the rabbis and a lay censure of their competition. Each rabbi signed his name to the proceedings by claiming the title "chief rabbi" after his signature.[16] But the lay-written regulations went a step further to avoid this kind of rabbinic strife, ruling that: "We have found and seen fitting to establish well that no complete synod to appoint electors should be held at all in any community in which the rabbi of the *medinah* dwells. We have come to add with full force that it should remain and continue as such, it being well known all of the excess expense that falls upon the citizens of the *medinah*."[17] By the time the synod was held in Kremsier, the Va'ad had declared its resolve not to repeat this fiasco. To the extent that they could, lay leaders would prevent such an episode, in which rabbis could be so influential, from recurring.

Oppenheim's coalition ultimately prevailed, not only over the question of location, but over the larger question of power-sharing in the Moravian chief rabbinate. By the next synod of the Va'ad, in Lundenburg in 1697, Oppenheim had won supremacy, forcing his rival's departure from Moravia to Jerusalem. His victory over Frankfurter was so complete that the latter acknowledged his financial dependence on Oppenheim and his relatives. He published a book that lavished praise upon Oppenheim and his courtly relatives for their support of both his move and the printing of this book.[18]

Oppenheim's successful campaign for primacy as Moravia's chief rabbi reveals the dissonance between the ideals of Jewish self-governance and the pragmatics of realpolitik. The very same session of the Va'ad in 1694 that had been so contentious in its location on account of the rabbis' appeals to state authority attempted to legislate against that sort of intercession by its constituents more generally. It declared: "We have agreed after seeing the great outbreak, that some men arise in their communities and disturb their ruler (*serarah*), bringing cases before the ruler before they approach the rabbi and judges of their community. Therefore we have agreed, all of us as one, that the householders that approach the ruler must pay a fine of 12 reichsthalers, half to his ruler and half to the trustee of the *medinah*."[19] The synod attempted to impose fines on Jews who would contravene Jewish legal courts and take their cases to non-Jewish authorities. The ruling that Jews may not circumvent the law was likely to have been directed at ordinary Jews rather than the procedural behavior of their governing elites, and yet its timing and insistence are telling for the aspirations of the synod to complete self-reliance in governance. The synod attempted, at the very least, to control this process by continuing, "when he [the householder] has received a ruling from the rabbi and the judges, the permission is in his hands to appeal that ruling (*ha-pesak zu aplirin*) before his ruler, in the manner in which he must, as before, leave a deposit with the rabbi of 12 reichsthalers. If his ruler should find that the ruling of the rabbi is good,

then he must give those 12 reichsthalers held by the rabbi to the ruler of
that community."[20] This inclusion of an appellate process recognized that
Jews would inevitably seek to take their cases to non-Jewish spheres. But
it attempted to exert control over the process. Oppenheim and his rival,
however, appeared to undermine that very protocol in the process of their
contest, demonstrating, paradoxically, that the institutions which sought
to handle affairs within the confines of Jewish self-governance rested upon
appeals to larger, state-centered, power structures.

Oppenheim's victory had come from a chain of relationships leading
back to the court of the ruler, and he continued to draw upon that noble support. In late February 1700, Oppenheim paid a visit to Vienna.[21] Within a few
weeks, on March 10, a letter by Leopold Ignaz von Dietrichstein (who succeeded his father in 1698 as prince of Nikolsburg) ordered that every synagogue in Nikolsburg post a copy of a letter in which the prince expressed
his "special displeasure" at learning that Oppenheim had been "not a little
perturbed" in his capacity of deciding civil cases, of Jew versus Jew, as well
as acts "against his person."[22] Although the circumstances of Oppenheim's
ire are unclear, the prince warned that those who would in the future create
difficulties for Oppenheim, in either word or deed, would incur not only
those sanctions of ceremonial practice, but also the "disfavor" of the prince
himself, the particulars of which were perhaps best left to the imagination.

Oppenheim's reliance on the favor of courts was multifarious; he did
not depend on his uncle's influence alone. Over the course of his contests
with competitors in Moravia, he drew upon the support of various Jewish contacts who in turn secured the intervention of their local sovereigns.
These sovereigns then communicated their special favor to colleagues of
their own rank across borders. In December 1701, Dietrichstein received a
letter of commendation for Oppenheim from the westernmost end of the
Holy Roman Empire, by elector Johann Wilhelm of the Palatinate (1658–
1716). The elector's resident Court Jew was Michael, son of Aaron Beer,
who had married Oppenheim's daughter Blümele only a few months before.[23] Still a further statement of support arrived in Dietrichstein's hands
from the elector of Hanover, where Oppenheim's father-in-law had brought
great gains to the house of Hanover.[24] On January 13, 1702, the elector formally extended his aegis over Oppenheim's travels, providing him with a

pass of safe conduct.[25] The fortunes of this extended family solidified the standing of its members, establishing alliances across space that generated further horizontal exchanges between Germany's princely courts.

So great was Oppenheim's standing as Moravian chief rabbi that the *Va'ad* of Moravia took two unprecedented actions on his behalf. In 1697, the council at Lundenburg decided to name the chief rabbi as the keeper of its records.[26] Up until this point the association had housed the ledgers of its proceedings together with any communication from the emperor in one of the three subdistricts of the province. But the leadership of the region's Jews departed from this practice and elected instead to henceforth place the manuscripts of their statutes under the stewardship of the chief rabbi, "who has been examined with seven tests and examinations, and found fitting."[27] For the first time in the history of the association of Jewish communities of Moravia, the records of its most fundamental governance would depend not on a location, but on the safekeeping of an individual. This decision was significant in two respects: first, Oppenheim's appointment as a warden of this foundational body of texts points to his supreme political image. In a certain respect, the Moravian council was acknowledging a near-complete identification between chief rabbi and regional statute. The decision was also an expression of trust and confidence in Oppenheim's technical know-how as a conservator and guardian of books.

Over the next twenty years, long after his Moravian tenure ended, Oppenheim maintained a careful watch over the development of these statutes: he preserved two distinct manuscript copies of this important text—one with the original 311 statutes and a second that included supplementary statutes until the year 1721. Each is written in a single hand, which indicates that they were not produced during the slow accumulation of law, but as conscious copies of record.[28] Neither of these works was the official item that had been delegated to Oppenheim's care in 1697; instead, they were personal copies that Oppenheim maintained in case of political contest. The copyist of one of these texts paid careful attention to rabbinic appointments: the name of each rabbi is underlined, as if to carefully work over the document in order to confirm the prerogatives of the chief rabbi and the precedents to Oppenheim's tenure (fig. 2.3).

Four years later, the *Va'ad* made a second exceptional decision. At

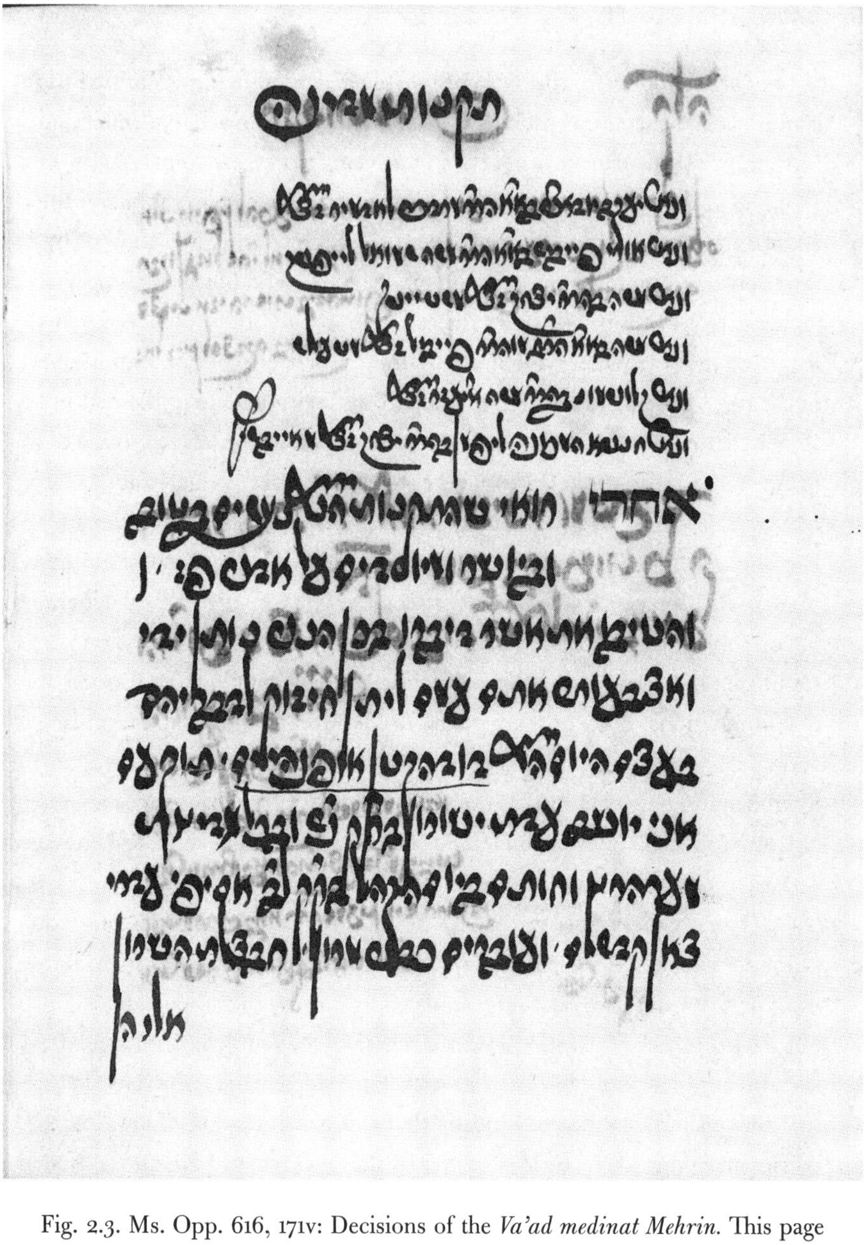

Fig. 2.3. Ms. Opp. 616, 171v: Decisions of the *Va'ad medinat Mehrin*. This page carries a transcription of the signatures of the leaders of this representative body, with Oppenheim's name underlined. Courtesy of the Bodleian Libraries, University of Oxford.

the meeting of the council in Broda, in the winter of 1701, the leadership of Moravia's Jews took the unusual step of naming David Oppenheim as their permanent chief rabbi:

> It has also been agreed—insofar as it is explicit in the statutes of the province regarding accepting the rabbi of the province that no rabbi should be appointed for more than three years—that all have consented as one to say: long live our master, teacher, and rabbi, the great David Oppenheim forever, and let us give him the honor to be received as chief rabbi for many days and years, as is written in his rabbinic contract that has been composed at great length, that he is worthy of all of this honor, on account of the great strength of his deeds, good and excellent, his giving to the poor, etc., He is clean of hands, hating of bribes, he founded several study houses and holy confraternities in our province, a holy and blessed man, who has the coat of arms and the great crown of Israel, the famed sage of this generation, all of the honors and merits are fitting for him, according to his contract. Accordingly, should he at some point need to leave the province, then any rabbis who come after him will not have these same conditions, and this honor will not be given to other rabbis that succeed him.[29]

The ruling of the synod pointed to both Oppenheim's leadership and his economic patronage as decisive elements in his new, permanent status. The establishment of "study houses and holy confraternities in our province" makes clear that his leadership had closely intertwined rabbinic ritual guidance with the materiality of daily life.[30] Oppenheim had used his personal wealth to sustain communal life, among them the establishment of a *beit midrash* (study house) and tuition support there for poor students.[31] Yet the decision of the synod was ill-timed. In just over a year after receiving this highest honor for a Moravian rabbi, Oppenheim was invited to move westward, to Prague, where he would serve for the next three decades.

Courtly Representation in a Jewish Fashion

Oppenheim's Moravian contests and the campaigns of his clients were deeply local matters, but their outcomes were shaped by regional forces. His father and mother lived in Worms, but his paternal uncles served the courts of Heidelberg and Vienna, and his maternal uncles were men of influence in Frankfurt. His father-in-law supported the court in Hanover. These individuals were in turn linked to other families with agents in Amsterdam, Bayreuth, Brandenburg, Cleves, and parts of Italy.

The members of this group behaved much like the nobles who populated these courts, adopting styles and manners that were fashionable within them. The activities of the Court Jews amounted to more than just political influence in Oppenheim's career; they also shaped culture. Court Jews, in their proximity to power, learned and expressed the significance of representation. A great revolution in style, taste, and manners on a grand scale, initiated in the Versailles of Louis XIV, was present in Vienna and Berlin as well.[32] Oppenheim's uncle, Samuel Oppenheimer, was one of the first German Jews to have his image preserved in portraiture, following the style of self-presentation so customary at court.[33] Court Jews directed their penchant for courtly fashion into the Jewish sphere as well, dedicating new communal buildings and donating elaborate religious artifacts for synagogue use. Lavish objects such as covers for the ark, gold cups, and ornaments for Torah scrolls gilded the traditional prayer space.[34] Oppenheim existed in the ambience of the Court Jews and imbibed their appreciation for fine things and, perhaps more importantly, the symbolism of power that fine things conveyed.[35] He, too, donated and dedicated ritual objects that projected his wealth and standing into communal spaces, such as a curtain for the ark that housed the Torah scrolls in one of Prague's synagogues.[36]

Within the space of the noble court and the Jewish elite estate, household and administration, pomp and politics were inextricably intertwined. Such mutual dependence was particularly clear in the realm of printed material—a lesson that Oppenheim learned well. One quite public instance of this association appears in a printed broadside, a paean to the benefactions of Samuel Oppenheimer and recognition of his material and spiritual heirs: his son and his nephew David. Broadsides are large sheets of paper commonly used for distribution and display, with printing on only a single side. They were inexpensive and easy to produce, so many publishers relied on the revenue from broadsides in order to fund more expensive projects such as books. Cheap publications such as these served a critical mobilizing function during the Reformation, as German *Flugschriften,* pamphlets, and posters fueled the promulgation of both the reformers' message and that of their Catholic opponents.[37] But this genre also served to entertain, inform, and delight. Among Jews the broadside was a similarly ubiquitous printed object for various ends: ordinances, calendars, commemorative poems, decorations for Sukkot and synagogues, settlements of commercial disputes, rabbinic responsa, and open letters.[38]

Broadsides also represented power. One early-eighteenth-century broadside sang the praises of the Court Jews but elevated Samuel Oppenheimer above the rest, placing his achievements as surpassing those of all the other Court Jews combined. The author of this broadside did not stop with Samuel's great merits, however. Instead, it named Samuel's son and his nephew as the heirs to his great achievements.[39] The designer of this decorative publication, and the readers who purchased and displayed it, identified not only Samuel as a great benefactor, but also his nephew, David Oppenheim, rabbi of Nikolsburg and "all of Ashkenaz," as a part of this championing force (fig. 2.4).[40]

A similar form of printed publicity appeared in the fall of 1701 when David Oppenheim's daughter Blümele married Michael, son of Aaron Beer of Frankfurt. The union of two prominent German Jewish families prompted the publication of a special booklet to commemorate their observance of a wedding custom that had fallen into disuse over the preceding centuries: a *Breileft,* a marriage ceremony held on Friday with the Sabbath following it as a day of celebration. In honor of this very special, very rare occasion—"nearly forty years had passed in which there was not such a celebration in our community, and the first ones had no memory of it"— Beer published a small handbook for the proceedings, a resource for others who would do the same.[41] Beer was no stranger to the affluent life. Like other Court Jews of his time, he did not exist exclusively in the world of

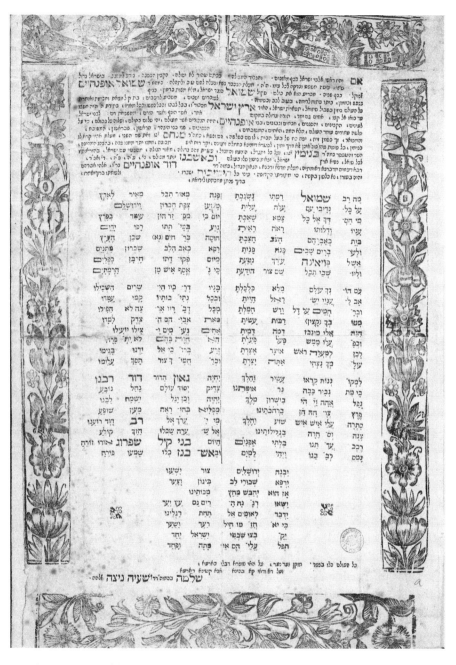

Fig. 2.4. Opp. Add. Fol. III 503, p. 1: Solomon b. Isaiah Nizza, "Poem on Death of Samuel Oppenheim" (Venice, ca. 1703). Courtesy of the Bodleian Libraries, University of Oxford.

the court: he translated courtly fashion into a Jewish idiom and labored for both his noble patrons and his Jewish community—his home was furnished with paintings and tapestries, and table utensils and knick-knacks like pocket watches were accentuated with gold, silver, and ivory trimmings.[42] Like the public declarations in the Oppenheim family broadside, the *Breileft* pamphlet served to harness the power of the printing press to represent a message of status, power, and service. The overlapping of such themes contributed mightily to Oppenheim's standing, especially in moments of competition with rabbinic rivals. Oppenheim's marital arrangements for his other children maintained this strategy of strategic alliances. In late summer 1707, the rabbinic and lay leadership of Worms received a flowery invitation to the wedding of the daughter of Samson Wertheimer, successor to Samuel Oppenheimer in Vienna, and the son of David Oppenheim.[43]

Oppenheim's network of kin—and the clients who relied on it—generated a host of opportunities and honors for him which transcended immediate geographic presence and which he expressed through print media. Over the course of the 1690s alone, he was able to claim for himself the titular leadership of a number of Jewish communities across Europe. In addition to his official chief rabbinate over Nikolsburg and Moravia, he also claimed positions over Slutsk and Brisk in the Polish-Lithuanian Commonwealth, titles that he appended to his name when writing letters through the 1690s.[44] In the summer of 1702, Oppenheim was consulted for advice about the appointment of a new rabbi in Worms, and his correspondents did not fail to acknowledge that they wished Oppenheim might choose to take up the position himself.[45]

Oppenheim harnessed the power of the broadside to publicize these appointments and to fashion an identity of social superiority for wider consumption. On March 25, 1698, he composed a letter to the community of Brisk, in response to their invitation for him to serve as their new chief rabbi. Gushing with thanks, humbly submitting that he lacked the qualifications for such an honor, Oppenheim emphasized his wish to repay this kindness with kindness, hinting at offers of financial support without directly committing to any. Carefully employing the language of family and philanthropy, Oppenheim cannily framed his rejection of the offer in terms of his commitment to his father-in-law, the Court Jew Leffman Behrens, who had enjoined him not to abandon the lands of Ashkenaz, that is, the German Holy Roman Empire. And while he noted in his missive that he was exceedingly sought after by students and colleagues and therefore very busy, his great love for Brisk demanded a letter of this length. In a closing flourish, he signed the letter "David Oppenheim . . . my flag, a flag of love, unfurled over the community of Brisk."[46] Without relocating beyond Central Europe to Brisk, Oppenheim appropriated the local title and affixed it to numerous responsa and letters that emerged from his pen.[47]

The broadside, with its implied publicity, served as a surrogate for the individual appointment. Since his presence in Brisk was not to be, Oppenheim fashioned a material representation of the invitation and his response, a reminder to others that he was the first choice (fig. 2.5). Had he taken up the position, a thing of this sort would not have been necessary. In place of the most obvious claim to a title—fulfilling its duties in situ—Oppenheim harnessed the power of print to transmute the personal letters of appointment into objects of public recognition and display. By commissioning the publication of these printed objects, he could direct the flow of information about his achievements and expand his own renown.

Oppenheim also harnessed the printed broadside to publicize those moments in which he physically took up a new, prestigious post. On Friday, August 18, 1702, two emissaries from Prague arrived at Oppenheim's home in Nikolsburg, carrying with them a letter of invitation to become chief rabbi of Prague, the largest urban Jewish community in all of Europe, with its ghetto population nearing eleven thousand Jews.[48] Oppenheim received the news of this appointment with surprise and honor, but it was the product of months of negotiation. Before this note was delivered into Oppenheim's hands, it had been vetted by the Jewish officials of Prague as well as the imperial offices. The official letter of appointment had been drafted, approved, and signed by eighty-four Jewish dignitaries of Prague on May 25, 1702, a full three months earlier.[49] On July 12, the offices of the exchequer in Bohemia (the imperial finance office of the Habsburg monarch) received notice of the selection of this candidate by the elders of the

Jewish town. This notice further requested official extension of protection to Oppenheim by the Bohemian chancellery in Vienna on the emperor's behalf, to be carried out by the local governor there; the final confirmation by the imperial offices came on August 5.[50] Oppenheim had been a part of the negotiations for some time before. On June 7, only two weeks after the rabbinic contract had been signed (fig. 2.6), he gave his approbation to a book with the words "a flag of love spread over the holy community of Prague."[51] His location at the time of writing: Vienna, with his uncle, Samuel Oppenheimer, who for years had been a donor to the Prague Jewish community and who likely played a part in securing his nephew's new position.[52]

Oppenheim's arrival in Prague was met with approval by the agents of the state. On February 18, 1704, the emperor issued an order bringing him under special protection, an act that was perhaps motivated by his repeat visit to Vienna in December 1703.[53] But much as in Moravia, Oppenheim faced Jewish rivals in Prague. The terms of his appointment named him as *av beit din* (chief justice of the rabbinical court), but a second rabbi, named Abraham Broda, enjoyed a status on par, as *rosh yeshiva* (headmaster of the yeshiva) in the city.[54] Each role conferred a certain sort of power upon its bearer—the former a say in ritual and economic practice, and the latter in its influence over a venerable institution and a population of young residents of the community.[55]

Reports by contemporaries suggest that relations between the two men were rocky. Over the course of the next half decade their rivalry spilled over into antagonisms between their students. One observer, coming to the city in 1708, described the students of each as "hating each other," noting his own unique situation of studying in both houses, an exception to the "young men who follow their hearts, deliberately causing controversy."[56] It was perhaps with an eye to a contest between official equals that Oppenheim took recourse to printed propaganda to enhance his standing. Even before taking up residence in the city in 1703, Oppenheim adopted his new title as chief rabbi in written correspondence and endorsements of newly printed books. He was so determined to assert supremacy over the man with whom he was meant to share power that he wrote to a scribe in Krakow to consult the communal ordinances of that community in the hopes

Fig. 2.6. Manuscript for Oppenheim's rabbinic contract of 1702 in Prague, complete with a Star of David surrounding a "Swedish hat," emblem of the Jewish community of Prague. Courtesy of the Jewish Museum in Prague.

of finding precedent for a hierarchy between the two rabbinic posts, but to little avail.[57]

Where a search for legal precedent faltered, however, media fortunes prevailed. To solidify his public standing, Oppenheim commissioned and disseminated not one but two broadsides to proclaim his new post. The first of these was a published edition of the manuscript offer of the rabbinate, complete with the transcribed signatures of the city's Jewish leadership and the peculiar icon of Prague's Jews: a Star of David surrounding a "Swedish hat," emblem of the Jewish community of Prague (fig. 2.7).[58]

The second broadside Oppenheim promulgated was his reply to his contract—a richly allusive letter of acceptance dated September 12, 1702, which once again revealed the importance not only of communication, but of familial association (fig. 2.8). In his open letter Oppenheim accepted the position and vowed to uphold the responsibilities of the Av Beit Din. The letter bursts with plays on words from biblical and Talmudic texts, to the point that it almost defies intelligibility even as it displays erudition. But the purpose of the letter appears to be less in its text than in its context. Oppenheim turned a semiprivate correspondence between himself and the Prague *kehillah* into a moment of publicity and print, and, in his signature, he indicated the location of his writing: Vienna, at the home of his uncle Samuel Oppenheimer.

As Oppenheim transformed these personal texts into public media, he reshaped and repurposed their function. As D. F. McKenzie, a pioneer in the history of the book, has argued, "forms effect meaning."[59] Oppenheim turned an illuminated manuscript contract into an object of open consumption, and an ostensibly private letter of acceptance into a vehicle for public self-representation. We cannot know what sort of circulation these broadsides achieved; as with other ephemera, the very nature of the medium makes their dissemination nearly impossible to recover. But Oppenheim preserved tens of copies of these broadsides, pasted into the front covers of the folio volumes in his collection. If the impact of these items remains unclear, the intention is within reach of reasonable conjecture: Oppenheim intended to harness the power of the printed word to widely disseminate news of his appointment and to display his literary talent—a level of political savvy appropriate to a man who knew the business of books.

Fig. 2.7. Opp. Fol. 23: Broadside pasted into front cover. Printed replica of manuscript contract. Notice, however, that in this version, above the "Swedish hat" emblem appear the Hebrew words "shield of David," perhaps Oppenheim's way of demonstrating the providence of Rabbi David taking up the leadership of the community associated with King David's shield. Courtesy of the Bodleian Libraries, University of Oxford.

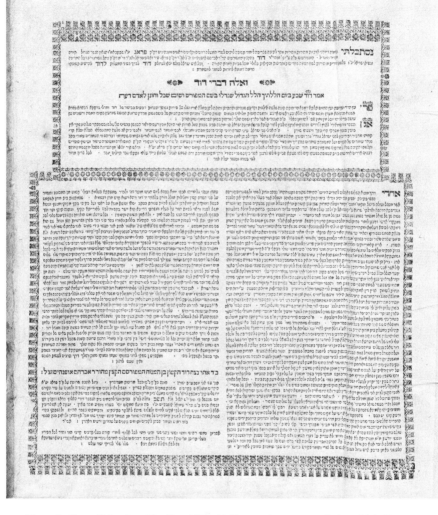

Fig. 2.8. Opp. Fol. 389: *Ele divrei David* (September 12, 1702), in which Oppenheim accepts the offer to become chief rabbi of Prague and states his intentions to relocate in June 1703; signed in the home of his uncle, Samuel, in Vienna. Courtesy of the Bodleian Libraries, University of Oxford.

In the years that followed, Oppenheim continued to operate within the rules of the courtly game, garnering the attention and favor of the royal court, which in turn enhanced his standing. On February 26, 1705, Emperor Leopold renewed Oppenheim's appointment as chief rabbi in Prague, lauding the history of his rabbinic career in Moravia and Nikolsburg with muted praise as being "without complaint."[60] The imperial rescript also commended Oppenheim for his stabilizing role, "on account of his good integrity and disinterest in change," not to mention his scholarship in Jewish law.[61] Three years after that, in January 1708 Emperor Joseph I promulgated an order confirming Oppenheim's position in Prague "for perpetuity" (or as long as he chose to keep the position), including special protection for him. The order extolled Oppenheim's popularity, noting that "not only has he earned everyone's favor and love, but even the Jewish Elders in the name of the entire Prague Jewish community" requested his renewed confirmation.[62] As in his earlier confirmations, Oppenheim's approval by the state was not a unilateral declaration, but was rather the product of sustained negotiations between the king, the community, and their intermediaries.[63]

One final professional conquest remained for Oppenheim. On February 9, 1713, gathering in the town of Brandeis, the representatives of the Bohemian *Landesjudenschaft* awarded Oppenheim jurisdiction over half of Bohemia, naming him "chief and first and head of the court and teacher of righteousness in all fifteen regions of Bohemia, with the great Wolf Spira [Wedeles]."[64] Wedeles died just less than two years later, on January 11, 1715, and by 1717 Oppenheim was confirmed by the Jews of Bohemia as chief rabbi of the entire province.[65]

Families and Favor, Patronage and Policy

Oppenheim benefited mightily from the favor of the royal court and the fortune of his family. Providing favors through personal connection was in fact part of the dominant form of "doing politics" in premodern Europe. Early modern politics in the German lands—especially in the realm of the court—inextricably linked "state service" and "household service."[66]

A web of patronage obligations strengthened the ties between center and periphery, drawing clients into a web of loyalty and accountability to those who had put them in office and upon whom their continued access to resources depended.[67] The political was deeply personal. A similar culture prevailed in the familial politics that dominated Jewish political culture in Central Europe. While Jews' numerical and cultural minority status provided them with a sense of solidarity and association, affective bonds and personal obligation were also at the core of the processes of communal self-governance, not just of compliance with its rules. In the noble courts, patronage linked central institutions with agents across a wider periphery. The same was true in the Jewish leading households, where a wide system of favors and debts determined the pace and practices of daily political life.

The importance of an economy of favors to the world of courtier and collector alike emerges from the advice manual of Gabriel Naudé. Keenly aware of the relationship between the book collector's passion and the possibilities it opened for others to reach a man of wealth and standing, Naudé wrote of how the library would induce many to "strive to aid this project and contribute to it," especially if its owner had "sufficient influence and authority to do favors for his friends."[68] Oppenheim would not have read this manual, but he practiced its basic principles, receiving books in the expectation of favors in return. An exchange of favors—seemingly nothing more than pure nepotism—was actually an essential and entirely acceptable means of conducting political activity at this time.[69]

Oppenheim positioned himself as, and was understood by others to be, a point of access for supplicants who hoped to benefit from his role not as a direct resource, but on account of an increasingly interdependent system. The extensive scope of the merchant families of the Court Jews set them apart from many of their fellow Jews (and non-Jews) of early modern Europe in their powerful networks. The success of their endeavors was predicated upon far-reaching ties between multiple centers that allowed their agents to marshal resources and transmit information efficiently and quickly.[70] Before the seventeenth and eighteenth centuries, Jewish attempts to coordinate their activities within an imperial framework had generally failed, often because of the resistance of individual communities to relinquish their independence to a supracommunal body, which they (reasonably) feared would be dominated by the largest communities (Frankfurt and Worms).[71] One of the few successful attempts at regional coordination on the part of German Jewry occurred in 1603 at the synod of Frankfurt, which was itself an expression of competition with Polish Jewry; it was convened as a rearguard action to fend off disrespect by the Jewish courts of Poland and Italy.[72] Despite these abortive institutional attempts, in the seventeenth and eighteenth centuries informal ties between Jews in the German lands thickened and intensified, often propelled by the wheels of commerce. The fact that commerce required cooperation meant that a leadership cadre emerged across the Jewish communities of Germany that was not formally appointed or elected. As personal ties between Jews in the German lands strengthened to meet the needs of commerce, their efforts on behalf of Jewish collective security coalesced as well.

To access the members of this class was another matter. In seeking political and economic resources, Jews would write to Oppenheim in the hopes of engaging him as a power broker who might intervene with his relatives to secure favorable outcomes for political hopefuls. Letters to Oppenheim represent a source outside of official communal documents, revealing actual practice rather than prescribed norms.[73] His epistolary exchanges offer a perspective that both links elites of multiple locations across the German lands of the seventeenth and eighteenth centuries and shows how individuals of lower rank might find a point of entry into the welfare provisions of these elites. In fact, letters of instruction for purposes exactly such as these circulated among students to train them in the art of supplication and ceremonial correspondence. For example, a letter guide from Prague called *Yefe nof* advertised its utility for students "so that they will know how to extend salutations in their letters, both to open and conclude them."[74] This manual was one of several printed during this period and may have instructed students and supplicants in the art of cultivating favoritism.

One such letter came Oppenheim's way on Sunday, September 1, 1709, from a Polish Jew temporarily staying in the German town of Halberstadt. The letter's author had hoped to make his final destination the nearby city of Hanover, but word had spread between fellow foreigners that Hanover was closed to Jews from Poland who wished to settle there. The weary traveler, who sought to join the ranks of the students in the *kloyz* (a privately funded Talmud study house) in the city, beseeched Oppenheim to intervene on his behalf with a powerful Jew in the city, who might gain him rights of residence.[75] The hopeful Polish traveler was not writing to Oppenheim in the latter's capacity as chief rabbi of Prague nor to draw upon the rabbi's expertise in halakhic matters or jurisprudential readings of communal statutes. Nor still was he attempting to access the voluminous and famed library of the Prague book collector. Instead, the young man made contact in an attempt to recruit Oppenheim as an intermediary between himself and the governing authorities of Hanover, hoping that Oppenheim might identify a sponsor to support his residency. But the letter's author also did not expect Oppenheim directly to intervene with Hanover's government. Instead, the Polish student reached out because Oppenheim was the son-in-law of Hanover's wealthiest and most influential Jew, Leffman Behrens, Court Jew of the elector of Hanover. The young Pole wrote in the hopes that a chain of diplomatic linkages might ultimately secure him a scholarship in the study house funded by Behrens, and by extension the rights of residence in Hanover.

Oppenheim's significance to the Polish Jew came not from the fact that he was closest to the elector, but that he was somewhat removed—and therefore accessible to ordinary Jews. Networks operate according to a system by which connections are established between distant people through a series of intermediaries.[76] Similarly, in 1709, Oppenheim was approached with a request from Wesel, in the Duchy of Cleves in the westernmost part of the Holy Roman Empire, to support the candidacy of the local rabbi, Meir, for an expanded role over the Münster rabbinate. Although Meir's access to Oppenheim emerged from their mutual inclusion in the world of rabbinic letters, he wrote to Oppenheim as a point of entry to court-Jewish patronage. He did not expect Oppenheim's direct intervention; instead, like the Polish student, he hoped that Oppenheim could prevail upon Behrens to intercede with the elector of Hanover on Meir's behalf. Meir was not the only one who had this idea. His rival similarly positioned himself vis-à-vis an influential Jewish relative at the court of the "hegemon" of

Cleves. Meir thus keenly understood that this would be a contest not of competence, but of patronage.[77]

As Meir learned, a request to a patron did not guarantee good favor: only a month later he wrote again to Oppenheim, dismayed that not only had he not heard back from his presumed advocate, but also that in the interim his rival had successfully secured the coveted post. For Meir, however, all was not lost, for he had discovered another opportunity in Hesse — perhaps Oppenheim could help him achieve this position? Since this post was outside of the jurisdiction of Hanover, the author hoped that Oppenheim could put in a good word with a different courtly contact, in this case Samson Wertheimer of Vienna.[78]

Such favors were not limited to individual placements, either. In 1702 Oppenheim received a request to intervene with cousins who were holding up a large donation. The letter, sent from Frankfurt, reveals that Oppenheim's uncle, the Court Jew Moses of Heidelberg, had pledged a donation of 1,000 reichsthalers to support a local *beit midrash* there — a pledge that his heir had yet to follow through with after the death of the donor.[79] Oppenheim's correspondent hoped that Oppenheim might secure the flow of cash to this *beit midrash,* the administrators of which had carefully calculated the uses of both the principal and the interest.

Oppenheim could be relied on — or at the very least approached — to secure positive ends for a portion of the Jewish population because the leading Jewish families of early modern Central Europe were not mercantile alone. Woven through every facet of their world were strategic marriages between daughters of wealthy families and sons of intellectual standing. Such marriages fused together capital and culture and produced a stratum of society that was decisive for shaping virtually every aspect of political and social life.[80] The strategies of marriage engendered a culture of regional cooperation between Jewish communities across the German lands.[81] The ties of kinship and commerce promoted informal alliances that traversed various imperial jurisdictions and created the conditions not simply to fund major military and political campaigns in German courts and battlefields, but to exert a significant influence over the structures of governance and administration that guided Jewish daily life.[82]

As these families strengthened the bonds between Jewish communities, they came to form something of a transregional oligarchy, akin in many ways to the patrimonial ruling blocs that dominated the political landscape of the Holy Roman Empire and the Netherlands, where a fusion of merchant capitalism and patrimonial rule was the usual political arrangement.[83] Rule by clans appears to have been the constitutional order of the *kehillot* as well. Although prescriptive communal documents offer the impression of local jurisdictions at work, letters to Oppenheim reveal the brokerage and negotiation behind the statues and ordinances, often transcending the jealously guarded local prerogatives of hermetic communal autonomy.

The letters—of request, of thanks, of solicitation—that traveled across these spaces and between the various members of this leading class do more than reflect the importance of the Court Jews; they reinforced the image and reality of the Court Jews as decisive.[84] Taken in the aggregate, such letters reflected and created a networked system of entrenched authority, dependence, and hierarchy. Oppenheim's letters are more than just the expected window on early modern rabbinic culture; marbled with references to those Court Jews, they are evidence of the structuring effect of those figures, who served no official communal role but generated the political context for much of the community's operations. Politics were conducted through personal contact, not solely through local legislation. Like the other personal states of early modern Europe that relied on loyalties and clientage as much as (if not more than) bureaucracy and paper regulations, Jewish politics relied on the personal within the political. By the same token, the trade in favors did not flow in only one direction. In many ways, this was a form of Jewish administrative bureaucracy. Much like royal officers appointed by state sovereigns, the leaders of Jewish communities depended on lower-order functionaries to carry out their decisions.[85] Official acts and orders were expressed through officiousness and obsequiousness, and political regimes were expressed and shaped by rites.[86] Like the political culture of the Holy Roman Empire itself, Jewish political culture was patrimonial, not abstract, and was conducted through assertions of presence, interest, and interpersonal ties, rather than by fixed and standard rules.

A Prince of the Land of Israel in Prague

Oppenheim's print publicity allowed him to demonstrate the range of his activities across Central and Eastern Europe, and beyond, into a realm that carried perhaps even greater prestige: the rabbinate of the Jews of Jerusalem. Over the course of the final decade of the seventeenth century, Oppenheim had kept up a series of regular exchanges with book agents in Jerusalem. Jerusalem was of particular interest to Oppenheim on account of its position as a hub in the transit of manuscripts, especially works of Iberian provenance. When the waves of exiles from medieval Iberia crashed across the Mediterranean basin and the Ottoman Empire, many of them brought rabbinic manuscripts in tow. These manuscripts were of particular interest for a bibliophile like Oppenheim, as the copying of manuscripts followed subethnic patterns of diffusion, and items of Iberian origin were far rarer in Ashkenazic Central Europe than in the new lands settled by the Sephardim. An Ashkenazic emigrant from Prague to the Holy Land in 1650 warned his continental colleagues of the subethnic dissonance in the city:

> Books can be found in Jerusalem, and their price is not costly, therefore do not load yourselves up with many books, because of the exertion. That said, each one should bring with him a thick prayer-book, a Pentateuch with three commentaries, *selihah* according to the Polish rites, Mishna with the [commentary of] *Tosafot Yom Tov, Levushim* by the great rabbi our master and teacher Mordecai Jaffe, *Shomrim la-boker,* a *Mahzor* according to the Prague rites, *Rabot, Ein Yaakov, Shulhan arukh, Yalkut;* the women should take *Daytsch-Humash, Daytsch-Mahzor, Daytsche-Tkhines,* and other books in the Ashkenazic language.[87]

This list, complied by Moses Prager (also known as Porges or Poryes/Poriyat), suggests that the only books one would need to take to Jerusalem would be those that accommodate Ashkenazic rites because all others could be found in Jerusalem with ease. In Jerusalem one could discover manuscripts with an inscription in which an owner identified himself as a descendant of "an exile from the Jerusalem that is Sepharad," that is, from Spain.[88]

Jerusalem was unique in that unlike the regional distinctions in continental Europe that prevailed between Ashkenazic and Sephardic Jews, the ancient Jewish city was home to members of both subethnic affiliations. Each of these groups maintained contact with respective members of a far-flung diaspora, but both proceeded with little intercourse between them. Thus the Sephardic Jews of Jerusalem corresponded with and dispatched emissaries to sister communities in Venice and Amsterdam; the Ashkenazim, by contrast, relied on Frankfurt and Prague.[89] Where the two distinct diasporas met, in cities like Jerusalem, the manuscripts of one group could be redistributed through the other.[90]

It was precisely with an eye to such acquisition that Oppenheim had been in contact with men in Jerusalem. And such contact was fruitful indeed. His collection came to include manuscript copies of important works of medieval rabbinic writings on the Talmud, including Nisim b. Reuben of Gerona (1320–1376) on Tractate *Bava Metzia,* Asher b. Yehiel (1259–1327) on Tractates *Zeraim* and *Taharot,* a Nahmanides commentary on Kethubbot, and the commentary of the Meiri on Tractate *Shabbat,* among others.[91] The trade with Jerusalem also facilitated the diffusion of kabbalah into Central Europe via the Italian peninsula (occasionally in the hands of crypto-Sabbateans).[92] These included the kabbalistic notes of Hayyim Vital that recorded the influential thought of the sixteenth-century kabbalist Isaac Luria. One such text was copied for Oppenheim from Vital's autographed manuscript in Jerusalem.[93] Another, completed in Vienna on August 31, 1716, had been brought to Central Europe by Meir Poppers, an important seventeenth-century agent for the diffusion of Lurianic kabbalah.[94] A copy of Luria's commentary to the Haggadah, composed in 1540, is likely to have joined the collection by a similar means.[95]

But the transit of these books was not merely an arrangement between individuals acting alone. Rather, Oppenheim's agents for distributing books from Jerusalem were chiefly involved in a different sort of circulation—that of funds to the needy. Jerusalem's Jews subsisted on the largesse of donations that came from abroad, and they conducted an economy that exchanged gifts, honors, and prayers for funds to maintain their buildings, purchase essentials, and pay their taxes. The solicitation and transit of charitable funds depended on the concerted activities of recipients, donors, collectors, and regulators of both state and nonstate provenance, across vast distances.[96] These disparate parts were linked together most frequently through the activities of emissaries — intermediaries whose travels abroad linked the fate of Palestinian Jewry to European *kehillot* and individual donors.[97] Both emissaries and the people they represented depended heavily on the charity of others; the philanthropic economy, however, benefited both the recipients and the donors themselves.

The culture of the court was an important ingredient of charitable activities as well. In the decades after the Thirty Years War, individual forms of charitable giving increasingly complemented more official channels of poor relief, often emanating from the rise of a princely or ducal court.[98] Such forms of noble giving enhanced the prestige of courtiers, as their bequests were public acts, the very buildings that they helped construct serving as daily reminders of a patron's generosity. This logic extended to the Court Jews as well because they funded the construction of synagogues and furnished their interiors with silver and textiles, all bearing inscriptions praising the donor and enhancing his or her prestige.[99]

It was with an eye to cultivating such a relationship, and with full cognizance of the power of prestige, that in 1699 Oppenheim's primary book dealer in Jerusalem sent him a packet of books accompanied by an invitation. The death of Jerusalem's Ashkenazic rabbi and charity officer had left a vacancy in two vital elements of the community's existence: the collection of funds from global donors and the local leadership of the community. Oppenheim was invited to migrate to Palestine to take up the post of rabbi.[100] In January 1701, the Ashkenazic Jews of Jerusalem drew up a formal letter of invitation to Oppenheim to become their rabbi and delivered it to him in Vienna, at the home of his uncle Samuel. His presence there confirmed his role as an influential broker of monetary transmissions that could be advantageous for Palestine's Jews.[101]

Oppenheim took his time in crafting a reply. When he finally wrote a lengthy letter of response, on July 23, 1702, he had already accepted the post of chief rabbi of Prague. Although he refused a move to the Holy Land, he willingly claimed the title that described it: *Nasi Eretz Yisrael,* Prince of the Land of Israel, and publicized that role in still another broadside printing (fig. 2.9).[102] The title appeared in salutations to letters to him, and he included it to sign off on his responsa and approbata for books.

The transit of books thus shaped not only the contents of a library but the direction of philanthropy. Oppenheim's decisions to champion the cause of his Jerusalem dependents were often informed by the purchase of his favor through books, and they were careful to maintain regular contact with this powerful patron. One emissary, Eleazer ha-Levi of Holleschau, repeatedly sent manuscripts to Oppenheim, often from exotic locales. Eleazer took the opportunity during his travels through Cairo in 1702 to locate the commentary of Nahmanides to the Pentateuch and send it to Oppenheim, with an inscription of good wishes.[103] In 1703, Eleazar sent another inscribed item to Oppenheim from Jerusalem titled "A Resolution of Three Contradictions in Rashi."[104]

As a book agent, Eleazar appears to have played an important role in calming a crisis that brewed in Jerusalem during 1704–1706 around the arrival of the followers of Judah Hasid. Although Oppenheim had provided material support for this group's migration from Europe to Palestine in 1700, their adoption of strange practices had generated rumors that they were clandestine followers of the messianic pretender Sabbatai Zevi.[105] In 1704, Oppenheim intervened in an attempt to impose order. He condemned the newly arrived group's deviation from custom, their abolition of fast days, and the factionalism they sowed. He threatened a ban of excommunication against them if they did not desist and buttressed his authority by noting his international standing, writing that "several holy communities and pleasant regions, the glory of the diaspora, hinge upon my word."[106] When the group began to dispatch emissaries to Europe that contravened the normal routes of charitable giving, Oppenheim threatened to stem the flow of cash to the Land of Israel entirely, a threat that was averted only through the intercession of his book agent, Eleazer ha-Levi.[107]

Eleazar thus felt comfortable maintaining contact with Oppenheim as the crisis drew out. In 1706 he wrote to Oppenheim, offering to transcribe

Fig. 2.9. Opp. Add. Fol. III 503, p. 4: Broadside publication of Oppenheim's letter to the Jewish community of Jerusalem, 1702, printed in Venice. Courtesy of the Bodleian Libraries, University of Oxford.

and send still more manuscripts, but requesting something in return—that Oppenheim hold fast to his commitment to "send a gift to his study house in Jerusalem" and prompt others to uphold their promise of monies as well. The letter signed off on a dire note with a more pressing concern: raising the specter of "the false prophet of Prossnitz," that is, the Sabbatean preacher Judah Leib "Leibele" of Prossnitz, who had been at the heart of recent controversy. Eleazar asked that Oppenheim send a copy of his recent letter excommunicating Leibele Prossnitz so that the truth could be publicized among "the men of Jerusalem who refuse to hear of it."[108]

The letters of the Jews of Jerusalem and the books that supplied a vehicle for tribute demonstrate that the greater significance to this system of favors was not simply that the very wealthy benefited from familial connections; it is in the ways that Jews of various segments of society participated in it and accessed its decisive actors. Jews wishing to enjoin Oppenheim for his mediation with relatives of power and influence consistently sent him books in an attempt to curry favor with him, much as Naudé had expected. His library was therefore more than the collection of a learned man—it was a putative currency in a Jewish economy of the exchange of favors.

Conclusion

By the first years of the eighteenth century, Oppenheim had demonstrated his mettle as a man who could use his courtly connections for his own political struggles and intervene on behalf of others. He continued to purchase books himself, but many Jews found that they had much to gain by giving him books as presents. These books-as-gifts came from as far away as Jerusalem and as near as local communities in Moravia, but all were given in the hopes that Oppenheim's favor might be converted into a form of political patronage. Oppenheim's world of favor and families—mediated through his library's contents and his personal character—represents an important instance of this widespread political culture, one that was conducted by Court Jews as much as by princely courtiers. In this system, patronage and clientage were not simply vital elements of individual fortunes or the callously corrupt, but were decisive for the operations of an entire structure of governance, securing the welfare of its constituents and the power of its leaders.

These acts of display reflected and reinforced the decisive influence of the Court Jews on political affairs within the Jewish communities of Central Europe. The memoirist Glikl of Hameln offers a sense of their reach, noting both their tremendous influence and the ways in which a faltering in their fortunes could affect other Jews adversely.[109] The Court Jews served both their sovereigns and the interests of fellows Jews as intermediaries and intercessors. Their ability to represent Jewish interests in the halls of power stemmed from the dynamics of the court as the primary institution of governing power during this period. The early modern court was the site where the activities of the early modern state were actually conceived, crafted, and practiced. The pomp and ceremony of the court was not a distraction from the business of politics — it was integral to it, and influence and intimacy left their marks on policy and procedure.[110] The "absolutism" of the Habsburg lands inhered not in the personage of a ruler with loyal bureaucrats, but in the court as a totality of state agents and offices, holding together the multinational monarchy of East-Central Europe. By the late seventeenth and early eighteenth centuries, the court had grown to mammoth proportions, comprising some two thousand to twenty-five hundred courtiers.[111] The court's significance lay not only in its numerical size, but in its administration of territory. It linked center and periphery and formed a site for both the ruler's hereditary holdings and his elective, imperial domains, acting as an assertion of the emperor's prerogatives against those of the electors and other claimants to decentralized authority in the Holy Roman Empire.[112]

As we have seen, letters seeking Oppenheim's favor and intervention with his relatives came from Wesel, Hanover, and Jerusalem, as well as from across his official jurisdictions in Bohemia and Moravia. But there were also important places they did *not* come from, namely, Poland. The reach of Oppenheim's courtly relations appears to have had little influence on the politics of communal appointment or the provisions of safe conducts or the rights of residence there. The fact that he has very few letters from Poland suggests that his influence meant different things in different domains. As we shall see, the Jews of Poland could write to Oppenheim to help them obtain books; but when it came to obtaining economic and material support, his lines extended more to Germany and the Land of Israel than to Brisk and Slutzk, which were more symbolic than material. The boundaries of his correspondence are just as telling as their extent. If Oppenheim's authority in the realm of rabbinical appointments and the disbursement of favors depended on courtly influence, then Jewish settlements in which German courts held no sway would have little reason to appeal to that aspect of Oppenheim's persona.

But in those lands in which Oppenheim had connections to relatives with the ear of the sovereign, he represented—for some Jews—an important point of access. And by extension, the ways in which Jews expected the intervention of Court Jews into local affairs reveals the *Jewish* impact of a sector of premodern society that is often taken to have been more "secular" than Jewish, more involved in the affairs of state than the spaces of community. Oppenheim's mediation between Court Jews and Jewish communities reveals the entanglements between the spaces of state administration and autonomous Jewish self-government.

THREE

Collecting, Recording, and Practical Knowledge

In vain does he strive to carry out any of the preceding suggestions
or go to any great expense for books who does not intend to
devote them to the public use and never to withhold
them from the humblest of those who may reap benefit thereby.
—Gabriel Naudé, *Advice on Establishing a Library,* 1627

IN 1706, THE JEWISH COMMUNAL elders of Hildesheim, located just thirty kilometers southeast of Hanover where Oppenheim's father-in-law served the court, took upon themselves the task of rewriting their constitution. The elders felt that this renewal was a long time coming, as some of their ordinances had been established as temporary measures by ancient predecessors, and some others appeared too onerous for the community to withstand. They therefore "answered and said with one voice, 'let us follow a fine court, since a wise man has arrived from the East, behold he is the great light, wonder of his age, the famed sage across all of Israel's dispersal, David Oppenheim . . .' and David conducted great justice, adding and removing from the ordinances according to his mind."[1] In response to their request, Oppenheim drafted twenty-one guiding statutes by which the community should administer itself, ranging from the selection of its leaders to the confirmation of ancient custom that "the community will have a special box with two keys, and within it shall place all of the ledgers and contracts and all of the items that relate to the *kahal.*"[2] With the additional signatures of four scholars to generate a quorum, this rabbi from

beyond the local community, who carried no official relationship to it, decisively shaped the politics and administration of the Jews of Hildesheim.

Oppenheim was known as a scholar and intellectual, and his library
functioned as a unique resource in the Jewish world that comprised a diverse array of books whose contents guided the conduct of Jewish daily,
communal, and ritual life. His library was consulted for information that
could inform rulings on kosher food, marriage and divorce, and the observance of Sabbath and holidays. Scholars traveled from around the continent to consult the material in his collection. Many more wrote letters requesting information when they were not able to view the books directly
and to request Oppenheim's legal consultation — evidence of his standing
and authority. He used many rare texts in his own rabbinic rulings, and his
status as a scholar of unparalleled resources led many Jews to consult his
legal opinions, much as the Jews of Hildesheim had. The collection also invited the curiosity of Christians, who toured the library and consulted it for
religious and scholarly ends of their own.

His distinctive collection took on a larger valence, both symbolic and
functional, as well. The world of books in early modern Europe encompassed more than individual affection for cherished volumes. Bibliophilia
belonged to a wider apparatus of learning, documenting, and archiving that
played a significant part in early modern social life.[3] Possession of a consolidated "archive" of the documents of Jewish life served a function much like
state archives had since their inception in the Middle Ages: they accumulated ever more knowledge about diplomacy and the peoples who resided
in the territories under the state's authority. In assembling archives, states
made power visible through paper and record-keeping, capturing and em-
bodying the reach of knowledge assembled by rulers about the governed,
which in turn shaped governance itself.[4] Knowledge is indeed power, and
a monopoly on knowledge conferred privileged authority upon the states
that gathered it and, in the Jewish case, upon those who behaved like states,
even if they lacked fully coercive power. In the words of one scholar of the
period, records operated as "arsenals of state authority."[5] That paper monopoly derived, in part, from the fact that these documents were not public
or widely disseminated but were enclosed within the confines of the state's

repository or the collector's abode. Manuscripts, whether of communal de-cisions or of rabbinic legal writing, were costly to reproduce and difficult to acquire. Their uniqueness made them all the more valuable and concen-trated authority in the hands of their privileged holders.[6]

Oppenheim's library was a product of this emergent pan-European development and provided him with a vehicle for shaping his place in the religious and social culture of the early modern period. His library-as-archive contributed to administering the autonomous life of early mod-ern Jews in Moravia and Bohemia, across the German lands, and into the Jewish courts of Italy. By amassing, archiving, and mobilizing information, Oppenheim used his collection to interweave personal prestige with insti-tutional practice. Acquired with family wealth, and symbolic of courtly in-fluence, the library was used by both Oppenheim and a constituency of rabbinic and communal leaders to shape the legal, ritual, and daily lives of an even wider array of ordinary Jews in early modern Europe.

Knowledge on Display

A quest for a large, all-encompassing library was not a fully formed ideal for most Jews before the early modern period. Jews across the ages had collected and preserved texts in manuscript form and, since the fifteenth century, in printed form.[7] But medieval Jews could satisfy themselves with a quite limited library, as a closely circumscribed canon was all that a basic yeshiva curriculum required or that a rabbinic authority needed to consult before issuing a ruling.[8] With the advent of print, new strands of thought emerged in the rabbinic mindset that advocated the supremacy of the mod-erns over the ancients because of the access rabbis had to a greater number of texts.[9] In their autonomous communities across Europe, Jews expanded the practice of keeping records — storing the affairs of their courts, confra-ternities, and burial societies in ledger books.

Oppenheim's collection took this desire to a new level, incorporating not simply scholarly material, but diplomatic and administrative documents as well. The early modern period witnessed the rise of new forms of docu-mentary and archival practices among Jews that paralleled the shifts in their ambient societies.[10] Early modern merchant capitalism, of which the Court Jews were an integral part, was intrinsically connected to the practices of literacy, record-keeping, copying, collecting, and archiving.[11] The skills required for careful accounting included a host of documentary practices for recording debits and credits and keeping track of a wide range of financial activities that included inventories, receipts, rates of exchange, and promissory notes.[12] Merchant accounting depended on extensive systems of reckoning and recollecting. An entire genre of "accounting books" appeared in the early modern period to train merchants in the skills of accounting, including measures for rates of exchange. Oppenheim's library bears witness to the literary ephemera that accompanied Jewish economic life: the binding of one of his books was recycled from a chart of rates of exchange (fig. 3.1). When such books lost their utility, as rates changed, their material could be recycled as the binding of other books.

In a spirit shared with the finest libraries of the rulers of his age, Oppenheim's library gained an increasingly professional structure as his stature grew: its contents were housed and stored as to be accessible and were staffed by a librarian. But this scenario was not entirely of Oppenheim's making. During the first decades of his collection, the library may have been split among various locations. In an entry in his personal catalogue from 1683, Oppenheim recorded the titles of twenty-five books that belonged to him "here, in Hanover."[13] He appears to have deposited some of his books at the home of his father-in-law there, while keeping others in Worms and presumably taking others with him to his various sites of study as a student. After his move to Nikolsburg in 1691, most of the library must have come with him, as he testified on one of his visits to Vienna that "the house of gum and dripping balm [i.e., his collection] is in Nikolsburg, for there is my home, a great place of gathering for sages, and at the time I am here, in Vienna."[14]

Oppenheim expressed discomfort at this temporary separation from his collection, but his move to Prague a decade later, in 1703, decisively and permanently placed the library at great remove from Oppenheim's home, a situation that lasted until the end of his life. During the period following the Thirty Years War (1618–1648), Habsburg authorities undertook a mission to re-Catholicize Bohemia's population, and central to this campaign was a renewed vigilance toward suspect books, conducted by the Jesuits from their stronghold at the Clementinum, their university in the city.[15] A 1669 Jesuit campaign resulted in the temporary closure of both of Prague's print houses, which reopened by 1674. Thereafter, Hebrew printed matter came under the watchful eyes of the Jesuit establishment in the city.[16] Oppenheim's relocation of the library to Prague would necessarily subject his collection to heightened scrutiny, which might ultimately result in its destruction. Fearing this scrutiny, Oppenheim opted not to take his collection to the city. Instead, he sent his entire library to Hanover where his father-in-law Leffman Behrens had petitioned Elector George Ludwig for the right of settlement in the city for David Oppenheim, his wife, and his children.[17]

The collection's move to Hanover perhaps made it safer but also removed it from Oppenheim's private keep and more fully transformed it into a professional library for a wider use (although not a fully public one). The great wealth of the Behrens estate granted Oppenheim the luxury of following the emergent practices of book collecting captured by Gabriel Naudé in *Advice for Establishing a Library,* which advocated situating a collection "as far removed as possible from hubbub and annoyance," in a space that was dry, airy, and light enough to facilitate both usage and preservation.[18] In Hanover the library acquired a steward in the person of Oppenheim's only son, Joseph (d. 1739). Joseph, joined by other occasional caretakers of the library such as David b. Moses of Sulz, provided a necessary condition for the library's functioning as an agent of knowledge-making that relied on Oppenheim's consent but did not require his immediate presence.[19]

The space and staff in Hanover lent the collection a structure and order that enabled its utility. Its caretakers marked every volume with both a Hebrew letter and an Arabic numeral for shelving, dividing the collection into 106 sections, with a corresponding catalogue directing the user toward the row and series number of each item in the physical library (fig. 3.2.).[20] Such marking enabled the retrieval and consultation of the books in the collection, and perhaps even the organization of memory itself. In the early modern library, the display of books was understood to affect the manner in which the knowledge they contained was apprehended—a sort of en-

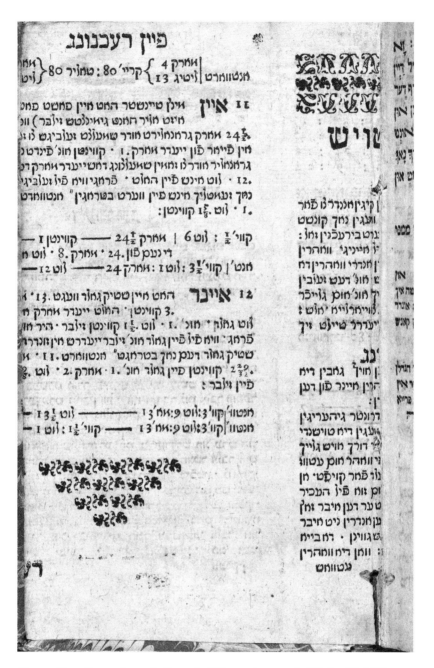

Fig. 3.1. Opp. 8° 919: Aaron b. Samuel of Hergershausen, *Leibliche tfillah* (Herger-shausen, 1709). A table for rates of exchange, recycled as the binding of a book—likely because its utility for exchange rates had expired. Courtesy of the Bodleian Libraries, University of Oxford.

לוט	אמרק	אמרק	לוט
11 ———		1 ———	3 : 17

אמט מיינר מיין שטיק זילבר וועגט 20. אמרק המלוט
וייא אמרק מינט פיין 1¼ לוט פאר קויפט צולביגט
זיין מוס 1¼ ½ טמויר וויא פיל בטראמגט מין גיזאמט
ומרט 21ג. טמויר 7ג. קרייגלר :

| 20 רק ——— 14 לוט ——— אמרק 1 |
| 280 ט ——— 12⅓ טמויר ——— אמרק 1 |

מודר

| 14 ט ——— 12⅓ טמויר ——— לוט16 |
| 20רק ——— 10½ 2/24 טמו ——— אמרק 1 |

ין איינטער המט מיין שטיק גמור וועגט 20.
אמרק · החמט דיא אמרק מיינט פיין 12. קרמט·
פיינירט צולביגט · דערם גטמלט דמט עט 15ן
· דיא פרמג מיזט · וויא פיל דענם נאך יערר אמרק
ין ווערט מינט פיין החלטין 16. קרמט:

| אמרק 20 ——— קרמט 12 ——— אמרק 1 |
| אמרק 1 ——— קרמט 240 ——— אמרק 15 |
| נמך דער רעגגוא דעטרי קומפערום דורך 1. זמן : |
| 20 ——— קרמט 12 ——— אמרק 1 |

מזהיר · 1· לוט · 12· ליטיג זילבר מוס 2ג. קרייגלר· 2.
הלוט ווערט · וויאפיל גביהרטזיך דענם נמך פאר· 1.
דר 16. ליטיג זילבר לו גענבין מטנווערט 12· טמויר :

| לוט 16 ⎰ שפעג 2 קריי' ג½ ⎱ לוט 1 |
| מרט ליטיג 16 ⎰ ⎱ ליטיג 12 |

פט 6¼ אמרק פיין זילבר מוס 80. טמויר
80. קרייגלר · וויא פיל גביהרטו זיך דענם
פאר· 4· אמרק 13. ליטיג זילבר · מטנווערט
40, קרייגלר :

מטנווערט

Fig. 3.2. The shelved material in Oppenheim's collection. The Hebrew and Arabic numerals at the tops of the spines represent the original shelf marks. Numbers at the bottom are the product of later cataloguing by the Bodleian Libraries. Courtesy of the Bodleian Libraries, University of Oxford.

cyclopedia writ large.[21] Visual perception was intended to aid memory and organize knowledge in the eye of the beholder, and wall-system furnishing was often adopted, not merely to impress but to conform to educational theory: material organization and knowledge organization were meant to cohere.[22] Naturally, such intentions were often more aspirational than fully possible. Since books entered most early modern collections as composite volumes of various texts, systems of cataloguing were often caught between preserving a recently acquired collection and dispersing its parts into thematic categories.[23]

Once in Hanover the library could receive visitors of varying stripes.

The most detailed description of such a visit comes from Christian lawyer and diplomat Johan Anderson (1674–1743) in December 1713. Anderson had a doctorate in law from the University of Leiden, and his talents brought him to the negotiating table at the Peace of Utrecht (which concluded the War of Spanish Succession). From there he traveled to the northern German town of Hanover to the home of Gerhard Wolter Molanus (1633–1722), who told him about Oppenheim's library. Anderson was stunned by the collection—noting its magnitude, comprehensiveness, and diversity of geographic provenance and paleography—all the more because its primary owner lived in Prague, rather than onsite. Writing to spread word of this Jewish marvel to other interested Christians, he reported that

> the owner himself was not present, but rather absent in Prague. But his son-in-law [*sic?*] showed me all civility, and the old cantor of the synagogue showed me the most noteworthy of the books, which I inquired after. There was no catalogue present, because Rabbi Oppenheimer traveled with it. He [the guide] could not really say the number of the books that were available. The approximate number which I estimate, however, was at least 6000 codices or volumes and surely 2000 manuscripts which were written all over the Jewish world, and it was a curiosity to behold their different, but always rabbinic, characters. Of them many, as he tells me, and also presumably, have still never been printed. Although I myself cannot read [the Hebrew language], he showed me an item of the Bible written on large parchment, consisting of the Torah, the Prophets, and the Writings, probably of very ancient age, and a similar one in small format written very neatly for a wealthy Jew a few years ago, with the Masora in the margin and on every side in special fashion borders, lines, and leaves, animals and fish, some of them microscopic. Among the printed volumes one can find an astounding quantity of Bibles, all of the editions of the Talmud, and prayers printed from entirely unknown locations and small villages—among other books.

> . . . The great correspondence, which Oppenheim's cou-
> riers undertake across the entire world, yields the advantage
> that he is held as rabbi throughout the imperial domains and
> Poland, as well as in Venice and Jerusalem.[24]

Anderson's account of the library at work highlights salient points regarding the collection and its representation. He grasped Oppenheim's far-flung contacts as an essential ingredient in his successes in amassing this collection, noting the rabbi's extensive, worldwide communications beyond the boundaries of German Central Europe to Venice, Poland, and as far as Jerusalem, where, as we have seen, he had been named Prince of the Land of Israel.[25] He also registered an observation of another seemingly minor point: that although Oppenheim was apart from his collection, he carried a physical manifestation of it on his person in the form of its catalogue. We have already seen that catalogues could offer a template for acquisition, but their functions were not limited to this. Early modern catalogues served as a form of "libraries without walls."[26] Traveling with a catalogue was a surrogate for the physical collection that allowed Oppenheim to virtually consult his holdings in absentia and to project the full force of his library even when he was far from it. Its synechdochal function assured that the rabbi's command of the entirety of his collection remained perpetually at his fingertips, and allowed him to demonstrate to himself and others that the full complement of knowledge was within his reach, even remotely.

Visitors and Users

As the library's fame grew, a wider public came to personally consult the collection, or wrote to its keeper to request replications and extracts from its stores. Although this was a personal collection, and not officially an institutional library akin to the great royal and princely libraries that arose during the second half of the seventeenth century, Oppenheim allowed it to serve a wider rabbinic republic of letters, thereby translating its private contents into a form of public service.[27] The transmission of information through travel, copying, and correspondence was a hallmark of the early modern republic of letters' system of knowledge-making, as scholars turned to distant colleagues to consult inaccessible material.[28] In fact, as early as the mid-1680s Oppenheim's teacher Isaac Benjamin Wolff had written to him to request that he write back with copies of what he had learned and studied.[29] Such lending activity was rare, but not sui generis: in the catalogue Oppenheim prepared during the 1680s, he noted the few occasions when he lent books to colleagues, as in the case of a Joseph Katz of Halberstadt who was in Hanover at the same time as Oppenheim in April 1683.[30] Jacob Rzeszów (Reischer), Oppenheim's relative by marriage, wrote from Prague to Nikolsburg in 1699 requesting that Oppenheim send him "his" book (it is not clear whether he means a book that Oppenheim wrote, or simply a book in his care).[31]

Oppenheim similarly permitted people to visit the collection in person. Thus Rzeszów made use of specific texts from the collection in crafting his rulings on various themes, noting, "and greater still, I found and saw in the responsa of the Rashba in manuscript, #108, in the noble collection of my in-law the great David Oppenheim."[32] In 1709 Oppenheim received a request from a man in Halberstadt who was in the process of composing his own commentary to the Talmudic tractate *Nazir*. He requested to visit Oppenheim to consult manuscript editions of the Talmud produced before the age of print in the hopes of discovering textual variants.[33] The author of the book *Noheg ke-tzon Yosef* recalled viewing a book of customs by Yuspe Hahn Norlingen "which is still not printed and can be found in the *bibliothek* of the famed sage."[34] A copyist and editor of kabbalistic manuscripts, R. Yerahmiel b. R. Menahem Nahum of Rzeszów visited the library in 1737 (after Oppenheim's death) and commented on his use of a manuscript edition of the book *Etz Hayyim* with provenance from Safed that "had additional sections . . . which are not found in the copies of *Etz Hayyim* in our lands."[35]

The library's visitors were many and varied. Although Christian censorship posed a problem to the world of Jewish books from some quarters, Oppenheim was not averse to allowing access to his formidable collection to Christians who were well-disposed toward its contents. Such collaborations were a feature of the early modern period. During the Renaissance, direct interaction between Jewish experts and Christian students was essential for Christian Hebraist learning to flourish. By the seventeenth century, however, a Christian scholar seeking to gain the requisite skills to read Judaic works could turn to textbooks produced by Christians, and to Christian teachers, attaining a complete education without interacting with a Jew.[36] But the materials of Jewish learning, in the form of books and manuscripts, were still more ubiquitously found in Jewish hands than elsewhere.[37] Oppenheim's house of artifacts offered a space for interaction across confessional lines. And although the work of Christian Hebraists and Jewish rabbis was clearly directed toward different ends, both could maintain contact out of their mutual affection for the Hebrew book. A semi-neutral sphere of a very different sort was created between the bookcases of Oppenheim's collection.

Johan Anderson's visit led to the arrival of other Christian visitors to the library. The great bibliographer of Hebrew literature Johann Christoff Wolff began communicating personally with David Oppenheim in 1713, sending him a book to facilitate conversation.[38] Wolff traveled in person to consult the contents of the library no fewer than four times, its contents leaving their mark on his massive *Bibliotheca Hebrea* (Hamburg, 1715–1727).[39] He marveled at the library's treasures, reporting on its contents to his colleague, the Christian Hebraist Johann Justus Losius, who also visited the library and recorded the books that impressed him the most.[40] Although a hiatus in correspondence appears to have occurred after 1714, contact resumed between Wolff and the collection's caretakers in 1719 when David Oppenheim's son, Joseph, renewed the correspondence. Joseph, speaking on his father's behalf, saw Wolff's interest as beneficial for the growth of the library and acknowledged the aid of the Christian Hebraist, particularly in his expertise in Latin, "a language which I do not know too well."[41] Wolff's visit to the library was decisive for its fate in future generations. His discussion of the library in volumes 1 and 3 of *Bibliotheca Hebrea* provided the critical assessment needed for future interest to blossom. Although during Oppenheim's lifetime his library was famed on account of his own activities, after his death it was Wolff's endorsement that provided the means by which marketers could raise interest for prospective buyers to purchase the collection.[42]

The visits of Christians to the collection continued throughout Oppenheim's lifetime. When the missionary Johann Georg Widmann (1696–1753) undertook a two-year journey from the Netherlands to the Balkans in 1730, a stop in Hanover brought him to the famous library. Widmann logged the events of his travels in a diary and recorded the dialogue that first brought the library to his attention:

> J E W : Would you not like to go to our library as well?
>
> M E : If it would be permitted.
>
> J E W : Why not? It holds a book that costs, by itself, 500 thalers.
>
> [M E :] What is it called?
>
> J E W : I do not know. The library is near the synagogue, and there is nothing in the world like it. . . . Indeed, there is no book in the world that you cannot find there.

Following some negotiation, Widmann gained access to the library and wove his visit there into a longer polemical dialogue in his diary about the interpretation of the Bible from a Christological perspective, as well as his own expertise in Jewish bibliography. He even encountered "an Oppenheim daughter" who granted him permission to return to the library at will.[43]

From Court Jews to Jewish Courts:
Oppenheim as Legal Authority

Others may have visited the collection, but it was not simply a storehouse of items from the past, of interest to antiquarians alone. The spheres of activity to which they related extended beyond the academic and intellectual and into the lived experience of early modern contemporaries. The library's contents had pressing relevance for the administration of Jewish collective and ritual life that came together in the autonomous communities of early modern Europe, and the collection operated as an important resource for the institutions of Jewish life. First and foremost, the collec-

tion was Oppenheim's own scholarly domain, and he used it for the practical adjudication of aspects of Jewish life. Consciously and conspicuously
mentioning sources that only he could know on account of his private collection allowed him to position himself as having a level of expertise un-
available to others—a tangible symbol of superiority in Jewish society's
most revered arena.

The library complemented a position of authority that was conferred
upon Oppenheim by communal appointment and the opinion of his peers.
His official position in Prague was to serve as the head of its rabbinical
court, a position of legal authority. Colleagues of various rankings across
parts of Europe solicited his legal opinions. In this regard he was both a
poseq (legal decisor) and a *dayyan* (judge), two roles with similar expertise but different functions.[44] A *dayyan* was a communal officer, locally appointed, whereas a *poseq*'s authority derived from the recognition of his
peers. In the writings of Oppenheim's teacher, Yair Hayyim Bachrach, the
poseq was superior to the *dayyan* partly on account of the intellectual independence he displayed. Oppenheim's legal oeuvre of rabbinic responsa
reflects his expertise as a *poseq* in matters of holidays and the Jewish ritual
cycle, prayer, marriage and divorce, jurisprudential procedure, kosher
food, and commerce. Jacob Rzeszów bore testimony to some of Oppenheim's activities as a *dayyan* in Prague. He recalled moments in which he
"sat in the place of the elders, the place of the Court, by the side of the great
and famed sage David Oppenheim," where the chief rabbi ruled on questions of marriage contracts and divorce laws, and other occasions when
Oppenheim was called upon to decide questions of liturgy and ritual, as on
a Saturday evening when the moon was not visible yet custom demanded
that a prayer for the new moon be read.[45]

Oppenheim's use of his library emerged most starkly not in his in
situ decisions in Prague but in his foreign correspondence, in the responsa
that he authored upon consultation by distant questioners and then edited
in preparation for publication and dissemination.[46] He authored legal decisions in reply to queries from Holleschau, Lundenburg, Krakow, Neustadt, Rotterdam, Frankfurt, Livorno, Venice, and Mantua.[47] Oppenheim
routinely furnished these writings with reference to his collection of rare,

and therefore privileged, information, using such references to enhance his legal standing when writing to colleagues and even teachers. From his responsa it is also clear that Oppenheim was perennially in transit between his post in Prague and his library in Hanover; many of the letters he received were addressed to him there, which indicates that his contemporaries knew that he was as likely to be with his books in Hanover as with his constituents in Prague.

From the library in Hanover, Oppenheim had recourse to materials that few others possessed. It was not so much that books did not circulate widely, but Oppenheim made use of the limited circulation of two kinds of manuscript writing: copies of titles that were difficult to acquire, and the manuscript glosses and annotations to printed books. These latter especially equipped him with an extra stratum of scholarship that he parlayed into a specialized expertise not readily available to others, which had come from the act of collecting not only single copies, but multiple copies of books. Marginalia and glosses converted copies of the same edition of a text into two unique and distinct books. In a responsum from 1694 Oppenheim wrote to his former tutor Yair Hayyim Bachrach regarding a question of marriage law; he followed the routine procedure of casuistic discussion and citation of pertinent texts common to this genre of rabbinic writing but also went a step further in writing, "the *Sefer Mordekhai* that I possess is annotated throughout, and also here [i.e., on this subject] it is annotated as follows. . . ."[48] In a 1692 responsum dealing with a case of illegitimate marriage, he invoked rules that he had discovered in "annotations in manuscript."[49] And when ruling on the unsuitability of a Torah scroll for ritual use on account of a scribal error, Oppenheim annotated a manuscript edition of his responsa by noting "and I discovered a proof . . . see an ancient book, a manuscript, from 5071 since the world's creation [1411], it is the work *Kupat ha-rokhlin* written by the great kabbalist our master Joseph Angelino."[50]

In each case he took recourse to manuscript material that his interlocutors would not have otherwise seen or known, thereby positioning himself as not just having read more, but as being the only one with the means to access such material to begin with. This ethos of bibliographic maximalism was relatively new, a departure from the canonical and limited body of texts of Jewish legal decisions of an earlier era, which had been replaced with a drive to read as widely and comprehensively as possible. This stance was articulated most fully by the Amsterdam rabbi Shimon Frankfurt (d. 1712), who charged that "whoever makes legal rulings should possess a sufficient quantity of books, such that he is able to follow the majority in all his legal decisions that are followed in these lands."[51]

Oppenheim's comprehensive yet restricted collection enabled him to fulfill this demand more than perhaps any of his contemporaries, and he therefore supplied individual decisors and rabbinical courts with vital information for adjudicating aspects of daily and family life that ranged from the procedural to the particular.[52] One example of his use of the library as a reflection not just of law, but of empirical data appears in the particularly vexing judicial problem of Jewish marriage and divorce. This field of law occupied the energies of rabbi-jurists who were tasked with precision in drafting writs of divorce, without which women could be permanently prevented from remarrying (a status that did not apply in the same way to men), their remarriages could be delegitimized, and the children of such unions could be relegated to second-class status in the Jewish community. In order to prevent such an abysmal scenario, rabbis were charged with meticulously conducting the rituals of divorce, but they could be stymied by procedural matters such as incomplete testimony and unreliable documentation. In addition, Central European rabbis could find themselves hindered by the fact that Jews often went by more than one name—one for ritual purposes and another "in the street" for daily use and for commerce with non-Jews.[53] Failure to use the correct name could invalidate divorce proceedings. Thus a Jewish court wrote to Oppenheim to consult about the name "Todros" (derived from Theodoros) for whom questioners feared the name was not sufficiently Jewish. In another case, there was uncertainty about whether to refer to a woman by her colloquial name "Tzippor" (or "Vogel") or by the proper biblical name "Tzipporah." At stake was the efficacy of the divorce contract and the ability for new marriages to be conducted by the authority of these courts. The frequency with which such questions emerged shows the problem to have been common.[54]

When confronted with such uncertainties, Oppenheim used his library not only to offer legal precedent, but to locate empirical and evidentiary bases to resolve these questions. It was not appeals to reason or tradition alone that made his library important, but its expansive scope, which enabled treatment of every conceivable question. On the question of the man named Todros, Oppenheim combed through his books to identify use of the name in the Jerusalem Talmud (a sufficient reference for canonical status) and in works of commentary to it (*Sefer sde Yehoshua* [Constantinople, 1662]); he offered further support from the book *Sefer shemot ha-gittin* (The Book of Names for Writs of Divorce).[55] To aid in resolving the question of the use of the name "Vogel," Oppenheim reached beyond published books into the texts and registers of Jewish daily life, noting, "I found in the book of memory of the holy community of Prague, may it be preserved, in the old synagogue, that it is written there the name of a man, our teacher and master R. Vogel, and we may therefore resolve that the woman's father and mother named her for that one."[56]

Ownership of reference matter that treated both the canonical and the ephemeral furnished Oppenheim and his interlocutors with the relevant information to resolve these would-be crises. Baffled writers could stand secure in writing to Oppenheim for inquiries about names, as he had dedicated a portion of his library to precisely this problem, collecting no fewer than eleven manuscripts on the theme. The manuscripts offered information about ceremonies of divorce performed by rabbis of the previous two centuries, including Jacob Margaliot (d. 1490),[57] Israel Isserlein (ca. 1390–1460), Yom Tov Lipmann Heller (1579–1654),[58] and Isaiah Horowitz (1565–1630),[59] as well as a volume of ceremonies from Frankfurt[60] and a concordance of names showing their Hebrew and German counterparts.[61] Such concordances and indexes of names belonged to a larger trend in the production of reference literature that was not based in antiquity alone but sought to manage contemporary information as well. Oppenheim's collection served not only to preserve a distant past, but to collect the practices of contemporaries in a systematic fashion. He utilized the library as an agent in the production of new knowledge and the application of that knowledge to new scenarios.[62]

This quasi-ethnographic approach to the practices of Jewish life in early modern Europe could range from the minutiae of law to the spheres of the supernatural. In 1696 Oppenheim drew upon the resources of his collection in the winter months when a recent arrival to Poland from Nikolsburg was struck with symptoms of spirit possession.[63] The afflicted boy had wandered across Eastern and Central Europe, performing strange acts and giving way to tremors and seizures as the foreign spirit tormented him. Oppenheim met with the boy before delegating responsibility for his spiritual treatment to a seasoned exorcist by the name of Moses Prager. In order to equip Prager for such a thaumaturgic task, Oppenheim scoured his collection and reported that he had "already prepared a book, found among my holy writings, packets here and there from oaths and charms that relate to these matters."[64] With the help of this text, Prager conducted his spiritual healing. Oppenheim was not present for the exorcism, but his place in the event, and more importantly in the legend thereafter, was firmly established on account of his book collection: two reports were produced about this episode, one in Hebrew and one in Yiddish, the only surviving copy of which is kept in Oppenheim's library.[65]

The uses of mystical texts from his collection could provoke concern from state authorities. When Oppenheim presided over the exorcism of a Jewish woman in Prague in 1708, the Prague appeals court and Bohemian chancellery quickly involved themselves by investigating both the ceremony and the texts that accompanied it. Bohemia's authorities convened an inquisitorial commission to fully examine the affair and returned a decision after a year and a half that condemned such Jewish activities and mandated more careful scrutiny of books and manuscripts that contained "false" kabbalistic knowledge.[66] The imperial offices proceeded to curtail Oppenheim's involvement by restricting such questionable books from Jewish schools and synagogues. As we shall later see, this was not the last time that Oppenheim's private actions as a collector of books ran counter to the expectations that the state authorities who guaranteed his position had of him.

A Rabbinic Republic of Letters

Oppenheim's resources were important for his support of Jewish courts of law and the individual judges who staffed them. But his library also elevated his standing within a community of religious decisors that transcended the jurisdictions of local courts, maintained contact with each other across space, and actively contributed to creating a new canon of legal decisions. They constituted a rabbinic "republic of letters," a transnational, urban, and highly mobile community of scholars who corresponded with one another about academic subjects and practical adjudication. As they wrote to each other, they did more than communicate knowledge; they shaped the way such knowledge was made, appraised, and accepted as authoritative by weaving together personal reputation, collegial consensus, and textual research.[67]

This rabbinic republic linked the events of daily life and local Jewish judiciaries to a wider, regional conversation exchanged between authorities across Central Europe, and its members repeatedly enlisted each other's support in recognition of their legal decisions.[68] Recognition, reputation, and personal credibility were as important as reason and textual interpretation when it came to making new knowledge. Anthony Grafton has argued that "by contacting a dominant figure in one of these glittering galaxies of talent and receiving a testimonial of warm approval, one could win credit in one's own local, competitive environment."[69]

An expression of this reliance on the consensus of peers to construct local decisions is evident from a dispute over the legality of marriage that broke out between the cities of Hamburg-Altona and Prague in 1707. The affair began when Hamburg's Ashkenazic rabbi, "Hakham" Zevi Ashkenazi (Zevi Hirsch b. Jacob Ashkenazi, 1656-1718), permitted the widowed daughter of Joseph Stadthagen to marry a man in Prague. Controversy erupted upon her arrival in Prague when Zevi's ruling was rebuffed by Oppenheim's rival in the city, Abraham Broda, who denied the legitimacy of the arrangement because the young widow was still a nursing mother, and the Talmud prohibits women from remarrying until a child has reached two years of age.[70] With divergent but accepted legal reasoning on the side of both rulings, rabbis across the German lands conveyed their thinking on the complicated matter.[71] The proportions of scholarly involvement were grand. One younger rabbi later recalled:

> In the days of my youth when I studied at the *yeshiva* of my master and teacher, the great one, rabbi of the entire diaspora, Abraham Broda, may he rest in peace, a question like this was posed to him of a woman whose doctors instructed her not to breastfeed (as it is referenced in the responsa *Beit Yaakov*), and all of the rabbis of Ashkenaz were perplexed by this matter. . . . and those who permitted [the marriage] opposed my teacher in Prague, and he was powerless because his colleagues, all of the leaders of Ashkenaz overwhelmed him.[72]

The emphasis on the widespread consensus of "all of the rabbis of Ashkenaz" demonstrates that rabbinic decision making did not happen in a one-to-one correlation between decisor and litigant. Rather, a widespread consensus often made a significant impact on the shaping of the law's outcome. Rabbis were deeply rooted in the immediate contexts in which they operated, but their local authority was buttressed by recognition by colleagues across the region, as they attempted to marshal support from prestigious allies outside of their locales.

Both general consensus within the rabbinic elite and communication of such consensus featured strongly for Oppenheim and his colleagues as they produced their legal decisions and captured those decisions in publications that justified their rulings. The pressures to marshal consensus in the face of competition emerged again during an acrimonious dispute about kosher butchering and the possibility of a chicken existing without a heart in the kitchen of a woman in Altona in 1709:

> It happened that a certain maiden opened the belly of a chicken to remove its innards at the edge of a table, and a cat stood below next to her, standing and anticipating eating whatever fell to the ground, and the maiden said that she found no heart

in the chicken, and the owner of the chicken said perhaps, almost certainly, the heart was cast to the floor and the cat that
was standing there, ready to eat, ate it, while the maiden says,
"I only tossed to the cat the *treifah hertz,* that is, the spleen,
but I did not toss the heart to the cat," and the chicken was fat
and healthy and good, it had no shortcomings, no rotting in its
belly, and no impress of the heart could be discerned, and not
because of some change in any part of its belly, and while it was
alive it was strong, healthy, with all of its power, to walk on its
feet, to fly with full might with all the powers as one of the best
and most healthy chickens, except that the maiden says that she
did not find the heart, and the matter came before the students,
and they declared it unkosher. Our master should teach us what
the law of the chicken is.[73]

This odd question was as important politically as it was ritually. Its author
was Zevi Ashkenazi, who shared his rabbinate with another rabbi, named
Rabbi Moses Rothenberg, in alternating terms of six months each—and
the rabbis had come to opposite conclusions about the case.[74] Zevi buttressed his empirical approach with authoritative texts, including infer-
ences from Maimonides's Code of Jewish Law and the mystical Zohar.[75]
Rothenberg decided otherwise, not least because this matter had arisen in
writings of Jewish authorities from previous centuries, who had accepted
the premise of a chicken's existence without a heart; to doubt it was to cast
aspersions on centuries of legal thinking and writing. Against Zevi's claims
of common sense ("for all whose hearts are the hearts of wise men within
them, and a mind in his head"), Rothenberg claimed that this was patently
incorrect, "the way of women, without any basis."[76]

   This regional dispute was initiated outside of his formal jurisdiction,
but Oppenheim was pulled into the fray. Letters poured into Altona at the
behest of the sparring chief rabbis and their proxies across Central Europe.
From Frankfurt Rabbi Naftali Kohen supported Zevi, his relative, while
letters from Meir of Prossnitz and Meir Eisenstadt sided with Rothenberg.[77] The letters occupied themselves not only with the law, but also with

the sources from which it was derived. A copy of the *Shulhan Arukh* surfaced that was purported to have belonged to the Maharal of Prague, whose
ruling that life without a heart was impossible lent considerable weight to
Zevi's position.[78] Oppenheim dispatched a former student, Jacob Zamartik, to the owner of this volume, who was a judge in the Frankfurt Jewish
court. Zamartik consulted the volume and found that it accorded with the
claim, and he consulted other books and manuscripts that cited the marginalia similarly.[79]

In his own responsum, Oppenheim presented a long-winded but
illustrative picture of the mood—one in which he did not hesitate to cast
himself again as an impartial arbitrator who was specially called in to resolve
this local argument:

> On account of a question, of which I have heard the roaring
> noise from a city full of sages and scribes, masters . . . in mat-
> ters of practical law . . . and they raise the call in the camp, the
> conflagration set out to divide and enflame, this one prohibiting
> and this one permitting. Yet they do not even agree on the ques-
> tion itself [literally, they do not prophecy in the same manner],
> this one as he will and that one as he will, and each points to
> the right at the fork in the road, its way pleasant, not destructive
> . . . and everyone is seeking that I give my weak opinion. And
> behold on account of love of the Torah and love of the world,
> which stands on a pillar of peace, a pillar that returns to the
> health of the soul, I have decided to uncover my ear to equally
> weigh each side, may God direct me on the true path, this is the
> language of the rabbi who permitted.

Oppenheim ruled against Zevi, but in the process he took the opportunity
to fashion an image of impartiality. Even as he took a side in the dispute, he
portrayed himself as standing above the fray of petty squabbles and intellectual discord. The framing of his legal argument within a larger narrative of his personal role served to project a superior legal authority, both
in terms of his ability to strike compromise between warring factions and

on account of his comprehensive collection. In rendering his decision, he referred, obliquely, to finding an "ancient compendium" that helped him make his ruling in a way that others were not able to imitate.[80]

The affair did not quickly abate. A full five years after the controversy began, Oppenheim wrote a letter, a rejoinder to yet another rebuttal from Zevi, in which he maintained his position that a chicken could indeed be born and live without a heart, which would make it unkosher. Offering his words "in every language of affection," Oppenheim stood his ground and leveraged his ruling both upon personal testimony of similar cases that had come before the Prague court in the years since the original question and upon books to which he alone had access. Oppenheim made repeated reference to "ancient books," especially a work of Rabbi Israel of Marburg. The text was particularly valuable because it bore a scribal colophon from 1530 in which the scribe attested to directly copying from the manuscript of the original author.[81] Such powerful evidence was especially important because, as we have seen, part of Zevi's case rested on the *Shulhan Arukh* thought to be owned by the Maharal of Prague. Yet Oppenheim did not extend to Zevi the same bibliographic confidence, and, invoking his own critical bibliographic reputation, he cast aspersions on the authenticity of the marginalia within Zevi's text, which had no scribal colophon and therefore could not be authenticated as Oppenheim's own could be. The battle over books and historical bibliography extended into the walls of Oppenheim's library: when Zevi visited Hanover in the spring of 1714, Oppenheim "showed this book to the permitting rabbi [i.e., Zevi], when he was with me, to gain wisdom and knowledge in the house of books."[82] Oppenheim thus positioned himself and his library as decisive repositories of knowledge that even his opponents were forced to recognize.

The case of the chicken without a heart was perhaps the most sensational halakhic debate of the period, but it was not the last of Oppenheim's career. More than fifteen years later, Oppenheim once again was embroiled in a controversy that pitted traditional codes of law against critical bibliography and natural science. In 1725, Oppenheim relied on regional networks to support his localized legal ruling against a challenge from an upstart rabbi by the name of Jonathan Eybeschütz, who had positioned himself as an antagonist of Oppenheim for some time, in part as a result of Oppenheim's competition with Abraham Broda more than two decades before. The debate between Oppenheim and Eybeschütz concerned the kosher status of an animal in whose intestines had been found a needle, which was covered in fat, the consumption of which was legally questionable. Oppenheim took a stringent position and prohibited the consumption of this fat, but Eybeschütz permitted it and seized on the opportunity of this dispute to instruct his students to question the authority of the city's chief rabbi.[83] Decades later, in the heat of his own clashes with Eybeschütz, Zevi's son, Jacob Emden, recalled Eybeschütz's use of his own scholarly networks who "did not only publicize his name locally in Prague, but rather they wrote stories of his wondrous deeds to all corners . . . until his reputation was widely known, all of Ashkenaz and Poland and even Turkey believed that he is unique."[84] Emden's framing of the affair in terms of student allegiance shows his keen awareness of the social foundations of legal dispute, which was not lost on either side. Oppenheim appealed to the court of opinion of his peers and wrote to colleagues beyond the city to buttress his claim. From Metz, Jacob Rzeszów responded that "out of great humility, David diminished himself with regard to one who is smaller than he," noting with equal humility that he had been called upon to take up the cudgel in Oppenheim's defense.[85] Adopting a page from Oppenheim's playbook, Rzeszów enhanced his opinion and that of Oppenheim by citing books that were not in wide circulation, specifically relying on the book *Elia rabbah* by Elia Spira Wedeles, which "was not yet printed."[86] Others, like Ezekiel Katzenellenbogen of Altona, was more hesitant. He respectfully disagreed with Oppenheim, hedging his dissent in deference to Oppenheim's stature even as he diverged in his ruling by interpreting the texts without recourse to changing them. Oppenheim, in turn, sent a rejoinder to the ruling, working to bring Katzenellenbogen to his point of view.[87]

The argument revolved around an interpretation of the *Shulhan Arukh*, the code of Jewish law by Rabbi Moses Isserles of Krakow, or Rema (1520–1572). Although Oppenheim appeared as the more conservative character with regard to practice, his interpretation hinged upon a greater preparedness to criticize the form of received texts. Where Eybeschütz and others who upheld the permissibility of consumption cited a

ruling by Rema, Oppenheim argued that this was based on a faulty printing of a text and argued for the emendation of that text in favor of the less
lenient approach.[88] In Oppenheim's case textual criticism combined with
legal conservatism—his access to books and manuscripts allowed him to
position himself as having greater authority to evaluate the authentic version of texts, but his ruling was more cautious and restrictive.[89] He wrote,
"it is a scribal error in the *Kol bo* [an anonymous medieval compilation that
included rulings of the Tosafists], and Rema, because of his youth, was not
discerning, and copied the words as they were before him."[90]

The exchange of letters, followed by rejoinders and replies, reveals
the intensity of rabbinic debate and the work that went into attempts to persuade colleagues to concur. The shaping of law was more than just coherence with legal norms and fidelity to ancient texts. Law required the work
of reputation, trust, and authority, which were recognized in the court of
opinion of a closed cadre of rabbinic elites.

Between a Communal Archive and
an Archive of the Community

Oppenheim's collection of manuscript materials of limited circulation
reached well beyond the realm of rabbinic law, ritual practice, or even mysticism, into the domains of communal governance as well. In this regard,
he was participating in a practice common to governments of various forms
in the early modern period. From as early as the rise of medieval states,
collecting, as a form of archiving, was a vital component of the administration of subjects and the exercise of power. The growth first of church archives during the early Middle Ages and the expansion of record-keeping
into the domain of states during the High Middle Ages were outpaced by
the explosion of documentary practices during the fourteenth and fifteenth
centuries in humanist centers such as northern Italy and the Low Countries. Libraries came to represent a crucial lynchpin in this process: Gabriel
Naudé, who achieved fame in his role as librarian to the French first minis-
ter Cardinal Mazarin, was also an advocate of a statecraft that relied on the
accumulation of knowledge.[91] Across the European landscape, the possession of libraries and the practices of good governance became allied with

each other—in terms of both the practical effects of learning and the symbolic authority learning could convey on the exercise of power.

Despite regional differences, the rise in archival practices took hold across the continent. Naudé's native French political theory, especially its endorsement of absolutism, was not popular in the German lands, where centralized power was kept in check through constitutional limitations; but German thinkers participated in an emerging political economy that saw government's task as promoting the prosperity and material welfare of a territory.[92] What both French and German theories had in common was a new approach to the relationship between the practice of power and the contribution of scholarship to such practice. Beginning in the mid-seventeenth century a slew of books addressed to German princes advocated for the establishment of a new academic discipline now known as cameralism.[93] This new "science of government" proposed to manage the administration of a state through the training of experts in the realities of that state's affairs.

An essential component of this new science of government was *Herrwissenschaft,* the idea that rulers must both have knowledge of the conditions of those they govern and know how to operate within those conditions. At the core of this knowledge was the gathering and preservation of information. Oppenheim was not likely to have read cameralist treatises, and there is no hint of such literary material in his collection, but he could participate in their approach to knowledge-gathering on account of his ties to the halls of power that were beginning to adopt cameralist stratagems for governance.[94] The Court Jews were intimately familiar with the world of governance on account of their place in the higher circles of statecraft. They could serve as conduits between different political contexts—the sovereign court and the *kehillah*—and subtly translate the political culture of one to the practices of the other. Rabbinic training, too, wrestled with the tension between study as a value in and of itself and study as a means toward practice.[95] Although Oppenheim's collection included tracts that would hardly have been accessible to the non-initiate, many of his books and manuscripts were directed toward the realm of the administrative, rather than the rabbinic, religious, or esoteric. This application of knowledge to practical affairs belongs to the sphere of politics—the putting into practice of principles, ideas, and precedents of governance. Collection and copying created troves of knowledge about politics and procedure, which in themselves were political acts with political ends.[96]

One striking instance of copying in the service of politics and administration appears as a bound manuscript volume comprising eighty-two exempla of contracts that might be issued by Prague's Jewish administration, ranging from marriage and divorce to business partnerships to, ultimately, contracts for rabbis.[97] Oppenheim's copy opened with a copper plate engraving with an inscription that identified the significance of this volume (fig. 3.3):

> *Tikkun Sofrim*
> Established upon plinths of gold, from the mouths of parents
>   and teachers,
> To teach the sons of Judah the inkwell of scribes and clerks,
> According to the law of Israel and the courts of others,
> To silence the claims of those who speak lies, and not to lock
>   the door before lenders and merchants,
> We have come with a pen of iron and lead
> To write at length in the *pinkas* of the holy community of
>   Prague, city of heroes . . .
> All this we have written for preservation (*le-mishmeret*) for
>   many generations to come.[98]

This descriptive epigraph and the book it introduces demonstrate important elements of the act of collecting that go beyond the assemblage of titles for preservation alone. Rather, they reveal the relevance of these works for Jewish communal and political life. The successful exercise of this knowledge in the service of power entailed navigation between the spheres of the autonomous Jewish community ("the law of Israel") and the institutions of Jews' ambient society ("the courts of others"), especially that of the court of the sovereign.

The title page on the volume of contracts from Prague also referenced another important body of texts: the *pinkas* (record-book of the communal

Fig. 3.3. Ms. Opp. 615: *Sefer tikun sofrim.* A formulary of contracts used by the Prague Jewish community, based on the communal ledger, or *pinkas.* Courtesy of the Bodleian Libraries, University of Oxford.

leaders). The use of this genre of Jewish text marks an important element of early modern culture that sets the period apart from both the medieval and the modern. Neither wholly sacred nor entirely secular, record books governed the constitutional lives of early modern Jews as a corporate entity—the *kehillah*—but were not part of their religious law derived from a chain of tradition of authority believed to have originated in biblical revelation and thereafter vested in the Talmud and its textual interpreters. Decisions taken by authoritative legislative bodies that were promulgated as statutes were called *takkanot*. Whereas rabbinic authority derived from Talmudic training, the laws enshrined in *takkanot* were buttressed by the authority of a local governing Jewish laity and communal consensus of their constituents.[99] The practice of drafting these statutes and regulations can be traced to the early Middle Ages and even before. Despite their importance for ordering communal life, *takkanot* do not, by and large, appear to have been recorded and preserved in volumes that were set aside for such a purpose.[100] In the early modern period, however, a shift in cultural attitudes toward preservation introduced the practice of registering *takkanot* in a designated ledger called the *pinkas*—an act that gave them greater force.[101]

Many communities had a *pinkas* for recording and consulting the regulations of the *kehillah* as a whole, but various corporations under the aegis of the Jewish community also took to enshrining their governing principles within particular *pinkassim,* such as charitable societies, burial confraternities, individual jurists, midwives, and ritual circumcisers.[102] Just as the towns of the Holy Roman Empire recognized the liberties of guilds and other corporations to regulate their own internal affairs, the official organization of the Jewish community similarly encompassed any number of voluntary associations that shaped the conduct of their members by establishing rules and regulations. And the records of the leadership of the community could vary as well. In 1702, when the tax system for Prague's Jewish community was overhauled, the leadership stipulated the creation of a ledger for the purpose of registering taxpayers:

> And within that ledger he [the official community scribe] shall put the names of all of the people of all of the *kehillah,* may the

Lord protect it, and of the women and young men and also the young women and even orphans who engage in trade and business, be it great or small, whatever it be of whatever the mouth may speak of, for which the *perdon* [the sales tax] must be paid, the bringer thereof will enumerate before the scribe . . . and the scribe must register it in the ledger beside the name that is registered in the *pinkas*.[103]

In registering the names of the taxpayers, the leadership of the community aimed to use the medium of record-keeping to accumulate information that could thereafter be used for administration and regulation. *Pinkassim* thus encompassed the descriptive acts of information-gathering and the prescriptive governing materials that attempted to order the social sphere.

Record in a ledger book did not alone confer status upon an ordinance — that ordinance had to be the product of an authoritative legislative body. But recording the decisions of that legislature within a designated material object created a regulated, fixed, textual constitution by which Jewish social and communal life was expected to be conducted. The simple technology of recording authoritative decisions in a designated book made concrete the process of lawmaking from legislation to registration. Such registration thereby converted abstract rules and accepted custom into formal, objective law. Reaching a decision was not sufficient; decisions had to be inscribed into a designated object (the *pinkas*) by a designated person (the salaried scribe). In his capacity as chief rabbi, Oppenheim had regular interaction with and recourse to the services of such scribes. In Nikolsburg he held the services of the Jewish "provincial scribe" (*sofer ha-medinah*) on retainer.[104] Prague, too, had an official communal scribe. When the democratic leadership of Prague was replaced by a permanent oligarchy by order of Emperor Leopold, the new Jewish governors issued a body of *takkanot*, listing among the new statutes an emphasis on the importance of registration by the officially appointed scribe, who held a key to the new synagogue where the communal ledger was kept.[105]

The creation of law did not end with inscription, however. By the late seventeenth century, preservation, the final step, was deemed crucial to the process. Registration enshrined law in the form of an object. The translation of a common possession of custom into a material object similarly demanded a designated individual to take hold of and preserve that object. Unlike the great act of preservation effected by large-scale textual reproduction by printing press, manuscripts demanded concerted care by a steward of skill and standing. The statutes from Hildesheim that Oppenheim helped craft specifically demanded the continuation of the practice of designating a room for storage in the building in which Jewish leaders conducted their business, that a trunk or chest house the statutes and other documents under lock and key, and that two copies of the key were held by the leaders of the community—a practice that Jewish communities across Europe maintained as well. Space, personnel, and objects converged to produce official administration.

A document relating to Oppenheim's own rabbinate reveals the interplay between the regulations of daily life and documents. In 1713, Prague's *rosh yeshiva*, Elia Spira Wedeles, who had replaced Abraham Broda after 1708, died during the outbreak of the plague.[106] In response to his death, the leadership of Prague's Jewish community under their primas, Samuel Taussig, renewed Oppenheim's rabbinic contract and expanded his role to encompass that of both *av beit din* and *rosh yeshiva*, finally and formally uniting the roles of the rabbinate that had been partitioned between two men over preceding decades and consolidating them under Oppenheim's control. The contract outlined Oppenheim's fitness for the role and stipulated matters of tax exemption and salary. It concluded by confirming that it has been drafted with the consent of state authorities, but then it invoked one further authority: the *pinkas* of Prague's officers (*ketzinim*). In the final sentence of the contact, in bold letters as large as the heading of the entire text and matching the name of the contract's beneficiary, the *pinkas* was given special mention, as the drafters assured all readers and challengers that "we have copied word for word from the rabbinic contract that is registered in the officers' *pinkas*, page 311" (fig. 3.4).[107]

But Oppenheim was careful to preserve copies of his own outside of the walls of the official communal buildings. One did not have to be a governor to be a preserver of records. Townspeople across early modern

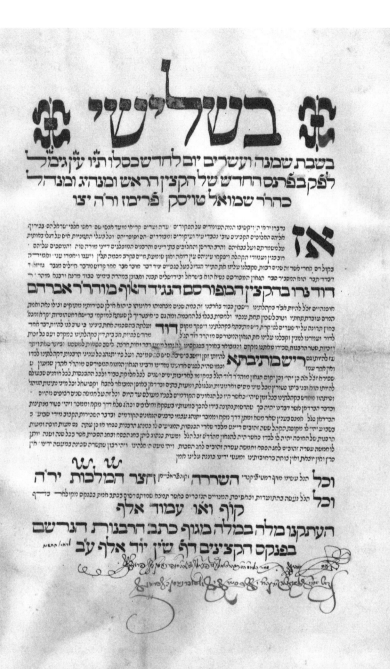

Fig. 3.4. Contract for David Oppenheim, 1713, signed by the leadership of the Prague community. The document closes with an assurance that its authors have copied the language "word for word from the rabbinic contract that is registered in the officers' *pinkas,* page 311." Courtesy of the Jewish Museum in Prague.

Germany, Italy, and other parts of Europe kept records and chronicled the events of their times in order to understand and give shape to their places in the passage of great and small events.[108] Whereas as chief rabbi Oppenheim had recourse to the official scribes of the community, he also had a *personal* scribe, as in 1721 he petitioned the government for special tax exemptions for his scribe by the name of Moses Leib (Moyses Löw).[109] Record-keeping was not the monopoly of the autonomous community, and perhaps authority followed the records, rather than the other way around. Oppenheim's record-keeping is particularly noteworthy on account of the fact that the preservation of records during the early modern period could be so precarious. When fire ravaged the Jewish Town in 1689, it extinguished decades of record-keeping, a fact often acknowledged by Prague's leadership in its formal correspondence with municipal and imperial bodies.[110] Perhaps they, too, took occasion to turn to Oppenheim's private archive to furnish their official dealings.

A formidable representation of the combination of scholarly and diplomatic roles that manifested in Oppenheim's person and his wider network can be found in the "Kopialbuch of David Oppenheim." The name, applied by modern archivists, refers to a hefty volume of some 205 documents covering 765 manuscript pages.[111] The documents' original provenance ranges from 1623 (some forty years before Oppenheim's birth and a full eighty years before his arrival in Prague) to 1724, twelve years before his death. With the exception of a handful of pages in western Yiddish, the compilation is made up entirely of German-language documents in the baroque hand, evidence of the mediating role of these records between the affairs of Jewish life and the affairs of the bureaucratizing Habsburg state. The lion's share comprise correspondence between the Habsburg imperial offices (predominantly the Bohemian chancellery) and the elders of the Prague Jewish community regarding the administration of Jewish life on matters such as taxation, electoral representation, sanitation, and construction of synagogues, schools, housing, and ghetto walls. A number of other documents record exchanges between the offices of the archbishopric and either Oppenheim himself or the Prague Jewish leadership more generally. These might include regulation of censorship and sermons, or even deputizing Oppenheim with ensuring Jewish orthodoxy.[112] Interspersed among these letters were also a number of texts that pertained more directly to the financial dealings of the Oppenheim family and its larger network: the sale of jewels by Court Jews or inheritance disputes regarding the estate of Leffman Behrens and the claims of Oppenheim's children to it.[113] Still others represent points of conflict within the community, such as challenges to Oppenheim's capacity to adjudicate intracommunal matters. And finally, one page is a fragment of Prague's *pinkas,* a governing record book that has since been lost.[114] Evidence suggests that the provincial scribe or a man of similar abilities collected and copied a body of diplomatic documents akin to the "Kopialbuch," which supplied Oppenheim's Prague years (1703–1736), by recording state correspondence from his Nikolsburg years (1690–1703) as well. These documents, produced by Mordekhai b. Menahem Menke of Leipnik in 1695, have since been lost.[115]

In straddling the boundaries between *poseq* and *dayyan,* Oppenheim served as the arbiter of the meaning of *takkanot* that were neither strictly within the realm of halakha nor too far from it. Jewish civil and statutory laws that were drafted by non-rabbinic leaders were sometimes referred to the chief rabbi for consultation and interpretation, even though they were not derived from the Talmud and codes whose study was the main purview of rabbis.[116] This did not require a new skill set on the part of rabbis, but it did represent an extension of those skills to a body of texts with a different sort of authoritative weight—a weight that came not from religious precept but from communal fiat.[117] A letter from the Moravian town of Leipnik to Oppenheim is instructive in this regard. The author, Abraham, had participated in a business arrangement that had gone sour. When local forms of adjudication did not return a favorable outcome for Abraham against his rival, Leizer, Abraham reached out to a court of higher appeal, the chief rabbi. Among the details of his grievance with his grim prospects, Abraham made special note of the fact that he had been particularly accommodating in this case toward his rival, appearing before a wider court "even though it is a violation of the *takkanot ha-medinah.*"[118] In his appeal to the chief rabbi, Abraham foregrounded the weight of communal statute and its formal application. His casual reference to this information proffers a sense of the significance of this body of law for domains of early modern Jewish life, and of his expectation that mention of these statutes would resonate with the region's chief rabbi, Oppenheim.

In the responsa that Oppenheim prepared for publication, he similarly extended his purview to the texts that had been produced by the lay governors of Jewish life. In a responsum from 1689 he commented on custom as it applied in the laws of taxation and included *takkanot* as a source for adjudication.[119] He ruled on the contents of *takkanot* and their application in a responsum penned in 1709 (by this point he had already left Nikolsburg for the chief rabbinate of Prague), when prompted by a query regarding the permissibility of relatives to serve on the same governing council. Drawing upon medieval halakhic texts, chief among them the work of Rabbi Asher b. Yehiel (d. 1327), Oppenheim praised the act of keeping careful statutes and ruled upon the practices of the community.[120]

Just as subordinate rabbis of Moravia appealed to Oppenheim's rulings of the *takkanot,* Oppenheim acted as researcher and archivist to uncover legal precedents for his own professional contests. In 1702, he wrote to the scribe of the community in Krakow for excerpts from the latter's *pinkas.* He wrote on the eve of his departure from the Moravian rabbinate to take up the position of chief rabbi of Prague, a position he would be sharing with an equal partner. Oppenheim therefore wrote to Krakow in search of precedents from the Polish *pinkassim* that might offer him grounds for supremacy over his supposedly equal partner, Abraham Broda, understanding that recourse to documents and records would provide the best means to achieve his aim. His gambit involved an attempt to discover which part of a rabbinic appointment was more important: administration of the rabbinical court or leadership of the yeshiva, and he attempted to lead his witness to uncover precedent for "the superiority that the rabbi and head of the court has over the *rosh yeshiva.*"[121] To his disappointment, the Krakow scribe returned with no such precedent.

Finally, the registers and records pointed toward the creation of new records. When the Jewish community of Prague drafted a new rabbinic contract for Oppenheim in 1713, they specifically noted that all of the terms were in accord with the prescriptions of the *pinkas ketzinim.* Like the contracts assembled in Oppenheim's *Tikkun Sofrim* exempla of contracts, the rules established by the deliberations of governors could set future forms of documents and records in motion. Printed matter itself promoted the proliferation of manuscript contracts: the precedents fixed by print permitted copyists of individuated texts to produce by hand according to the models established in the printer's shop. The printed word gave renewed impetus to writing by hand as well.[122]

Conclusion

Since the Middle Ages, Ashkenazic rabbinic culture adopted an approach to legal knowledge-making that involved a network of discussants. Such diversity of legal opinion may reflect the entrenchment of local prerogative as a supreme value in the halakhic decision-making process, in which each local authority felt the need to internalize the questions and localize them to his immediate geographic context. Although a similar networked structure persisted in the eighteenth century, it may actually represent a different set of motivations. Rather than work to localize scholarly authority in an immediate communal space, many controversies saw the export of immediate contests in the hopes that support from neighboring communities might provide the necessary leverage to overcome opposition. As such, engagement with a particular controversy transcended, even undermined, local hermeticism, and—like other aspects of Jewish commerce and politics in the Holy Roman Empire—bound disparate Jewish communities more closely together, even if only for their representatives to disagree with one another.[123]

The contours of this rabbinic republic of letters shifted over time and place. But Oppenheim's library offered him a means to assert superiority over his rabbinic colleagues on account of his ability to marshal and manage an ever-growing body of documentation and knowledge. Using the contents of his library, Oppenheim combined formal learning and bureaucratic administration into a central resource deposit that shared many features with the archives of centralizing states. This entailed a process of careful commission, reproduction, curation, and preservation and a system of managing materials in an early age of "information overload."[124] Paradoxically, the physical separation between Oppenheim (in Prague) and his collection (in Hanover) cemented his identification with his collection and the use of it as a vehicle for his professional standing. Removed to Hanover, in the care of guardians and librarians, the collection's books and manuscripts became the shared province not simply of Oppenheim and his family, but of a wider literary-administrative elite that consulted the collection to shed light on the affairs of courts and *kehillot*. Rabbis and judges appealed to both the collection and its collector—who operated with the authority of the library at his fingertips—to inform their decisions in ritual matters, social relations, taxation, and administration. Christians and Jews alike traveled to visit and marvel at a library that might hold the key to pressing questions about Jewish life and culture in ancient times and in the streets of early modern Europe.

"To Make Books Without End"

From the Library to the Printing Press

It would be most unfortunate, and should be a cause for regret, that the
lucubrations and labors of an infinity of great men who have labored and sweated
perhaps all their lives long to give us knowledge of something that had never been
known before, or to elucidate some profitable and necessary matter, should be
lost or should rot away in the hands of some ignorant possessor.
—Gabriel Naudé, *Advice on Establishing a Library,* 1627

THE TITLE PAGE OF A MANUSCRIPT copied for Oppenheim in
1712 describes the contents of the volume as "a book of mourning practices"
by Maharam of Rothenburg (fig. 4.1). The inscription elaborates, pointing
out that the book was cited by prominent medieval Jewish authorities, the
Rosh (Asher b. Yehiel, 1250–1327) and the Mordekhai (Mordekhai b. Hillel
ha-Kohen, ca. 1250–1298), "but it cannot yet be found in printed form."[1]
This description of the contents of the volume and the self-referentiality of
the object as a manuscript reveals the sense by its handlers of the relationship between a printed book and its manuscript siblings. The words "it
cannot yet" imply that the widespread diffusion of classical material via the
printing press was a desideratum which might be rectified in the future.
But the fact that this ideal could not "yet" be fulfilled—and was therefore
limited and as a result precious—served as an important basis for Oppenheim's unique access to the material, and concomitantly, to his prestige.

The social life of Oppenheim's library extended beyond the exchange
of used items or the consultation of books and manuscripts by courts and

ספר
התשבץ : ספר
הלכות אבל לֵמֵ״ה
רֵם וֵספר זה מובא
בהרֵא״ש ובמרדכי
ולא נמצֵא עדֵין
בדפוס

ℐ. 500

תע״ב לפ״ק

Fig. 4.1. Title page of Ms. Opp. 94, *Sefer ha-tashbetz* (copied in 1712). Courtesy of
the Bodleian Libraries, University of Oxford.

communities and into the production and publication of new titles, both original works and ancient manuscripts only recently discovered. Although Oppenheim and his colleagues studied printed books alongside manuscripts with equal scholarly weight, the form of each was not insignificant when it came to constituting his authority.

Oppenheim acted as an important motor of this process. From the first moments of his self-conscious collecting, he expressed the will to "make books without end," and he promoted that mission in a variety of material and cultural ways. Much as the circulation of books permitted a vantage point for discovering relationships of power and prestige, the production of books represented an equally fraught political field. To print a Jewish book required the cooperation of Jews and Christians, authors and printers, artisans and wealthy sponsors, censors and endorsers. Oppenheim stood at the meeting place of such concerted action: while his library offered a source of discovery for unpublished manuscripts, he also was personally involved in the publication process on account of his familial wealth to sponsor publications and the cachet he possessed, as a bibliophile and scholar, to discriminate between works that deserved publication and those that did not.[2] Oppenheim and his wealthy relatives played a vital role in this economy. They were not just the representatives of Jewish concerns in the halls of power; they were also the financing force behind the production of the most important items in the idealized normative rabbinic culture of the early modern period, books — items whose publication shaped the contours of the Jewish canon and curriculum for centuries to follow.

The Printer's Altar: Sourcing the Market

The introduction of printing technology into the world of books in early modern Europe produced a host of predictions and lamentations about what such an innovation might mean for scribes, scholars, and readers, and how a more easily facilitated production of books might impact the world of learning. Sir Francis Bacon applauded its contribution, enumerating the invention of printing among the three most important technological innovations in human history, alongside gunpowder and the compass.[3] But printing also produced its share of anxious critics. From the moment of its introduction, intellectuals rushed to condemn the new medium and the threat to order and quality that it portended.[4] The advent of print presented opportunities to unseat hierarchies of knowledge and power, creating spaces for new elites and circumventions of the authority of tradition and its representatives.[5]

Some Jewish thinkers joined the chorus of critics of the printing press and the potential of newly published books to overwhelm the classics. Two full centuries after the introduction of the press, Joseph Solomon Delmedigo (1591–1655), an avid collector of books, fretted that "the entire business of publishers is with new books, and they give no care to the ancient works . . . and because of the printing press the world is turned upside-down."[6] A verse from the book of Ecclesiastes gave voice to anxiety about the proliferation of the printed word and furnished skeptics of the press with a clear sentiment: "And furthermore, my son, be admonished: of making many books there is no end; and much study is a weariness of the flesh" (Eccl 12:12). A predecessor of Oppenheim's in Prague, Rabbi Ephraim Luntschitz (1550–1619) read this text with dramatic resonance. He took "there is no end" to mean that the redemption of humankind—the expected "end of days"—would be forestalled by the ceaseless multiplication of books.[7] In his view, the growth of printed texts robbed the ancients of their due and created a culture of novelty and the pursuit of self-aggrandizement.

But Oppenheim took a very different stance. Rather than rejecting the dangers of publishing, he embraced the power of the press and facilitated the production of an ever-growing roster of print matter, from both new authors and ancient sources. As we have seen, he took the admonition of Solomon not as a warning, but as a mandate, adopting it as his motto. In the catalogue of his youth, he explicitly invoked the phrase to imbue it with the inverse of its original meaning: "May God grant me to collect and accrue them / that God's Torah in Israel may spread far and wide / and to make books without end."[8] Oppenheim elevated the task of publication to a holy mission, often referring to the process as offering books "on the printer's altar"—a casting of the printing press as a sacred space, upon which the holiest offerings, books, were put before a wider reading world.[9]

Premodern responsibility for "making" books was a messy business.

Of all of the participants in a book's publication, the author was hardly the most important. An "author," as an autonomous creative individual who produces a work based on singular genius that is his or her own intellectual property, is an invention of the modern age. It was only in protracted legal battles in Western Europe over the course of the eighteenth century that debates over the rights of property contributed to this notion of an autonomous, creative author who was uniquely and most fundamentally responsible for the genesis of a work of intellect.[10] In the world in which Oppenheim operated, the "makers" of books included all of the workers in the process—not only the author, but also printers, publishers, and sponsors. This principle held especially when the "author" in question was long deceased—as was the case with so many medieval manuscripts in Oppenheim's collection. The ambiguous intermediate role of a "publisher" might be combined with that of printer or bookseller, and the title pages of books acknowledged them as partners in a book's production. The front matter of Hebrew books often included a preface by the publisher, who told the story of his labor to bring the book to print.[11] This intermediary role was labeled as the "*mevi le-defus,*" literally, "the one who brings [the item] to print," which captured the distinction between technical printer, original author, and the more expansive role of publisher.[12] This sort of "publisher" was a more amorphous role that could encompass financiers, agents, children of deceased writers, and people who had invested energy in facilitating the printing of works by authors long gone by bringing the works to the printing presses.

On some occasions, manuscript copies of texts preserved a sense of the authors' intention to publish their works, giving voice to the long and winding road from manuscript to print book. When Petahiah b. Joseph of Frankfurt hoped to published his manuscript copy of the commentary of Elijah Loans of Worms to the Zohar, he prefaced the manuscript with a poem describing his desire to print: "I thus spoke to his heart [i.e., persuaded him] to print it in order to grant it . . . to all who seek wisdom."[13] An inscription in the manuscript copy of *She'elot menuhot Shalom* by Shalom b. Leib Shalom of Lvov records a note by the author's son that "my father left this book with me in order to be brought to print."[14] The author's own introduction to the work made the circumstances even more clear, as he recalled a childless life with his spouse for more than twenty-four years. His respite from this familial emptiness was the act of writing, and he told his readers that he wrote the book to create a legacy in the absence of offspring. This author did not remain childless, but he did not live to see his book printed—a task his son took up. Despite the express wishes of aspiring authors, the business of books required far more than will alone.

Oppenheim's collection represented a space even further removed from the printer's altar in the chain from author to reader—the supply of unpublished manuscripts to those people who would become a *mevi ledefus*. When Jonathan b. Jacob, a Jewish refugee from besieged Ofen (in Hungary), took refuge in Nikolsburg during Oppenheim's tenure as chief rabbi there, he found his way to the bibliophile's library.[15] There he discovered a manuscript copy of a text by the Italian kabbalist Menaham Azaria da Fano (1548–1620). Fano had written a series of ten kabbalistic essays titled *Asara ma-amarot* (Ten Utterances), of which only three were published during his lifetime.[16] Oppenheim had purchased an unpublished portion of this series—the seventh essay of the collection—in 1686 (for half a reichsthaler).[17] By granting Jonathan permission to enter the collection, Oppenheim exposed him to the book and authorized his labors to publish the text under the title *Maamar ha-itim* in 1694 at the print shop of Shabbetai Bass, in Dyhernfurth.[18]

Credit for Oppenheim's role in the publication of Fano's kabbalistic manuscript was somewhat muted, appearing in the introduction to the book but without great fanfare on its title page. A very different situation obtained a decade later, with the publication of a text long thought lost: the commentary to the Bible by Rabbi Samuel b. Meir of Troyes, or Rashbam (ca. 1085–ca. 1158). Like the Fano manuscript, Oppenheim acquired a copy of this text during the earliest phases of his collecting, in the 1680s in Worms. Unlike the simple purchase of a manuscript, however, the story of its acquisition was far more adventurous and, in Oppenheim's telling, providential. While he was still just a young man, hoping to build a great collection but far from realizing that end, his relationship with a bookseller in Worms in the 1680s led him to a trove of documents in a synagogue *genizah,* that is, a deposit of discarded Jewish texts.[19] According to the seller, the discarded materials included "thousands of manuscripts" that were abandoned (*hefker*) on the upper level of a synagogue; they were fetid, dusty, moldy, infested with vermin, and rotting from exposure to rain.[20] Oppenheim described this moment as an epiphany, convinced that "the Lord brought this book into my hands . . . a writing of truth, of ink on parchment," especially as he discovered two remarkable works for the heritage of Worms Jewry: Rashbam's biblical commentary and a copy of the *Mahzor Vitry,* the first complete prayer book of medieval Ashkenaz.[21]

Oppenheim did not race to publish the manuscript, however. In fact, twenty years elapsed between its discovery and publication, even though he recognized the significance of the text early on. Rashbam's commentary is distinct from many other medieval readings of the Bible in its fidelity to the plain and literal interpretation of the words of Scripture. It is perhaps even more noteworthy because of all the commentaries that attended the printed page since the earliest publications of the Rabbinic Bible, none other than Rashi had an Ashkenazic provenance. Yet Oppenheim hesitated. His doubt of the author's desire to circulate the text led him to resist publication for two decades after its discovery. With the passage of time, Oppenheim revealed the manuscript to colleagues, friends, and students, but he refused their suggestions to publish the work, reticent to print a manuscript that might never have been intended for the public eye.

After twenty years of resisting the book's publication, in 1705, Oppenheim decided that the circumstances were propitious for a change. One influential intermediary in this process for the Rashbam manuscript was a man by the name of Joseph b. Moses of Premysl, or Joseph Darshan ("the preacher").[22] It was this Joseph, from his station in Berlin, who arranged the circumstances of the manuscript's printing. It is no accident that Berlin housed a press that was willing to invest in endeavors like this. In that same year, a new noble academy, the Berlin Academy of Sciences, was founded, with its mandate being research rather than what its founders saw as an earlier and outmoded model of mere "curiosity."[23] Berlin did not have a Jewish-owned printing house at this time, but it was home to an enthusiastic Christian scholar of Hebraica, the professor and court preacher

Daniel Ernst Jablonski, who cofounded the Berlin Academy with Gottfried Wilhelm Leibniz. Jablonski opened the first Hebrew printing house in the city and employed Jewish workers there.[24] Joseph, the intermediary, did not survive to see the work published. Instead, the labor was carried on by his wife, Hayale, who descended from a rabbinic family in Luntschitz.[25]

When the text was published, it featured an eight-page preface by Oppenheim, one of the longest pieces of his writing published during his lifetime. The preface began with a declaration of a ban of copyright, lasting fifteen years from the date of the completion of publication, but it was far more than a mere assertion of intellectual property. Oppenheim directed his preface to two tasks: a paean to Rashbam and his work, and a description of the process by which the long-lost manuscript had come to light. Weaving citations of biblical verses together — a style quite characteristic of his particular authorial voice and of rabbinic introductions to books in general — Oppenheim linked great biblical ancients with moderns, cloaking more recent authority in ever greater symbolism of Israel's influential prophets. In the course of his preface, he demonstrated the evidence for identifying the text as authentically authored by Rashbam, adamant that he had done due diligence in matching the manuscript against references to statements by Rashbam in other texts ("everything which I have seen in printed books in the name of Rashbam can be found in this composition"), and noting instances in which the author explicitly mentioned debates with his maternal grandfather, Rashi.[26]

Oppenheim's narrative carried a providential tone to it: a discovery akin to a Sinaitic epiphany, a pressure to print as fulfillment of a divine mission. And in the nature of printing that was intimately bound up with patronage and prestige, the finished product offered material testimony to Oppenheim's indispensable role. The book appeared with not one, but two title pages. The first appeared immediately after the binding and identified the work as the first volume of the Five Books of Moses, advertising the multiplicity of commentaries and attendant texts that accompanied the biblical material. But following eight pages of introductory material, and immediately preceding the opening of the biblical verses, a second title page appeared (fig. 4.2), which proudly proclaimed:

Fig. 4.2. *Hamishah Humshe Torah* (Opp. 8° 49). This is the second of two title pages that appear in the volume. Oppenheim owned two copies of this edition. Courtesy of the Bodleian Libraries, University of Oxford.

> This is the Book of Rashbam, discovered in the trove of holy
> books of our master, our teacher, and our rabbi, rabbi of all of the
> diaspora, David Oppenheim, may his creator protect him, he is
> the chief rabbi and *rosh yeshiva* of the holy community of Nikols-
> burg, and the flag of his love is spread over all of the provinces of
> Moravia, and he has given permission to print it, with the aid of
> the One who dwells in heaven. May God grant him many days
> and years, and may he live to see sons and grandsons, Amen.

A banner of text framing the page offered verses in tribute of Oppenheim's
biblical, kingly namesake: "And David had great success in all his ways; and
the Lord was with him" (1 Sam 18:14) and "David reigned over all Israel;
and David executed justice and righteousness unto all his people" (2 Sam
8:15), as well as the Talmudic phrase "and in all circumstances the law follows him." The book's physical layout offered tribute to the nobility of the
man who had enabled it to be printed.

Supporting the Market: Courtly Culture and Conspicuous Consumption

The 1705 printing of the first volume of this new edition was received with
great success. Within months Jablonski began work on the second volume
and again contacted Oppenheim for his support, this time not for texts to
publish, but for financial backing. On October 12, 1705, Jablonski wrote
to Oppenheim, in German and Hebrew, asking the rabbi to purchase fifty
copies of the recently printed *Arba turim*, the halakhic work of the medieval
scholar Jacob b. Asher (1270–1340). The revenue from Oppenheim's purchase of these fifty copies, in Jablonski's plan, would go to the express purpose of printing the second volume of the Pentateuch with accompanying
commentaries.[27] The complete new edition of the Pentateuch was complete
by 1708, and a second edition was published in Dyhernfurth in 1728 (this
time without Oppenheim's lengthy preface).[28] In addition to an ordinary
version of the printed product, Oppenheim owned a special vellum copy
of the four-volume series, bound in a velvet, dark pinkish-crimson cover,
which was perhaps given to him by the publisher as well.[29]

When Jablonski reached out to Oppenheim to purchase fifty copies of the *Arba turim,* he understood that Oppenheim was more than bibliophile or antiquarian. He was also an agent of economic investment in the press. Books may be crucial bearers of knowledge and can often be items of deep emotional attachment, but they are also fundamentally commodities. Their production depends on market forces: they require capital outlay and sufficient demand for financiers to recover their outlay and gain at least moderate returns. The costs of printing included the purchase or rent of a press (actually the least expensive aspect of the industry), the purchase of type (which frequently wore down and needed to be replaced), a semi-skilled labor force, and, most expensive of all, paper.[30] In the majority of cases, this was far too great an expenditure for the entrepreneurial printer to cover alone. Rather, capital came from investors who saw opportunity for profit. It was for this reason that the first centers of printing did not spring up in intellectual centers and university towns, but rather in hubs of commerce that were near enough to those towns to bring together material supply with intellectual demand.[31] In the world beyond the little market of the Hebrew book, changes were already taking place that may have allowed the author to occasionally liberate himself (and occasionally herself) from patronage. The market for Jewish books was, on the other hand, comparatively small and therefore required subvention by patrons and funders.[32]

Oppenheim and his family members repeatedly contributed to the financing of Hebrew books. As Jablonski perhaps intuited, personal ties to Oppenheim opened doors to a wider network of financiers. When a student of Oppenheim's wished to publish a book of his father's writings in 1698, Oppenheim secured the sponsorship of both Leffman Behrens in Hanover and Samuel Oppenheimer in Vienna.[33] In 1715, Oppenheim's student Elyakim Getz published a volume of Talmudic commentaries and defenses of Rashi by the Krakow rabbi Joshua b. Joseph (Getz's uncle), a work funded with the support of Oppenheim; Oppenheim's son, Joseph; Feibush Katz of Hanover; and Behrend Lehmann, the Court Jew of Halberstadt.[34] When the Amsterdam press of Aaron de Solomon Antonis published an edition of *Midrash rabot* in 1725, the publisher fondly recalled his days as a student of Oppenheim's student in Nikolsburg and made clear that the arrival of this text in print form would have been impossible without the material support of the Prague rabbi, "who contributed to purchase a fixed number of the books and purchased the word of God [i.e., these books] in their full amount."[35]

Oppenheim's financial sponsorship of the book trade was expressed both in obtaining financing for publications and in committing to purchase multiple copies of a work once it was printed. This commitment of Oppenheim's may also have served a wider Jewish reading public: it stands to reason that while Oppenheim would keep one or two copies of each publication, his purchase of tens of duplicate copies would go to supplying study houses and individual libraries as well. Indeed, communities across Europe seem to have depended on Oppenheim as a *distributor* of books. In 1704, he received a letter from the scribe of Krakow's Jewish community, Moses Liberles, who wrote to thank Oppenheim for sending a book and to remind him of the commitment he had made to send two copies of the recently printed Talmud.[36] In requesting copies of the Talmud, perhaps the most fundamental text of Jewish study, Liberles was not writing to get his hands on an exotic work. Rather, he, and by extension the community of Krakow, placed his hope in Oppenheim because he believed Oppenheim could be relied on not just as a depot of books, or as a sponsor of printing, but as someone capable of aiding communities without access to presses by sending books to them, and perhaps sending them without charge.

Patronage of new books—both their production and dissemination—was thus the driving force of the Jewish book trade. The practice of sponsorship extended beyond Oppenheim, however, and books might even have many sponsors. When a compendium of rabbinic commentaries to the Talmud was published in 1721 under the title *Sefer asefat zekenim* (also called the *Shita mekubezet*), the publisher listed no fewer than seven sponsors who had pledged their commitment to forthcoming volumes in the series.[37] Chief among these was Samson Wertheimer, but Oppenheim's name was conspicuously absent from the roster. Not only did Oppenheim patently *not* hold a monopoly on book patronage, it also may have been the case that competition to sponsor Jewish books obtained between and even within Jewish moneyed families. Oppenheim and Wertheimer were relatives whose life stories were closely intertwined, most immediately in the marriage of their children, but also in their mutual candidacy for the Prague rabbinate. Just as Oppenheim's name became synonymous with his collecting activities, it is entirely possible that Wertheimer was party to a similar project of self-fashioning, one that excluded Oppenheim where it could.[38]

Benefactors like Oppenheim and Wertheimer were often rewarded with unique copies of the books they sponsored, produced on higher-quality paper, with special bindings and inscriptions. Moreover, the books they sponsored featured a concise recognition of the patronage involved in the book's production — not quite a dedication along the lines of the works of science and art produced specifically for the aggrandizement of a court, but an acknowledgment of the impact of the personal subventions granted by members of an influential class.[39] The Court Jews' financial contributions to the provisions of the materials of Jewish life were consonant with a larger culture of consumption and sponsorship in which they participated and were reflected both in the fact of the provision and in the decorous form that these books took. Oppenheim imbibed the courtly appreciation for fine things, and, perhaps more importantly, the symbolism of power that fine things convey. Having fine items was a way of conveying "taste" — that intangible quality that confers prestige upon its bearer.[40] Learning and politics went together in this culture in which advances in the sciences were produced in the service of the state, not merely as technological know-how to productive ends, but as part of the prestige of the court.

Mingling an appreciation of learning with an appreciation for objects, Oppenheim spared no expense in augmenting his collection with uniquely adorned copies of books. Rather than simply purchase books that were already in circulation, he also had specific copies of books printed for him in special print runs on blue or other colored paper.[41] This practice had been started in Italy during the early years of Hebrew print and was a particular favorite of Oppenheim's in the presses of Amsterdam, Frankfurt, and Berlin.[42] Oppenheim owned fifty-seven such books, all but eleven of which were printed during his lifetime.[43] This did not escape the attention of Johann Jakob Schudt, the Christian Hebraist and observer of Jewish practices, who remarked in his *Jüdische Merkwürdigkeiten* on Oppenheim's books printed in blue, "which is supposedly good for the vision."[44] Blue paper, colored and hefty, was so costly that for many buyers of books, it served as a binding. But Oppenheim's wealth was so extensive that he could afford to take what for others was the most expensive aspect of book production and make it mundane and routine. His palette was not limited to this hue, however. He also ordered a copy of the Passover Haggadah, titled *Mah nishtanah*, printed in Prague in 1713, which was produced on orange cardboard.[45] He set the precedent for print runs on grey paper (owning seven volumes in that color), and ordered two copies of *Seder keriah ve-tikkun* on yellow paper, and held colorfully illuminated copies of printed editions.[46]

Oppenheim's library brimmed with expensive objects of these sorts alongside the inexpensive and mundane. He ordered some forty vellum editions of books between 1705 and 1735. His edition of the Talmud on vellum cost him 1,000 gulden.[47] He also owned vellum copies of incunabula, books published during the first decades of print, such as a 1484 Talmud *Berakhot*.[48] Both the color and material of these books point to the materiality of Oppenheim's collection, artifacts of a cultural élan among the Court Jews and wealthy Jews like them, who brought material luxury to religious artifacts.[49] Much as the contents of the library symbolized the authority of knowledge in the service of governance and administration, the materiality of its contents demonstrated conspicuous consumption and distinctions of social standing.[50] The binding of his books similarly conveyed wealth and power, as in the gold-embossed cover of a heptaglot lexicon (of Hebrew, Chaldaic, Syriac, Samaritan, Ethiopian, Arabic, and Persian) printed in London in 1669 (fig. 4.3). In the thirty years or so following its initial printing, it was specially bound either by Oppenheim or by someone who wished to submit it to him as a gift, recognizing the man's appreciation for "Jewish books" even beyond the rabbinic canon.

The Talmud

The entanglements of literary material, economic investment, and personal credit converged in Oppenheim's involvement in the appearance of new

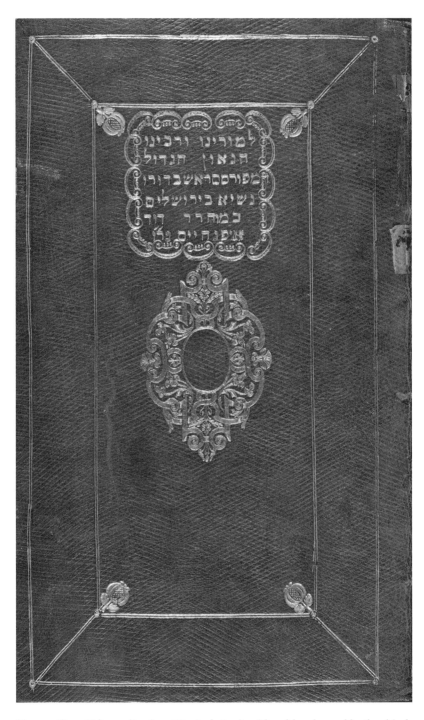

Fig. 4.3. Opp. Fol. 322 (Lexicon Heptaglotton), with gold embossed leather binding naming the owner as David Oppenheim, "Prince in Jerusalem." Courtesy of the
Bodleian Libraries, University of Oxford.

editions of the Babylonian Talmud at the start of the eighteenth century. Although the sixteenth and seventeenth centuries witnessed a period of prolific printing as publishers presented the Jewish reading public with ever more material, one item in particular made it off the presses with some difficulty: the Talmud.[51] Foundational as it was to Jewish study, complete editions of the Talmud nonetheless were scarce. To begin with, the Talmud was an enduring battlefield between Jewish students and Christian censors, subject to special scrutiny especially in Catholic lands.[52] But material conditions were equally determinative of the Talmud's scarcity, especially in Eastern Europe. Although Krakow had once been a center of Talmud printing, the ravages of the Khmelnitsky uprising in 1648 had left the Jewish libraries of Eastern Europe denuded and had shifted the center of gravity in Jewish cultural production from east to west.[53] Half a century had elapsed since the publication of Immanuel Benveniste's Amsterdam Talmud (1644–1648) when, in the 1690s, the wealth of Court Jews was recruited to finance a new edition in Frankfurt an der Oder, on the eastern edge of the Holy Roman Empire.

The initiative for this new edition emerged during the final decade of the seventeenth century in the persons of Johann Christoph Beckman, professor of theology at the University of Frankfurt, and Michael Gottschalk, a Frankfurt printer. Beckman had dedicated more than two decades of his life to Talmud study, with the help of a Jewish tutor, Jacob Abendana.[54] Shrewdly observing that an effort to print the Talmud in Sulzbach in 1694 had foundered, the partners seized upon the well-perceived market demand and the well-situated location of Frankfurt (Oder) as a distribution point for markets in both the empire and the Polish-Lithuanian Commonwealth, especially through the fairs at nearby Leipzig (a distance of some two hundred kilometers).[55]

In order to secure their financial standing, Beckman and Gottschalk applied for a printing privilege from the imperial and territorial authorities and secured a commitment of investment from wealthy local Jews.[56] All publishers of the early modern period sought the protective aegis of territorial sovereigns to guard their exclusive right to print a work and fend off economic competitors; in the case of Jewish books, and especially the

Talmud, an extra assurance was required to contain the heresies and anti-Christian sentiments the book was widely believed to hold.[57] As early as the thirteenth century, the Talmud had occupied pride of place in the eyes of Christians as a work of Jewish sedition and was subject to the most scrupulous surveillance and polemic.[58] The most striking and scandalous instance of censorial intervention in the publication of the Talmudic text is the infamous Basel Talmud published by Ambrosius Froben, printed between 1578 and 1581, which many Jews eschewed entirely as an inauthentic and deeply corrupted perversion of the ancient text.[59]

Beckman and Gottschalk also enlisted the investment of wealthy Jewish patrons. Although the Christian printers first approached the Saxon-Anhalt Court Jew Moses Benjamin Wulff (1661–1729), who had already established a printing press of his own in Dessau, his shifting financial fortunes (typical of the Court Jews as well) soon made him a poor candidate for a major publishing endeavor.[60] Into the breach stepped another Court Jew, Behrend Lehmann of Halberstadt, to save the enterprise. Lehmann had secured the post of Court Jew to the elector of Saxony, Augustus "the Strong," in 1696 and was instrumental in the drama surrounding the successful bid of Augustus for the Polish throne.[61] With Lehmann's support, publication began in 1697 and rapidly reached completion by 1699.

This new edition met with rabbinic encomia and market demand. The occasion of print called for introductory approbata by a number of high-profile rabbis, including Oppenheim, Naftali Kohen of Poznan, Josef Samuel of Krakow in Frankfurt am Main, Moses Judah b. Kalonymus ha-Kohen, and Jacob Sasportas, both of Amsterdam. Each acknowledged the need for a new edition and the paucity of volumes of the Talmud in the communities over which they presided. Oppenheim, in his introduction and approbation to the work, wrote of the general state of affairs in which copies of the Talmud were difficult to procure, "the Shas [i.e., the "Six Orders" of the Talmud] could not be found, merely one in a town and two in a family."[62] The chief rabbi of Posznan offered an even more evocative image, conjuring visions of "ten men wrapped in a single shawl around a single *gemara* [volume of the Talmud]."[63] Each, moreover, paid homage to the financing by Behrend Lehmann, underscoring the crucial connection between economic patronage and the Jewish book trade.[64]

Despite this shared vision for opportunity, the partnership between the Court Jew Lehmann and the printer Gottschalk frayed and dissolved into competition over the next two decades.[65] They eventually parted ways, and each labored to produce his own new edition of the Talmud for a still-thirsty market. While each of the erstwhile partners adopted different strategies for market dominance, and drew upon multiple sources of power and influence, both explicitly sought out Oppenheim's involvement in their projects, albeit in different ways.

Gottschalk aimed to achieve dominance over his partner-turned-competitor in the legal sphere. He worked to secure protections in the form of imperial and royal privileges to produce and sell the books, beginning with Emperor Joseph I in Vienna, which he then supplemented with further protections from the Prussian and Saxon electors as well, holding overlapping monopolies by 1710 for a period of ten years.[66] Attempting to attain as many aspects of legal cover as he could, Gottschalk also worked to obtain rabbinic bans on unlicensed reproduction and turned to Oppenheim to write an approbation that would prohibit other Jews from competing with his endeavor. In order to represent the best possible work, Gottschalk printed thirty pages of his proposed complete edition on vellum and sent them to Oppenheim. Oppenheim carefully inspected the materials and replied favorably, yet cautiously, on June 30, 1714. Gottschalk sent him still more pages, this time on blue paper, in the hopes that Oppenheim might also aid him in obtaining financial backing. Oppenheim was far less impressed with the blue paper edition, and to this added further reservations. He noted the need to include his colleague in Prague, Simon Jeiteles, who was the officially appointed censor of Hebrew books there, but also registered hesitation on account of a competing edition of the Talmud being prepared in Amsterdam at that very moment.[67]

It was to Amsterdam that Gottschalk's competitor Behrend Lehmann had turned to produce his new edition of the Talmud, in partnership with a new publisher, Rabbi Judah Arye Loeb b. Samuel of Frankfurt am Main, and the printers Samuel b. Solomon Marcheses and Raphael b. Joshua de Palacio. Amsterdam was beyond the legal jurisdiction of the Holy Roman Empire and therefore immune to the proprietary rights accorded to Gottschalk within its boundaries. Where Gottschalk appealed to Oppenheim for legal and financial support, Lehmann and Loeb sought access to the treasures of his library. Loeb recognized that economic competition depended on presenting to the public a text that was better than its rivals. He therefore turned to Oppenheim's collection in Hanover in search of previously unpublished Talmudic commentaries; there, he found, among other titles, the medieval commentary of Asher b. Yehiel to the first order of the Talmud.[68] In his introduction to the new edition, Loeb laid out the importance of quality in drafting his new edition. Loeb's introduction told a story that began in the age of manuscripts, an era, in his assessment, that had produced an unwieldy diversity of versions which then coupled with the diffusion of the printed word to produce a widely disseminated and highly flawed text. He credited the emendation activities of sixteenth-century rabbis of the Polish-Lithuanian Commonwealth, especially rabbis Solomon Luria (the Maharshal) and Samuel Eidels (the Maharsha), with returning the text to its "truth." Moreover, noted Loeb, citing new rabbinic ideas about curricular reform, a new edition of the Talmud would be a significant motivator for individuals to return to Talmud study and away from simple halakhic information.[69]

But Loeb's edition had a further benefit: it incorporated unique and previously inaccessible material from Oppenheim's shelves. As Loeb described it:

> God rewarded me and placed in my hands the commentary of the Rosh on *Seder Zeraim* and *Tohorot* that had entirely disappeared, and the Rosh referenced it himself in Tractate *Bava Kama* chapter seven, and the *Beit Yosef* referenced it in *Yoreh de'ah*, and the *Kesef Mishneh* several times in portions seven and eight of *Taharah*, and these were also copied by the author of the *Ein Yaakov* in Tractate *Pe'ah*, and it [the manuscript] is located in the holy treasury of the famed David Oppenheim, chief rabbi and *rosh yeshiva* in Prague.[70]

As described by Loeb, this was a text that many had known about, so it could therefore rest on a strong foundation as the authentic text, but it had escaped complete publication and usage because of its scarcity. Only the resources of the Oppenheim collection kept it preserved, and only access to that collection by its gatekeeper made its publication possible. Loeb continued to list further rarities that he had unearthed in the collection, including *Tosefot Yeshenim* on Tractate *Yoma*,[71] Nahmanides on Tractate *Ketubbot*,[72] *Tosefot ha-Rosh* on Tractate *Bava Metzia*,[73] and still more.[74] Many of these manuscripts had originated in the Land of Israel, where Oppenheim's agents had copied, sold, or sent them to him as gifts.[75]

Lehmann and Loeb's edition appeared between 1714 and 1717 and met with an enthusiastic reception, albeit with an acknowledgment that the edition may not have accorded with the fairest economic practices.[76] At least one of the approbators emphasized his initial reticence to write an approbation, but seeing as how well the first volumes were spoken of, he was persuaded to lend his name. Other approbators offered careful cover to Loeb, noting that although the period of copyright asserted by the approbata to Lehmann's Talmud had not yet expired (it was valid until 1720), the Court Jew himself desired this new print run, and it was therefore exempt from the ban's original conditions.[77]

Gottschalk's edition appeared between 1715 and 1722, but the competition between the two former partners did not abate. As Gottschalk's privilege expired, the Amsterdam printers encroached on imperial terrain, moving their enterprise to Frankfurt am Main. They did not succeed in procuring an imperial privilege, however, despite the intercession of the Court Jew in Vienna, Samson Wertheimer, who was also a funder of this new edition. Nonetheless, with the lapsing of Gottschalk's monopoly, the printers produced a second run of the Amsterdam edition in Frankfurt am Main between 1720 and 1722. In the year following the end of that print run, Gottschalk attempted once again to enlist imperial authority. In 1723 he inaugurated a process by which representatives of the Jewish community in the city of Prague and the province of Moravia were consulted by imperial authorities regarding how to proceed with Gottschalk's request for a renewed privilege.

The story of the new editions of the Talmud published during the final years of the seventeenth century and the first decades of the eighteenth bring together the host of concerns that converged on the Jewish book trade: learned culture, preservation, the business of printing, Christian Hebraism, government oversight, and intercommunal relations between Jews of different settlements. Oppenheim's involvement in competing editions represent both his political savvy and his demand as scholar-collector and wealthy donor. But his activities in this regard did not end with patronage or supply. In an almost complete circle, the products of Oppenheim's participation fed back into the expansion of his library. His collection maintained not simply copies of the editions, but the documentation that surrounded the publication of these items. He retained copies of the decisions rendered by the Habsburg court, preserving them as part of his larger archival repository for the administration of the Jews of Bohemia. He added to these still more government decrees about the status of the Talmud, especially those that related to censorship and regulation of the text at the hands of the Jesuits of Prague.[78]

Publishing in Prague

The Talmud looms largely as the cornerstone of traditional Jewish thought and study, but Oppenheim also contributed to making books outside of the study hall, beyond the ranks of the learned elite. Such literature, often inexpensively or hastily produced and sometimes in Yiddish—the domain of popular piety, leisure reading, news, and storytelling—was often printed without extensive paratextual material offering prefatory introductions that reveal the history of these works.[79] Much as his earliest collecting reflected his heritage in Worms, these works often carried a local coloration as well and reflected aspects of his rabbinate as it played out on the Prague stage. Prague was a significant hub in the publication of Yiddish books, in competition with only Amsterdam as a major center for literature in the language of Jewish daily life.[80] Oppenheim could exert an influence over the Prague presses, often impelling them to produce material in an ad hoc manner to meet the needs of the moment in the city.

One such need was liturgical. When plague began to engulf the Jews of Prague in 1713, Oppenheim commissioned special prayers of forgiveness—*selikhot*—to be included in their daily liturgy for protection against illness. The text, produced under Oppenheim's directive "with the cooperation of illustrious rabbis," opened with a twenty-six-line acrostic in which the word "Prague" was spelled out through the repetition of the four letters it comprises in the Hebrew alphabet (fig. 4.4).[81] He commissioned a further prayer similarly designed to avert the path of illness, which concluded, according to its opening paragraph, "with mention of the name of the great David Oppenheim."[82] Oppenheim did not remain in the city during the worst moments of the plague—like other men of means, he fled the city and sought refuge beyond the reach of disease. But he still preserved the poems and songs that told of the tale—even those that spoke critically of his departure—and maintained a copy of women's prayers that were written in 1719, five years after the plague subsided, to be recited over the graves of those who perished.[83] And although these prayer books were thin—only six folios—and consisted mostly of psalms (which required little intellectual labor to compile), Oppenheim still managed to turn them into collectors' items: he had one printed on vellum.[84] In his role as chief rabbi, Oppenheim also directed the production of other ritual texts as called for by desperate circumstances. In 1708 he ordered the publication of a special prayer for rain to combat a particularly dry season.[85]

Catastrophe was not the only impetus for making these books; sometimes joy and celebration demanded new publications. In 1720 the Prague press operated by the Back family produced a pamphlet called *Acta Ester mit Ahashverosh*—a parodic Purim performance, *Purim Spiel,* that had been performed that year by the students of Oppenheim's yeshiva (fig. 4.5).[86]

It was also in the context of the yeshiva that Oppenheim personally engaged in the process of "making" original books of his own. With only a few exceptions, these books existed solely as manuscripts and did not make the journey to the printer's altar.[87] Rather, they were products of the oral culture of study, revisions of the lectures he delivered to students according to the cycle of study in his yeshiva.[88] Oppenheim assigned titles to these works, such as his *Mei shilo'ah,* on Tractate Gittin, produced during the 1724 winter session of his yeshiva in Prague,[89] or his commentary on the Talmudic tractates dealing with festivals, which he labeled *Moed David.*

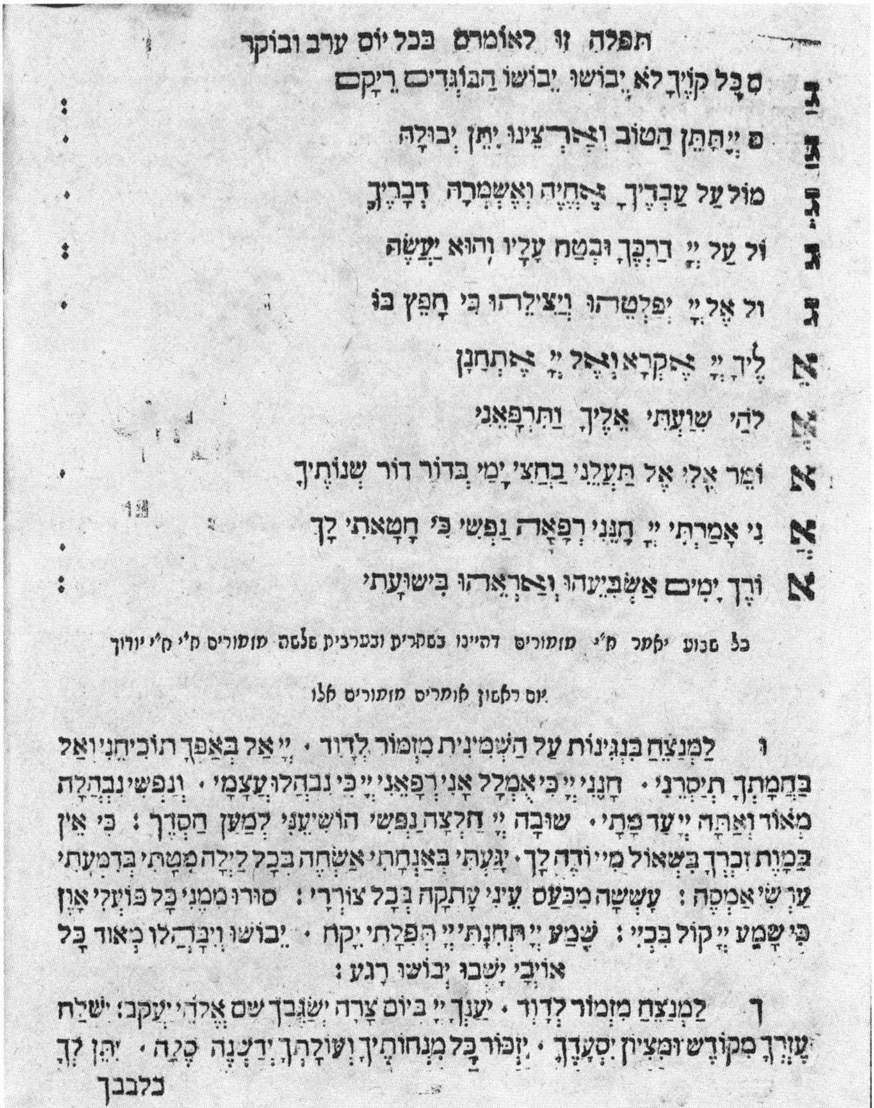

אָ סָבַּל קֹוֶךָ לֹא יֵבוֹשׁוּ יֵבוֹשׁוּ הַבּוֹגְדִים רֵיקָם

בְּג פ יֵתֵּן הַטוֹב וְאַרְצֵנוּ יִתֵּן יְבוּלָהּ

בְּגּ מוֹל עַל עַבְדְּךָ אֶחְיֶה וְאֶשְׁמְרָה דְּבָרֶךָ

גָ וֹל עַל יְיָ דַּרְכֶּךָ וּבְטַח עָלָיו וְהוּא יַעֲשֶׂה

גֵ וֹל אֵל יְיָ יְפַלְטֵהוּ וְיַצִּילֵהוּ כִּי חָפֵץ בּוֹ

אָ לֵיךָ יְיָ אֶקְרָא וְאֶל יְיָ אֶתְחַנָּן

אָ לֹהַי שִׁוַּעְתִּי אֵלֶיךָ וַתִּרְפָּאֵנִי

אָ וֹמַר אֵלִי אַל תַּעֲלֵנִי בַּחֲצִי יָמַי בְּדוֹר דּוֹר שְׁנוֹתֶיךָ

אָ נִי אָמַרְתִּי יְיָ חָנֵּנִי רְפָאָה נַפְשִׁי כִּי חָטָאתִי לָךְ

אָ וֹרֶךְ יָמִים אַשְׂבִּיעֵהוּ וְאַרְאֵהוּ בִּישׁוּעָתִי

כֹּל סְנוּעַ יֹאמַר מ' מִזְמוֹרִים דְּהַיְנוּ בְּשַׁחֲרִית וּבְעַרְבִית שְׁלֹשָׁה מִזְמוֹרִים ק"י ק"י יֹורוּךְ

יֹום רִאשׁוֹן אוֹמְרִים מִזְמוֹרִים אֵלּוּ

ו לַמְנַצֵּחַ בִּנְגִינוֹת עַל הַשְּׁמִינִית מִזְמוֹר לְדָוִד · יְיָ אַל בְּאַפְּךָ תוֹכִיחֵנִי וְאַל בַּחֲמָתְךָ תְיַסְּרֵנִי · חָנֵּנִי יְיָ כִּי אֻמְלַל אָנִי רְפָאֵנִי יְיָ כִּי נִבְהֲלוּ עֲצָמָי · וְנַפְשִׁי נִבְהֲלָה מְאֹד וְאַתָּה יְיָ עַד מָתָי · שׁוּבָה יְיָ חַלְּצָה נַפְשִׁי הוֹשִׁיעֵנִי לְמַעַן חַסְדֶּךָ : כִּי אֵין בַּמָּוֶת זִכְרֶךָ בִּשְׁאוֹל מִי יוֹדֶה לָּךְ · יָגַעְתִּי בְּאַנְחָתִי אַשְׂחֶה בְכָל לַיְלָה מִטָּתִי בְּדִמְעָתִי עַרְשִׂי אַמְסֶה : עָשְׁשָׁה מִכַּעַס עֵינִי עָתְקָה בְּכָל צוֹרְרָי · סוּרוּ מִמֶּנִּי כָּל פֹּעֲלֵי אָוֶן כִּי שָׁמַע יְיָ קוֹל בִּכְיִי · שָׁמַע יְיָ תְּחִנָּתִי יְיָ תְּפִלָּתִי יִקָּח · יֵבֹשׁוּ וְיִבָּהֲלוּ כְאֹד כָּל אֹיְבָי יָשֻׁבוּ יֵבֹשׁוּ רָגַע :

ז לַמְנַצֵּחַ מִזְמוֹר לְדָוִד · יַעַנְךָ יְיָ בְּיוֹם צָרָה יְשַׂגֶּבְךָ שֵׁם אֱלֹהֵי יַעֲקֹב: יִשְׁלַח עֶזְרְךָ מִקֹּדֶשׁ וּמִצִּיּוֹן יִסְעָדֶךָּ · יִזְכּוֹר כָּל מִנְחֹתֶיךָ וְעוֹלָתְךָ יְדַשְּׁנֶה סֶלָה · יִתֶּן לְךָ כלבבך

Fig. 4.4. Opp. 4° 1241: The opening lines read, "This prayer was printed by in-struction of our master, teacher, and rabbi the great and famous head of the court and *rosh yeshiva* of our community of Prague and all of Bohemia, may they endure forever, whose fortress extends over Jerusalem (the holy city, may it be swiftly re-

תְּפִלָּה לְאוֹמְרָהּ בְּכָל יוֹם עֶרֶב וָבוֹקֶר

תפלה זו נדפס במקודש לאדונינו מורינו ורבינו הגאון הגדול המפורסם אב"ד ור"מ דקהלתינו ק"ק פראג ואב
ובמדינות מיהם יע"א ומנ"ם בירושלים עה"ק קוב"ץ כבוד מהור"ר דוד אופנהיים נר"ו בניקוף הרבנים
מופלגים ב'ד עורם זוה נר"ס נעשה בי"ו'ם'ז' ימים לחדש אדר לפרט כי **בָּא עֵת** להחנה לפם

פ׳ פְּתְחוּ לִי שַׁעֲרֵי צֶדֶק אָבֹא בָם אוֹדֶה יָהּ

פ׳ נָה אֵל תְּפִלַּת הָעַרְעָר וְלֹא בָזָה אֶת תְּפִלָּתָם ׃

פ׳ נֵה אֵלַי וְחָנֵּנִי כִּי יָחִיד וְעָנִי אָנִי ׃

פ׳ נֵה אֵלַי וְחָנֵּנִי תְּנָה עֻזְּךָ לְעַבְדֶּךָ וְהוֹשִׁיעָה לְבֶן אֲמָתֶךָ

פ׳ נֵה אֵלַי וְחָנֵּנִי כְּמִשְׁפָּט לְאוֹהֲבֵי שְׁמֶךָ

פ׳ יְסַפֵּר צִדְקָתֶךָ כָּל הַיּוֹם תְּשׁוּעָתֶךָ כִּי לֹא יָדַעְתִּי סְפֹרוֹת

פ׳ דוֹרֹת שָׁלַח לְעַמּוֹ צִוָּה לְעוֹלָם בְּרִיתוֹ קָדוֹשׁ וְנוֹרָא שְׁמוֹ

פ׳ וּדְה יְיָ נֶפֶשׁ עֲבָדָיו וְלֹא יֶאְשְׁמוּ כָּל הַחוֹסִים בּוֹ

פ׳ דָה בְשָׁלוֹם נַפְשִׁי מִקְּרָב לִי כִּי בְרַבִּים הָיוּ עִמָּדִי

פ׳ דֵה אֱלֹהִים אֶת יִשְׂרָאֵל מִכֹּל צָרוֹתָיו ׃

ר׳ אֵה עָנְיִי וַעֲמָלִי וְשָׂא לְכָל חַטֹּאתִי

ר׳ אֵה עָנְיִי וְחַלְּצֵנִי כִּי תוֹרָתְךָ לֹא שָׁכָחְתִּי

ר׳ צֹאן יְרִיאַי יַעֲשֶׂה וְאֶת שַׁוְעָתָם יִשְׁמַע וְיוֹשִׁיעֵם

ר׳ אֶה כִּי פִקּוּדֶיךָ אָהַבְתִּי יְיָ כְּחַסְדְּךָ חַיֵּנִי

ר׳ חַמִּין רַבִּים יְיָ כְּמִשְׁפָּטֶךָ חַיֵּנִי

ג׳ ס עַד זִקְנָה וְשֵׂיבָה אֱלֹהִים אַל תַּעַזְבֵנִי עַד אַגִּיד זְרוֹעֲךָ לְדוֹר לְכָל יָבוֹא גְּבוּרָתֶךָ

ם א

built) our rabbi and teacher Rabbi David Oppenheim may his creator guard and protect him, with the cooperation of illustrious rabbis . . . 7th of Adar, 5473 [Sunday, March 5, 1713].” The acrostic of the first letters of each line spells the word “Prague.” Courtesy of the Bodleian Libraries, University of Oxford.

Fig. 4.5. Opp. 8° 595: *Acta Ester mit Ahashverosh* (Prague, 1720). Courtesy of the Bodleian Libraries, University of Oxford.

He did not limit himself to Talmudic commentary; he also wrote on biblical and Talmudic Aggadah, a series of expositions of the weekly Torah portions, as well as later books of the Bible, expositions based on resolving inconsistencies in the narrative through recourse to midrashic texts and his own midrashic reasoning. But the fact of their existence as manuscripts rather than printed matter did not mean that these items were not "books." Oppenheim's students studied the titles, copied them, and referred to them in their questions to him.[90] In his own writing, Oppenheim often made intertextual references to his other writings, encouraging readers to look further into his other compositions.[91] Unlike the printed book, these works maintained a certain flexibility unique to manuscripts, and Oppenheim emended and adjusted his thinking over time. Portions of his commentary *Mo'ed David* appeared in print in 1698, but two further manuscript editions derived from later occasions in Oppenheim's career, in 1718 and 1723.[92]

It is clear that Oppenheim expected to ultimately see these books through to publication, as he organized his collection of responsa into a coherent body, nearly ready for the press. In the process of preparing a responsum for this larger planned work, *Nish'al David* (It Was Asked of David), Oppenheim wrote to Behrend Lehmann as follows: "Since it is my intent in life and in peace to bring my book *Nish'al David* to the printer with the help of God, may he be my aid, blessed be his name, and among them this ruling will be included, please notify me if I should excise your name and the name of your city, in which there was a ruling between you and the community of Halberstadt . . . or if this should be sealed."[93]

Oppenheim wrote the vast majority of these responsa between 1690 and 1711 (with perhaps one exception from 1716) and appears to have intended them for publication. In fact, contemporaries also expected to see Oppenheim's words in print. In 1709 Meir of Wesel included some good wishes to Oppenheim, saying "my son has written to me that my master the great one will raise to the press [i.e., publish] an attractive book, and may it be his [God's] will that we merit to enjoy his light, the light of Torah."[94] But something stood between Oppenheim's plans to publish and his accomplishment of that aim. He was such a careful critic of books and manuscripts that he may have been too much of a perfectionist to release his own writings to a wider public. When Jacob Rzeszów sent an inquiry to Oppenheim regarding a rare instance of a published piece of Oppenheim's writing—a 1698 excursus on the laws of Hanukkah—Oppenheim replied by dismissing the published words as "intermittent discussion," a work that had been abbreviated in the extreme, creating closure and finality where it should not have been.[95] In a different responsum he again derided a printer who "shortened when he ought to have lengthened . . . and I told him to copy from the body of the book *Mo'ed David* which is still written and sealed in the treasury in its shape and form."[96] Perhaps, once chastened, Oppenheim adopted a more tentative approach to committing his own texts to print. Partly conscious of his own perfectionism, Oppenheim also blamed circumstance as a factor in the delay in his printing. In the introduction to his book *Nir David* (an unpublished work), Oppenheim gave some indication of the will to print, with hesitation:

> When I sat upon the throne of teaching in the great city of Nikolsburg and all of Moravia, I planted a tree for scholars to take shade under . . .
>
>   . . . and I revealed new concepts on all of the Talmud, innovations in Talmud, Rashi, and Tosafot. But on account of the great demands upon me, I was without the time to compose them together, to weave them into a single composition, and I said to myself, "for the vision is yet for the appointed time" [Hab 2:3].[97]

In crafting a narrative of his preparation of a book, Oppenheim explicitly acknowledged his decision to postpone publication. But the decision to preserve a single manuscript rather than the security of multiple printed copies had disastrous and unforeseen consequences:

> But then, suddenly, the plunderer came upon us, with the raucous trumpets of war, and I at that time was not in my home to save the sacks of writing that were in my store, the fortress, my palace for an array of books. And in the great hurly-burly, with the fear of the enemy engulfing all around, it was finder's

keepers. . . . But the ark traveled throughout the diaspora, until
I became the rabbi of Prague.[98]

The constraints of time, the ravages of circumstance, and his own will combined to prevent his works from reaching a wider audience, and his name
to continue in print. More than a decade after Oppenheim's death, in 1749,
Jacob Emden attested that "in my youth, twenty-five years ago, I saw a responsum of the Gaon, our teacher R. David Oppenheim, of blessed memory, who sent a few pages from his book which he wanted to publish in
Amsterdam, but changed his mind."[99]

And so Oppenheim's career offered the paradox of a "man whose
greatest delight is in books," who was not at a material loss to produce
them, but who barely published a word. Decades later, when Hayyim Yosef David Azulai compiled his bibliographic survey of rabbinic authors, he
could write of Oppenheim that only "a few of his *hiddushim* were printed
at the beginning of *Sefer beit Yehudah* and in the responsa of *Havot Yair*
and *Shvut Yaakov* there are responsa by the rabbi."[100] Oppenheim's writings and thought did not infiltrate yeshiva curricula or shape subsequent
intellectual developments. As he knew so well, the printing press was the
arbiter of literary posterity, even the absence of his own.[101]

A Library of Ashkenaz

Much as Oppenheim aimed to "make books without end," in practice he
was often engaging in a much more particular and even parochial sort of activity. Although his library encompassed works whose provenance spanned
the Jewish cultural world, his use of the library as an agent of cultural production often maintained an inflection toward his native Rhineland, with
augmentation from Prague (as well as Amsterdam's Yiddish presses). As
Oppenheim's preference for Ashkenazic handwriting demonstrated, he was
an Ashkenazic Jew in both medium and message. And yet in the process
of working as a collector, he reshaped and reformed the Ashkenazic canon
of biblical and Talmudic commentators, weaving lost Sephardic commentaries into a common Jewish diet of medieval legacies.

Just as Oppenheim's library was both a product of and an agent in a networked culture of patronage and mutual benefit, it presented opposing, sometimes competing contributions to the textual community of early modern Ashkenaz. On one hand, the library was an agent of restoration, a revival of a particularly medieval Ashkenazic heritage. The Pentateuch of 1705 was a part of a chain of publication of rabbinic biblical commentary that had begun with Daniel Bomberg's Bible of 1517. That first edition placed medieval rabbinic texts on the same page and in the same volumes as the biblical text, and while it included the commentary of Rashi, it was predominantly an anthology of the biblical thought of medieval Iberia.[102] Including Rashbam within the Rabbinic Bible represented an act of "Ashkenazification," a part of the same cultural impulse that led others among Oppenheim's contemporaries to work to restore a unique Ashkenazic heritage.

This restorative project resonated in other parts of Central Europe's Jewish literary production. During the middle decades of the seventeenth century, a number of authors dedicated themselves to the composition of *Minhagbücher,* collections of the local customs of the Jews of Frankfurt and Worms, evincing a sense that they were facing an era of profound cultural transition, an erosion of the old ways in the face of something new.[103] The same decades witnessed the publication of Sabbath hymnals particular to Frankfurt[104] and rituals for the close of the Sabbath from a family's heritage in Prague.[105]

A concern for "local knowledge" was consonant with the trends of knowledge-making in inventories and compendia about the natural world produced by non-Jewish naturalists of the German lands. While some German *Wunderkammer* were dedicated to eclectic collections with little attention to provenance or coherence, an increasing number of collectors turned their attention to capturing specimens from their most local environments. The exotic and wondrous encounters with the New World inspired interest in the particulars of the Old World, and naturalists, amateur scientists, and other collectors invested their resources in discovering the terrain beneath their feet.[106] Oppenheim's literary collection similarly embraced this dynamic. While he strove for universal inclusion of Jewish materials—defined largely by publication in Hebrew characters—he betrayed a particular proclivity for texts of a provenance local to Central Europe.

At the same time, Oppenheim's library served to reshape the textual horizons of Ashkenaz. Since at least the sixteenth century, Ashkenazic Jews had incorporated Sephardic works into their literary diet. This process, inaugurated by the mobility of the sixteenth century and accelerated by the engine of the printing press, intensified during the eighteenth century.[107] An invigorated turn to the Talmudic heritage of medieval Iberia took on new life in the early eighteenth century with the publication of texts that had never before appeared in print, which in turn had important ramifications for the direction of Jewish study in the modern period.[108] This phenomenon took place through multiple presses in Central Europe, some of which were independent of Oppenheim and his library, but crucial commentaries surfaced only and uniquely as a result of David Oppenheim's extensive collection.

His manuscript collection supplied materials for the first publication of the Talmudic commentary of Yom Tov b. Abraham Asevilli (Ritva, 1250-1330) to Tractates *Eruvin, Ta'anit, Mo'ed Katan,* and *Bava Metziah* in Amsterdam in 1729. The published text derived from a manuscript copy that had been held by the family of Isaiah Horowitz of Prague (1555-1630), but in order to complete the edition, the publisher wrote to Joseph Oppenheim in Hanover, who sent a supplementary manuscript to Amsterdam to complete the edition.[109] Six years later, in 1735, the Katz printing house in Prague published Ritva's commentary to Tractate *Hullin,* again by relying on Oppenheim's manuscript collection.[110] The title page declares the revelation of the hidden manuscript from the possessions of Samuel Oppenheimer of Vienna, but the introductions, by the author and by David Oppenheim himself, reveal that while this collection once belonged to Samuel, its care was now in the hands of his nephew David (and probably David's son, Joseph). The agent who found the manuscript, Elijah b. Asher of Podheitz, was a student of Oppenheim's who was granted permission to bring the text to the publisher's floor.[111] And in that same year, Elisha b. Abraham of Altona published the commentary to Tractate *Zeraim* of Asher b. Yehiel (the Rosh), accompanied by his own early modern glosses.[112]

As we have seen in the case of his preference for manuscripts in the Ashkenazic hand, Oppenheim's library often transposed Jewish works of other subdiasporas into an Ashkenazic key, reshaping the Ashkenazic textual community from a canon that drew upon the Rhineland to an enlarged canon that came to include the Iberian Talmudic heritage within it. Important ingredients in this process flowed from the eastern Mediterranean home of the Iberian diaspora into the Ashkenazic curriculum by way of Oppenheim's ties to the east and his patronage of the press in Central Europe. The introduction of the Rosh, Ritva, Rashba, and Rambam, seemingly subtle shifts, point toward new intellectual trends that would continue to grow. The medieval Spanish works published during the first decades of the eighteenth century soon became foundation material for the curricula of the great Lithuanian yeshivot, an indispensable element of an intellectual diet for a significant element of traditional male Jewish society in the succeeding centuries. They fueled (or perhaps responded to a call for) a turn away from the dominant pattern of early modern pedagogy—derided as *pilpul*—and made way for new directions in Jewish study and research—a Sephardic influence on Ashkenazic circles.[113] The making of books "without end" could be turned to new ends indeed.

Conclusion

Oppenheim's library generated new books as much as it preserved old ones and even determined the way ancient texts might be reconceptualized and received. Even critics of the proliferation of books and skeptics of the ever-expanding print market could not avoid his grand collection. The critic of Ashkenazi educational practices Isaac Wetzlar (ca. 1680–1751) visited the Oppenheim library, only to gain from the experience a memory of seeing a prohibition on publishing new books, and perhaps deriving a sense of the overwhelming size of the ever-growing Jewish library, which could not possibly find a readership. Wetzlar recalled:

> They [an advanced group of Torah scholars] study diligently and write what they think are novella on the Torah, part halakhic novellae (*hiddushim oyf halakha tosefes*) and part casuistry (*pshatim*), and finally publish a book. They travel around

with it or send it out to be sold. However, I wish to write that I saw in the library of David Oppenheim, the Rabbi of Prague, a printed book, the name of which I forgot, because of our many sins, in which it says that eighty years ago, several great scholars of the land proposed a ban of excommunication that no new book should be printed, whether commentary on the Torah or halakhic work. We have enough, thank God, with our Talmud, *Tosafot,* Rabbi Asher, Alfasi, Maimonides, and many other commentators. I do not know who has any use for these new commentaries.[114]

Ironically, Wetzlar sought to enlist this library, an agent of making books "without end," in a campaign against the production of an excess of books.

Oppenheim struggled with the most personal act of making books—the role of the author. But he facilitated the making of books as a conservator of ancient texts and as a financier of newly written material. His participation in these book-making acts was colored by his social horizons. His patronage of aspiring authors generally emerged out of preexisting relationships to his students or other young men in his scholarly milieu. And similarly, his investment in publishing "old" manuscripts was partially determined by his personal proclivities and affective associations with the cultural heritage of the place of his birth.

Endorsing and Incriminating

Oppenheim and Approbata in the Court
of Opinion and the Courts of Law

Because he has a library he may with reason call himself cosmopolite,
or citizen of the whole world; since with it he may know all,
see all, and be ignorant of nothing.
—Gabriel Naudé, *Advice on Establishing a Library,* 1627

AS WE SAW IN THE PREVIOUS CHAPTERS, Oppenheim's ex-
clusive recourse to manuscripts held only in his collection allowed him to
flaunt his private collection, which was made all the more valuable because
of the scarcity of some of its contents and the selective access to it—its wisdom was available to others by his permission alone. He used printed books
in the exact opposite fashion. Printed matter provided Oppenheim with a
medium for publicity, a means to establish his authority by diffusing his
name, his influence, and his impact on the making of books. Manuscripts
conferred intellectual authority by means of limitation, but printed books
offered a means to the same goal on account of their ubiquity. Oppenheim
used the printed word to fashion a wider sense of credibility and to extend
that credit of reputation to scholars of lesser rank. But at times this public
expression of his influence could work against him.

If books were made by writers and published by their affiliates and
patrons, they reached a reading public through a concerted system of mar-
keting and distribution. As we have seen, Oppenheim's library was nur-
tured by the transit of books and facilitated new publications; their cir-

culations in turn generated praise and controversy. Because of his special
relationship with the making of books, Oppenheim acted as a lynchpin in a
system of literary promotion and the reception—both positively and critically—of books once they were released into circulation that was exem-
plary of rabbinic culture in the early modern period. Between the contents
of the books themselves and the commodities that carried them stood a
community of gatekeepers and promoters. Their activities fueled accolades,
gossip, and occasionally furor over the books that left the printer's altar and
entered into the world of readers and respondents, both friend and foe.

Reaching Readers: Establishing
Authority Through Endorsements

The act of making books "without end" depended on scholarly labor and
financial backing, but it also required a less immediately tangible contribution in the regulation and direction of the book trade. If books were intrinsically (though not exclusively) commodities that followed the rules of
industry and production, publishers and governing officials attempted to
shape the contours of such rules in order to protect the interests of their
investors, promote the productivity of the craft, and control the content of
the texts.[1] In Jewish circles, one vehicle for shaping this domain was the
approbation. Approbata (Hebrew: *haskamot*) are brief letters of endorsement that appear in the front matter of books, generally after the title page
and before the introduction of the author or publisher. They consist of a
few sentences of praise for the author and usually the imposition of a ban
on reproduction until a given period of time has elapsed. But within their
generic constraints, *haskamot* also operated to showcase the erudition of
their authors and to highlight the social ties they held to a book's author
and beyond. They are therefore significant sources for contemplating the
social dimensions of authoritative knowledge-making and the importance
of reputational patronage in constituting trust.

   Hebrew book approbata bore a number of functions. They served as
letters of recommendations to other rabbinic colleagues, and they encouraged others to purchase the book in question.[2] They also had an economic

function. Like privileges designated by local rulers to particular publishers, which granted them the exclusive right to print a text, approbata to Hebrew books functioned as a form of rabbinic copyright aimed at protecting capital outlay and curbing excessive market competition. The first such defense of Jewish intellectual property appeared in 1518 on the work of Elijah Levita Bahur, and many *haskamot* thereafter declared a moratorium on reprinting a work for a specified number of years, usually ten to fifteen.[3]

Where commercial agents feared competition and piracy, religious and governing leaders feared deviance and dissent. Just as the papacy and the governments of confessional states directed their efforts to suppress or expunge offensive material from books, Jewish leaders attempted to impose an audit of material before publication to ensure that its contents were licit and appropriate for a Jewish reading public.[4] In the early seventeenth century assemblies in Frankfurt and the Polish Council of Four Lands issued decrees geared toward staunching the flow of suspect literature from abroad and into their local print shops, and rabbis such as Moses Hagiz worked to rehabilitate the *haskamah* as an agent of rabbinic power in the pursuit of heresy.[5]

The task of securing *haskamot* often fell to the author or publisher of a new book. Manuscripts from Oppenheim's collection reveal something of the process of obtaining and reproducing *haskamot*. In some instances, authors sent manuscript copies of their books for review by prospective approbators and requested a letter of endorsement.[6] These letters might be returned to the author or inscribed directly onto blank pages of the manuscript-in-preparation.[7] On other occasions the collected letters were transcribed into the manuscript by a single scribe, as in the case of a book of responsa by Nathan Noteh Kahana, rabbi of Ostrava, composed around 1640, whose grandson secured approbata half a century later, in 1695–1696, in preparation to publish the book.[8] It was not entirely atypical for a significant span of time to elapse between authorship of a text, approbation, and publication. A manuscript of *Sefer beit avot,* a commentary on the Mishnah Tractate *Avot,* received a recommendation to print in 1700 and did not appear in print until 1712.[9] Approbata were not, however, a guarantee that a book would ultimately be printed, as a colophon to an unprinted but approbated manuscript titled *Devarim atikim* made clear in stating "this book has not yet been printed" (fig. 5.1).[10] And even after a book was printed, the rights to copy could be transferred as well. A 1715 printing of a letter-writing manual from Amsterdam features an addendum to its *haskamah*—a note by the work's original author indicating that he had sold the rights to the volume for 10 gold pieces and relinquished all future rights to it.[11]

Approbata were supposed to have been forged in a system of supervision, but the most common way an approbation was produced was for a rabbi to do so without having seen much of the book at all. It's little wonder that rabbis and readers of the early modern period viewed approbata with both expectation and skepticism.[12] Isaac Wetzlar drew upon Oppenheim's collection to criticize the practice when, among Oppenheim's thousands of published and manuscript texts, he read about a ban, issued eighty years before, against the publication of new works—an effort to stem the tide of an ever-increasing deluge of Jewish literature whose quantity and quality had challenged the monopoly of the religious learned male elite. Wetzlar lamented this excess of books, which "not only contain lies and falsehoods, but also contain, because of our many sins, vile insults and abuses," but he held himself back from enumerating their titles. The books were shielded from Wetzlar's full-throated criticism on account of his respect for "the great rabbis who gave their approbata to such books." Wetzlar wondered in amazement at "how such sages could allow themselves to be deceived. How could they allow themselves to be shown a few pages by the author and believe the whole book is good? The authors are then very expansive with the approbation and, because of our many sins, the public is deceived."[13] Wetzlar was not entirely exaggerating. Many rabbinic approbata, Oppenheim's included, acknowledged that the reviewer had not read the entire book and had seen "only a few pages" of the text.[14] Oppenheim had written no fewer than seventy-two approbata, often for books he had never seen.[15]

But the fact that rabbinic approbata could not conceivably vouch for the content of a text that had not been read did not mean that they were wholly impotent devices. Rather, as Wetzlar's concern with public deception makes clear, they served a social function in the world of Jewish books. *Haskamot* stood between a market economy and an economy of patronage.

As a genre, approbata belong to the wider category of paratexts, the accessories that accompany printed material and plot the coordinates of their usage to prospective audiences. With the advent of the printing press and the potential for widespread dissemination of the written word, paratexts were called into existence to direct market forces and guide readers through the intentions of a book's producers.[16]

Like book dedications and extensively wordy title pages, which revealed the dimensions of economic patronage in the production of a book, *haskamot* reflected social ties as well, albeit of a different sort. Rather than a dependence on an external legitimizing authority like the court or a financier, they represent the judgment of intellectuals and members of the class of cultural producers as legitimating agents of the creation.[17] Although they participated in the practice of control, they were distinct from the acts of censorship or copyright regulation. Rather, they represented *reputational* patronage, a different form of support and sustenance from the financial backing of the Court Jews but a vital component of the book trade nonetheless. Even as *haskamot* claimed to serve as evidence of a process of review or as guarantors of intellectual property, they forged an association in the literary present between the producers of the work and the people who lent the credence of their authority to the character of the author.

An assessment of authorial credibility was essential to the making of early modern knowledge.[18] Despite claims to the production of universal truths, knowledge-making is a deeply personal act, which rests (and rested) on the reputation and recognition of a community of scholars. To assert the credibility of a book was to express approval not primarily for its contents, but for its author. An approbation created the conditions for what Adrian Johns has characterized as "the merging of trust in people with trust in things."[19] Assessing the authority of a book, like assessing the authority of knowledge more generally, demanded trust not only in objective knowledge, but in the people who had produced such knowledge.[20] The introductory material to these books informed readers of the scholarly credentials of an author—chiefly by situating him within a rabbinic republic of letters—and assured them that the book was worth reading because the author was of credible character and credentials.

If familiarity with a book's content was not decisive for issuing an approbation, credit and credibility did not need to be confirmed by first-hand experience with the author either. For example, when a guide to the grace after meals was published in Offenbach in 1721, it was accompanied by an approbation of Abraham Broda (once Oppenheim's rival rabbi in Prague), written more than twenty years before, in 1700. Published after Broda's death in 1717, the approbation carried little direct power to enforce any form of copyright, and yet it was included insofar as its testified to the credentials of the author. But Broda acknowledged that it was not direct knowledge of the author that had motived him to provide an endorsement. In writing that "when my students, the members of my yeshiva, gave their testimony, I relied upon them," Broda revealed that credibility was a transitive property and could be assessed by the testimony of a third party.[21]

Not only was credibility available without direct knowledge of the item or author in question, at times the credibility of the author was less important than the fact that a potential approbator's rabbinic peers had already signed on to the endeavor. In 1698 Oppenheim lent a conditional *haskamah* to a book, stipulating that "should this book come before some great rabbis and they read in this book of God's Torah explicitly and dedicate their thought to it, and understand its words as worthy for inscription with an iron pen, behold my hand and finger are with them to assent to bring it to light and to grant a privilege to print this book."[22] Oppenheim's wager on the diligence of others reveals a different relational dimension: that of an approbator to his peers. The standing of other approbators who had already agreed to lend their names to the book could be forceful enough to compel the granting of an approbation. This multilateral context of the *haskamah* carries a further implication. The credit created by a *haskamah* worked both to establish an author as reliable and to mark the approbator as authoritative to assess that reliability, at least in theory. Withholding one's approbation could potentially consign an authority to oblivion.[23] Hedging his bets on this book and refusing to fully lend his name without the careful scrutiny of another, Oppenheim opted to situate himself conditionally between the Scylla of negligence and the Charybdis of obsolescence.

Aspiring authors appear to have been alert to the peer-related pressures of approbata and knew how to leverage that pressure into requests. In the 1690s David Oppenheim received a letter from a writer in Boskowice in Moravia, a text thick with requests for economic support, that concluded with a more modest request: that Oppenheim add his name to the list of rabbis ("the rest of the great sages") who had already guaranteed a moratorium on reprinting the book for the next fifteen years.[24] Although the primary aim of the request was to ensure economic rights over a literary product, the means by which the supplicant made his request was through a subtle appeal to peer pressure.

Even skeptics and opponents of the practice could not escape entanglement within it. In the introduction to his own work *Kreti u-fleti,* Jonathan Eybeschütz railed against the nonsensical practice of seeking approbata, explaining that he himself sought no such frills that "place the measure of the author among the stars," indicting *haskamot* with the responsibility for the proliferation of casuistry and the ignorance of classical texts.[25] And yet even he protested too much: oftentimes books appeared with a printed letter by Eybeschütz that vigorously denied itself the label of approbation while still vouching for the author's character and the book's worthiness.[26] Eybeschütz's teacher, Abraham Broda, occasionally displayed a similar reticence to grant an approbation and yet joined the chorus of endorsement all the same. In a reluctant order to issue an approbation to the posthumous publication of the *hiddushim* of Gerson Ashkenazi, his predecessor in Metz, Broda highlighted the exceptionality of his action—an exceptionality that was noted by both the publishing editor of the material and the men who released the approbation in his name.[27] Despite their professed disavowal of the institution, both Broda and Eybeschütz repeatedly wrote letters of support for aspiring publishers, in each case assailing with words the very institution they were in practice maintaining.[28]

The writers of approbata were not simply instrumentalized by authors of lower rank and publishers that sought an advantage in a market economy. Approbata were also vehicles for self-fashioning. Many approbators used the opportunity to delight in wordplay, to create sentences of rhyming prose, or to offer evidence of their literary prowess. For Oppenheim, approbata constituted virtually the only published texts of all his writings to appear during his lifetime. Although he wrote extensive commentaries on the Bible and Talmud as well as numerous responsa, only his approbata appeared in print before the twentieth century. They thus offered a unique medium for him to reach the widest possible audience in the rabbinic republic of letters and presented one of the sole opportunities available to him to craft his public persona. Oppenheim's approbata featured much rhetorical flourish; he carefully stylized these would-be formulaic texts to showcase his erudition, employing alliterative phrases and biblical allusions. Asserting his stature, Oppenheim plucked quotations from the Bible about King David and turned them into statements about his own worth. Other writers used the opportunity to promote their own writings. Eybeschütz used the approbation, even as he derided it, to notify readers of his own publishing endeavors. Thus he included in a 1745 approbation: "and in truth we had already started in 1725 to print this in Prague, and I laid out from my pocket great sums, but I only succeeded in publishing on Tractate *Berakhot*," referring to his controversial new edition of the Talmud.[29]

Where literary allusions offered subtle acts of self-presentation, the bold typeface that headed an approbation could offer a space in which one could expressly proclaim one's title and assert mastery over others. During the final decade of the seventeenth century, when David Oppenheim was locked in a struggle for supremacy over the rabbinate of Moravia in which both he and a rival claimed the mantle of chief rabbi of the entire region, acts of competition spilled over from Jewish regional councils and territorial princely courts onto the printed page. Approbata served as a further arena in which the struggle could be waged. In the 1692 publication of the book *Meginei eretz* both Oppenheim and his rival, Issachar Baer Frankfurter, claimed the title (in print) "chief rabbi of Moravia."[30] Both asserted that they were writing by invitation and commission of the book's publisher, Shabbetai Bass, and both added their names to the roster of rabbis who had extended their aegis of copyright to the book.[31] As Oppenheim's career progressed, the honors adorning his name in printed approbata grew as well. It became quite common for printers to include his honorific titles over the rabbinates of Brisk, Slutzk, and, of course, the entire Land of Israel.

It is noteworthy that not *all* Jewish books carried approbata. Books geared toward rabbinic learning contained the approbation of rabbis, but literature for the wider reading market—particularly in Yiddish—seldom featured endorsements of any sort.[32] If literary property is the primary function of a *haskamah,* this is a strange set of circumstances. Despite all of their gestures toward a defense of property, rabbinic approbata were not particularly effective forms of copyright and served instead a more "internal" function regarding the practices of peer recognition.[33] When the book *Yosippon* was marketed toward a Yiddish reading audience, the publishers made a case (in Yiddish) for the merits of a book not just for lay readers (the primary audience for Yiddish texts), but for scholars and students as well. An endorsement by a rabbi was not necessary; the publisher's words could accomplish the same task.[34] Precisely that absence of approbata in some books and their presence in others reveals the important role that they played in the domains of knowledge-making and mutual recognition. Those aims, however, could sometimes be subverted.

Sabbatean Sympathies?: Approbata and Accusations

If an approbation could bring credit and credibility by association, it could also invite criticism and condemnation. Isaac Wetzlar bore witness to the perils of this system:

> I saw a kabbalistic book which is considered to be a light unto Israel. I do not want to name the author because several rabbis, known throughout the diaspora, whose souls are bound up in the bonds of eternal life, gave their approbation to this book. All of them called the author an eminent and pious sage. He was supposed to be in reality pious and all his life acted piously and ascetically. Yet, I was shown and saw with my own eyes that in this book on pages 13 and 39a and 39b Sabbatai Zevi is clearly called the messiah. I knew several of these great sages, and—let us distinguish as between the living and the dead—served some of them. The whole public is aware that these same scholars

were the greatest persecutors of the evil believers in Sabbatai
Zevi, in order to exterminate them. Were not these sages misled,
to so easily give their approbation to this book?[35]

The tenuous relationship between endorsing an author and vouching for
content generated acute problems for Oppenheim in another realm of
Jewish culture: the Sabbatean controversies. His reputation was so well-
respected that its power sometimes had quite unforeseen circumstances
and brought with it heightened expectations. In the winter of 1711–1712 the
suspected Sabbatean Nehemiah Hayon visited Prague and found hospitality in the home of David Oppenheim with his son Joseph and son-in-
law Hayyim Yonah Teomim Fränkel.[36] Joseph became enamored of Hayon,
whose endorsement resulted in his father issuing a *haskamah* for Hayon
that appeared in his two books that were printed in 1713: *Divrei Nehemiah*
and *Oz le-Elohim.* Oppenheim's approbation joined those of others who
had already seen fit to support this book, including Naftali Kohen, then of
Frankfurt; Gabriel Eskeles, rabbi in Nikolsburg and all of Moravia; Aaron
of Berlin; and Judah Leib of Glogau.[37] Oppenheim acknowledged in his
approbation that he had "only seen one page from each book" and that "it
would be appropriate to stay my hand from it," but the fact that the students
of his yeshiva vouched for Hayon's great learning encouraged Oppenheim
to endorse these books as well.[38]

Controversy erupted almost as soon as the books left the presses, as
Hayon came under scrutiny and condemnation by Moses Hagiz, the re-
lentless heresy hunter, and Hakham Zevi Ashkenazi, at the time the rabbi
of the Ashkenazic community of Amsterdam. Zevi led the charge against
not only Hayon, but the rabbis who had supported Hayon by lending
their endorsements to his work; however, he was rebuffed by supporters
of Hayon (including Zevi's colleague, the Sephardic chief rabbi of Amsterdam, Solomon Ayallon), who counterclaimed that Zevi was slandering the
work and reputation of a fine scholar.[39] Both the Amsterdam Ashkenazic
chief rabbinate and Hayon himself sent letters to Oppenheim trying to enlist his unequivocal support in the controversy. Oppenheim responded with
a letter not to either party directly, but rather to Amsterdam's Jewish com-

munity leaders that cannily aimed to appease the heresy hunters without fully alienating their opponents.[40] As he outlined a policy that called for a person's innocence until proved guilty, Oppenheim also betrayed a sense of personal abuse by both parties with regard to his treasured medium, the printing press. He took umbrage at the fact that although he had written a longer letter to Zevi Ashkenazi, the latter had printed only excerpts from it, thereby doing violence to Oppenheim's words. He also disparaged Hayon's unauthorized duplication of Oppenheim's endorsement of one book (*Divrei Nehemiah*) in the front matter of the other (*Oz le-Elohim*).[41] At the conclusion of this fiery letter, Oppenheim refrained from passing judgment, calling on local officials to carefully scrutinize the words of Hayon's text and to give it a fair hearing. In playing to neutrality, Oppenheim raised the ire of his colleagues who counted on him to join the campaign against Sabbateanism. When, in 1714, Zevi and Oppenheim met in Hanover, Zevi publicly rebuked Oppenheim before all of the assembled community leaders present "for aiding Hayon and clandestinely strengthening his hand."[42]

But Oppenheim's reticence to condemn suspect literature was not at all out of character. The Hayon affair was among the most famous episodes involving rabbinic approval for suspect literature, but it was not the only time that Oppenheim associated himself with questionable texts and authors yet managed to preserve his reputation intact. In 1701, he lent his approbation to Mordecai Ashkenazi's edition of Abraham Rovigo's *Eshel Avraham,* a work that Oppenheim's son-in-law Michael Beer Oppenheim worked to bar from reprint in Frankfurt two decades later, in 1720.[43] Another questionable book bearing Oppenheim's approbation was written by Hayyim b. Moses Lipschitz. The book, *Derekh Hayyim,* was a compendium of laws for travelers, prayers, and kabbalistic *segulot.* Among them the author included a prayer written by Nathan of Gaza, prophet of Sabbatai Zevi.[44]

Oppenheim's ties to Sabbatean literature went far deeper. His library was rich with printed and manuscript materials (often in duplicate copies) of the literature of the Sabbatean movement and other messianic movements that preceded it. Oppenheim did not explicitly approve of this heretical sect, but he may have tacitly ignored its activities, as books and manuscripts of Sabbatean provenance repeatedly found their way into his collection, including a number of works by Nathan of Gaza, such as his treatise *Sefer ha-beriah*,[45] *Tikkun ha-yom*,[46] and *Tikkunei teshuva*.[47] Oppenheim also possessed manuscripts that related to Zevi's messianic predecessor, Solomon Molkho.[48] A Yiddish text in his collection, *Ayn shayn naye lid fun mashiah,* offered a popular account of the events of Sabbatai Zevi's arrival.[49] Throughout the eighteenth century Sabbatean literature, even in its most explicit forms, proved difficult to distill and eradicate, even from the libraries of rabbis with impeccably orthodox credentials.[50] These blurred lines were both intellectual and social. In a letter to the Jews of Jerusalem of 1706, Oppenheim referred fondly to a Moses b. Isaac, who had ties to the Sabbatean movement, had studied in Italy with Benjamin Kohen, and may have immigrated to Palestine with the movement of Judah Hasid—a movement that Oppenheim both financially supported and publicly condemned.[51] In the early eighteenth century, Sabbatean sympathizers and heresy hunters were often impossible to distinguish. For a man like Oppenheim, who delighted in books, no measure of heresy was sufficient to exclude a Jewish book from his ever-expanding library—a collection that strove to preserve, not proscribe or censor, Jewish literature.

Reception and Repression: Catholic Censorship and Jewish Approbata

If Oppenheim escaped demands from Jewish contemporaries to suppress books in his library or even consign them to oblivion, he faced other constraints from an entirely different quarter: the Catholic Church and the Habsburg monarchy that patronized it. In the years following the Thirty Years War the Habsburg monarchy embarked on a campaign of robust Counter-Reformation Catholicization, an enterprise geared primarily toward non-Catholic Christians of the realm, but with significant implications for Jewish life as well. The Jesuit offices were, for many of Prague's residents, a source of fear and repression and the energy behind forced sermons, conversionary campaigns, and the baptism of Jewish youth.[52] But patronage of the Catholic Church was not simply or even primarily a device for conflict. Rather, it served the Habsburgs in centralizing their domains and circumventing the privileges of the nobility—a road to absolutism quite different from the bureaucratization of their neighbors to the west. Catholic learning and culture, especially in its Central European articulation by the Jesuits and other orders, formed the sole unifying device of the composite Habsburg monarchy.[53] This process of "confessional absolutism" began in the seventeenth century under the reigns of Ferdinand II (1619–1637) and Ferdinand III (1637–1657), and after a limited retreat under the short reign of Joseph I, it continued into the early decades of the eighteenth century.[54]

A policy of repression and toleration took time to develop with regards to Jewish books. From the Habsburg victory at White Mountain in 1620 until Empress Maria Theresa's expulsion of the Jews from Prague in 1744, policy toward the Jews was carefully balanced between on one hand, the protective interests of imperial finances and on the other, the anti-Jewish sentiment shared by the Counter-Reformation church and the local economics of Prague's municipal authorities, with the former often prevailing over the latter.[55] But the Habsburg monarchy, Prague's local administrators, and the Jesuits of the archbishopric made common cause to suppress, scrutinize, and sanitize Jewish literacy. In 1669 the offices of the Habsburg governor of Bohemia ordered the closure of the two Jewish printing houses in Prague—operated by the Back and Löbl families, respectively—and confiscation of all the books found within them. The consistory of the archbishop—with its members who specialized in reading Hebrew—undertook scrutiny of the Talmud and "other forbidden Jewish books," which resulted in the establishment of a committee of oversight and the confiscation, in January 1670, of several hundred volumes of the Talmud and more than a thousand other Hebrew books.[56] When the appeals of the printers resulted in the reinstatement of one printer in 1672 and the other in 1674, new terms and conditions prevailed over their operation. Henceforth, Jesuit professors of Hebrew were mandated as censors of Jewish books, and royal privileges to print books would be issued only after applications were submitted through the inspectors of the texts.[57]

During the decade following Oppenheim's arrival in Prague in 1703—when he parted with his library to protect its contents from confiscation—

censorship of Jewish material became increasingly harsh.[58] In 1706, two Prague Jews, Berl Back and Israel Kettwies, were severely punished for publishing Hebrew prayer books without first subjecting them to review by the censor, Father Johannes Gall. Pinhas Katzenellinbogen recalled an owner, in Prague, of a silver-bound volume of the Amsterdam printing who kept his Talmud stored in safety in the marketplace rather than in his own home for fear of discovery.[59] Even the transit of books through Bohemia to other termini was carefully monitored. When Naftali Kohen of Frankfurt sought to travel through Bohemia to deliver books to Poland in 1707, Emperor Joseph I issued regulations about the storage, passage, and taxing of these objects.[60] In 1712 some forty-two Jewish families were searched by an Inquisition commission composed of the Jesuits Johannes Gall, Georgius Thomas, and Franciscus Haselbauer. Pointing to the blasphemous content especially of Tractates *Sanhedrin* and *Gittin,* two commonly studied tractates of the Talmud, the commission called for their destruction. In 1714, these calls were finally heeded, with an auto-da-fé of Hebrew books in the center of the town.[61]

The censorial activities of Haselbauer were not strictly suppressive. Haselbauer was a professor of Sacred Languages at the Jesuit University in Prague, the Clementinum, and as elsewhere on the continent, the role of the censor was not to destroy Hebrew books, but to generate Hebrew books that were purged of offense. In 1713 Haselbauer facilitated the publication of the Talmud Tractate *Pesahim* by cleansing it of offending material.[62] Moreover, censors, who were also scholars in their own right, labored to fashion acceptable canons of literature that removed offensive material from texts and generated texts that might bridge the divide between faiths, often in the name of conversion.[63] Rather than repressing the activities of readers, Haselbauer and others used literacy as a key to winning souls. In 1719/1720 he published a book titled *A Basic Report on Christianity: What the Christians believe and do not believe, that all of the Children of Israel may come to know the Truth* (*Des gründlichen Berichts von dem Christenthum, Erster Theil. Was die Christen glauben, und nicht glauben. Allen Kindern Israel zur Erkanntnus der Wahrheit*). The purpose of this book was apiece with a larger conversionary strategy, and he explained that "the source of Jewish ignorance is because most Jews, even if they wanted to, cannot read Christian books, and they are, from childhood, so little acquainted with Christians."[64] The book was printed in both Yiddish (or, more precisely, Judeo-German, or Western Yiddish) and German and was intentionally brief and laconic—a diglossic invitation for Jews to seek out a Christian partner in reading "so that the Jew may present his doubts, and the Christian can easily explain."[65] Rather than provide comprehensive guidance, the book was intended to whet the Jewish appetite and direct Jews to initiates for further instruction. In 1729 he published a primer on Christian practice for Jews, "A brief content of Christian law in 100 instructions."[66] Unlike the best-known Hebraic scholars of the Renaissance and Baroque ages—the Buxtorfs, Johann Andreas Eisenmenger, and Johann Jakob Schudt—who produced writing about the Jews in ethnographical fashion in order to introduce Jewish themes to interested Christians, Haselbauer imagined a *Jewish* audience for his work and wanted to convey Christian concepts in a Jewish idiom.[67]

The Jesuits were not the only agents in the regulation of Jewish books. Much as the Habsburgs relied on Jesuit expertise in religious affairs, they made efforts to incorporate the institutions of Jewish self-rule into a larger state apparatus. Despite their efforts to create an integrated polity, the Habsburgs consistently lagged behind in the process of absolutist state-building, and relied, instead, on co-opting elites whose agendas did not always neatly align with the court in Vienna. In Oppenheim's Prague and the surrounding province of Bohemia, government policy relied not on an army of bureaucrats, but rather on a symbiotic relationship between the Habsburg monarchy and the corporations and institutions within it, including the Jewish autonomous *kehillah*. In 1703, for example, in an attempt to rationalize Jewish tax collection and bring it into harmony with the practices of other corporate entities, Emperor Leopold abolished the entire electoral procedure of Prague's Jewish leadership, replacing it with a permanent governing oligarchy "in order to achieve the goal of a steadfast tranquility both for the Jewish community itself and for the general need for stability."[68] Leopold justified the action by describing the new arrangement for Jews to administer their affairs "just as the Christian faithful do"—an attempt to impose order and uniformity on a monarchy marked by diversity.

In keeping with a policy of co-opting elites to carry out policy, the monarchy tasked the chief rabbi with the oversight of books. These duties were delegated to the chief rabbi after the publication of an unapprobated exemplum of a prayer book in Prague in 1710, making Oppenheim not just chief rabbi, but a de facto state-mandated agent of the local print market. On June 28, 1713, Oppenheim wrote to the imperial offices to protest the imposition of this duty "ex post facto"—ten years after his initial appointment and confirmation as chief rabbi in the city.[69] Oppenheim cited historical precedent, an overburdened workload, fear of accidental incrimination, and finally bodily frailty as excuses to be recused from the task, to which the imperial offices eventually acquiesced, replacing Oppenheim with another Prague resident by the name of Simon Jeiteles.[70]

Where Oppenheim refused to alter Jewish books to the standards of outside forces, others saw opportunity in collaboration with the Jesuits. His younger contemporary, Jonathan Eybeschütz, who had already demonstrated his fierce opposition to Oppenheim and Prague's rabbinic establishment, cultivated a relationship with the Jesuits of Prague—Haselbauer in particular. Eybeschütz joined Haselbauer in an endeavor to produce new Jewish books, creating first a prayer book and then a new edition of the Talmud that would satisfy censorial demands and excise material disparaging of non-Jews, especially Christians.[71] Eybeschütz contributed "great sums from out of pocket" in order to finance the edition and claimed that his unique role as a disputant with the Jesuits had actually positioned him to collaborate with them and moderate their interests.[72]

The project immediately aroused a furor. According to Jacob Emden, a "great cry in Bohemia and the Lands of Ashkenaz" provoked the rabbis of Frankfurt am Main to raise 1,100 gold pieces in 1728 to dissuade the emperor from allowing this to proceed.[73] David Oppenheim joined the campaign to preserve the Talmud from alteration by banding together with the rabbis of Frankfurt am Main to block any further printing of the Talmud by Eybeschütz.[74] Eybeschütz responded in an anonymous apologetic in 1727 that justified this new edition of the Talmud on the grounds that not only Jews, but also (especially) Lutheran books had come under critical surveillance, and argued that although this situation was not ideal, it was better than the alternative of no printed Talmud at all.[75] The print run pro-

ceeded apace, with the appearance of *The Laws of Berakhot* (a title more
circumspect than the title "Tractate" or "Talmud" *Berakhot*) in 1728. Despite his opposition to the text's publication and his energies at halting its
production, a man whose greatest delight was in books could not resist the
allure of acquisition; Oppenheim acquired a copy and preserved it in his
collection.[76]

Titles on Trial, Approbata in Evidence

Entanglement between the various agents of book regulation in Prague
most directly affected Oppenheim when he was personally accused of abet-
ting treasonous activity. Unlike controversies and disputes over the making
of acceptable content within books, it was the content of books that stood
as the most forceful testimony against him. The very approbata that he wrote
had come under careful scrutiny by the censor who Oppenheim had suggested could execute the task more suitably: Franciscus Haselbauer. Haselbauer's expert testimony became a lynchpin in a case that was ostensibly
about the transit of funds to the Land of Israel but had important implications for the publication and circulation of Jewish books.[77]

The primary mover of this affair was a relative newcomer to the
city named Georgio Diodato. A native of Damascus, Diodato imported
his knowledge of the coffee trade from the Ottoman Middle East to open
Prague's first such institution, on the so-called Jesuit Street (*Jesuiter
Gassen*), which ran along the south side of the imposing complex of the
Clementinum, the city's Jesuit College. At Diodato's shop, students and
faculty of the university could mingle with merchants, traders, artisans, and
Jews. Unlike most other European cities, which boasted of several if not
hundreds of coffeehouses by 1700, this was Prague's only one, making such
interaction inevitable.[78] Although both Jewish and Christian authorities
occasionally looked askance at such interfaith mingling, Diodato's shop was
recognized by Franciscus Haselbauer as rich with potential.[79] This coffeehouse became the primary distributor of Haselbauer's primer for Jews on
Christianity. Its title page explicitly named Diodato as its distributor: "To
be found with Georgio Diodato, resident of the Old City and proprietor of
the coffeehouse on the Jesuit Street." Born into a Christian family in Da-

mascus, Diodato had not been raised Catholic but belonged, in his words, to a "schismatic" sect. By the age of eight he had come into contact with Jesuit teachings in the local Jesuit school, which housed eighty students, many of whom were not Catholic. Diodato was thus the beneficiary of the renowned educational services of the Jesuits, where he gained facility with European languages.[80] In 1698, following several years of travel around the eastern Mediterranean as a partner in his family's business, Diodato journeyed to Rome for the Jubilee of the Catholic Church. He remained in the Eternal City for four years before attempting the return journey but was further waylaid by the outbreak of revolt in the Hungarian lands led by Prince Ferenc II Rákóczi (1703-1711). He remained, therefore, in Central Europe and settled in Prague, where he founded the city's first coffeehouse.[81]

A newcomer both to Prague and to Western Christendom, Diodato was an enthusiastic promoter of Catholicism. In 1716, he published his first work, a fifteen-page pamphlet titled *Wail or Lamentation of the Asian Christians to the Anointed Heads of European Christians, especially the most powerful, most high, and most insurmountable Roman Emperor Charles VI* (*Wehe-Klag oder Lamentation der Asiatischen Christen zu den Christglaubigen Europaeischen gesalbten Häuptern; Absonderlich: zu den Großmächtigsten Durchleüchtigsten und Unüberwindlichsten Römischen Kayser Carolum VI.*). In this *Lamentation*—a book that highlights the benighted status of Christianity in the East and its perseverance as testament to its truth—he pointed to the presence of worldwide missions, despite great adversity, as a confirmation of the supremacy of Catholicism.[82] He pressed his claim that the presence of specifically Catholic missionaries across the Ottoman lands—in contrast to the absence of representatives of Islam, "schismatic" Christianity, or Judaism in Western Christendom—demonstrated Catholic dedication and superiority over all other faiths. Diodato adhered to the standard bearers of global Catholicism—the Jesuits—and sought to aid them in their mission. Their cooperation set the stage for a campaign that Diodato would wage, with Haselbauer's help, against David Oppenheim, taking particular aim at his purported role as Prince of the Land of Israel.

The pretext for this affair emerged in 1711 on the eastern shores of the Mediterranean, in Ottoman Palestine, where the Ashkenazic Jewish community of Jerusalem was in the throes of a financial crisis.[83] Having failed to pay a debt to the Ottoman pasha, some of the community's rabbis had been imprisoned. In a panic, the Jews of the city mobilized, sending letters to the Jewish diaspora, to Poland and Central Europe, in search of material aid to divert the complete impoverishment of Jewish life in the Holy Land at the hands of one of its debtors.[84] One of the addressees of these impassioned pleas was David Oppenheim in Prague, whose position as Prince brought with it an expectation that he would marshal the requisite financial support to redeem Jerusalem's Jews from bankruptcy and imprisonment. Relief came, however, from a more immediate presence in the city. A visitor to Jerusalem by the name of Jacob Siman Toff, a Jew from Smyrna, provided the 300 gold ducats needed to redeem the captive Jews in exchange for a promissory note.[85] This note, signed by sixteen of the community's rabbis, lauded Toff for his generosity and guaranteed repayment by either of two of Jerusalem's charity agents currently in Constantinople or by Joseph Beer, a Jewish native of Prague serving as the sultan's primary physician and occasional intercessor for Ottoman Jewry.[86] Toff traveled to Constantinople in search of his reimbursement, but Beer relayed him farther on to Prague, where, Beer assured him, the Prince of the Land of Israel could surely help him. Toff arrived in Prague in March 1713 and received lodging, a weekly stipend, and a generally warm reception from Oppenheim.[87]

This initial favor, however, soon turned sour. While Toff's promissory note stipulated a remission of his loan of 300 ducats with 1,200 gulden to cover the expenses of travel and interest, Oppenheim offered only 844 gulden to cover the capital outlay. Notwithstanding Toff's promissory note supporting his claim, Oppenheim would not budge.[88] Disadvantaged and ignorant of the vernaculars of the Bohemian lands, Toff sought an ally in his cause and found one in another Levantine: Diodato, operator of the Prague coffeehouse.[89] The Ottoman compatriots (Jew and Christian) made common cause, and Diodato agreed to serve as translator and intermediary between Oppenheim and Toff.[90]

Diodato aided Toff in negotiations with Oppenheim and, when they reached their limit, asked the chief rabbi to fund his return journey. Oppenheim granted the request, but rather than returning to Constantinople, Toff revised his plan and brought the case to the magistrate of Prague's Old

Town.[91] The suit was delayed by the outbreak of plague in the city, which sent Oppenheim in search of a safe refuge and left the litigants in Prague waiting. They followed the rabbi to Vienna, where Toff decided to convert to Catholicism—a process he did not complete until April 13, 1717, when Diodato christened him Ferdinand Paul Diodato Toff.[92] Diodato and Toff, now coreligionists, took up their suit against Oppenheim with renewed vigor, retaining a lawyer and appearing before the magistrate of Prague's Old Town only months later, in July 1717.[93]

Since directly suing Oppenheim had not worked, the pair now denounced Oppenheim's illegal use of a royal title, Prince of the Land of Israel, assaulting his character and shifting the focus away from a mere monetary dispute to an attack on Jewish perfidy. Diodato began "to publicize the great and important secret for the entire beloved Christendom, especially the Jewish king, his profits, and finally the export of large sums of money out of Europe into the Turkish Empire; since I have learned of his large, important secret *in authentico* against God, against his Imperial Majesty, and also against the entire meritorious Christendom."[94] These accusations captured the attention of the magistrate's court, which carefully considered Diodato and Toff's allegations. The centerpieces of this hearing were three documents that had initially set Toff's journey in motion: Toff's promissory note, a letter to Oppenheim describing the troubles in the Holy Land, and a second letter to Oppenheim reporting on Toff's generosity—all issued by the Jews of Jerusalem in 1711. The court subjected these letters to special scrutiny, enlisting two "sworn" officers of Prague's Jewish community—Elias Strackowitz, the scribe, and Wolff Selig, the *Schulklopper* (beadle)—to translate them into German so that it could effectively assess the way in which Oppenheim was addressed.[95] Both Diodato and Oppenheim proved themselves to be quite litigious; the elders of the Jewish Old Town countersued on Oppenheim's behalf, demonstrating that they saw this as larger than a private, interpersonal matter.[96] By July 1, 1718, the court found for the chief rabbi, ruling that he was "absolved from the denunciation."[97]

Unsatisfied with this outcome, Diodato and Toff initiated a series of appeals, which garnered imperial notice, and invited state incursion into the affair, perhaps in more direct ways than either party might have imagined. On September 26, 1721, Emperor Charles VI dispatched the Jewish Economic Commission, an imperial body dedicated to oversight of Jewish affairs, to investigate.[98] Diodato and Toff's appearance before the commission was not a rehearsal of their arguments before the municipal court of 1717–1718. Since their evidence there—the correspondence between Oppenheim and Jerusalem—had proved impotent for their purposes, they identified two different, more incriminating bodies of evidence that demonstrated Oppenheim's sedition.[99] Diodato amassed witnesses to attest to the traffic in people and currency toward Jerusalem.[100] Accordingly, the two men also turned away from Jewish agents to act as translators on the court's behalf and toward a more sympathetic and authoritative ally, the Jesuit professor and Hebraist Haselbauer, whose familiarity with Jewish books might provide a new direction of attack.[101]

The shift in both evidence and its expert witness moved the trial in a different direction than either Toff or Diodato had initially intended. Although Diodato was driven to publicize Oppenheim's title in order to reveal the "secrecy" of the Jews for the benefit of "worldwide Christendom," and Toff was largely in search of returns on his loan, Haselbauer's preoccupations were far more practical.[102] The Jesuit professor was brought in as an expert witness to translate Hebrew books that bore Oppenheim's illegitimate title, but he was far less concerned with the title itself than with the uses to which it was put: the dissemination of Hebrew books and the control of Jewish knowledge. Whereas the commission had difficulty with the translation of the *letters* exchanged between the Jerusalem Jews and Oppenheim, Haselbauer definitively showed Oppenheim's illegitimate titles by translating material from Hebrew *books,* especially their approbata. Together with another Hebraist named Petrus Paulus Christianus of Heidelberg and Vienna and the officers of the Prague archbishopric, Haselbauer supplied the imperial court with a list of books attesting to the use of Oppenheim's princely moniker by both the rabbi himself and the wider Jewish reading public. Haselbauer produced at least nine books or pamphlets that carried Oppenheim's princely designation in approbata he had written. Of these, four were included in books printed in Prague, and the rest in Frankfurt or Sulzbach.

Although the initial inquiry had demanded approbata as a body of evidence to compensate for the insufficient testimony provided by the Jerusalem letters, the introduction of printed books lent an entirely new dimension to the trial. In the hands of the Jewish commission that was trying the case, Haselbauer's testimony was used to show that not only did Oppenheim's signature appear adorned with royal trappings, it was used functionally to approve of books that had not been officially censored by the Prague consistory.[103] Oppenheim had gone from declining to precensor books to facilitating books that had not been censored at all.

Given the opportunity to present his defense, Oppenheim argued that his approbata to Hebrew books was only "adhortative," and not an imprimatur, denying the regulatory force of his words.[104] Remarkably, more than half of the books under investigation actually bore a censor's seal of some sort. All of the texts printed in Sulzbach, in Catholic Bavaria, carried the phrase *Cum Licentia Serinissimi* and Oppenheim's approbata asserted that the books had first been reviewed by figures "appointed by the emperor."[105] In the fragmented and confessionalized jurisdictions of the eighteenth-century Holy Roman Empire—where approved books were not reciprocally recognized in disparate territories—Haselbauer's claims with respect to Oppenheim's pretensions of censorship may have had more to do with jealously guarded local territorial prerogative by Bohemia's religious elite than with offensive content.[106]

Yet a further, silent party may have been involved in the attack on these approbata as well. Although he did not appear before the tribunal, Jonathan Eybeschütz may have had his part to play in this affair, as an antagonist of Oppenheim's and a budding partner of the Jesuit consistory. Eybeschütz had little to lose by bringing the institution of approbata under scrutiny; it was a crusade he had been waging for some time. He feared that conferring approbata encouraged a proliferation of casuistic commentaries and thereby ignorance of classical texts. Unlike Oppenheim, who penned more than seventy such approbata, Eybeschütz broke with rabbinic publishing conventions by printing his books without the introductory praises of colleagues.[107]

When the commission finally reached a decision on January 27, 1723, it dismissed many of the original pretexts for the suit, relieving Oppenheim of any obligation to pay Diodato and Toff, a victory that may have been facilitated by Oppenheim's courtly relatives in Vienna.[108] But the larger political dimensions of the affair remained a matter of imperial scrutiny. Although the commission "lacked the requisite evidence" to indict Oppenheim for illicit trafficking of funds, the imperial offices expressly forbade future collections for the Land of Israel on the grounds that such collections directly enriched the coffers of the Ottomans.[109] Moreover, the commission had found Oppenheim's title of Prince of the Land of Israel to be a direct affront to Christian interpretation of the messianic prophecies of the Hebrew Bible and recommended a recall of all Hebrew books that bore the title.[110] The emperor similarly forbade Oppenheim from using the title to facilitate printing books without appropriate censorship.[111]

The affair brought misfortune on all sides. Diodato faced financial ruination. In his account of the trial, titled *Anfang der Weißheit ist die Furcht Gottes* (The Beginning of Wisdom Is the Fear of God), he reported that he was bereft of his "business, worth more than twenty thousand thaler, from which I registered a yearly 2,000 Gulden, but I have also hereby lost my best days, my health, and have fallen to such a miserable state," which he credited with ruining his family life and causing the death of five of his eight children.[112] He soon thereafter left Prague for Leipzig, where his associations with Lutherans further distanced him from the Jesuits of Prague. While Oppenheim dodged personal penalty, he does not appear to have given his approbation to another book until more than a decade later, during the years immediately preceding his death. In the final approbation of his lifetime, Oppenheim was careful to express, even in his Hebrew introduction, that the work had already received the approval of the imperial censor before being published.[113] In at least that regard, Diodato and Haselbauer had successfully targeted an instrument of Jewish culture.

Conclusion

That books have a social life does not mean that their production and dissemination is always congenial. Books are deeply political objects, forged at the meeting place between commerce and knowledge and easily subverted to ends at odds with regnant regimes. The distribution of books relies not simply on their content, but fundamentally on the wider structures of the authority, recognition, and reputation of both the author and the complex of characters who lend their credence to the work and the person who produces it.

As early modern Europe's most renowned bibliophile who was also a man of governing influence and familial wealth, Oppenheim was in particular demand to bridge the space between assessments of a book's worth and enlistment of a community of regard. Despite his reticence to publish his own writings, his approbata populated the pages of numerous books that entered the market during his lifetime. But his approbata also provided others with evidence of misdoings, giving antagonists, Jewish and Christian alike, fodder for assaults against him. The spaces between endorsement and incrimination, between censorship and treason, and between hospitality and heresy reveal the thin boundaries between books as objects and the social worlds that created them. They showed the importance of credit and credibility for the making of books, and the ways by which extension of personal credit could, in return, incriminate the people who doled it out in the first place.

Epilogue and Conclusion
The Library Moves On

Actually, inheritance is the soundest way of acquiring a collection.
—Walter Benjamin, *Unpacking My Library: A Talk About Book Collecting*, 1931

OPPENHEIM'S LIBRARY WAS A PRODUCT of his unique family fortune, social standing, and personal taste. Because it was so closely tied up with the personhood of its collector—a man "whose greatest delight is in books"—its meaning and purpose dramatically changed after Oppenheim's death in 1736, and the untimely death of his son only three years later in 1739. With the death of these two men, the library traveled between different owners and users, and ideas for configuring new purposes for it were mooted for more than a hundred years. Much as the movement of the library's individual components revealed a map of power relations in premodern Europe, the wanderings of the entire collection similarly reflected commensurate shifts in Jewish political culture. Proposals for (and rejections of) new homes for the library indicated that Jewish patronage culture was being left behind, replaced with new models of accommodation and advocacy, and the library's contents were imagined as a basis for new forms of Judaism and Jewish political life in the modern world.

Family and Fortune: The Travels of a Collection

The deeply personal nature of a library built by personal patronage—rather than by institutions—meant the absence of a durable, sustained, institutional grounding for it.[1] Oppenheim's library was not helmed by a communally funded body of stewards and was answerable to nobody but its founder. After occupying the Prague rabbinate for more than thirty years, and holding the chief rabbinate of all of Bohemia for nearly twenty years, Oppenheim died at the age of seventy-two. His son, Joseph, had shared in the library's upkeep for decades, but at his death in 1739, the library was orphaned of all of its original caretakers.

It is a strange fact of the Court Jewish phenomenon that despite the strength of marriage alliances and lateral ties, such families often rose and fell within the span of a few generations, spectacularly attaining fortune and rapidly falling from grace.[2] Oppenheim was born into wealth, and there is no evidence that he ever became impoverished, yet his immediate family did not carry his standard forward. His eldest daughter Sara (who wrote her own megillah) died in 1713; his daughter Blümele (wife of Michael Beer, whose marriage was commemorated by the *Breileft*) died only two years after Oppenheim in 1738. His two surviving daughters, Jente and Tolze, were married to Selig Kohen of Hanover and Baer Cleve (of the Gumpertz family of Court Jews), respectively.[3] The library passed first to Oppenheim's only son Joseph and then onward to Joseph's daughter, Gnendel, who was named for Oppenheim's first wife.

This inheritance entailed a change of location. The fortunes of Oppenheim's father-in-law's family had been on the wane for two decades. Following the death of Leffman Behrens in 1714, his grandsons, Gumpert and Isaac Behrens, took up the post of Court Jew, as their father Hirz had died in 1709. Yet by 1721, both men had been subjected to criminal charges, under suspicion of defrauding their creditors through bankruptcy. Their imprisonment lasted until 1726, after which point their assets were in ruins and they were forced to leave Hanover.[4] The library, however, does not appear to have been relocated at this point. But with David and Joseph Oppenheim's deaths, the library was bequeathed to Joseph's daughter, Gnendel, and her husband, Hirschel Isaac Oppenheim, in Hildesheim, where the library was then relocated.[5]

The library's move to new, less familiar, caretakers obliged a new reckoning with its contents. And so, much as the collection had begun in a cata-

logue, the death of its owner propelled a new cataloging activity. Oppenheim had used catalogues to grasp the horizons of the Jewish bookshelf,
and a catalogue was now needed to map the terrain that Oppenheim had
traversed. Even before his death, the library, once the product of booklists,
became an authority against which to build a more comprehensive and up-
to-date bibliography. The *Bibliotheca Hebrea* of Wolff was the most notable
among these, but not the only such project. One visitor to the library used
his admission as an opportunity to create a manuscript addendum to Shabbetai Bass's catalogue, *Siftei yeshenim* (Amsterdam, 1680), which had perhaps inspired Oppenheim's own first reckoning of his collection in 1682,
providing a list of 546 books "from the library of the great sage our master and teacher David Oppenheim Av Beit Din of Prague, books that are
owned by the sage whose names are not mentioned in the book *Siftei yeshenim* in its two volumes." The author of the manuscript also identified a further 488 manuscripts of texts not in circulation.[6] Because Oppenheim once
had used Bass's catalogue as a blueprint for building a library, the library
could then serve, dialectically, as the model against which an enhanced bibliography could be drafted.

Oppenheim's heirs, however, produced an inventory of the collection
for more prosaic ends. Faced with an unfamiliarity with the intricacies of
the collection, lacking the personal zeal for its contents, and experiencing
deteriorating financial circumstances, Gnendel's family itemized the library
in its entirety (fig. 6.1).[7] The resulting catalogue represents the oldest extant
complete itemization of the collection; it is divided into three sections—
Hebrew printed books, non-Hebrew works, and manuscripts—the contents of each arranged alphabetically, and provides information about publication date and location for printed matter. Three copies of this catalogue
survive, one of which was written by a scribe in Hildesheim by the name of
Judah Benjamin b. Jonah Katz, who had conducted some scribal work for
Oppenheim.[8] A subtle but important shift in the treatment of books accompanied this endeavor. Whereas Oppenheim's earliest catalogue of his collection had made no distinction between manuscripts and books—all were
simply texts—by the middle of the eighteenth century the gap between
the handwritten and the machine-printed word had widened. The earliest

Fig. 6.1. Ms. Opp. Add. 4° 135, f. 1r. The first page of the complete manuscript catalogue. The right-hand column numerals indicate the size of the work (folio, quarto, octavo, etc.), the wide central column gives the title and a brief description of the work, and the left-hand columns give the date and location of publication. Courtesy of the Bodleian Libraries, University of Oxford.

stages of modern bibliography, codicology, and paleography had begun to effect a conceptual division between these two media that conveyed the written word in catalogues and collections across the continent, and this ethos penetrated Oppenheim's holdings as well.[9]

Understandings of the relationship between manuscripts and printed books may have shifted, but the multiplication of copies of this catalogue demonstrate that the library still captured the interest of contemporaries. In fact, Oppenheim's library was of interest not only for its individual items, but as a blueprint for aspiring collectors to chart their own collecting paths, much as Bass's catalogue had once guided Oppenheim's acquisitions. One catalogue later made its way into the possession of Heimann Joseph Michael (1792–1846), who came to acquire 5,400 books and 860 manuscripts of his own.[10] Michael seems to have been deeply inspired by Oppenheim. His collection of manuscripts contains some of the sole copies of commentaries, responsa, and Talmudic casuistry produced by Oppenheim and, even more strikingly, more than three hundred letters that were sent to Oppenheim during his lifetime—a veritable Oppenheim archive.[11] In constructing this archive, Michael also aimed to retrieve items that had belonged to Oppenheim, or manuscripts that had been commissioned by him, and incorporated them into his own collection.[12]

Unlike Michael's wish to emulate the master collector, Oppenheim's heirs worked to inventory the collection in order to part with the library as a scholarly reservoir and use it for its monetary potential. On the brink of bankruptcy, Gnendel sought debt relief by liquidating some of her assets. She made overtures to profit from a piece of the collection in 1764 with an attempted sale of 614 items.[13] Even as she was in need of financial aid, Gnendel was still a woman with significant contacts and the influence to enlist people of renown. By 1775, with creditors enlisting the state to force Gnendel to pay her debts, the catalogue was reviewed by two of the most well-known men in the field of Jewish knowledge, outside of rabbinic circles: Moses Mendelssohn and Johann David Michaelis, professor of oriental studies at Göttingen.[14]

Mendelssohn, known as the father of Jewish Enlightenment, wrote of the collection: "It contains not only many individual rarities, the price of which cannot be determined, but also the totality has such great worth that I cannot assign [a price] to it . . . fifty or sixty thousand reichsthalers would certainly not be too expensive to pay."[15] Michaelis, on the other hand, hesitated even to hazard an estimated value for the collection until a thorough assessment of the value of each book was made, but he nevertheless declared that "the value of the library is exceedingly great."[16] In order to attract the greatest possible sums from the sale of the library, Michaelis emphasized its value "not only for Jews, but also for Christians; and not merely for both in Germany, but rather in Europe."[17] As attentive to the aesthetics of an auctioneer's catalogue as the collector was to each individual item, Michaelis produced detailed recommendations as to how best to present the material for it to find buyers in "England, Holland, France and Italy." He argued for the importance of appealing to buyers in multiple languages, including rabbinic Hebrew. Michaelis also was sensitive to location: "Hildesheim must not be the place where the auction will be held, because foreigners know it too little, and there are presumably not many local buyers. Instead Hamburg (on account of its easy transport to foreign lands and the strong Altona Jewish community) or Göttingen, because foreign scholars know it well, and because at Göttingen auctions university libraries bid very high. Of the two, I would select Hamburg."[18]

Perhaps the attention of these two prominent men raised the profile of the collection, which was assuredly the point. Rumors circulated that the Berlin Court Jew Daniel Itzig might have been contemplating a bid on the collection in 1774, and in 1777 the Christian Hebraist Oluf Gerhard Tychsen reported that the collection had been pawned to a merchant in Altona.[19] Still, Hamburg became the collection's next home, and the books remained, for a time, within the Oppenheim family. Gnendel was in such dire straits that she could not wait for a full appraisal of the collection. A family member, Isaac Seeligmann Berend Salomon Kohen — Gnendel's cousin, a nephew of Joseph Oppenheim, and grandson of Samson Wertheimer — appears to have relieved her of some of her debt in exchange for the collection and other Jewish artistic and ritual objects, though at a far lower sum than the recommended 50,000–60,000 reichsthalers put forward by Mendelsson.[20] But Kohen's acquisition was only a temporary measure. Under his ownership, a new catalogue, this one printed, was produced in 1782 for the explicit purpose of auctioning off the contents of the collection. Absorbing some of Michaelis's recommendations that the library might find interest beyond Jewish circles, the catalogue included a Hebrew title page and second title page in German and Latin that advertised its value (fig. 6.2). Whereas the Hebrew simply advertised the "ancient and famous" collection, the German page listed the contents as including "Kabbalistic, Theological, Talmudic, Philological, Mathematical, Medicinal, and other scholarly fields," recognizing that a Christian Hebraist reader would find greater interest in the mystical and theological than in the curriculum of the yeshiva (it also gave no mention at all of the Yiddish and liturgical items in the collection).[21]

The compilers of the catalogue further relied on two sources of name recognition for the library, appealing to both Jewish and Christian library sensibilities. In its German forward a brief description of the contents invoked the expert authority of Johann Christoph Wolff, who had visited the collection and used its contents to construct his survey of Hebrew literature, *Bibliotheca Hebrea,* in which he specifically referenced Oppenheim. Similarly, but with a different audience in mind, perhaps, the manuscript listing of the catalogue assured readers that the manuscripts listed had been noted according to the catalogue produced by Shabbetai Bass. Oppenheim's collection was thus framed against and mentioned in relation to other libraries and other catalogues—from both the Jewish and Christian worlds.

Winds of Change: Shifts in Knowledge and the Dynamics of Jewish Political Culture

When the library ceased to be the patrimony of the Oppenheim family, it flared the imagination of thinkers and activists in an age of revolution and reform who sought to forge new forms of Jewish culture out of the materials of the Jewish past. These men were acting in line with new ideas about collecting and display that were rapidly gaining currency as the eighteenth century drew to a close. As the nation emerged as the political legitimate par excellence, collections and museums came to represent the body politic, not the courtly patron.[22] The logic behind a personal library was receding, to be replaced with libraries that would serve newly constituted collectives: the nation, the state, and its citizenry. What might this mean for Jews, who at precisely this moment in Western Europe, were being warned that they did not constitute a nation at all?

These changes in political thought coincided with new approaches to the organization of knowledge as well. The men of the eighteenth-century Enlightenment inaugurated an epistemological shift in early modern ways of knowing. They derided the catchall character of the cabinet of curiosities and personal collections as idiosyncratic and unsystematic, replacing them with classifications and taxonomies. Various intermediaries and champions of the library emerged, often not as buyers, but rather to urge the actions of prospective buyers, and to put forth their own ideas about how the collection might be repurposed.

The production of the catalogue in Hamburg inspired renewed notice among scholars, who advertised its importance for an age of enlightenment and absolutism. Michaelis returned to comment on the library in *Orientalische und exegetische Bibliothek* (vol. 21). Despite its current owner's ignorance of Michaelis's prior evaluation of the library, Michaelis proceeded to speculate about prospective buyers for the collection:

> The first and natural (although this ranking is without prejudice) are the wealthy sons of Abraham in Germany, especially in a capital city, who operate not in tons of gold, but in millions. For one of them it would be a trifle, and still a very patriotic deed, were they to find a stable place for such a library in a capital city where there are many Jews, and young Jews who conduct scholarship. . . . Clearly not all of its students must be Jews . . . there must also be other students who are interested in eastern philology, as there are among Christians, and philosophy. . . .
>
> The second [potential buyers] are kings and princes: not just for them, but as a form of patriotism for scholarship.[23]

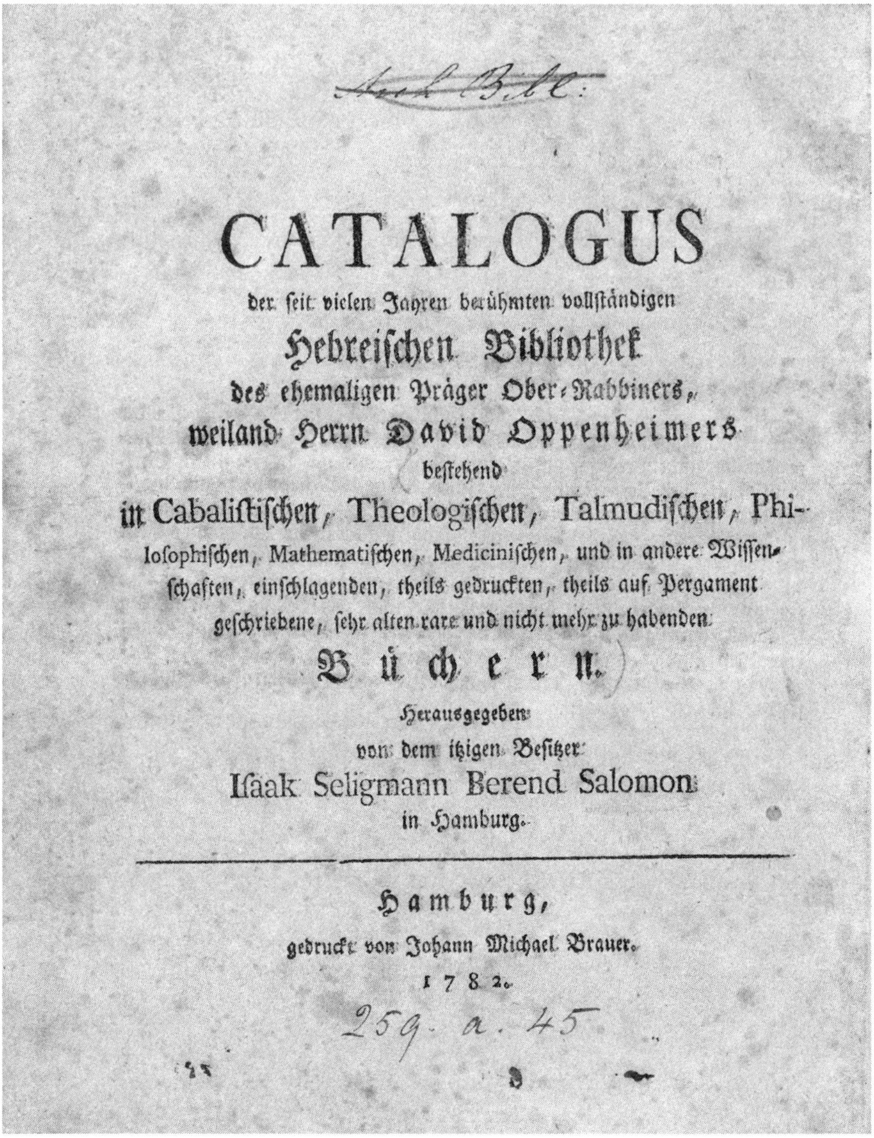

CATALOGUS

der seit vielen Jahren berühmten vollständigen

Hebreischen Bibliothek

des ehemaligen Präger Ober-Rabbiners,

weiland Herrn David Oppenheimers

bestehend

in Cabalistischen, Theologischen, Talmudischen, Phi-
losophischen, Mathematischen, Medicinischen, und in andere Wissen-
schaften, einschlagenden, theils gedruckten, theils auf Pergament
geschriebene, sehr alten rare und nicht mehr zu habenden

Büchern.

Herausgegeben

von dem itzigen Besitzer

Isaak Seligmann Berend Salomon

in Hamburg.

Hamburg,

gedruckt von Johann Michael Brauer.

1 7 8 2.

259. a. 45

Fig. 6.2. Johann Michael Brauer, *Catalogus . . . hebraischen Bibliothek . . . David Oppenheimers* (Hamburg, 1782). Note the duplicate title pages, one in German (with some Latin) (left) and the other in Hebrew (right), produced to advertise the collection for sale to quite different buyers. Courtesy of the Bodleian Libraries, University of Oxford.

רשימה

תמה ומתואמה בסידור א״ב מסיפה

מן קבוצת ספרים

ונקראה בשם

ביבליותיקי

העתיקה המפורסמה והרוממה אשר מאז מקדם קיבץ ריבה ואסף
איש טהור וקדוש הגבר הקים עולה של תורה הרב הגאון נשיא אאלהים

מהורר דוד אופנהיים זצ״ל

אין ערוך אליה

והיא מכמה אלפים ספרים חשובים ורבים נדפסים על קלף וכמה מאות

כתובים יד

אשר לגודל חשיבותם ויקים לא נמצאו זולתם
(והמה הוצגו באחרונה בסידור א״ב ברשימה לבדהם)

הכל בכתב יפה אף נעים

ועם רוב יושנם עוד לא פנה הוד תפארת מכתבם וזיו כריםותם
ההדורות לא נשתנה ורמה לא היתה בם

בעת במצות ה׳ ה׳ה האלוף הקצין התורני המרומם כבוד הרר

איצק כהן נרו

בן השר המפורסם הנגיד מהורר נעליגמן כהן זצל

נדפסה פה המבורג, יע״א ה׳ תקט״ב

נעשה בשקידה נאמנת ותיקון נפלא

על ידי איש מהור״ר במלאכתו

בשנת ודברך היה יקר ליצירה

Tychsen, the Christian Hebraist, personally visited the collection for three weeks, and he corresponded with the Italian Christian Hebraist Giovanni Bernardo De Rossi to report on its manuscripts. Tychsen endeavored to excite the interest of prospective buyers, ranging from Catherine the Great, empress of Russia, to more local figures, such as Duke Karl Eugen of Württemberg and Archduke Frederick Francis I of Mecklenburg-Schwerin.[24] Despite enthusiastic speculation and lobbying, the library found no owner and remained in Hamburg in possession of the family.

The cause of new ownership was taken up again in the age of revolution and emancipation. As French forces moved across the continent, the domestic reform of Jewish practices came under significant consideration, not least with the convocation of the Parisian Sanhedrin by Napoleon I. After Napoleon's armies occupied neighboring Westphalia, established a monarchy under the emperor's brother, Jerome, and emancipated the Jews in 1807, Jews were organized into a *consistoire*, a central organization of the Jews of the kingdom. When a new spirit called for a regeneration of Jewish values in alignment with a state that was finally prepared to accord them full civic equality, the library found renewed interest, for a very different purpose than its initial creation a century before. The educator and author Jeremiah Heinemann (1778–1855) attempted to purchase the library for the *consistoire*, bringing the plan before its president, the Court Jew Israel Jacobson.[25] The men labored to produce a holding company that would raise the funds for the books and intended to sell duplicate copies in order to fund the other activities of the *consistoire*. With the demise of the kingdom of Westphalia in 1813 and the *consistoire* shortly thereafter, Heinemann attempted to enlist the interest of the Prussian state to support the regeneration project, but to no avail.[26]

Following the failure of plans to use the library in the service of national regeneration, a theology professor at Rostock, Anton Theodor Hartmann (1774–1838), attempted to muster interest in the library by publishing a report in the journal *Jedidja, eine religiöse, moralische und pädagogische Zeitschrift*. He reported that "the books have been packed for sale for so long . . . the curators will thank the heavens to sell the books at the low price of 5,000 reichsthalers."[27] They currently, he assured his readers, were stored in twenty-eight boxes, were free of worms, and had previously been insured against fire to the sum of 30,000 Marks.[28] He further attempted to peddle the library to a prospective "Bibliotheca Palatina" based in Heidelberg—the Rhineland city from which the Oppenheim family's fortunes had first been launched—the ownership of which would benefit studies in oriental philology and biblical studies, and then to the Prussian monarchy.[29] These efforts were in vain as well.

After ten years of uninterest, the library was given over to a seller of antique books, who unpacked the collection in order to stage a new auction. As in the past, a catalogue was produced in preparation for the auction, to garner interest in the collection that everyone agreed someone should buy yet no one seemed to want. The catalogue, printed in 1826 and prepared by Isaac Metz, announced the forthcoming sale of the collection in its entirety but indicated that a failure to find a suitable buyer in the course of a year and a half would result in a piecemeal sale of the collection by auction, scheduled for June 11, 1827.[30] The catalogue bore parallel Hebrew and Latin titles (*Kohelet David/Collectio Davidis*), featured two unique introductions that appealed to different clientele, and included a linear translation into Latin of the body of the catalogue. Unlike previous catalogues, which had been organized according to print versus manuscript or alphabetically, this catalogue was produced with an eye to the packing, shipping, and storage constraints of potential buyers and therefore was organized according to the size of the books and only thereafter by topic and then name, although it did preserve a distinction between books and manuscripts. For the discerning bibliophile the catalogue also indicated the quality and color of the paper, revealing those editions printed on vellum, grey, blue, or other colored paper, as well as pointing out copies that had been produced as exemplaria.

Unpacking Oppenheim's library breathed some new life into it. Some interest was piqued by David Friedlander, who sought to produce a joint-stock company to take hold of the collection, and Leopold Zunz attempted to persuade the Berlin Royal Library to house the collection, but to little avail.[31] From Tarnopol in Habsburg Galicia it attracted the attention of the young rabbi, *maskil*, and *Wissenschaftler* rabbi Solomon Judah Rapoport (1790–1867). Rapoport's contact with works of the Haskalah had propelled him to produce monographs on Jewish personalities from the Middle Ages. He prevailed upon a colleague to make copies of books in the collection in Hamburg and to bring them back to him, much as Oppenheim had done in his own time through his wide epistolary network. Rapoport used these copies to produce a more accurate edition of a number of texts in manuscript, including works of Abraham, son of Maimonides; a letter of Moses Maimonides for the sultan and other writings; commentaries on Maimonides's *Guide for the Perplexed;* the book *Sefer ha-melamed;* and others.[32]

Although an auction was scheduled for June 1827, by late 1826 negotiations opened between the estate's executor in Hamburg and officials at the Bodleian Libraries at the University of Oxford, under the direction of the Rev. Dr. Alexander Nicoll, and his agent in Hamburg, Dr. J. J. C. Pappe.[33] The library's value was a complicated matter, perhaps exacerbated by Mendelssohn's and Michaelis's appraisals. An awareness of the collection's worth within the family had prompted speculation by its owners, and "the intended sale of the library had given birth to many pretensions on account of debts, which were contracted upon it." A "Mistress Oppenheim, residing in the city of Hildesheim," had done exactly that and then involved the Prussian government, "which has interfered on her behalf and has commissioned a lawyer of this place, to take the necessary steps in order to satisfy her pretensions."[34] Creditors to the estate in Hildesheim (apparently from the unresolved bankruptcy of Gnendel) had maintained a lien on the library that had to be satisfied in this auction/bankruptcy of the family. An early offer to the family by "some person in England" of 1,850 pounds had apparently been rejected by the family as too low, and they requested a sum of 2,200 pounds to cover the cost of the library as well as the incidentals of the executor's fees and the catalogue's publication.

Pappe, from his station in Hamburg, did not share the family's expectations: "According to my firm opinion," he told his future buyer, "this rare collection will never reach the sum, which is asked for it by the lump, if it should actually be resolved upon to detail it in auction."[35] Nicoll replied with his counteroffer of 2,000 pounds on January 23, and by February 6 Pappe reported that the family's lawyer was prepared to accept the sum but required the approval of the family's trustees, which would require a further four weeks. Pappe stood his ground, advising Nicoll "not to be precipitate in granting their request, or consenting to an additional sum."[36] Only three and a half months later, on May 25, Pappe was "at last enabled to give you some information about the Hebrew library of the late Mr. Oppenheimer." With its public auction imminent, Pappe hedged his bets and betrayed his own initial confidence, suggesting that Nicoll "might authorize me to add a few pounds" in the off chance that a higher bidder appear.[37]

With the auction approaching, Nicoll undertook his own visit to evaluate the library in person. Although he left despondent in the face of seemingly "insuperable impediments," on May 2, 1828, nearly a full year later, the family agreed to a final sum of 2,080 pounds.[38] Pappe wrote to apprise Nicoll of these circumstances, expressing his concern that he had not heard from Nicoll since the Oxford librarian's visit. By this time Nicoll had contracted a terminal disease. He did not witness the fruits of his labor, dying only a few months later on September 25. The arrangements for the library's relocation came a year after that, on May 22, 1829, with the itemization of thirty-four crates required to move the collection from northern Germany to Oxford. The crates were put in transit in the summer months—when hopes of good weather were higher—and made their way to England and became the cornerstone of Oxford's Judaica collection (fig. 6.3).[39]

Oxford remains the collection's final resting place, although not without some discontent: scholars visiting the collection in the nineteenth and the first half of the twentieth centuries lamented its presence outside of Jewish ownership. In some ways, the relocation of an "oriental" collection from Jewish ownership to England paralleled the processes of imperial "collecting" occurring in contemporary British cultural institutions, most notably the sensational arrivals of the Rosetta Stone and the Elgin Marbles at the British Museum in 1802 and 1816, respectively. An act of cultural plunder, even when the bill was paid, was noticed by contemporaries. In his *Die gottesdienstlichen Voträge der Juden* (1832) Zunz deplored the fact that "even the incomparable library of Oppenheimer had to emigrate to Oxford despite all the rich and pious Jews and the erudite and powerful Christians, and could not find a refuge in Germany, which precisely in this field ranks quite significantly behind foreign countries (Parma, Florence,

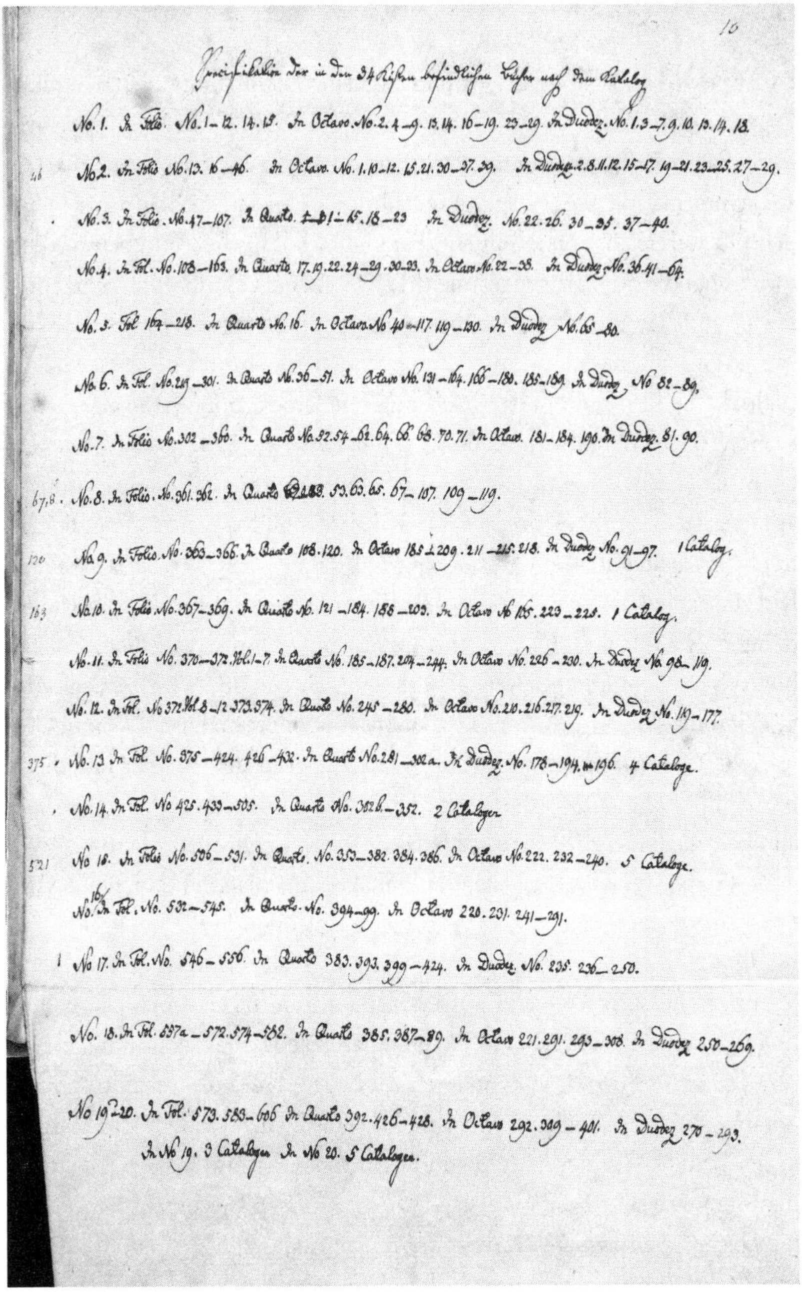

Fig. 6.3. Bodleian Ms. Add. C 166, f. 10r (left) and 11r (right): List of the contents of the crates containing the Oppenheim collection in transit between Hamburg and Oxford, according to their shelf marks. Courtesy of the Bodleian Libraries, University of Oxford.

Sr. Hochedlen den Herrn Canning,
Königl. Großbritannischen General-Consul in Hamburg
für die Bodleianische Bibliothek in Oxford.

Nota

Für meine 2 jährige Bemühung &c für den Ankauf der Oppenheimerschen Hebräischen Bibliothek, deren Revision und Verpackung 2 Procent von der Probiessit? Summa oder   42 Ltr Pistol.

An Auslagen: für 34 Kisten à 3 mk Cour. — — —   102 mk

Dem Tischler für Packlatten u Nägeln, Erstigung des Arbeitslohn —   15 ß

für das Zeichen der Kisten — — — —   3 "

an Trinkgeld — — — — — — —   2 "

_____

Summa 42 Ltr Pistol und 122 mk Cour.

Hamburg, den 22ten Mai 1829.

J. J. C. Heyne &c &c.

Rome, Leiden, Paris, Oxford)."[40] This sentiment intensified with time. In *Zur Geschichte und Literatur* (1845) Leopold Zunz described the collection as "belonging to the few memorials that Jews established and Christians preserve."[41] Nearly a century later, without a hint of irony or a glimmer of historical prescience, Oppenheim's biographer, C. Duschinsky, despaired in 1930 that "it cannot, with the best possible good will, be considered lucky for the library or for Jewish learning that fate has decreed Oxford to be the home of the Oppenheimer library," lamenting its distance from London, or, the centers of Jewish learning in Germany.[42] This twist of fate, however, also left the library in one of the few English sites that was not bombed during the Second World War.

A Jewish National Library?

The lamentations of Zunz and Duschinsky, separated by nearly a century, share a sentiment that the Oppenheim library *ought* to be the natural patrimony predominantly of Jews, and of German Jews in particular. They each captured what appear to be the two important registers—at times at odds with each other—for making sense of the collection as it was assembled by its collector. Oppenheim sought to make books "without end," but linguistic and cultural boundaries hemmed the texts of the collection into a shared framework, bounding this endless collection and limiting it. On one hand, the collector's expansive impulse was synonymous, to the best of his ability, with the reaches of Jewish settlement. His contacts with Jews and Christians across Central Europe, the Netherlands, the Italian peninsula, and the Ottoman Empire resulted in the ingathering of materials from medieval Ashkenaz and Sepharad, the mysticism of Safed, the flowering of early Yiddish literature in Poland and Amsterdam, and the humanist reference materials of Christian Hebraists. All contributed to the growth of a protean Jewish "national library," a complete collection of material on every facet of Jewish intellectual and cultural life.

But on the other hand, as both Zunz and Duschinsky noted, the collection had a more regional, even local flavor to it. It was undoubtedly not strictly a Jewish library, but first a library of Ashkenaz, and at times an

Ashkenazic library with a particular inflection toward Worms, with augmentation from Prague (as well as Amsterdam's Yiddish presses). As Oppenheim's preference for Ashkenazic handwriting demonstrated, he was an Ashkenazic Jew in both medium and message. And yet in the process of working as a collector, he reshaped and reformed the Ashkenazic canon of biblical and Talmudic commentators, weaving lost Sephardic commentaries into a common Jewish diet of medieval legacies.

In some ways, Oppenheim's assemblage of Jewish books paralleled an activity happening in the courts and academies of Western and Central Europe: the emergence of national libraries. As later eighteenth- and nineteenth-century activists recognized, a library might be an important element not necessarily of reflecting a nation, but of making one. In Oppenheim's combination of collecting and power, his books represented aspects of this theme on a smaller, premodern scale. This "man whose greatest delight is in books" tapped into a Jewish mode of doing politics, across borders and bodies of water, and intertwined those politics with culture and personality. Perhaps intentionally, perhaps not, Oppenheim created a monument to Jewish life in Europe throughout the ages, a monument of a Jewish past of diverse languages, subjects, and themes, of men and women and of Jews and Christians. The movement of his books followed the flows of power and influence to which he was uniquely privileged, and he in turn used those books to shape the legal, procedural, and personal elements of the workings of premodern Jewish communal life in Central Europe.

Abbreviations

CAHJP	Central Archives for the History of the Jewish People
EH	Even ha-ezer
HM	Hoshen mishpat
JMP	Jewish Museum in Prague
Ms. Mich.	Manuscripts of the Michael collection, held by the Bodleian Libraries
Ms. Opp.	Manuscripts of the Oppenheim collection, held by the Bodleian Libraries
NA	Národni archiv (National Archives, Czech Republic), Prague
NLI	National Library of Israel
NM	Národni Muzeum
OH	Orah hayyim
Opp.	Printed books of the Oppenheim collection, held by the Bodleian Libraries
YD	Yore de'ah

Notes

A methodological underpinning of this book is the contention that the personalizing inscriptions, bindings, and pasting of ephemera by Oppenheim into his printed books offer important "archival" material for a reconstruction of his life and times. In effect, this requires a treatment of individual copies of books as unique items without replica or parallels—a collapsing of the distinction between books and manuscripts.

Therefore, whenever I have used a printed book in the collection *not* for its printed content but for the unique marginalia or other personalized data, I have given the particular shelf mark of the book—much as one would for a manuscript—and only thereafter given the publication information, which often is not relevant. I have placed the shelf mark number before the bibliographic reference itself in order to convey to the reader the sense of the uniqueness of the material artifact. In the bibliography, I itemize these items according to their shelf marks, which represent the specific material copy of the book, not the idealized expression of the work, and which can be consulted only in the Bodleian Library. For the ease of the reader, I have also given the title and publication information.

In cases where evidence is drawn from the *printed* content of a book, however, I have refrained from giving the shelf mark in order to maintain the convention by which this evidence might be consulted in any available copy of the printed matter—whether physical or digital. In the bibliography, I itemize these items according to the more familiar model of author, title, and publication information.

Readers familiar with the manuscripts of the Oppenheim collection may have grown accustomed to referencing the material according to the numbers assigned by Adolf Neubauer in his indispensable reference *Catalogue of the Hebrew Manuscripts in the Bodleian Library and in the College Libraries of Oxford* (Oxford: Clarendon, 1886). Neubauer's numbers describe entries in a catalogue but do not correspond to the books themselves. I have therefore chosen to give the "Opp." numbers rather than the "Neu." numbers for two reasons: first, since this book is about Oppenheim and the historical use of these books, I found it fitting to link the items to his name rather than to Neubauer's. But more significantly, I adopted this practice because a visitor to the Bodleian Library who wishes to consult books from Oppenheim's collection must use the "Opp." shelf marks, not Neubauer's catalogue numbers, in ordering books. Nonetheless, for both convenience and concordance, I have provided the corresponding Neubauer numbers ("Neu.") in the bibliography so that readers may consult Neubauer's work and Malachie Beit-Arié's instructive supplement to his catalogue.

Hebrew titles have been transliterated following the guidelines of the *AJS Review*, capitalizing on the first word of a title and proper nouns. Diacritical marks have largely been excluded, unless necessary to avoid confusion.

In making use of Oppenheim's responsa, I have provided references to the printed edition prepared by Isaac Dov Feld (Oppenheim, *She'elot ve-teshuvot Nish'al David*), so that readers interested in consulting these sources may do so with greater ease than a return to the original manuscripts.

Introduction

1. Ascertaining the precise numbers of the collection's holding is something of a challenge. The conventional enumeration of 7,000 books and 1,000 manuscripts originated with the reportage of Johann Christoph Wolff in his *Bibliotheca Hebrea*, vol. 1 (Hamburg, 1715): 290. A figure approximating 4,500 printed books is more accurate, and although the Bodleian has 782 volumes of manuscripts, the presence of multiple items in single bindings makes the estimate of 1,000 a more realistic figure. For a breakdown of the figures according to size, see Zunz, *Zur Geschichte und Literatur*, 235.
2. Israel, *European Jewry in the Age of Mercantilism*, 123–144.
3. Stern, *The Court Jew*, 15–37. A foundational study of Samuel Oppenheimer remains Grunwald, *Samuel Oppenheimer*.
4. Lieben, "David Oppenheim," 20–21. The Oppenheim family was extraordinary but not unique in this pattern of strategic marriage alliances. Glikl of Hameln, the famed Jewish female memoirist, was a relative of Leffman Behrens of Hanover as well through her husband's sister, and no fewer than three of her children were married to Court Jews: her daughter Zipporah was married to Elias Gomperz of Cleves (Court Jew in Brandenburg), her son Zanwil married a niece of Samson Wertheimer's, and her son Moses married the daughter of the Court Factor in Bayreuth. Davis, "Riches and Dangers," 49.
5. For writings on Oppenheim's biography, see Löwenstein, "David Oppenheim"; Freudenthal, "David Oppenheim"; Duschinsky, *Toldot ha-ga'on rav David Openhaymer;* Lieben, "David Oppenheim"; Duschinsky, "Rabbi David Oppenheimer"; and Teplitsky, "Between Court Jew and Jewish Court."
6. Benjamin, "Unpacking My Library," 60.

7. See, for example, Findlen, *Possessing Nature.* The literature on early modern collecting is vast. For further examples of inquiries into its theory and practice, see Pomian, *Collectors and Curiosities;* Pearce, *On Collecting;* and Swann, *Curiosities and Texts.*

8. Naudé, *Advice on Establishing a Library,* 6.

9. See Pearce, *On Collecting,* 109–121.

10. "Objectivity" as a scientific notion preserves the linguistic register of knowledge inhering in objects as a material, object-based experience. Cook, *Matters of Exchange,* 13–33; Smith, *The Business of Alchemy.*

11. See also Benedict, *Curiosity.*

12. Gordan, *Two Renaissance Book Hunters;* Jardine, *Worldly Goods.* On the blurred boundaries, both conceptual and spatial, between collections of artifacts and documents, see Clark, "On the Bureaucratic Plots of the Research Library," 190.

13. One outstanding example of scholarship's relation to politics and the exercise of power is Peter N. Miller, *Peiresc's Europe.*

14. For some examples, see Evans, *The Making of the Habsburg Monarchy,* 312–318; Hochner, "Reshitah shel ha-sifriyah ha-malkhutit be-Tsarfat"; and Raines, "Tafkidam shel ha-sifriyot ve-ha-archiyonim ha-pratiyim be-hinukham ha-foliti shel ha-patrikim ha-Venezianim".

15. Bepler, "Vicissitudo Temporum," 955–956; Brady, *German Histories in the Age of Reformations,* 378.

16. Blair, "Reading Strategies"; Pollmann, "Archiving the Present and Chronicling for the Future."

17. Israel, *Radical Enlightenment,* 119–127; Evans, *The Making of the Habsburg Monarchy,* 312–318.

18. On patronage as an essential ingredient in scholarship, see Biagioli, *Galileo, Courtier.*

19. Biale, *Power and Powerlessness in Jewish History,* 47–53.

20. For a social history of pious practices in medieval Ashkenazic Jewry that reaches beyond textual prescription, see Baumgarten, *Practicing Piety in Medieval Ashkenaz.*

21. See Boyarin, *Unheroic Conduct.*

22. See Soloveitchik, "Religious Law and Change"; and Fram, *Ideals Face Reality.* The sources for such constructions of authority are, by and large, products of rabbinic writers themselves and therefore are to be taken with a measure of skepticism. It was not an accident, however, that even records of communal statutes, those literary products that bore a lighter touch of rabbinic authorship, were often organized by placing the establishment of study houses and

the provision of scholars among their first regulations. See, for example, the communal records of Worms collected in Litt, ed., *Jüdische Gemeindestatuten*. See also the statutes of Moravian Jewry in Halpern, *Takkanot medinat Mehrin*. See also Breuer, "Makom ha-yeshiva be-ma'arakh ha-irgun he-atzmi ha-Yehudi."

23. On the distinction between power and authority, see Arendt, *On Violence*, 44–45.

24. Voit, "Ornamentation of Prague Hebrew Books," 123–151; Veselá, "Hebrew Typography at Non-Jewish Bohemian Printing Houses," 165–175.

25. See, for example, Heller, "Earliest Printings of the Talmud"; and David Stern, "The Rabbinic Bible."

26. Opp. Fol. 1305: Avicenna, *Canon* (1491).

27. Opp. 4° 1422 (1): *Kenig Artur's Hof* (Prague, ca. 1652–1659?).

28. Opp. Fol. 1347: Buxtorfi, *Concordantiae Bibliorum Hebraicae* (Basel, 1632); Opp. Fol. 1159: Aquinas, *Ma'arikh ha-ma'arakhot* (Paris, 1629).

29. Opp. 8° 1159: *Vara de Iuda* (Amsterdam, 1640). For Morteira, see Opp. 4° 1102 (1): Morteira, *Sermaô funeral* (Amsterdam, 1652). For Oliveyra, see Opp. 4° 320: *Sermoes Que Pragaraō* (Amsterdam, 1675) and Opp. 8° 324 (4): *Ilan she-anafav merubin* (Amsterdam, 1665).

30. Opp. 8° 969 (1): Judah b. Samuel ha-Levi, *Mi kamoha* (Mantua, 1557); Opp. 8° 969 (2): *Shir naeh le-simhat Purim* (Mantua, 1619); Opp. 8° 1025 (4): *Yezamru be-se'udat Purim* (Mantua, 1700). For a London text, see Opp. 4° 612: Johanan b. Isaac, *Ma'ase rav po K"K London* (Amsterdam, 1707).

31. Appadurai, "Commodities and the Politics of Value," 5 (emphasis in original). See also Brown, "Thing Theory"; Siebenhüner, "Things That Matter"; and Füssel, "Die Materialität der Frühen Neuzeit."

32. For important studies of Jewish communal and political history based on documents of this nature, see, for example, Baron, *The Jewish Community;* and Baer, *A History of the Jews in Christian Spain*. See also the more recent material surveyed in Bell, *Jews in the Early Modern World*, 93–141. Records produced by non-Jewish institutions are vitally important for our understanding of Jewish communal and cultural life as well and will be given due consideration throughout the book.

33. Studies of political culture are indebted to innovative histories of the French Revolution. See, for example, Hunt, *Politics, Culture, and Class;* Baker, *The French Revolution;* Schorsch, "On the Political Judgement of the Jew"; Yerushalmi, *The Lisbon Massacre;* Yerushalmi, *"Servants of Kings";* and Biale, *Power and Powerlessness*.

34. For similar theorization of the practical, rather than the theoretical, see

Crowston, *Credit, Fashion, Sex,* 15–18. Crowston bases her theory on the work of Pierre Bourdieu (*Outline of a Theory of Practice* and *The Logic of Practice*) and Michel de Certeau (*The Practice of Everyday Life*).

35. Whaley, *Germany and the Holy Roman Empire,* 6–8. On the relationship between war and finance, see also Parker, *The Military Revolution;* Black, *Beyond the Military Revolution;* and Parrott, *The Business of War.*

36. On the economic crisis even outside of war spending, as well as the new state that arose from the ashes, see Wilson, *Europe's Tragedy,* 795–812.

37. An emergent science of government, *Kameralwissenschaft,* recognized an uncanny ability on the part of Jews to marshal funds and other resources, and they operated as a party at court in favor of soliciting Jewish agents. Gömmel, "Hofjuden und Wirtschaft im Merkantilismus," 59–65; Battenberg, "Die Jüdische Wirtschaftselite."

38. Höbelt, "The Westphalian Peace"; Wilson, "Still a Monstrosity?," 573–576.

39. Whaley, *Germany and the Holy Roman Empire,* 280–281.

40. Battenberg, "Die Jüdische Wirtschaftselite."

41. Israel, *European Jewry in the Age of Mercantilism,* 101.

42. See, for example, the efforts of Samson Wertheimer to block the publication of an anti-Jewish book, or that of Leffman Behrens to sponsor a Jewish spokesman in a disputation. Wolf, "Der Prozeß Eisenmenger"; Friedrich, *Zwischen Abwehr und Bekehrung,* 173–174.

43. Whereas Jacob Katz (*Tradition and Crisis,* 90–91) asserted the essentially democratic character of the administration of Jewish communities, arguing that "change of personnel prevented individuals from monopolizing offices and turning them into permanent sources of income or bases of power," the historical evidence appears to indicate otherwise. For an instance of oligarchicization in Frankfurt, see Halpern, "Mahloket 'al breirat ha-kahal be-Frankfurt de-Main ve-hedeha be-Folin u-ve-Bihem"; and Wolf, "Zur Geschichte des Jüdischen Gemeinwesens in Prag."

44. According to Mack Walker (*German Home Towns,* 56), a system obtained in German towns in which they were dominated by "a regime not of oligarchs but of communarchs, a regime of uncles," who sustained but also held sway over the conduct of these communities.

45. On the Polish case, see, for example, Ury, "The 'Shtadlan' of the Polish-Lithuanian Commonwealth." For discussions of different political circumstances and political representatives between Central and Eastern Europe, see Hundert, "Was There an East European Analogue to Court Jews?"; and Teller, "Telling the Difference."

46. On the expulsion of Jews from Vienna in 1670, see Kaufmann, *Die Letzte*

Vertreibung der Juden aus Wien. See also Spielman, *The City and the Crown,* 123–135; and Cerman, "Anti-Jewish Superstitions."

47. For an analysis of the impact of this book once published, see Carlebach, *Divided Souls,* 212–221.

48. Stadthagen and Berliner, *Religionsgespräch Gehalten am Kurfürstlichen Hofe.* On this disputation, see Friedrich, *Zwischen Abwehr und Bekehrung,* 173–174. Although the age of high disputations was over, Jews continued to produce polemical literature in response to Christian provocation. See, for example, *Judscher Tiryak,* which was published in three editions: Hanau, 1615 (Opp. 4° 886); Altdorf, 1680 (Opp. 4° 868); and Amsterdam, 1737 (Opp. 8° 406).

49. Cohen, "Creating an Elite Norm of Behaviour," 148–150.

50. Watanabe-O'Kelly, "Literature and the Court."

51. Shapin, *A Social History of Truth;* Johns, *The Nature of the Book.*

52. Biagioli, "Galileo's System of Patronage."

53. A play on Gen 37:25.

54. Mishnah Tractate *Avot* 1:4.

55. Ms. Mich. 479, f. 26r. Oppenheim, *Nish'al David,* vol. 2, §HM, no. 9. For similar statements by others that lack the personal injury, see Ms. Mich. 466, f. 41r (Letter of Aharon Shmuel, new appointee in Frankfurt).

56. On collecting as identity formation, see Findlen, *Possessing Nature,* 291, 294. On self-fashioning in the early modern period more generally, see Natalie Davis, *The Return of Martin Guerre;* and Stephen Greenblatt, *Renaissance Self-Fashioning.* On the entanglements of objects and identity, see Parkin, "Mementoes as Transitional Objects."

Chapter 1. Creating a Collector

1. Marx, "Some Jewish Book Collectors," 214–215. For some considerations on the meaning of the category "Jewish book," see Dweck, "What Is a Jewish Book?" For the purposes of this study, a "Jewish" book is understood in the broadest possible definition, inclusive of any work printed in Hebrew characters (including in non-Hebrew languages such as Yiddish or Ladino) as well as in other European languages if their contents pertain to Judaic material, even if they are produced by Christian scholars with aims that might be considered at odds with or even hostile to Jewish orthodoxies.

2. Ms. Opp. 699: Oppenheim catalogue (ca. 1685), ff. 63–89.

3. Naudé, *Advice on Establishing a Library,* 52.

4. On evidence of origins, see Chazan, *The Jews of Medieval Western Christendom,* 171–174; and Roemer, *German City, Jewish Memory,* 11–12.

5. Juspe Schammes, *Mayse nissim* (Amsterdam, 1696): §1. On the *Mayse nissim,* see Baumgarten and Frakes, *Introduction to Old Yiddish Literature,* 316–317. This myth was current among seventeenth-century Jews as well as Christian Hebraists. For a version of the myth of the antiquity of the Jewish community in Worms (and Regensburg) in a Christian Hebraist source, see Wagenseil, *Belehrung der jüdisch-teutschen Red- und Schreibart,* A3r. This myth of antiquity neatly captures the tensions of a Jewish feeling of being at home in the city alongside an awareness of the periodic persecutions that were characteristic of medieval Jewish life. Like Virgil's Aeneas, who established Rome as a refugee from Troy, genealogy produced a sense of stability, continuity, and even cultural superiority by anchoring the living community in the mists of antiquity. The literature on genealogy, historiography, and medieval and early modern memory is vast. For some theoretical approaches, see Spiegel, *The Past as Text;* and Yerushalmi, *Zakhor, Jewish History and Jewish Memory,* 31–52. See also Vehlow, *Abraham Ibn Daud's Dorot 'Olam.*

6. Nils Roemer (*German City, Jewish Memory,* 15) has argued for a "distinct culture of remembrance in Worms that recalled Jewish unity in the face of danger and the unwavering piety of the community." Their legalists occasionally asserted their laws and customs as standing on firmer grounds than their younger counterparts in Poland-Lithuania. Berkovitz, "Crisis and Authority in Early Modern Ashkenaz."

7. Transier, "Die Schum-Gemeinden."

8. For the expulsions and new settlement arrangements of the sixteenth century, see Israel, *European Jewry in the Age of Mercantilism,* 6–13; Benjamin J. Kaplan, *Divided by Faith,* 28–34; and Debra Kaplan, *Beyond Expulsion.*

9. On the complex of legal jurisdictions claiming authority over the city, see Fritz Reuter, "Mehrkonfessionalität in der Freien Stadt Worms," 10–13.

10. Ibid., 30.

11. Fritz Reuter, *Warmaisa,* 216–217; Ursula Reuter, "Die Wormser Judengasse."

12. Ursula Reuter, "Die Wormser Judengasse," 232–236.

13. The regulation also stipulated a fine to the Jewish participant in the conversation, which would be used to fund synagogue lighting. Litt, ed., *Jüdische Gemeindestatuten,* 90 (item 27). On ghetto life in Worms, see Raspe, "Die Lebensbedingungen des Ghettos."

14. Juspe Schammes, *Mayse nissim,* §20, p. 29r. Also cited in Ursula Reuter, "Die Wormser Judengasse."

15. Grunwald, *Samuel Oppenheimer,* 36–37; Eidelberg, ed., *R. Yuzpa Shamash di-kehilat Vermaisa,* 100 (Hebrew section). For the daughters, see Berliner, "Sefer hazakarat neshamot kehillat Vermaiza," 18–19.

16. The *Wormser Memorbuch* contains barely a page without mention of a member of the family and the family's contributions to the community. For a fuller discussion of the genre of *Memorbücher,* see Bell, *Jewish Identity in Early Modern Germany,* 72–76. Note especially pp. 75–76, in which Bell argues that *Memorbücher* often memorialized those who were not directly from or buried in the locality of the text, thereby pointing to a larger regional association and identity for German Jewry beyond its narrower communal boundaries.

17. Eidelberg, *R. Yuzpa Shamash di-kehilat Vermaisa,* 120.

18. Inscription on end flyleaf of Opp. 8° 1137: Solomon ibn Verga, *Shevet Yehuda* (Amsterdam, 1655).

19. Berliner, "Sefer hazakarat neshamot kehillat Vermaiza," 21.

20. On Jewish life in Worms and the Oppenheim family there, see Berliner, *Wormser Memorbuch,* esp. 21. See also Fritz Reuter, *Warmaisa;* and Roemer, *German City, Jewish Memory.*

21. Lieben, "David Oppenheim," 3.

22. Berliner, "Sefer hazakarat neshamot kehillat Vermaiza," 19–20.

23. Traces of evidence about Oppenheim's nuclear family can be gleaned from inscriptions in his collection, but his familial energies appear to have been directed toward a wider network of kin. For limited information about his sisters, see Berliner, "Sefer hazakarat neshamot kehillat Vermaiza," 21–23. While his brother, Simon Wolff, is largely absent from Oppenheim's personal archive, some correspondence exists between him and Oppenheim's son Joseph in Ms. Opp. 702 f. 68r. See also Mann, Cohen, and Backhaus, eds., *From Court Jews to the Rothschilds,* 166.

24. Medieval Ashkenazic Jews began their children's schooling around this age, somewhere between three and six years old. Marcus, *Rituals of Childhood,* 1, n. 1. Oppenheim's contemporary, Pinhas Katzenellinbogen, who would later become head of the Boskowice Jewish court, was "delayed" in beginning his studies on account of illness and did not begin until somewhere between four and a half and five and a half years of age. It thus stands to reason that generally Jewish boys began their educations before this age. Katzenellinbogen, *Sefer yesh manhilin,* ch. 59. Oppenheim's own tribute to his parents and their impact on his childhood education appear in his introduction to the unpublished *Tehillah le-David* (Ms. Mich. 447).

25. On Bachrach and the circumstances of his career, see Kaufmann, "Jair Chayim Bacharach," 303; Twersky, "Law and Spirituality in the Seventeenth Century"; and Berkovitz, "Dyukono he-azmi."

26. For Bachrach's curricular program of study, see Yair Hayyim Bachrach, *Havot Yair,* no. 123.

27. Ibid., no. 152.

28. Ms. Mich. 466, 156r.

29. For example, Bachrach had a warm relationship with Oppenheim's teacher in Metz, Gerson Ulif Ashkenazi, prompting correspondence, occasional visits, moments of refuge, and a funeral oration for the Metz rabbi upon his death in 1693. The latter paid a visit to Bachrach in 1679. It was to Ashkenazi in Metz that Bachrach and his family fled following the destruction of Worms in 1689, and the two maintained a correspondence beyond moments of tragedy as well. Kaufmann, "Jair Chayim Bacharach," 493, 500–519; Berkovitz, "Dyukono he-azmi," 45.

30. He served in Prossnitz, Hanau, Nikolsburg, and Vienna. In 1670, he was expelled from Vienna alongside all of its other Jewish residents. From there he made his way to Metz, where he was elected to the rabbinate in 1670 to succeed R. Yonah Teomim Fränkel and where he remained until his death in 1693. Cahen, "Le Rabbinat de Metz," 8: 1255.

31. See Ms. Mich. 466, f. 7r. See also Oppenheim's responsum to the Jews of Lundenburg, who uncovered human remains while renovating their synagogue, and Oppenheim's citation of Ashkenazi's ruling to ask forgiveness of the dead for disturbing their eternal rest. Oppenheim, *Nish'al David*, vol. 1, §YD, no. 27.

32. Lieben, "David Oppenheim," 4; Löwenstein, "David Oppenheim," 539.

33. Ms. Opp. 699, f. 78r.

34. Leibetseder, "Across Europe." See also Walker, *German Home Towns*, 128–133.

35. Goldgar, *Impolite Learning*, 1–2; Grafton, "A Sketch Map of a Lost Continent," 6.

36. Shmeruk, "Bahurim mi-Ashkenaz be-yeshivot Polin."

37. For a lively debate on the standardization and fixity of the printed book, see Eisenstein, *The Printing Revolution in Early Modern Europe;* Johns, *The Nature of the Book;* See also the exchange in Eisenstein, "An Unacknowledged Revolution Revisited"; Johns, "How to Acknowledge a Revolution"; and Eisenstein, "Reply."

38. Jackson, *Marginalia*. On the role of the buyer in shaping the material conditions of the book, see Knight, *Bound to Read*.

39. Inscription on flyleaf of Opp. 8° 473: Moses b. Yakar Ashkenazi, *Sefer petah einayim* (Amsterdam, 1664); poems and other creative inscriptions of this sort abound from prior owners whose books ultimately ended up on Oppenheim's shelves. For limited further examples, see Opp. 4° 1018: *Ot emet* (Salonika, 1565), which carries a poem on it about the little person who, despite

his unimportance, still wants his books returned; Opp. Fol. 834: *Mordekhai* (Riva di Trento, 1558), in which an owner similarly comments on the merits of asserting possession; ironically, the name of that owner was effaced by later possessors. There was also a defensive posture to inscribing a name: Opp. 4° 219: *Devek tov* (Venice, 1588) carries a similar note about warding off accusations of theft.

40. For example, the admonition by the medieval *Sefer Hasidim* against writing "calculations" or testing ink in books. See Freehof, "Some Autographs on Title Pages," 108.

41. For a fifteenth-century articulation of the overlapping of ownership and intellectual mastery, see Isaac Canpanton, as cited in Bar-Levav, "Bein toda'at ha-sifriyah le-republika ha-sifrutit ha-Yehudit," 203–204. For similar impulses in Michel de Montaigne, see Nelles, "Stocking a Library," 4.

42. Inscription at end of Ms. Opp. 246: Commentary on Avot; other examples can be found in Ms. Mich. 181 at the end of which the owner, a young man, repeatedly wrote his name (Leib Poppers) and recorded that he had studied in a yeshiva that had *semikha,* that which is patronized by Wolf Wertheim, led by Moses, chief rabbi of Darmstadt; see also the multiple owners' signatures of a volume of Opp. Fol. 858: *Alfasi* (Krakow, 1597). A further example with no relationship to immediate "practical" knowledge may be found in Opp. 4° 49: *Hamishah humshe Torah* (Amsterdam, 1680), in which the student writes, "I have studied from this intensively and with logic."

43. Wedeles, *Sefer Elia rabbah,* §133:5. See, for example, the appearance of the phrase in the blank pages of Opp. 4° 248, Opp. 8° 619, and numerous others.

44. Inscription at end of Opp. 4° 605 (1): *Sefer tikkunei zevah* (Prague, 1604). See also Ms. Opp. 156 and the discussion in *Shulhan arukh,* §YD 1:1–2, regarding certification and Fram, *My Dear Daughter,* 20, n. 84.

45. See Opp. 4° 541: Jacob Weil, *Shehitot u-vedikot* (Krakow, 1577); Opp. 4° 544: Jacob Weil, *Shehitot u-vedikot* (Basel, 1602).

46. Rohden, ed., *Meneket Rivkah,* 169. Rebecca paraphrased and modified the Talmud's suggestion, which reads "one writes [i.e., copies out] Scripture and lends it to others" with a more expansive *purchase* of various books, not limited to Scripture alone.

47. See Opp. Fol. 1174 (2): Elijah Levita, *Meturgeman* (Isny, 1541).

48. On the expense of paper, see Febvre and Martin, *The Coming of the Book,* 112–115. On German paper markets, see Schmidt, "Die Internationale Papierversorgung der Buchproduktion."

49. For examples of family birthdates, see Ms. Opp. 78, f. 203v; Ms. Opp. 156; Ms. Opp. 200, f. 260v; Ms. Opp. 231; Ms. Opp. 238; Ms. Opp. 338, f. 160; Ms. Opp. 643; Ms. Opp. 648; Ms. Opp. 650; Ms. Opp. 665; and Ms. Opp. 775.

50. Opp. 4° 1342: f. 36r, *Midrash be-hiddush perush le-haggadat Pesah* (Venice, 1641). On the phenomenon of "private Purims," especially in the Bohemian lands, see Rachel L. Greenblatt, *To Tell Their Children.*

51. Opp. 8° 1137, *Shevet Yehuda.* This book had only recently come into his care, as the inscription inside its cover gives its owner as a Samuel in Hanover, who left his mark on the book on September 10, 1687, only two years before the destruction of Worms.

52. Cser, "Zwischen Stadtverfassung und Absolutistischen," 62–65. For a contemporary description of the destruction of the city and the fate of its Jews, see Juspe Schammes, *Mayse nissim,* §25. Later still, Oppenheim preserved a broadside that memorialized the recently destroyed Jewish quarter. See Opp. 4° 959: Eliezer Lieberman b. Juspe Schammes, Broadside (Amsterdam, 1692).

53. On the dissonance between the modern concept of the individuated title and the early modern composite volume, see Knight, "Fast Bind, Fast Find." The question of binding in the Oppenheim collection is a difficult one. Some compiled volumes were bound by earlier owners, but there is evidence that in some cases the binding had to have happened after Oppenheim had purchased the books. Such appears to be the case for Opp. 4° 468, which includes items published after the time of sale from the earliest owner. Compare with the titles listed in Ms. Opp. 699, 77v.

54. Clark, "On the Bureaucratic Plots of the Research Library," 192.

55. Opp. 8° 930: *Iggeret ha-Ramban* (Amsterdam, 1652). For other similar book lists within books, see Ms. Opp. 214, Ms. Opp. 42, and Ms. Mich. 541.

56. Ms. Opp. 699. On the inclusion of calendrical calculation in the early modern Jewish curriculum, see Carlebach, *Palaces of Time,* 76. Chronology was a "hot field in its day" according to Grafton, "A Sketch Map of a Lost Continent," 14. Oppenheim maintained this awareness of chronology throughout his career: a sermon on the Passover Haggadah involves an excursus on the calendrical calculation of the dates of the Exodus. See Oppenheim, "Drush al Hagadah Shel Pesah."

57. See, for example, items in Oppenheim's manuscript collection that are based on printed items: Ms. Opp. 334: "Notes on Maimonides' book of commandments." Malachi Beit-Arie has suggested that at least half of all medieval manuscripts were copied by their owners. Fram, *My Dear Daughter,* 9, n. 27. A different Prague Jew, Elazar Altschul, followed a similar path a century earlier, as noted by Elhanan Reiner ("A Biography of an Agent of Culture," 238–239), whose study has suggested that Altschul's later career in publishing ought to be understood as a direct "sequel" to his youthful activities as a copyist, and that we might see a natural connection between activities in the

world of books to a yeshiva education in copying and collecting. For analogous activity of commonplacing in other disciplines, see Blair, *Too Much to Know.*

58. The word *kiton* appears in rabbinic contexts with the meaning "ladle" or "pitcher." I have given the meaning here as "vessel" under the assumption that the poetic meaning Oppenheim intended was about the proper sorting of the books.

59. Ms. Opp. 699, f. 63r.

60. Years later, the Sephardic scholar Hayyim David Azulai characterized Oppenheim as one who weaves great allusive chains from the language of the Talmud. See Azulai, *Shem ha-Gedolim,* vol. 1, 17v.

61. Jewish commentators tended to adopt the Talmudic exegesis of the text as instructive of the relationship between oral law (the words of the sages) and the written law of the Pentateuch. See also Blair, *Too Much to Know,* 15–16.

62. Oppenheim was not the only rabbi to play with this phrase, which was often used as fodder for various sides of a polemic over the place of print in rabbinic culture. See the discussion in Chapter 4.

63. Chartier, *The Order of Books;* Blair, *Too Much to Know,* 160–166; Nelles, "The Library as an Agent of Discovery," 42.

64. Shabbetai b. Yosef Bass, *Siftei yeshenim.* (Oppenheim's two copies: Opp. 4° 758 and Opp. 4° 759; for his acquisition of Bass's bibliography in 1689, see Ms. Opp. 699, 78r.) On this book, see Bar-Levav, "The Religious Order of Jewish Books," 1–27.

65. Bar-Levav, "Ha-merhav ha-kadosh shel moledet ha-mitaltelet." For other senses of comprehensive library awareness in the second half of the seventeenth century, see Schotte, "'Books for the Use of the Learned and Studious.'" On the tension between the quest for comprehensiveness and the reality of incompletion in libraries and book collections, see the essays collected in Crawford, ed., *The Meaning of the Library.*

66. Naudé, *Advice on Establishing a Library,* 11–12.

67. Opp. 4° 792: *Hesed le-Avraham* (Sulzbach, 1685); *Sefer Hasidim* (Sulzbach, 1685); *Ta'anugei shabbat* (Sulzbach, 1685); *Davar she-bi-kedusha* (Sulzbach, 1685); *Zera Avraham* (Sulzbach, 1685).

68. Ms. Opp. 699, f. 79r.

69. Ibid., f. 79v.

70. Naudé (*Advice on Establishing a Library,* 32) similarly instructed his audience to make concessions to the particular popularity of local vogue. See also Raspe, "Die Schum-Gemeinden in der Narrativen Überlieferung," 322–323.

71. Ms. Opp. 186: Pentateuch and Megillat Esther; manuscript copies of the bib-

lical prophetic books, Ms. Opp. 1 and Ms. Opp. 2, both similarly date their scribal provenance to the sixteenth century in Worms.

72. On the Rhineland Pietists, see Ms. Opp. 340: "Sefer Hasidut," possibly the oldest edition of "Sefer Hasidim I"; Ms. Opp. 467; Ms. Opp. 506; Ms. Opp. 614; and Ms. Opp. 667: *Selihot* and *tekhinot* from Sefer Hasidim. See also Ivan G. Marcus, "The Recensions and Structure of 'Sefer Hasidim,'" 131–153; and Soloveitchik, "Piety, Pietism and German Pietism." See also Ms. Opp. 111, Ms. Opp. 540, and Dan, *Iyunim be-sifrut Hasidei Ashkenaz.*

73. For a book in Loans's own hand, see Ms. Opp. 199: Loans's commentary on Bereshit Rabba.

74. Ms. Opp. 175: "*Selihot* according to the custom of Worms"; Ms. Opp. 680: "Verses recited before *selihot*"; Ms. Opp. 674: *Yotzrot Worms.* Prayer books, Mahzors, and other liturgical texts represent a significant part of the collection.

75. Ms. Opp. 750–751.

76. Ms. Opp. 355: Commentary of Shmuel Bachrach of Worms.

77. Ms. Opp. 716.

78. Ms. Opp. 715.

79. Ms. Opp. 711: Yom Tov Lippman Heller, "Megillat Eivah."

80. Ms. Opp. 716: "Pinkas shel Kahal Worms mi-mahzor R"T," which lists the martyrs of Worms and Budapest, 1687.

81. This was a common practice. Oppenheim's near contemporary, Pinhas Katzenellinbogen, made a gift of more than sixty books to his son on the occasion of his marriage. Katzenellinbogen, *Sefer yesh manhilin,* 41–42.

82. Lieben, "David Oppenheim," 4.

83. Behrens provided such services to other German nobles as well: in 1701, he was involved in the successful attainment of the Prussian crown for Frederick I. See Breuer, "Part 1," 108–109. For a full study of Behrens, see Schedlitz, *Leffmann Behrens.*

84. Selma Stern, *The Court Jew,* 28.

85. On marriage practices, see Sabean, "Kinship and Prohibited Marriages." See also Duhamelle, "The Making of Stability."

86. For only a limited survey of the expansive historical and anthropological literature on the gift, see Mauss and Halls, *The Gift.* See also Sykes, *Arguing with Anthropology;* and Godelier, *The Enigma of the Gift.* For a historiographical study of the gift in European thought, see Liebersohn, *The Return of the Gift;* and Godelier, *Enigma of the Gift,* 12. See also Natalie Zemon Davis, *The Gift in Sixteenth-Century France;* Algazi, Groebner, and Jussen, *Negotiating the Gift;* Heal, *The Power of Gifts;* Graeber, *Debt;* Ilana Krausman Ben-Amos, *The*

Culture of Giving; Offer, "Between the Gift and the Market"; and Crowston, *Credit, Fashion, Sex.*

87. Ms. Opp. 699 79r–79v. This may have been the Humash with *Siftei hakhamim* (Amsterdam, 1680) listed in the alphabetical portion of the catalogue.

88. Isaac of Duren b. Meir, *Sha'arei dura;* Elijah Loans b. Moses, *Rinat dudim;* Ms. Opp. 699, f. 79r.

89. Ms. Opp. 699, f. 77r–77v. See also the inscription on the title page of Opp. 4° 643 in which the owner records the purchase of the book from a widow in Freising.

90. Turniansky, ed., *Glikl: Zikhronot,* 52–53.

91. *Pinkas* Worms, col. 39. Reproduced in Eidelberg, *R. Yuzpa Shamash di-kehilat Vermaisa,* 126.

92. Ms. Mich. 465, 146r–147v.

93. See Katzenellinbogen, *Sefer yesh manhilin,* 53. For a comparable scenario, see the will of David Todros Kozuchowski, 1647, who bequeathed all of his possessions to his widow "except she has no share in my books" (57).

94. Natalie Zemon Davis (*The Gift in Sixteenth-Century France,* 45) has even suggested that in the early modern world a belief prevailed that "property in a book was as much collective as private and that God himself had some special rights in that object." For another instance of disputed inheritance, and an appeal to Oppenheim to resolve a question of how to divide up multiple editions and volumes of the *Arba Turim,* see Oppenheim, *Nish'al David,* vol. 2, §HM, no. 13. See a similar case of inheritance between a stepson and a grandson when a dying man specified merely "son" in Rzeszów, *Shvut Yaakov,* vol. 1, no. 169.

95. Opp. Fol. 265: Moses b. Nahman Gerondi, *Biur al ha-Torah* (Venice, 1580), inscription on title page.

96. Opp. 4° 903 (1): Don Isaac Abarbanel, *Sefer rosh amanah* (Venice, 1545).

97. Weissler, " 'For Women and for Men Who Are Like Women.' "

98. Naudé, *Advice on Establishing a Library,* 36. For the barest introduction to early modern Yiddish texts and their production, see Baumgarten and Frakes, *Introduction to Old Yiddish Literature;* Shlomo Z. Berger, "Yiddish Books in Early Modern Prague"; and Shlomo Berger, "The Oppenheim Collection." See also the important studies of Chava Turniansky listed in Rosenzweig, "Kitve Hava Turniansky"; and Dauber, *In the Demon's Bedroom.*

99. Benjamin Slonik, *Seder Mitzvot Nashim:* Krakow, 1577 (Opp. 4° 518); Basel, 1602 (Opp. 4° 517); Hanau, 1627 (Opp. 4° 519); Dessau, 1699 (Opp. 8° 292); and Frankfurt am Main, 1714 (Opp. 8° 293). See Fram, *My Dear Daughter;* and Weissler, *Voices of the Matriarchs.*

100. On salting meat, a Yiddish translation of *Torat ha-hatat:* Opp. 8° 634 (2): *Dinim ve-seder* (Venice, 1701–1702); on medical manuals, see Opp. 8° 1035: *Dimyon ha-refuot/Harmonia Wallachia Medica* (Frankfurt am Main, 1700); Opp. 8° 1036: *Yerushat Moshe* (1677); Opp. 8° 1037: *Sefer segulot ve-refuot* (Prague, 1694); and Opp. 8° 1038: *Segulot ve-refuot* (n.d.).

101. Opp. 4° 1401.

102. Ms. Opp. 19.

103. After only half a year together in Hanover (and a brief stint with the groom's family in Worms for the high holidays of 1682), Oppenheim and his wife parted so that he could resume his yeshiva study, this time in Landsberg. Oppenheim's teachers praised the dedication of this young man who "left his house to study in yeshiva, a groom from his room half a year after his wedding," and Oppenheim acknowledged his wife's patience in his own introduction to his book *Tehillah le-David* (Ms. Mich. 447). Published in Oppenheim, *Nish'al David*, vol. 3, 8–10.

104. On the Frankfurt fair, see Flood, *"Omnium Totius Orbis Emporiorum Compendium,"* 27–30.

105. Burnett, *From Christian Hebraism to Jewish Studies,* 36, 44–45.

106. Ms. Opp. 699, f. 75.

107. Oppenheim, *Nish'al David*, vol. 1, §OH, no. 19. Freudenthal, "Zum Jubiläum Des Ersten Talmuddrucks in Deutschland," 140–141. It was often at these fairs that he would make new contacts, at times to his benefit, at times to theirs. See the letter of appeal from a prospective client in NLI Ms. Heb. 4° 966, 5. See also Lehmstedt, " 'Ein Notwendiges Übel' "; and Freudenthal, *Leipziger Messegäste.*

108. Oppenheim listed all of these personal transactions in Ms. Opp. 699, 79v: Judah Leib Puchawitzer of Pinsk, *Derekh hokhmah* and *Kaneh hokhmah* (Frankfurt [Oder], 1681–1683); Moses b. Eliezer Morawchik, *Sefer be-shartei tzedek* (Amsterdam, 1686); Samuel Zoreph b. Joseph, *Metsoref la-kasef* (Frankfurt [Oder], 1681); Jacob Koppel b. Aaron Saslawer, *Nahalat Yaakov* (Sulzbach, 1686); David Gruenhut b. Nathan's notes on Hayyim Vital's *Sefer ha-gilgulim* (1684).

109. This was the case, for example, with the book *Magen David,* by David b. Solomo Avi Zimra (Radbaz). See *Magen David* (Amsterdam, 1713). For a discussion of the publication of this book, see Benayahu, "Sfarim she-hibram rabi Moshe Hagiz ve-sfarim she-hotziam le-or," esp. 154–162. See also Ms. Mich. 479, f. 15r, in which an author sends material in the hopes of receiving an approbation.

110. Ms. Opp. 699, 80r. Another item in his collection, however, reveals account-

ing for binding. In the flyleaf of Opp. Fol. 40, a previous owner has left the price breakdown of printing and binding.

111. See, for example, a number of Oppenheim's volumes that bound together printed books with manuscripts (Ms. Opp. 139, 259, 279), while others still were copies of printed books (e.g., Ms. Opp. 685).

112. Only the modern tactics of bibliography and preservation have separated the two media from each other, which has more to do with conservation than historical function. On the mingling of book and manuscript in seventeenth-century catalogues from the French Royal Library, the Bodleian, and Leiden, see McKitterick, *Print, Manuscript, and the Search for Order*, 12–13.

113. Ms. Opp. 700: *Evronot* of Zevi Hirsch Kaidenover.

114. Ms. Opp. 699, f. 79v.

115. Oppenheim, *Nish'al David*, vol. 2, §HM, no. 10.

116. Fram, *My Dear Daughter*, 8, esp. n. 24. On medieval scribal reproduction, see Gullick, "How Fast Did Scribes Write?" Oppenheim, *Nish'al David*, vol. 3, §OH, no. 3.

117. Oppenheim, *Nish'al David*, vol. 3, §OH, no. 3.

118. Ms. Opp. 289: Moses of Brussels, *Haze ha-tenufah*, copied Vienna, 1716, f. 2r.

119. Azriel was not solely in Oppenheim's employ. In 1698/1707 he copied a manuscript for Naphtali b. Uri of *Hakdamat Etz Hayyim*. See Ms. Mich. 194.

120. See Scholem, *Halomotav shel Ha-Shabtai'i R. Mordekhai Ashkenazi*; Benayahu, "Shemu'ot Shabtai'iyot"; Scholem, *Sabbatai Sevi*; Carlebach, *The Pursuit of Heresy*; and Avivi, *Kabalat he-Ari*, vol. 2, 724–746.

121. Ms. Opp. 545.

122. Azriel appears to have copied some forty manuscripts total. See Avivi, *Kabalat he-Ari*, vol. 2, 767.

123. Ms. Mich. 465, f. 253r. Oppenheim was not the only Ashkenazic Jew who had trouble with the Sephardic hand. In his travels to German lands, Hayyim David Azulai noted the difficulty with presenting letters of introduction to Ashkenazic Jews who "are not expert in the handwriting of the men of Sepharad." *Ma'agal tov*, 16. On Azulai's travels, see Lehmann, "Rabbinic Emissaries," 1238.

124. Ms. Opp. 429: *Sefer likutim*; Ms. Opp. 469: *Sefer likutim* al Tanakh; Ms. Opp. 380/381; Ms. Opp. 329/392. See also Ms. Opp. 353, a series of *hiddushim* on Gittin and Qiddushin, copied for Oppenheim from a Sephardic manuscript in 1697; and Ms. Opp. 358: Bezalel Ashkenazi on Zevahim (Prague, 1713).

125. Ms. Opp. Add. 4° 68: *Sefer Abualbar*, copied by Eliezer b. Shlomo Zalman Lipschütz. Note the shelf mark, which indicates that the book does not appear to have been a part of the Oppenheim collection at the time it was purchased

by the Bodleian Library, even though the scribal inscription specifically indicates that the work from which it was copied belonged to Oppenheim.

126. Neumark, *Shoresh David.*

127. Steinschneider, "Mathematik bei den Juden," 590.

128. Ms. Opp. 184. It is not clear whether Frankfurt was a home to only Meir or to his entire family, which would account for his father's publishing his work there when we know that he had affiliations with a print shop in Berlin.

129. This was Meir's third literary achievement. Between his first and second translations he wrote a *sefer melitzot* titled *Meir netiv* (Ms. Opp. 184). Although Neumark tells us that he translated the work from *la'az* ("a foreign tongue"), without specifying what the language of origin was, Steinschneider ("Mathematik bei den Juden," 592) doubts Neubauer's assertion that this was from German and believes instead that this refers to Latin. This is a somewhat odd conclusion, given the colophon that reads "*mi-lashon alemmania.*"

130. Ms. Opp. 708.

131. On science in Jewish circles, see Ruderman, *Jewish Thought and Scientific Discovery.* Oppenheim and his family contributed to what Shmuel Feiner (*The Jewish Enlightenment,* 39–40; 388, n. 323) and David Sorkin ("The Early Haskalah") have called "the early Haskalah" through their patronage of men like Neumark and the Hebrew grammarian Solomon Hanau (1687–1746), who worked for Oppenheim's son-in-law Michael, son of Aaron Beer, in Frankfurt am Main.

132. Perles, *Megillat sefer,* 50b. See also the discussion in Fleckeles, *Teshuva me-ahavah,* vol. 2, 47a. Oppenheim himself produced a responsum in 1704 regarding whether or not a *megillah* written by a woman was suitable for use and concluded in the affirmative, noting that the fact "that we have not seen this before is not proof [that it is prohibited]." His responsum did not make reference to his daughter's skill in this area. Oppenheim, *Nish'al David,* vol. 1, §OH, no. 20.

Chapter 2. Politics, Patronage, and Paper

1. Peter N. Miller, *Peiresc's Europe,* 8.

2. Ms. Opp. 258: "Biurei Maharan" of Nathan Spiro to *Tur Orah Hayyim,* copied by Samuel b. Moses.

3. Oppenheim's early biographers displayed some uncertainty about the dates of his arrival in Nikolsburg. Although Leopold Löwenstein ("David Oppenheim," 3) dated Oppenheim's arrival there to late summer 1689, Max Freudenthal ("David Oppenheim," 262), on the basis of our knowledge of his

meeting with Yair Hayyim Bachrach in 1690 in Frankfurt (Oppenheim, *Nish'al David*, vol. 2, §HM, no. 10), surmised that he would not have arrived in the city until 1690. Brunn, cited by Lieben ("David Oppenheim," 4–5), concurs that Oppenheim would not have come to the city before 1690, since his predecessor, R. Eliezer Fanta, died on June 9 of that year. This may not have been his first time in Nikolsburg; a responsum dated September (Tishrei) 1689 suggests that he may have paid a visit there before his appointment (Oppenheim, *Nish'al David*, vol. 2, §EH, no. 26). In 1705, Emperor Leopold recognized Oppenheim in his "rabbinic post in Nikolsburg in our Margravate of Moravia for fifteen years." See NA Ms. SM 1505 J4/23 ("Election of chief rabbi David Oppenheim").

4. Kaufmann, "Jair Chayim Bacharach," 501, n. 501.
5. Oppenheim, *Nish'al David*, vol. 1, §YD, no. 15.
6. On Jewish settlement patterns in Moravia, see Engel, "Die Ausweisung der Juden"; and Michael Laurence Miller, *Rabbis and Revolution*, 16–35. On the rural conditions of German Jewry, see Breuer, "Part 1," 191–208; and Debra Kaplan, *Beyond Expulsion*. On demographic challenges to Jewish ritual life in Bohemia, see Oppenheim, *Nish'al David*, vol. 1, §OH, no. 5.
7. Halpern, *Takkanot medinat Mehrin (410–508)*, 9; Michael Miller, *Rabbis and Revolution*, 22–23. In both the demographic circumstances of its constitution and its practices, the regional body resembled a Polish counterpart in the *Va'ad Arba Arazot* (Council of Four Lands). On the latter, see Halpern and Bartal, *Pinkas Va'ad Arba Aratsot*.
8. In 1754 the acts were translated into German and published under the title *General Polizei-, Prozess- und Kommerzialordnung für die Judenschaft des Markgraftums Mähren*. Historian Hillel Kieval (*Languages of Community*, 25) has called this collection "nothing less than a body of constitutional law governing the lives of Moravian Jewry." For more on the history of the survival of the statutes (two copies of which were preserved by Oppenheim), see Halpern, *Takkanot medinat Mehrin (410–508)*, 15–16.
9. Ms. Opp. 616, 169r.
10. Ibid., 158r. On Moravia's Jewish book industry, see Jelinková, "Hebrew Printing in Moravia"; and Marvin J. Heller, "Often Overlooked."
11. A number of approbata from the early years of the decade reveal each rabbi claiming for himself the title *rav medinah*. See approbata to *Meginei eretz* (Dyhernfurth, 1692) and Meir of Eistenstadt b. Hayyim, *Mishte yayin* (Furth, 1737). In both cases Oppenheim's approbation appears before Frankfurter's.
12. For the extended details of this affair, see Freudenthal, "David Oppenheim," 262–274.
13. Ibid., 266.

14. Original documents published in ibid., 265–267.

15. Evans, *The Making of the Habsburg Monarchy*, 172.

16. Freudenthal, "David Oppenheim," 265–271.

17. Halpern, *Takkanot medinat Mehrin (410–508)*, no. 454.

18. In the introduction to his *Shelosha serigim* (Venice, 1701), Frankfurter bowed his head to David Oppenheim, recognizing him as chief rabbi and thanking him for his personal aid in supporting his immigration to the Land of Israel. Just as striking is the fact that the very first approbation to this book was by none other than David Oppenheim. In case any doubts lingered about Oppenheim's relationship to the power of the court, he signed the approbation from the house of his uncle, Samuel Oppenheimer, in Vienna, in the spring of 1701. Frankfurter, for his part, gave special thanks to David Oppenheim, his uncle Samuel, and his cousin Samson Wertheimer—any hint of irony or grudge cannot be discerned.

19. Halpern, *Takkanot medinat Mehrin (410–508)*, no. 467.

20. Ibid.

21. Other Jews testified to the importance of Vienna's Jews in shaping the Moravian rabbinate. Pinhas Katzenellinbogen (*Sefer yesh manhilin*, 83–84) recalled a payment of the leadership in Vienna to the noble ruler of Holleschau to secure a rabbinic position for their chosen candidate. (Meanwhile, in Katzenellinbogen's telling, the ruler was ultimately dissuaded from taking the payment by a local rival faction.)

22. Freudenthal, "David Oppenheim," 269. For evidence of Oppenheim's Vienna visit, see his approbation to Judah Liva b. Samuel Zanwill Oppenheim, *Sefer mateh Yehudah* (Offenbach, 1721), dated February 26, 1700.

23. Freudenthal, "David Oppenheim," 271.

24. Behrens had been essential to shaping backwater Hanover into a major continental player: he orchestrated a return of Hanover to the Habsburg alliance after a brief dalliance in league with France, and raised 1.1 million thalers in order to purchase the electoral title for his patron. Selma Stern, *The Court Jew*, 69–72; Breuer, "Part 1," 108–109.

25. Printed in Freudenthal, "David Oppenheim," 273. On travel and attempts to create security for people in motion, see Groebner, *Who Are You?*

26. Halpern, *Takkanot medinat Mehrin (410–508)*. Compare no. 301 (ca. 1650) with no. 476 (1697).

27. Ms. Opp. 616 (*Takkanot medinat Mehrin*), f. 167r–168v. The "seven tests" are not a literal battery of tests but a reference to the Mishnah Tractate Sanhedrin (5:1), which calls for a cross-examination of witnesses according to seven inquiries and denotes comprehensiveness.

28. Ms. Opp. 149 and 616. Neither of these was used as the basis for Israel

Halpern's printed edition, according to Malachie Beit Arie's entries for them in his *Catalogue of the Hebrew Manuscripts in the Bodleian Library: Supplement of Addenda and Corrigenda.*

29. Halpern, *Takkanot medinat Mehrin (410–508),* no. 490. For the rabbinic contract, see reproductions and transcriptions in Lieben, "Oppenheimiana," 471–477, 484; and Oppenheim, *Nish'al David,* vol. 3, 21–22.

30. For acknowledgment of Oppenheim's support of local confraternities in Nikolsburg, see *Meoznei zedek* (Dyhernfurth, 1707), a book of psalms that explicitly thanks him for his support. On the importance of confraternities in the establishment of rabbinic power during the eighteenth century, see Carlebach, *The Pursuit of Heresy,* 11–12.

31. On Oppenheim's establishment of a study house in Nikolsburg and the approval of state authorities, see CAHJP HM 2/8202.

32. See Duindam, *Vienna and Versailles.*

33. Only a few others followed his example in the first half of the century, such as Samson Wertheimer, Oppenheimer's successor in Vienna, but the practice gained traction as the century proceeded. Cohen, "Creating an Elite Norm of Behaviour," 144.

34. Ibid., 148–150.

35. Cook, *Matters of Exchange,* 14–15; Bourdieu, *Distinction.*

36. See Jewish Museum in Prague, Plášťík na Tóru, Morava, 1695, http://collec tions.jewishmuseum.cz/index.php/Detail/Object/Show/object_id/200817. The curtain was donated in 1695, a full seven years before Oppenheim became chief rabbi of the Jews in the city.

37. Stallybrass, "'Little Jobs.'"

38. Oppenheim's collection contains a number of broadsides that, if not unique, are quite rare, such as a poster on Hebrew grammar (Amsterdam, 1685; pasted into Opp. Fol. 1347), blessings of good fortune to decorate the home (Dyhernfurth, 1693; Opp. Fol. 1334, front and back flyleaves), and a poem in honor of destroyed Worms (Eliezer Lieberman b. Juspe Schammes, Amsterdam, 1694; Opp. 4° 959), as well as several relating directly to promoting his own prestige in the Jewish world. Gabriel Naudé advised the collector to attain these more ephemeral sorts of publications for a library, as they were sure to be rarer and therefore of worth to later generations. See Nelles, "The Library as an Agent of Discovery," 43–44.

39. The mythmaking of the relationship between David and his uncle the Court Jew is so forceful that a legend suggested that Oppenheim's library was based in a bequest of books given from Prince Eugene of Savoy, the Habsburg military commander, to Samuel Oppenheimer, which Eugene discovered upon his conquest of the Balkans in the 1680s. No evidence of this transaction

exists, and elements of the chronology throw the story into further doubt. For the story, see Grunwald, *Samuel Oppenheimer,* 147, n. 141; Marx, "The History of David Oppenheimer's Library," 243–244; and Duschinsky, *Toldot ha-ga'on Rav David Openhaymer,* 78–79. Some books were, however, owned by Samuel. A manuscript copy of *Pelah ha-rimon* (Ms. Opp. 242) is inscribed in the front cover "this book belongs to Samuel Heidelberg."

40. Opp. Add. Fol. III 503 (1): Solomon b. Isaiah Nizza, "Poem on Death of Samuel Oppenheim" (Venice, ca. 1703).

41. *Seder ve-hanhaga shel nisuin ha-hatunah breileft ke-minhag shel k"k Vrankfurt de-Main* (Frankfurt, 1701). According to this practice, in the middle of Sabbath morning prayers, the entire congregation would leave the synagogue and greet the groom at his home, escorting him back to the synagogue for the remainder of the service. The groom was then placed in a special seat at the front of the synagogue, surrounded by the celebrants, and given the highest ritual honors. The rest of the wedding proceeded with similar fanfare. Shammes, *Minhagim de-K"K Virmaiza,* no. 235. For a complete discussion of this text and tradition, see Debra Kaplan, "Rituals of Marriage and Communal Prestige." For a manuscript copied for Beer with reference to his father-in-law, see Ms. Mich. 385, f. 168r.

42. On Beer, see Stern, *The Court Jew,* 100, 198. The use of printing for public display was not limited to Oppenheim's family. To commemorate the marriage of another family in Frankfurt, a broadside was published in 1701. See broadside inserted into the cover of Opp. Fol. 283: Aaron Teomim, *Sefer bigdei Aharon* (Frankfurt, 1710).

43. Kaufmann, *Urkundliches aus dem Leven Samson Wertheimers,* 123–124. A more recent, more complete, and more correct publication appears in Oppenheim, *Nish'al David,* vol. 3, "Tosefet le-naspahim," no. 3.

44. See Oppenheim, *Nish'al David,* vol. 1, §OH, no. 21; §YD, no. 18; vol. 2, §HM no. 29.

45. See Lewinsky, "Ein Brief." My thanks to Debra Kaplan, who discovered this source and shared it with me.

46. Opp. Add. Fol. III 503 (2): Broadside letter by David Oppenheim to the Jewish community of Brisk (written March 25, 1698).

47. See Oppenheim, *Nish'al David,* vol. 1, §OH, no. 16; §YD, nos. 7, 8, 9, 12, 13, 16, 24, 27; vol. 2, §EH, no. 1. See also Oppenheim's Haskamah to Judah b. Nisan Av Beit Din of Kalisch, *Beit Yehuda* (Dessau, 1698).

48. See Oppenheim's details of their arrival written to his son-in-law August 20, 1702. Oppenheim, *Nish'al David,* §HM, no. 6.

49. Lieben, "Oppenheimiana," 477–483. It is likely that even these letters of ap-

pointment were preceded by overtures and invitations from the Prague Jewish community to Oppenheim. One scholar has conjectured that it was the
product of collusion during tax negotiations in the fall of 1701. See Putík,
"Prague Jews and Judah Hasid," 37.

50. This was consonant with the procedures that elders of the Jewish community described (two decades later) as being part of their ancient customs. According to this scheme, the Prague Jewish elders, jurists, and other officials,
as well as contributors of large sums of money, would assess the caliber of a
candidate for the rabbinic position. Following a decision, they would send a
form letter of appointment to the candidate, informing him of their invitation
and the provisions for his tenure. After this point, a request would be sent to
the offices of the emperor to ratify the Jewish selection. Were the emperor to
decline the request, the Jewish representatives would return to the drawing
board to forward a new candidate. NA SM J4/23, 98–99 (1718), and 72–73,
100–101 (copy of the original, produced in 1718). See also Lieben, "David
Oppenheim," 13.

51. See approbation to Lipschitz, *Sefer derekh Hayyim,* dated June 7, 1702,
Vienna; see also Ms. Mich. 479, f. 63v (letter of David Oppenheim, signed
and dated March 6, 1702, Vienna).

52. The Klaus Synagogue in Prague prominently displays the name of Samuel
Oppenheimer over its ark, which was dedicated in 1696, boldly demonstrat-
ing the patronage of the Vienna financier. See also Cohen, *Jewish Icons,* 78;
Greenblatt, *To Tell Their Children,* 29–30.

53. NA SM J4/23, 74–75.

54. For the technical meaning of these titles in the early modern Jewish community, see the literature cited in Reiner, "Temurot be-yeshivot Polin ve-
Ashkenaz," 29, n. 33.

55. Jakobovits, "Das Prager und Böhmische Landesrabbinat," 110–112. On the
yeshiva within the early modern community, see Breuer, "Makom ha-yeshiva
be-ma'arakh ha-irgun he-atzmi ha-Yehudi," esp. 248–249.

56. Katzenellenbogen, *Sefer yesh manhilin,* 182–183 (see chapters 186–190 passim). Although Oppenheim was appointed as chief rabbi and was meant to
share the role with a partner, Abraham Broda, who would oversee Prague's
yeshiva, within a few years Oppenheim had established a yeshiva of his own.
Katzenellenbogen's memoir reveals how intimidating students could find
Oppenheim to be, as well as how gracious (and also teaches us that the chief
rabbi regularly enjoyed a midafternoon nap).

57. See Fram, "Bein ma'arav le-mizrah u-mizrah le-ma'arav."

58. More than thirty copies of this broadside are extant in the Oppenheim col-

lection, as well as copies in the Jewish Museum in Prague and the Jewish Theological Seminary of America. On the history of the "Swedish hat" icon, see Putík, "The Origin of the Symbols." On the star of David in depictions of Prague Jewry, see Spicer, "Star of David."

59. McKenzie, *Bibliography and the Sociology of Texts*, 4; McKitterick, *Print, Manuscript, and the Search for Order*, 18. Both studies are indebted to Marshall McLuhan's dictum "the medium is the message" (*Understanding Media*, 7).

60. NA SM J4/23, 78b. For some time, it was believed that the only copy of this document was in Hamburg, as published by Max Grunwald in *Aus dem Hamburger Staatsarchiv*. An extant copy survives in the Narodní Archiv in Prague.

61. NA SM J4/23, 78.

62. Ibid., 87.

63. For analogous activities in Poland, see Teller, "The Laicization of Early Modern Jewish Society," 336.

64. Rabbinic contract published by Feld in Oppenheim, *Nish'al David*, vol. 3, pp. 23–28. The incidental details of the contract also offer some insights into the workings of the Bohemian *Landesjudenschaft*.

65. Jakobovits, "Das Prager und Böhmische Landesrabbinat," 114.

66. Duindam, "Versailles, Vienna and Beyond," 402–403. On linkages between the ordered home and the ordered state, see Foucault, "Governmentality."

67. Evans, "The Court," 488; Duindam, "Versailles, Vienna and Beyond," 425.

68. Naudé, *Advice on Establishing a Library*, 48.

69. Moraw, "Soziale Verflechtungen," 1–18.

70. Selma Stern, *The Court Jew;* Graetz, "Court Jews in Economics and Politics"; Battenberg, "Die Jüdische Wirtschaftselite."

71. On the Frankfurt Synod, see Finkelstein, *Jewish Self-Government*, 79–81, 257–264; and Klein, "The 1603 Assembly in Frankfurt."

72. Yitshak Zimmer, "Hanhaga u-manhigut be-kehillot Germanyah be-me'ot ha-16 ve-ha-17," 265–266. Even the successes of the career of Josel of Rosheim rested on imperial activism and assent, not intra-Jewish election. This is hardly surprising: Jews participated in the legal culture of the Holy Roman Empire in its jealous embrace of local prerogative and its suspicion of efforts at imperial integration or incursion.

73. Moraw, "Soziale Verflechtungen," 6–7.

74. Opp. 8° 563 (12). Oppenheim owned many books of letter formulae. See, for example, the letter formulae of Solomon Altschul B. Joshua, *Megillat sefer*, with editions from Venice, 1552 (Opp. 8° 603 [2]; Opp. 8° 627 [8]), Cremona,

1566 (Opp. 8° 557A); Basel, 1611 (Opp. 8° 557B); and Frankfurt am Main (Opp. 8° 592); the formulae of Joseph Maarsen, Opp. 8° 545, Opp. 8° 565: *Hanokh le-na'ar* (Amsterdam, 1713); Opp. 8° 593: *Tikun sohrim ve-tikun hilufin* (Amsterdam, 1714); Opp. 8° 568: *Leshon zahav* (Amsterdam, 1715); and Opp. 4° 1064, Eliakim b. Jacob Melammed, *Leshon limmudim* (Amsterdam, 1686). For a comprehensive list of Hebrew epistolary manuals, see Zwick, *Toldot sifrut ha-igronim.* On the political importance of formality in letters, see Sternberg, "Epistolary Ceremonial." On Jewish letter writing, see Carlebach, "Letter into Text." See also Davis, "Concepts of Family and Friendship." On Hebrew letter writing beyond Jewish circles, see Dunkelgrün, "The Humanist Discovery of Hebrew Epistolography."

75. On the operations of these privately funded study houses, see Reiner, "Hon, ma'amad hevrati ve-talmud Torah."

76. Buchanan, *Nexus.*

77. Ms. Mich. 465, 217. On similar practices across Europe at this time, see Horowski, "'Such a Great Advantage for My Son.'"

78. Ms. Mich. 465, 219.

79. Ibid., f. 140.

80. Ulbrich, *Shulamit and Margarete.* On the stabilizing function of kinship networks, see Duhamelle, "The Making of Stability."

81. During the early seventeenth century, German Jews had actually attempted institutional coordination, but to no avail. Only the extraordinary circumstances of Josel of Rosheim in the sixteenth century produced large-scale cooperation, and his successes may be the exception that proved the rule, as individual communities were generally loath to relinquish their independence to a supracommunal body. On Josel of Rosheim, see Stern, *Josel of Rosheim;* and Fraenkel-Goldschmidt, *R. Yosef me-Rosheim.* On efforts at coordination by the Frankfurt Synod, see Finkelstein, *Jewish Self-Government in the Middle Ages,* 79–81, 257–264; and Klein, "The 1603 Assembly in Frankfurt."

82. Between approximately 1650 and 1750 some twelve hundred Court Jews were active in various capacities, some at the highest echelons of state power, like Samuel Oppenheimer and Samson Wertheimer in the imperial capital in Vienna; others at the service of electors, like Behrend Lehmann and Leffman Behrens; and others who fulfilled important roles in the courts of nobles, such as the Bohemian Abraham Lichtenstadt or Salomon Koppel Deitsch, a protected and Court Jew in Nikolsburg. See Battenberg, "Die Jüdische Wirtschaftselite." For Deitsch, see CAHJP HM 2/8202. For Lichtenstadt, see NA Ms. SM 1505 J4/27, 4v, 5r. See also Jakobovits, "Wer ist Abraham Aron Lichtenstadt."

83. Adams, *The Familial State,* 4.

84. On epistolary politics, see Rustow, *Heresy and the Politics of Community,* xix. Burke, *The Art of Conversation.* See also Sternberg, "Epistolary Ceremonial."

85. Duindam, "Versailles, Vienna and Beyond," 425.

86. Stollberg-Rilinger, *The Emperor's Old Clothes,* 5–10.

87. Poriyat (Porges), *Darkhei Ziyyon,* 1650.

88. Asher b. Yehiel, commentary, Ms. Opp. 383; Ms. Opp. 384, Fol. 386r. On expulsion as a constitutive element of Sephardic identity, see Ray, *After Expulsion.*

89. On relations between the two populations in Jerusalem, see Ben-Naeh, " 'Veki lo aheihem anahnu?' " On the larger patterns of distinct Jewish communities existing side by side in the Ottoman Empire and the Venetian Republic, see Hacker, "The Sephardim in the Ottoman Empire"; and Malkiel, "The Ghetto Republic." On the ties within diasporas, see Trivellato, *The Familiarity of Strangers;* and Lehmann, *Emissaries from the Holy Land.*

90. This dissemination of Sephardic commentaries occurred despite an explicit prohibition against the Sephardic Jews of Jerusalem removing books from Palestine. See Benayahu, "Ha-takanah she-lo le-hotsi sefarim mi-Yerushalayim ve-hishtalshelutah."

91. Respectively, Ms. Opp. 369 (Nisim b. Reuben), Ms. Opp. 383 (Asher b. Yehiel), Ms. Opp. 361 (Nahmanides), and Ms. Opp. 96 (Meiri). Benayahu, "Halifat iggerot bein ha-kehillah he-Ashkenazit be-Yerushalayim ve-R David Oppenheim," 112–113.

92. For kabbalistic material that made the journey, see the various volumes of Moses Zacuto on the Zohar, Bodleian Ms. Opp. 511–517, 618. See also Idel, "Italy in Safed"; Avivi, *Kabalat he-Ari,* 2; and Weinstein, *Shivru et ha-kelim.*

93. Ms. Opp. 11: "Sefer derekh etz he-hayyim"

94. Autograph to Moses Zacuto on the Zohar, Ms. Opp. 618: 1r, 28 (Heb)/29v. Poppers was part of an editorial triumvirate that redacted and diffused the work of Isaac Luria in the mid-seventeenth century, alongside Jacob Tzemah and Samuel Vital. Born in 1624 in Krakow, Poppers was part of the Jerusalem circle that redacted Luria's work. He then traveled to Poland shortly after the 1648–1649 massacres, where he diffused Lurianic literature and knowledge (just as Tzemah did in Italy). He returned to the Holy Land by 1659, spending time in Constantinople in 1654. He died in Jerusalem in 1662. See Avivi, *Kabalat He-Ari,* vol. 2, 717–718, 891–892. Another manuscript, *Sefer ha-kaneh,* bore a colophon that similarly traced its provenance to an Iberian exile via a copyist in Safed (Ms. Opp. 548).

95. Ms. Opp. 508. Other kabbalistic works that originated in Palestine included

Sefer Leket ha-Pardes (Ms. Opp. 463), *Sefer ha-merkavah* (Ms. Opp. 741) from Hebron, and Ms. Opp. 721.

96. On the agents that traversed these lands to forge linkages, see Yaari, *Sheluhe Erets Yisrael;* and Lehmann, "Rabbinic Emissaries."

97. Travel in the service of alms-collecting was a tried and typical propeller for global sojourners during the early modern period. Spanish Catholic emissaries marshaled support in the New World for captives in North Africa, and Middle Eastern Catholics traversed the Mediterranean and Atlantic in their search for aid—all often emphasizing their belonging to a global faith with mutual responsibility. For a few examples, see Melvin, "Charity Without Borders," and Ghobrial, "The Secret Life of Elias of Babylon." On the early modern world as an interconnected sphere, see Subrahmanyam, "Connected Histories."

98. Cavallo, *Charity and Power in Early Modern Italy,* 98–152.

99. On the gendered dimensions of giving, see also Baumgarten, "Charitable like Abigail."

100. Arye Judah Leib Katz to David Oppenheim, July 2, 1699, in Ms. Opp. 361.

101. Regrettably, the contract does not appear to have survived, but its terms can be deduced from Oppenheim's reply, which was published as a broadside, "Shir ha-Ma'alot le-David . . ." (Venice, 1702). For extant copies, see the inside covers of Opp. Fol. 364, 390–391, 394–396, 481; Opp. Add. Fol. III 503. See also Lieben, "Oppenheimiana," 437–485.

102. On this episode, see Teplitsky, "A 'Prince of the Land of Israel.'"

103. On Eleazer, see Yaari, *Sheluhe Erets Yisrael,* 327, 847. Ms. Opp. Add 4° 43, Nahmanides on Pentateuch.

104. Ms. Opp. 197.

105. Frankfurter, *Shelosha serigim.* Oppenheim's relationship to Judah's movement remains somewhat opaque. Some scholars have suggested that his financial contributions to the migration of Judah and his followers directly contributed to his appointment. Others believe that he may have been offered the title "Prince of the Land of Israel" as a counterweight to the Sabbatean influx. Benayahu, "He-hevra kedosha' shel rabi yehuda hasid ve-aliyata le-Erets Yisrael," 151–152.

106. NLI Ms. Heb. 4° 966, Fol. 229.

107. For details about this emissary, see Yaari, *Sheluhe Erets Yisrael,* 327, 847.

108. Ms. Mich. 465, ff. 253–254.

109. Davis, "Riches and Dangers," 45–57.

110. Duindam, "Versailles, Vienna and Beyond," 402–403. In fact, the very thing signified by the word *Staat, état,* or "state" in the early modern period was

actually the personnel registered on official court lists. See Evans, "The Court," 483.

111. Duindam, "The Courts of the Austrian Habsburgs," 168–171.

112. Evans, "The Court," 487; Press, "The Habsburg Court as Center of the Imperial Government."

Chapter 3. Collecting, Recording, and Practical Knowledge

1. Oppenheim, *Nish'al David,* vol. 3, Appendix, no. 12.

2. Ibid.

3. Soll, *The Information Master,* 25–27.

4. Head, "Knowing Like a State," 747–752.

5. Greengrass, *Christendom Destroyed,* 538.

6. See, for example, Clanchy, *From Memory to Written Record in England.* Even medieval peasants understood that power and documentation went hand in glove and that power struggles could be mounted by destroying administrators' archives. Such destruction was not just about attacking power; by undermining the sole record of tax rolls or other administrative matters, the rationales for extracting resources from peasants could be extinguished in a flash. See Justice, *Writing and Rebellion.*

7. For profiles of various historical Jewish collectors, see Marx, "Some Jewish Book Collectors"; Bonfil, "Sifriyotehem shel Yehudei Italiah"; and Sluhovsky and Kaplan, *Sifriyot ve-osfe sefarim.*

8. This canon comprised primarily the *Arba Turim* of Jacob b. Asher, the *Sefer ha-Mordekhai, Sha'arei dura, Sefer mitzvot gadol,* and *Sefer mitzvot kattan.* Reiner, "Temurot be-yeshivot Polin ve-Ashkenaz," 21–22. See also Reiner, "'Ein tsarikh shum Yehudi lilmod davar rak ha-Talmud levado.'"

9. Bar-Levav, "The Religious Order of Jewish Books," 6.

10. Berkovitz, *Protocols of Justice,* vol. 1, 5–6.

11. Merchant transactions over distance depended on a reliable exchange of information through letters, messengers, and the post. Rabbinic learning similarly made use of such communicative devices. No fewer than four volumes of letters survive of Oppenheim's correspondence (Bodleian Ms. Mich. 479, Ms. Mich. 465, and Ms. Mich. 466 and NLI Ms. Heb. 4° 966).

12. As Jacob Soll (*The Information Master,* 57) argues, "at this time, being a successful merchant meant being a financier, an archival manager, and a record-keeper."

13. Ms. Opp. 688, f. 81v.

14. Ms. Mich. 479, f. 26r. ND HM 9.

15. On Baroque Bohemia and its confessionalization, see Louthan, *Converting Bohemia;* and Ducreux, "Reading unto Death." Efforts to regulate Hebrew books had preceded the Thirty Years War as well. Jewish chronicles of the sixteenth century paid special attention to a confiscation of Hebrew books in Prague in 1559. Putík, "Censorship of Hebrew Books in Prague," 199–200.

16. Prokeš, "Der Antisemitismus der Behörden," 81; see also Kisch, "Die Zensur Judischer Bücher in Böhmen"; and Popper, *The Censorship of Hebrew Books.*

17. Schedlitz, *Leffmann Behrens,* 138.

18. Naudé, *Advice on Establishing a Library,* 60.

19. On David b. Moses of Sulz, see Johann Christoff Wolff, *Bibliotheca Hebrea,* vol. 1 (1715): 321, item 507; and 290, item 475, in which the author reports the publication of a *haskamah* issued by Oppenheim for a book that was not properly censored and never appeared. In one letter, Joseph reported to Wolf that the regular librarian, or *bibliothécaire,* had already been absent from the library for a quarter of a year. Meyer, "Materialien zur Geschichte der Bibliothek David Oppenheims," 65.

20. Zunz, *Zur Geschichte und Literatur,* 235–236.

21. For the identity between a library and the information it houses, and the slippage between the two as representative of epistemological conceptions, see Chartier, *The Order of Books,* ch. 3.

22. Garberson, "Libraries, Memory and the Space of Knowledge."

23. Clark, "On the Bureaucratic Plots of the Research Library."

24. Meyer, "Materialien zur Geschichte der Bibliothek David Oppenheims," 62.

25. Ibid., 59–61, Letters I–II.

26. Chartier, *The Order of Books,* ch. 3.

27. Israel, *Radical Enlightenment,* 119–120.

28. Goldgar, *Impolite Learning,* 13.

29. Ms. Mich. 466, f. 12r, published in Oppenheim, *Nish'al David,* vol. 3, no. 1.

30. Marx, "The History of David Oppenheimer's Library," 243.

31. Ms. Mich. 466, 71r. For an expression of skepticism about Oppenheim's actual use of the library, see Marx, "Some Jewish Book Collectors," 217.

32. Rzeszów, *Shvut Yaakov,* vol. 1, no. 29. Rzeszów knew the value of such a library, having lost his own in his youth, at the age of nineteen, in Prague's fire of 1689. See ibid., §§5, 84, 94. See also Shilo, "Ha-Rav Ya'akov Raischer ba'al ha-sefer *Shevut Ya'akov,*" 68, esp. n. 43.

33. Ms. Mich. 479, 15r.

34. Quoted in Kinarti, ed., *Yosef Ometz,* 22.

35. Quoted in Avivi, *Kabalat he-Ari,* 2, 771.

36. Burnett, *From Christian Hebraism to Jewish Studies,* 5. See also Coudert and Shoulson, *Hebraica Veritas?;* and Elyada, *A Goy Who Speaks Yiddish.*

37. Elisheva Carlebach ("The Status of the Talmud," 87) has argued that despite aspirations to the contrary, the utility of Jewish tutors to Christian scholars did not cease.

38. Grunwald, "Handschriftliches aus der Hamburger Stadtbibliothek," 1895/1896, no. 9: 424–425; Meyer, "Materialien zur Geschichte der Bibliothek David Oppenheims," 62–63, Letters III–IV.

39. References to "Biblioth. R. Oppenheimeri" are scattered throughout Johann Christoff Wolff's volumes, *Bibliotheca Hebrea,* vol. 3 (Hamburg, 1727), 723. See also Marx, "Some Jewish Book Collectors," 217.

40. Meyer, "Materialien zur Geschichte der Bibliothek David Oppenheims," 65–66, Letter VIII.

41. Ibid., 64, Letter VI.

42. See, for example, the introduction to 1782 Catalogue, 1826 Catalogue, and the various other documents.

43. Archiv der Franckeschen Stiftung/Hauptarchiv (AFSt/H) K 55, f. 153–155, 193–200. I am deeply indebted to Avi Siluk, who brought these texts to my attention and shared the documents and his own transcriptions with me. On Widmann, see Doktór, "Georg Widmann."

44. For distinctions between the scholarly decisor and the institutional jurist, see Berkovitz, "The Persona of a 'Poseq.'"

45. Rzeszów, *Shvut Yaakov,* vol. 1, §§106, 122; vol. 3, §31.

46. On responsa, see Fram, *Ideals Face Reality,* 7. The still-classic work on the use of responsa as historical sources is Soloveitchik, *Shut Ke-Makor Histori.*

47. See the list of court and rabbinic correspondence in Duschinsky, *Toldot Ha-Ga'on Rav David Openhaymer,* 42–70.

48. Oppenheim is likely referring to Opp. Fol. 833: Mordekhai b. Hillel, *Sefer rav Mordekhai,* Shvuot 83a; see Oppenheim, *Nish'al David,* §YD, no. 15.

49. Oppenheim, *Nish'al David,* vol. 2, §EH, no. 26.

50. See Rambam Library, Tel Aviv, Ms. Nish'al David. Elbaum and Elbaum, "Mahadurah genuzah shel shut nish'al David," 16. The authors identified the manuscript as Ms. Opp. 228.

51. Frankfurt quoted in Bar-Levav, "The Religious Order of Jewish Books," 6.

52. In 1706 the Jews of Venice wrote to him because they possessed no standing rabbinic court and called for his ruling on how to conduct their jurispruden-tial procedures. Oppenheim, *Nish'al David,* vol. 2, §HM, no. 2.

53. Observers of various sorts noted this persistent phenomenon among early modern Jews. The Christian Hebraist Christian Teofilo Unger of Herrenlaur-

schitz noted the multiplicity of names as a German-Jewish phenomenon. Unlike in Italy, "in Ashkenaz there is occasionally the custom that some Israelites are better known by the names of their fathers than their own names." Unger, "Schreiben des Pastor Unger an Dr. Cantarini," 142.

54. In a responsum published in a volume of decisions by his teacher Yair Hayyim Bachrach, Oppenheim relayed a matter of discussion in his Beit Midrash over the spelling of the name "Axelrod" in writs of divorce. See Yair Hayyim Bachrach, *Havot Yair,* 249r. Indexes of biblical (and Tannaitic) names were one genre of literature that emerged during the early modern period alongside other sorts of reference texts that would have aided the man in his search. These included *Leket Shmuel* (Venice, 1694 — more a commonplace book than an index) and *Nahalat Shimoni* (Wandsbeck, 1728).

55. Ms. Mich. 466, f. 6–7.

56. Ms. Heb. 4° 966, fol. 242 (written in Hanover, Elul 1711). Oppenheim, *Nish'al David,* vol. 3, §EH, no. 12. See also a 1720 responsum on the name Bat-Sheva. NLI Ms. Heb. 4° 966, fol. 243, printed in Oppenheim, *Nish'al David,* vol. 3, §EH, no. 13. For further instances of queries to Oppenheim regarding names, see Ms. Mich. 465, f. 259, 260–262, as well as a manuscript letter from the court of Metz to David Oppenheim in the 1720s, CAHJP Ms. FME264.

57. "On the ceremonies of divorce and Halizah of R. Yaqob Margalioth," Ms. Opp. 302; Ms. Opp. 304.

58. "Yom Tov Lipmann Heller on names in letters of divorce, responsa on divorce law by Judah b. Nisan of Kalisch, Isaac b. Abaraham of Posen, and Yaski," Ms. Opp. 305.

59. "On the names occurring in letters of divorce, collected from the decisions of different rabbis, chiefly from R. Isaiah Horowitz," Ms. Opp. 316.

60. "On the ceremonies of divorce according to the usage of Frankfurt 1662–1706," Ms. Opp. 730. For still more on marriage and divorce, see Ms. Opp. 273 and Ms. Opp. 274. Portions of these items are published in Baruchson-Arbib, "Hamesh iggerot me-hakhmei Ashkenaz be-me'ah aa-16."

61. "Alphabetical list in Hebrew and German of persons and places listed in letters of divorce, extracted from works of R. Isaiah b. Sheftl and Solomon Luria," Ms. Opp. 71.

62. See the analogous outcomes of the library envisioned by Gabriel Naudé, as discussed in Nelles, "The Library as an Agent of Discovery."

63. "Ma'ase Hashem ki nora hu," in Prager, *Zera kodesh matzevata,* 28b.

64. Ibid.

65. Two accounts relate the events of this episode: Graf, *Zera kodesh matzevata;* and *Mayse shel ha-Ru'ah de-k"k N"Sh* (Opp. 8° 1122). For a detailed recon-

struction of the episode and the various ties of the people involved in it, see Zfatman, *Ze Tmeh.* Zfatman argues persuasively for an identification of the exorcism manual in question as Ms. Opp. 485. For another mention of spirit possession in relation to Oppenheim, see the letter sent to him in 1691 regarding an encounter with a disembodied voice in a cemetery, and the untimely death of the two men who heard the voice. Ms. Mich. 466, f. 170r (published in Oppenheim, *Nish'al David,* vol. 3, §YD, no. 22).

66. See Oppenheim's copy of the Prague archbishopric's involvement in JMP Ms. 120064 ("Kopialbuch of David Oppenheim"): §69 (pp. 252–254). The archbishopric had become increasingly involved in the regulation of "internal" Jewish affairs during that time. In 1709 marriage affairs were submitted to his jurisdiction as well. Ha-yisraeli, "Toldot kehilat Prag," 126.

67. On the relationship between knowledge and the people who make and promulgate it, see Goodman, *The Republic of Letters,* 2; Outram, *The Enlightenment,* 18–21; Darnton, *The Forbidden Best-Sellers of Pre-Revolutionary France,* 181–182; and Burke, *A Social History of Knowledge,* 20.

68. Rabbinic correspondence networks offer an opportunity to trace the flows of authority and approaches to the legal process either as a closed discussion between questioner and respondent or as a more open conversation between multiple discussants. Such a divergence obtained between the more binary structure of medieval Spanish Jewry and that of their more diffuse German counterparts. See Ta-Shma, "Mevo le-sifrut ha-shu"t shel rishoni Ashkenaz ve-Tzarfat," 122–123.

69. Grafton, "A Sketch Map of a Lost Continent," 6.

70. The Babylonian Talmud accords to a nursing mother the status of *meniqa* and defines a woman as such for twenty-four months after the birth of a child. The law exempts such a woman from certain religious obligations, such as participation in fast days, but also limits her in one important respect: "A nursing mother whose husband died—she should not be betrothed nor should she wed until twenty-four months have been completed" (Babylonian Talmud *Ketubbot,* 60a). Motivated perhaps by fears of conflicting pressures between a new husband and children from a previous marriage that could result in infanticide or the abandonment of children, medieval halakhists strengthened this approach and adopted a hard line, prohibiting such marriages and often compelling divorce if marriages were carried out in violation of the law. See Baumgarten, *Mothers and Children,* 122–125, 148–152. Ta-Shma, "Le-Toldot ha-Yehudim be-Folin."

71. Ashkenazi, *She'elot ve-teshuvot* (Amsterdam, 1712), no. 63; Rzeszów, *Shvut Yaakov,* vol. 1, nos. 95–97. Oppenheim was absent from the city in the late

summer, having traveled to Vienna for the wedding of his son, Joseph, to the daughter of the Court Jew Samson Wertheimer.

72. Samuel b. Elkana of Altona, *Mekom Shmuel* (Altona, 1738): no. 84.

73. Ashkenazi, *She'elot ve-teshuvot*, no. 74.

74. Schacter, "Rabbi Jacob Emden," 24.

75. Zevi took special care to note that Jewish law follows Zoharic mystical teachings only when such teachings pose no contradiction to Talmudic rulings. On the relationship between mysticism and Talmudism, which makes use of Zevi's responsa as proof text, see Katz, "Post-Zoharic Relations."

76. Mordekhai Zusskind Rotenberg, *She'elot teshuvot (Amsterdam, 1746)*, no. 33. Zevi's claim was not wholly "rational" either. To buttress his commonsense approach, he also cited the authority of the mystical Zohar, in which it was written that no living being can exist for even a moment without a heart. Ashkenazi, *She'elot ve-teshuvot*, no. 74.

77. Ashkenazi, *She'elot ve-teshuvot*, nos. 76–78. Naftali Kohen does not appear to have been Zevi Ashkenazi's first choice. In his responsum, he indicated that a letter had arrived for his son, Arye Leib, who had already departed the city to take up a post in Broda. With the letter open, Naftali found their arguments so compelling that he immediately agreed. The letter was lost, and a second letter came, this time soliciting his support (rather than his son's). He replied right away. Ashkenazi, *Hakham Zevi,* §76. Margaliot, "Le-toldot 'anshe shem' be-Lvov," 385.

78. Ashkenazi, *She'elot ve-teshuvot*, no. 76.

79. Ms. Mich. 466, f. 164r. Printed also in Oppenheim, *Nish'al David,* vol. 3, §YD, no. 4. Note, however, the date incorrectly transcribed as 1706, when it reads 1709 in the manuscript.

80. Oppenheim, *Nish'al David,* vol. 3, no. 35. For a study of the decisor's self-image as represented in his responsa, see Berkovitz, "Dyukono ha-azmi" On the importance of narrativity to all legal systems, see Cover, "Nomos and Narrative."

81. NLI Ms. Heb. 4° 966, f. 264, printed in Oppenheim, *Nish'al David,* vol. 3, §YD, no. 3.

82. Ibid. For another instance in which Oppenheim dissented from Zevi's opinion, see Elbaum and Elbaum, "Mahadurah genuzah shel shut nish'al David," who compare Ashkenazi, *She'elot ve-teshuvot,* no. 54, to the inscription in Rambam Library, Tel Aviv, Ms. Nish'al David 18 (in Oppenheim, *Nish'al David,* vol. 1, §YD, no. 21).

83. Emden, *Akizat akrav,* 17b. This was not the only time that Oppenheim took a more conservative approach in the face of Eybeschütz's permissiveness. Eleazar Fleckeles of Prague recounted his father's memory of a declaration

promulgated by Oppenheim in all of Prague's synagogues prohibiting Jews to drink milk on Passover. Eybeschütz disagreed with this ruling and permitted the practice. Fleckeles, *Teshuva me-ahava*, vol. 3, no. 325, cf. Eybeschütz, *Kreti u-fleti*, 60. See also Klemperer, "The Rabbis of Prague," (1950): 63.

84. Emden, *Bet Yehonatan hasofer*, 1a. According to Emden, Eybeschütz and Oppenheim had a lasting adversarial relationship. Eybeschütz subjected Oppenheim to mockery that was unheard of, doing something to his clothes (?) and erecting a tombstone for a bastard child, writing "here lies" (where presumably he should not have). Emden, *Shevirat luhot ha-aven*, 39a. See also Emden, *Edut be-Yaakov*, 76 (noted as 56).

85. Rzeszów, *Shvut Yaakov*, vol. 3, no. 65.

86. The book was only published in 1768 in Fürth.

87. Katzenellinbogen, *Knesset Yehezkel*, §§25–26. See also Poppers, *Shev Yaakov*, §26.

88. Rema's ruling was derived from the book *Kol bo*, an anonymous legal code compiled some time in the late Middle Ages.

89. Even this textual criticism rested upon family ties. This was a position first upheld by Elias Spira Wedeles, who shared the Prague rabbinate with Oppenheim for a very short time and was a relative of both Oppenheim and Jacob Rzeszów. Wedeles published this opinion in his book *Elia zuta*, first published in 1689, alongside Mordecai Jaffee's *Levush tekhelet*. Relation did not always mean agreement; Eybeschütz, who departed from this ruling, was a relative as well.

90. Oppenheim, *Nish'al David*, vol. 3, §YD, no. 6.

91. Soll, *The Information Master*, 39–40.

92. See, for example, Holenstein, "'Gute Policey.'"

93. Chief among the works dealing with record-keeping and governance was Aebbtlin, *Anfürung zu der Registratur-Kunst*. See Head, "Knowing Like a State"; and Tribe, "Cameralism and the Science of Government." On a variety of cameralist authors and their thinking, see Whaley, *Germany and the Holy Roman Empire, Vol. 2*, 192–201. Cameralism, in turn, was part of a larger move toward bridging the distance between experience and intellect. On the science of government during this period, see also Foucault, "Governmentality."

94. Cameralists, for their part, largely returned the favor of mutual disregard. Their academic interest in Jews emerged in earnest only in the middle of the eighteenth century. See Joskowicz, "Toleration in the Age of Projects."

95. Oppenheim led a yeshiva, a place of study that was not exclusively oriented toward practice but also toward the supreme value traditional Jews placed upon engagement with the text. The yeshivot of early modern Europe had

pioneered a system of study that drew ever further from study in the name of practice. See Dimitrovsky, "Al derekh ha-pilpul."

96. For the antiquarian as guide to constitutions, politics, and war, see Miller, *Peiresc's Europe,* 76–81.

97. Other manuscripts in Oppenheim's collection include formulas for civil codes. See Ms. Opp. 340 (dated 1299) and Ms. Opp. 337 (dated 1382). On the blurring of distinctions between manuscript and printed book with respect to the concept of "publication," see Dweck, *The Scandal of Kabbalah.*

98. Ms. Opp. 615: "Tikun sofrim"; a small number of these items were published in Katz, "Le-toldot ha-rabanut be-motzaei yeme ha-benayim."

99. They were remarkably akin to the guiding principle in the administration of German towns that "custom overrides law" (*Willkür bricht Landrecht*), which was grounded in the localism and communalism of custom. Walker, *German Home Towns,* 38. Religious tradition gave its imprimatur to this subordinate form of legislation, approving of such regulations if they are reached by a majority of resident Jews who are presided over by men of standing. On the tensions between communal consensus and scholarly expertise in the formation of Jewish regulations in the Middle Ages, see Kanarfogel, "Unanimity, Majority, and Communal Government."

100. *Takkanot* of medieval Jewish communities survive from the Middle Ages largely on account of their discussion in rabbinic texts, which were in turn copied and studied by later Jewish scholars and later still were printed. On the development of *takkanot* as a part of the evolution of the *kehillah,* see Katz, *Tradition and Crisis,* 66–68. For a discussion of the place of *takkanot* and *pinkassim* in the Jewish courts and communities of the Middle Ages, see Furst, "Unrecorded Justice." I am grateful to Dr. Furst for sharing this essay with me in advance of its publication. See also her discussion in Furst, *Striving for Justice,* 50–57.

101. The name is probably derived from ancient Greek, as transmitted (and transformed) by rabbinic Hebrew. The Greek word *pinax*—meaning list, register, or board—gave rise to words that serviced the field of rudimentary bibliography in the form of the *Pinakes,* an ancient reference tool that inventoried and summarized the holdings of libraries. See Blair, *Too Much to Know,* 16–27.

102. For examples of *pinkassim* of different varieties, see Litt, *Jüdische Gemeindestatuten;* Fram, *A Window on Their World;* Carlebach, "Community, Authority, and Jewish Midwives"; and Putík, "Prague Jews and Judah Hasid, Part 1."

103. Opp. 4° 557: Takkanot of the Perdons Kontract (Prague, 1702): §4.

104. Duschinsky, *Toldot ha-ga'on rav David Openhaymer,* 24.

105. Prague's Jews were repeatedly instructed by these *takkanot* to submit to the

register of this scribe for assessment, regardless of whether their dealings were retail or on commission, with Jews or gentiles, within the city limits or beyond them (in the countryside or at trade fairs), and whether they dealt in foodstuffs like wine and meat or artisanal products; even the fees of matchmakers were not exempt. Various mechanisms of enforcement were put into place, such as forestalling the wedding of a bridegroom until he produced a certificate from the Jewish leadership confirming that he had paid the 5-reichsthaler tax levied upon him. See Opp. 4° 557: Takkanot of the Perdons Contract, §6, 31. On this novel situation in Prague, see Wolf, "Zur Geschichte Des Jüdischen Gemeinwesens in Prag," 255–257; and Putík, "Prague Jews and Judah Hasid, Part 3," 34–44.

106. At first, Elia's father, Wolf Wedeles, was confirmed in the position, apparently an error by the imperial order, which was then rectified. See JMP 109493, nos. 8, 10. See also Jakobovits, "Das Prager und Böhmische Landesrabbinat," 112. For laments in response to Elias's death on account of the plague, see *Ayn naye klog lid* (Amsterdam, 1714), 2; *Ipesh lid fun Prague* (Prague, ca. 1714), 1.

107. JMP Ms. Hsg. 060786.

108. Pollmann, "Archiving the Present and Chronicling for the Future."

109. JMP 120064 ("Kopialbuch of David Oppenheim"): §58–59 (pp. 185–198); Ha-yisraeli, "Toldot kehillat Prag," 77. See also Opp 4° 325 (Sermon of Barukh Austerlitz), which was transcribed for publication by "Aaron son of the great Meir Austerlitz of blessed memory, the scribe of the great famed sage and chief rabbi here in Prague" in 1713. On instructions to the official scribe of Moravia's supracommunal organization, see Halperin, *Takkanot medinat Mehrin*, nos. 302, 304.

110. See, for example, mention of the destructive impact of the fire in records referenced by the community during the course of negotiating the Jews' taxation in 1707. NA SM 1505 J4/28, Section iv.

111. For a study of this collection of documents, see Ha-yisraeli, "Toldot kehillat Prag." Many of the archival items offer important data for reconstructing the events of Oppenheim's career; in the aggregate they also represent an important archiving "meta-practice" that was just as central to the constitution of his authority. On the emergence of copybooks in the Habsburg domains during the sixteenth century, see Head, "Configuring European Archives," 505–506.

112. JMP 120064 ("Kopialbuch of David Oppenheim"): §159 (pp. 519–571, ca. 1712-1724: on regulating the book trade); §127 (pp. 417–420, 1696: on pre-censorship of sermons); §69 (pp. 252–254, 1708: on conducting an exorcism and superstitious practices).

113. Ibid., §39 (p. 113); §6 (pp. 11–21).

114. Ibid., §27 (p. 78, 1718).

115. Lieben, "David Oppenheim," 24–25, n. 23.

116. As Jacob Katz (*Tradition and Crisis*, 67) noted, "halakhists were assumed to be the ones to rule on unclear or doubtful issues in the interpretation of written *takkanot*." Katz cites Krochmal, *She'elot ve-teshuvot tsemah tsedek*, no. 33; and Rzeszów, *Shvut Yaakov*, vol. 3, no. 83.

117. Oppenheim's predecessor in Moravia, Menahem Mendel Krochmal (1600–1661), had such a role. A number of his published responsa take as their object not the texts generated by the rabbinic chain of tradition rooted in Talmudic law, but instead those in the newly generated statutes of the semiautonomous Jewish community. Krochmal adjudicated issues regarding the weight that members of a higher tax bracket ought to exert in communal decisions, the election of rabbis, and the salaries of beadles. His role as an interpreter of communal statutes finds expression in the contents to his published work, which includes, among the book's more traditional topics (such as prayer, festivals, kosher food, and menstrual purity), a section dedicated to "the laws of *takkanot* and communal decisions." Krochmal, *She'elot ve-teshuvot tsemah tsedek*, 6b. See also responsa items, nos. 1, 2, 16, 28, 37, 44, 109. The *takkanot* of Moravia's supracommunal body similarly delegated such responsibilities to the chief rabbi. See Halpern, *Takkanot medinat Mehrin*, no. 292.

118. Ms. Mich. 479 ("Shalal David"), f. 3r.

119. ND HM 10.

120. Oppenheim, *Nish'al David*, §HM 4.

121. Ms. Mich. 466, 2r–3v. For a full treatment of this text's Polish context, see Fram, "Bein ma'arav le-mizrah u-mizrah le-ma'arav." Oppenheim had an awareness of other places in which the rabbinate was split. In his letter to Brisk upon receiving an invitation to head the city's rabbinate in 1698, Oppenheim made sure to remark that the position had once been divided. Opp. Add. Fol. III 503 (2).

122. Stallybrass, "Printing and the Manuscript Revolution."

123. One testament to the particularly regional character of the rabbinic republic of letters is in a collection of various homilies and novella written by German rabbis, and almost exclusively German rabbis, including Oppenheim. The compiler of the collection studied in Hamburg in 1734. Probing the collection shows once again a sense of regional belonging, as the biographies of the homilies and novella included are all of German provenance. Ms. Mich. 325.

124. See Blair, *Too Much to Know;* and Soll, *The Information Master.*

Chapter 4. "To Make Books Without End"

1. Ms. Opp. 94, *Sefer ha-Tashbetz*, title page.

2. On such roles as "virtues" in the early modern world, see Miller, *Peiresc's Europe*, 17.

3. Grafton and Rice, *Foundations of Early Modern Europe*; Boruchoff, "The Three Greatest Inventions of Modern Times."

4. See, for example, the ca. 1470 screed by Filippo de Strata, "Polemic Against Printing." See also the discussion in Pettegree, *The Book in the Renaissance*, 43–62.

5. On such challenges to authority in rabbinic circles, see Reiner, "Aliyat 'Ha-Kehilla Ha-Gedola.'"

6. Delmedigo, *Sefer novelot hokhmah*, 13. See also Marx, "Some Jewish Book Collectors," 207–208.

7. Luntschitz, *Olelot Ephraim*. A full century later, Luntschitz's exegesis was cited with approval by the education reformer Isaac Wetzlar (Wetzlar and Faierstein, *The Libes Briv of Isaac Wetzlar*, 29a–29b), who recommended "that every scholar read what the famous sage Ephraim writes in the introduction to his book *Olelot Ephraim*." Other contemporary sages adopted a similar line of transvaluation as Oppenheim's. See, for example, the publisher's epigraph of Isaac b. Aaron Prostitz to the title page of Judah Leow b. Bezalel, *Sefer gevurot Hashem* (Krakow, 1582); Bar-Levav, "Bein Toda'at ha-Sifriyah le-Republika ha-Sifrutit ha-Yehudit," 211.

8. Ms. Opp. 699, f. 63r (emphasis in original). Oppenheim was not the only one to assign a positive valence to this phrase. For a hope "to purchase books endlessly," see inscription to Moses b. Mordecai Galante, *She'elot u-teshuvot*, held by the Spertus Library.

9. On the sacred dimensions of books as divine gifts that resisted private property, see Davis, "Beyond the Market," 72.

10. The German philosopher Immanuel Kant was highly influential in shaping modern conceptions of authorship, laid out most prominently in his essay *On the Wrongfulness of Unauthorized Publication of Books* (1785). In that work, Kant identified the rights of the author as emerging from the creative self, a right that publishers could acquire, but only as a result of the alienation by the author of his or her property. Rose, *Authors and Owners*, 16–30. See also Baldwin, *The Copyright Wars*; and Johns, *Piracy*. For significant qualifications regarding the relationship between authorship and legal rights, see Chartier, *The Order of Books*, ch. 2. See also Chartier and Stallybrass, "What Is a Book?"

11. See, for example, *Meginei Eretz* (Dyhernfurth, 1692), introduction. At other times, rabbinic approbata and introductions might fulfill this function. When the responsa of Oppenheim's teacher Gerson Ulif Ashkenazi (*Avodat ha-Gershuni*) were published posthumously, Oppenheim wrote a lengthy introduction to the work, crediting the author's son with the labor of organizing the material for publication.

12. Gries, "le-demuto shel ha-mevi le-defus ha-yehudi be-shilhei yeme ha-beinayim."

13. Ms. Opp. 395.

14. Ms. Opp. 234: Shalom b. Leib Shalom of Lvov, *She'elot minhat Shalom* (seventeenth century).

15. For references to Jonathan's capture and ransom, see the approbata by Oppenheim and Abraham Naftali Hirsch Levi b. Moses Spitz to Jonathan b. Jacob, *Keset yehonatan* (Prague, 1697).

16. On the work and difficulties with assigning numbers to the titles, see Avivi, "Kitvei ha-RM"A mi-Fano be-hokhmat ha-kabbalah."

17. Ms. Opp. 699, f. 80r. In ever-widening circles of Oppenheim's network, a surviving copy of this book now held by the Chabad-Lubavitch Library carries the inscription of Aaron b. Eliezer Lippman Katz, Oppenheim's brother-in-law, son of the Court Jew Leffman Behrens.

18. Although Oppenheim was not the author, printer, or publisher, an introduction to the volume by Abraham Naftali Hirsch Levi b. Moses Spitz of Nikolsburg credits his role as the collector and owner of the manuscript. See Fano, "Introduction," *Maamar ha-itim*.

19. Jewish law requires that sacred texts receive a proper burial, rather than be discarded with ordinary refuse. A *genizah* served often as an interim repository for these texts before their burial. The most famous *genizah* is the one discovered in Fustat (Cairo) and studied by Solomon Schechter and S. D. Goitein. For a lively account of that discovery, see Hoffman and Cole, *Sacred Trash*. For *genizot* (plural) in the German lands, see Lehnardt, "Genisa."

20. Ms. Opp. 8° 53.

21. Ibid., 3r. This copy of the Rashbam manuscript may have been the second such that Oppenheim acquired, as he also writes of purchasing a thirteen-page manuscript of the medieval commentator. That text, itself missing portions, was sufficiently preserved that the two texts could be brought together in an act of careful textual reconstruction in order to fully obtain the commentary. On the mahzor, its editions, and its significance, see Ta-Shma, "Al kama inyanei Mahzor Vitry."

22. Joseph was attuned to the world of publishing, having a commentary on the Passover Haggadah, *Kutonet passim, Tzafnat pa'aneah,* and *Haluka de-rabanan.* On the relationship between preaching and publishing, see Reiner, "Darshan noded madpis et sefarav."

23. Burke, *A Social History of Knowledge,* 45–46.

24. See Heller, *Printing the Talmud: Individual Treatises,* 179. The paths of Jablonski and Oppenheim would cross repeatedly through their involvement in new editions of the Talmud at the end of the seventeenth and into the eighteenth centuries. Moreover, the manager of Jablonski's Berlin print shop was Judah Leib Neumark, whose relative Nathan Gruenhut had published part of Oppenheim's work and whose son, Meir, worked as a translator of scientific texts for Oppenheim. Neumark likely forged the crucial link between these two men, further demonstrating the importance of social networks in shaping material and intellectual exchange and output. Another son of Judah Leib Neumark, Nathan Neumark, later operated his own press in Berlin from 1719 to 1727. Ibid., 178–190. Contacts with agents of print in Berlin may have also served to establish Oppenheim's authoritative reputation there. In the same year as the first Rashbam publication, the relatively young Berlin Jewish community turned to Oppenheim (alongside a number of other rabbis) to request a ban declaring right of residence for only those already there, giving them the religious backing to limit migration to the city for those outside of its initial settlers. Oppenheim, *Nish'al David,* vol. 2, §HM, no. 8. It was reasonable that the Jews of Berlin would turn to Oppenheim for halakhic advice. The chief rabbi of Brandenburg and Pomerania had been Isaac Benjamin Wolff, Oppenheim's teacher who ordained Oppenheim as a rabbi in 1683. Moreover, Wolff was related to Leffman Behrens. Heller, "Moses Benjamin Wulff," 209.

25. The publisher told of the circuitous path of the manuscript's travels in a brief introduction to the volume titled "El ayin ha-kore," *Hamisha Humshe Torah* (Berlin, 1705). The manuscript, which appears to have been held by the Breslau Seminary in the nineteenth century, has since been lost. See Marx, "The History of David Oppenheimer's Library," 239, n. 234.

26. I am thankful to Prof. Ephraim Kanarfogel for discussing with me the means by which this manuscript would have been authenticated by Oppenheim and his contemporaries.

27. Talabardon, "Die Biblia Hebraica des Daniel Ernst Jablonski," 475–476.

28. *Hamisha Humshe Torah* (Dyhernfurth, 1728).

29. *Hamisha Humshe Torah* (4 vols.), Opp. 8° 49–52. Oppenheim's second copy, unadorned, is Opp. 8° 53–56.

30. Febvre et al., *The Coming of the Book*, 109–115.

31. Pettegree, *The Book in the Renaissance, 33.*

32. In the vast majority of cases, our knowledge about the print run of early modern Jewish books is still minimal, leaving us with little concrete sense about the size of the market and the cost of printing.

33. See Abraham, son of Judah b. Nisan, chief rabbi of Kalisch, "Introduction of the author's son," in Nisan, *Beit Yehudah.* A few pages of Oppenheim's own writings, his commentary on Tractate Shabbat titled *Moed David,* appeared in print as part of this volume as well.

34. Joshua b. Joseph of Krakow, *Sefer meginei Shlomo.* On Lehmann, see Raspe, "Individueller Ruhm und Kollektiver Nutzen." One of Oppenheim's responsa later appeared in Getz, *Even ha-shoham u-meirat einayim.* Oppenheim extended this support not only to his students, but to the works of his teachers as well. In 1710 he lent his support to the grandson of his teacher in Metz, Gerson Ashkenazi. Although Ashkenazi had died in 1693, his son, Nahum, had served as an emissary from Palestine to Central Europe, and his grandson had made a pilgrimage to Metz where he unearthed some of his grandfather's unpublished notes. But it was only with Oppenheim's aid that he could make the step to the printing press. Ashkenazi, *Sefer hiddushei ha-Gershuni* (Frankfurt am Main, 1710): "Introduction of the composer's grandson."

35. "Introduction of the great rabbi the son of the composer," *Midrash rabbot* (Amsterdam, 1725).

36. See Fram, "Bein ma'arav le-mizrah u-mizrah le-ma'arav," 161–164.

37. Bezalel b. Abraham Ashkenazi, *Sefer asefat zekenim ve-hu hiddushei bava metziah.* The story of the book's publication was remarkable in and of itself: Its publisher, Jonah b. Jacob, was a refugee from Constantinople to Poland, and ultimately to Amsterdam. While he traveled by land, he sent his books aboard a ship, which sank, consigning his library to oblivion. He had kept the manuscript for this work with him, however, which saved it from loss and made its publication possible.

38. Of course, even exclusion from the process of publication did not mean exclusion from a book's acquisition. Oppenheim owned two copies of the book (Opp. Fol. 1066, 1067), but Wertheimer's edition—printed on blue paper with a special leather binding upon which the words "Ha-gaon ha-gadol mofet ha-dor kmhr"r Samson Wertheimer" were emblazoned—far outshone Oppenheim's. Wertheimer's personal copy is preserved as JTSA 1870:2: *Sefer asifat zekenim ve-hu hiddushei bava metziah.* My thanks to David Sclar for bringing this item to my attention.

39. On patronage in the creation of science and art, see Biagioli, *Galileo, Courtier;* and Moran, *Patronage and Institutions.* Adrian Johns (*The Nature of the*

Book, 114) has perhaps gone furthest in linking patronage with book production in writing, "one can thus see the book trade as representative of a society conceiving of itself as an aggregate of patriarchal households, held together by fragile attributions of credit."

40. Cook, *Matters of Exchange,* 14–15.
41. Zunz, *Zur Geschichte und Literatur,* 235–236; Hill, "Hebrew Printing on Blue and Other Coloured Papers," 89.
42. "Hebrew Printing on Blue and Other Coloured Papers," 86–87.
43. Marx, "Some Jewish Book Collectors," 218.
44. Schudt, *Jüdisches Merwürdigkeiten,* I, 582.
45. Opp. Fol. 1299: Haggadah *Mah Nishtanah* (Prague, 1713).
46. Hill, "Hebrew Printing on Blue and Other Coloured Papers," 95. For an illuminated printed book, see Opp. Fol. 1292: *Seder haggadah shel Pesah* (Sulzbach, 1711).
47. According to Alexander Marx ("Some Jewish Book Collectors," 216–218), only two hundred vellum books were printed between 1475 and 1905, making Oppenheim's personal orders a full 20 percent of the total Hebrew books published on vellum.
48. Opp. Fol. 583.
49. Yudlov, "Hebrew Books Printed on Vellum," 58; Knight, "'Furnished' for Action."
50. On the proliferation of libraries during the late seventeenth century in the Habsburg lands, and the dynasty's patronage of scholarship and culture, see Evans, *The Making of the Habsburg Monarchy,* 312–318. See also Smith, *The Business of Alchemy.*
51. This discussion is of the Babylonian Talmud, but it is worth noting that Oppenheim was also involved in printing the Jerusalem (or Palestinian) Talmud during these decades. See, for example, the "Composer's introduction," *Talmud Yerushalmi* (Amsterdam, 1710), which acknowledges the financial patronage of Oppenheim and his son, Joseph. See also Heller, *Printing the Talmud: Individual Treatises,* 225–234.
52. Heller, *Printing the Talmud: Earliest Printed Editions,* Appendix B, 400. Oppenheim's "Kopialbuch" preserves numerous documents in which church and state authorities express their suspicion of this text.
53. Rosman, "Dimuyav shel beit Yisrael be-Folin ke-merkaz Torah aharei Gezerot 408–409"; Fram, "Bein ma'arav le-mizrah u-mizrah le-ma'arav."
54. Carlebach, "The Status of the Talmud in Early Modern Europe," 87.
55. Freudenthal, "Zum Jubiläum des Ersten Talmuddrucks in Deutschland," 80–81.
56. Ibid., 82.

57. On the premodern privilege system and the production of Hebrew books, see Netanel, *From Maimonides to Microsoft*.

58. Heller, *Printing the Talmud: Earliest Printed Editions*, Appendix B, 400. On the long history of the Talmud between Jews and Christians, see Funkenstein, *Perceptions of Jewish History*, 172–200; Cohen, *The Friars and the Jews*; and Chazan, "Christian Condemnation, Censorship, and Exploitation of the Talmud." For a recent study that has attributed enhanced interest to the Talmud's finalization as a coherent whole emerging only in the High Middle Ages, see Fishman, *Becoming the People of the Talmud*, 167–174.

59. Heller, *Printing the Talmud: Earliest Printed Editions*, 241–265. Oppenheim did, however, own a copy of this as well; see Opp. Fol. 390–396.

60. Freudenthal, "Zum Jubiläum des Ersten Talmuddrucks in Deutschland," 83; Heller, "Moses Benjamin Wulff," 214. Oppenheim had tangential links to Wulff as well; the broadside proclaiming his rejection of the invitation to serve as chief rabbi of Brisk was published at Wulff's press. See "Iggeret le-Hokhmei Brisk" (broadside letter by David Oppenheim to the Jewish community of Brisk written March 25, 1698, published at the press of Moses Benjamin Wulff, Opp. Add. Fol. III 503).

61. Stern, *The Court Jew*, 75–85.

62. "*Haskamah* of David Oppenheim," Tractate *Berakhot* (Frankfurt an der Oder, 1697).

63. "*Haskamah* of the chief rabbi of Posen," Tractate *Berakhot* (Frankfurt an der Oder, 1697).

64. On Lehmann's place as patron, see Raspe, "Individueller Ruhm und Kollektiver Nutzen."

65. Freudenthal, "Zum Jubiläum des Ersten Talmuddrucks in Deutschland."

66. Ibid., 86–89, 229–230.

67. Ibid., 139–142.

68. Tractate *Shabbat* (Amsterdam, 1714), publisher's introduction.

69. In making such an argument, Loeb invoked the curricular reforms advocated by Oppenheim's teacher Yair Hayyim Bachrach. See Bachrach, *Havot Yair*, no. 123. Bachrach appears to have been accurately describing the shifting interests of a scholarly generation. See Shear, *The Kuzari and the Shaping of Jewish Identity*, 180–193.

70. Tractate *Shabbat* (Amsterdam, 1714), publisher's introduction.

71. Ms. Opp. 98.

72. Ms. Opp. 361.

73. Ms. Opp. 99.

74. Tractate *Shabbat* (Amsterdam, 1714), publisher's introduction.

75. Benayahu, "Halifat iggerot bein ha-kehillah he-Ashkenazit be-Yerushalayim ve-r David Oppenheim," 112–113.

76. Freudenthal, "Zum Jubiläum des Ersten Talmuddrucks in Deutschland," 135–137. Interestingly, Tractate *Berakhot* of this edition bears no approbata whatsoever. The only historical "paratext" accompanying the volume is a justification for print by Solomon Proops on the final page of the volume. There, Proops speaks of his own renown and reputation as a competent printer and emphasizes his financial outlay for this comprehensive project. See Tractate *Berakhot* (Amsterdam, 1714).

77. Approbation of Shmuel b. Yosef Shattin of Frankfurt/Darmstadt.

78. JMP Ms. 120064: §§93–94, 174–178, 195–201, and the discussion thereof in Ha-yisraeli, "Toldot kehillat Prag." Oppenheim's clashes with the Jesuits and Eybeschütz are covered in Chapter 5.

79. This was especially the case for approbata. Only 30 of the 320 Yiddish books published in Amsterdam between 1650 and 1750 bore approbata. See Berger, *Producing Redemption in Amsterdam,* 78.

80. Berger, "Yiddish Books in Early Modern Prague," 177–185.

81. Opp. 4° 1241: *Tefillah le-omram be-khol yom erev va-voker* (Prague, 1713). See also Opp. 4° 1239: *Tefillah le-omram be-khol yom erev va-voker* (Prague, 1713). The date of this text from the spring of 1713 is surprising and perhaps an error given that the plague did not break out in the city until the summer of that year, according to contemporary accounts. See also Turniansky, "Yiddish Song as Historical Source Material."

82. Opp. 4° 1240: *Selihot* (Prague, 1713).

83. See Opp. 8° 632; Opp. 8° 643 (4); Opp. 8° 645 (4); and Opp. 8° 652. For the *tkhines,* see Opp. 8° 644 (3). On *tkhine* literature, see Weissler, *Voices of the Matriarchs.*

84. Opp. 4° 1239: *Tefillah le-omram be-khol yom erev va-voker* (Prague, 1713).

85. Opp. 4° 803: *Ata zan* (Prague, 1708).

86. The book was reprinted at least two more times over the course of the eighteenth century, once in 1763 (Prague) and then in 1774 (Amsterdam). For a discussion of the text and its images, see Shmeruk, *MahAzot Mikra'iyim be-Yidish,* 405–532.

87. Stallybrass, "Printing and the Manuscript Revolution."

88. This was a common practice within the educational sphere of the early modern yeshiva. On the shifting bibliographic boundaries of early modern Jewish study in the context of the yeshiva and the creation of new compositions, see Reiner, "Yashan mipnei hadash," 185–189.

89. Ms. Mich. 591.

90. See notes by students, which read "thus far I have copied from the book *Mo'ed David*," and similarly, "thus far from his book of responsa *Lev David*" as well as from "*Makom David.*" Ms. Mich. 466, 6r–7r. See also Ms. Mich. 90, f. 43r (42r in Hebrew pagination), in which Oppenheim writes "and see also in our book *Yad David*, there are some pleasant items where I resolved difficulties" (also many other references in the first pages of the text). There is evidence that another student copied Oppenheim's responsa. The library of Berlin's rabbinical seminary once held a manuscript copy of Oppenheim's responsa, which were copied by Meir Austerlitz (probably now lost). *Megillat Shmuel*, 14, n. 11.

91. See, for example, his responsum (dated February 26, 1719), which he closes by advising his reader to further consult "my composition *Nish'al David* in the *Yoreh Deah* portion, and in my commentaries to Talmud on Tractate Pesahim in my composition *Mo'ed David.*" NLI Heb. Ms. 4° 966, 25; Oppenheim, *Nish'al David*, vol. 3, §YD, no. 7.

92. Ms. Opp. Add. Fol. 6–7. On the persistence of manuscript well into the age of print in the Jewish world, see Dweck, *The Scandal of Kabbalah*, 17–21.

93. Ms. Mich. 544, f. 145r, printed in Oppenheim, *Nish'al David*, vol. 3, Appendix §11.

94. Ms. Mich. 465, f. 217v.

95. Rzeszów, *Shvut Yaakov*, vol. 1, §OH 39.

96. Ms. Mich. 438, f. 22r (§15).

97. Oppenheim, *Nish'al David*, vol. 3, p. 7.

98. "Intro to *Mo'ed David*" as printed in Oppenheim, *Nish'al David*, vol. 3, 7, from Ms. Mich. 431, f. 126a. This was not the only time that papers in his care were lost. In 1700, as summer turned to autumn, Oppenheim replied belatedly to a question from Samuel Katz, the head of the court and rabbi of the *kloyz* in Frankfurt, that Katz had sent the year before. The reason for the delayed reply? "And my teacher, may his Torah study be honored, must believe me in the confusion in the city of Vienna last year the questions and letters he sent to me, appropriately and correctly, were lost, and I was tormented over this, and a few days ago I found my heart's desire, a copy of his questions." Oppenheim, *Nish'al David*, vol. 2, §EH, no. 2. He may have been referring to the ransacking of his uncle's estate by unruly mobs; see also Ms. Mich. 466, printed in Oppenheim, *Nish'al David*, vol. 3, 175.

99. Jacob Emden, *She'elat Yavez*, vol. 1, responsum 41 (Altona, 1739), 69a, translated by Shai Alleson-Gerberg for the Early Modern Workshop: Resources in Jewish History, at https://fordham.bepress.com/emw/.

100. Azulai, *Shem ha-Gedolim* (Livorno, 1774): Daled, no. 13.

101. On books and reputation for posterity, see also Greenblatt, "'Asot sfarim ad eyn ketz.'"

102. David Stern, "The Rabbinic Bible in Its Sixteenth-Century Context," 99–100. On Ashkenazic umbrage toward the Spanish inflection of the Bomberg text, see Reiner, "'Ein Tsarikh Shum Yehudi Lilmod Davar Rak Ha-Talmud Levado," 735–740.

103. On this sense in both custom literature and legal reasoning, see Berkovitz, "Crisis and Authority in Early Modern Ashkenaz."

104. Opp. 8° 1023: Akiva b. Jacob Ginzburg, *Elu ha-zemirot* (Berlin, 1713). Oppenheim's copy was printed on blue paper.

105. Opp. 8° 1025: Isaac b. Eleazar Perles, *Tikkun motzaei Shabbat* (Amsterdam, 1660). The case of the *Breileft* pamphlet that commemorated Oppenheim's daughter's 1701 wedding represents but a single case of this widespread nostalgia, a constructed memory of time gone by. *Seder ve-hanhaga shel nisuin ha-hatunah breileft ke-minhag shel k"k vrankfurt de-main* (Johan Wusst, 1701). See Chapter 2. On the defensive posture of Ashkenazic Jews toward local custom, see also the literary battles between Central and Eastern Europe depicted in Reiner, "Aliyat 'ha-kehilla ha-gedola.'"

106. Cooper, *Inventing the Indigenous.*

107. The most robust pronouncement of this assessment is Elbaum, *Petihut ve-histagrut,* 24–25.

108. See Ta-Shma, "Seder hadpasatam shel hiddushei ha-Rishonim le-Talmud," and Eliyahu Stern, *The Genius,* 114–142.

109. "Introduction," *Sefer hidushei ha-Ritva* (Amsterdam, 1729). See Ta-Shma, "Seder hadpasatam shel hiddushei ha-Rishonim le-Talmud," 226–227.

110. Asevilli, *Hidushei Hulin le-ha-Ritva.*

111. "Introduction," in ibid.

112. *Pi shnayim* (Altona, 1735).

113. These were also the decades of the activity of the Jessnitz Press, which Moses Mendelssohn credited as being responsible for his earliest intellectual awakenings. See Feiner, *Moses Mendelssohn,* 26–28. On the intellectual modes of Talmud study in the early modern period, see Dimitrovsky, "Al derekh ha-pilpul"; and Reiner, "Temurot be-yeshivot Polin ve-Ashkenaz be-me'ot ha-16-ha-17 ve-ha-vikuah 'al ha-pilpul."

114. Wetzlar and Faierstein, *The Libes Briv of Isaac Wetzlar,* 28b–29a. On Wetzlar, see also Sorkin, "The Early Haskalah," 15–17.

Chapter 5. Endorsing and Incriminating

1. Johns, "The Coming of Print to Europe," 114–119.

2. Berger, "An Invitation to Buy and Read."

3. On the privilege system, see Febvre et al., *The Coming of the Book*, 109, 239–244; and Pettegree, *The Book in the Renaissance*, 41. Armstrong, *Before Copyright*. On Jewish copyright, see Rakower, "Ha-yesod ha-mishpati shel isur ha-hadpasah be-'haskamot' le-sfarim"; Rakower, *Zekhut ha-yozrim be-mekorot ha-Yehudiim;* Hurvitz, "The Rabbinic Perception of Printing," 17–18; and Netanel, *From Maimonides to Microsoft.*

4. Febvre et al., *The Coming of the Book*, 244–247; Eisenhardt, *Die Kaiserliche Aufsicht über Buchdruck.* On the complicated nexus between promotion of the book trade and suppression of suspect material, see Burnett, "The Regulation of Hebrew Printing in Germany"; and Freedman, *Books Without Borders.*

5. In 1603, the Frankfurt synod of rabbis forbade the publication of books, "old or new," without the permission of the *"Batei Avot Bet Din,"* especially of books published in Basel, presumably in response to the recent publication of the heavily censored Basel Talmud printed by Ambrosius Froben. Zimmer, *Jewish Synods in Germany*, 176; Burnett, "Hebrew Censorship in Hanau." On Froben's Talmud, see Heller, *Printing the Talmud: Earliest Printed Editions*, 241–265. In 1607, the Polish-Lithuanian Jewish Council of Four Lands combined economic protectionism with orthodoxy in calling for *medakdekim* (inspectors) to examine prayer books of recent provenance from Basel and Moravia. Burnett, *From Christian Hebraism to Jewish Studies*, 45–46. The governing body of the Polish-Lithuanian Commonwealth placed the responsibility for this regulation in the hands of rabbis and lay leaders in individual communities. Halpern, "Haskamot Va'ad Arba Arazot," 108. Regulation of the content of printed material was never a site of concord. The career of Moses Hagiz, as studied by Elisheva Carlebach (*The Pursuit of Heresy*, 11–12), saw the potential power of the *haskamah* for those jealously guarding the prerogatives of rabbinic authority and religious orthodoxy in an age of heresy. Francesca Bregoli (*Mediterranean Enlightenment*, 190) has pointed toward the diligence exercised by Jewish lay leaders, who initiated the regulatory process by commissioning rabbis of the *publica Jesiba* to assess a text's suitability and then to issue an approbation, which was in and of itself subject to the approval of the lay council.

6. Such a letter came to Oppenheim in 1709 from a man who also sent a manuscript of his new book, hoping Oppenheim would write a *haskamah* (Ms. Mich. 479, 15r).

7. See Ms. Mich. 181, which has approbata in different hands in the front matter of the manuscript.

8. Ms. Opp. 75, 80v–82r.

9. Ms. Opp. 243: Moses Heilberg b. Israel, *Sefer beit avot.* Recommendation to print from 1700. The book was ultimately published in Wilmersdorf in 1712 (Oppenheim owned a copy as Opp. 4° 215).

10. Ms. Opp. 103, *Devarim atikim,* with approbata from ca. 1642–1643, f. 290r–291v. It is entirely possible that the presence of the items in Oppenheim's collection are exceptions that prove the rule, as manuscript texts that were ultimately published might have terminated with the printer — making them beyond the scope of this study and outside of the surviving source base — rather than remained in circulation or in Oppenheim's library.

11. Opp. 8° 568: *Leshon zahav* (Part II of *Mikhtam le-David*) (Amsterdam, 1715).

12. On approbata as instruments of rabbinic control in contest with the power of Jewish lay communal leadership, see Carlebach, *The Pursuit of Heresy,* 11–12.

13. Wetzlar and Faierstein, *The Libes Briv of Isaac Wetzlar,* 72–73.

14. See, for example, Samuel Ashkenazi, *Yefe anaf.* In still other cases, Oppenheim never even saw the book but simply vouched for the character of the author, as he did in his May 1703 approbation to *Avak sofrim* by Abraham Cuenque, whom he met while he was in Hanover.

15. For lists of approbata, see Löwenstein, *Index Approbationum.*

16. As theorized by Gérard Genette (*Paratexts,* 1), the paratext is "what enables a text to become a book and to be offered as such to its readers and, more generally, to the public." See also Sherman, "On the Threshold." Using evocative spatial imagery, Genette invoked the literary figurations of Jorge Luis Borges in likening these paratexts to a "threshold" or "vestibule" that directs readers inward toward the text. Thresholds and vestibules, however, lead both inward and outward; they are liminal and connective.

17. Bourdieu, "Intellectual Field and Creative Project." Bourdieu offers a narrative in which an autonomous cultural field supplants a patronage system. The evidence from rabbinic production reveals that the two existed simultaneously, and different aspects of a book's topography appealed to and revealed the workings of these fields. See also Bourdieu, *Distinction.*

18. *Haskamot* have endured well into the modern, contemporary period as well, especially in the ultra-orthodox domains of book production. See Ahrend, "Haskamot le-sifrei kodesh be-doreinu."

19. Johns, *The Nature of the Book,* 36–37.

20. On the importance of trust in the knowledge communities of early modern English science, with implications for knowledge communities beyond both

the English context and the specific field of science, see Shapin, *A Social History of Truth,* esp. 3–41. See also Shapin, *The Scientific Life.*

21. Abraham Broda, "Haskamah," in Judah Liva b. Samuel Zanwill Oppenheim, *Sefer mateh yehuda.*

22. *Zot torah asher sam Moshe* (Amsterdam, 1698).

23. For the multiply refracted set of images and ideas of the authority of colleagues and critics in this reverberating field of relations, see Bourdieu, "Intellectual Field and Creative Project," 104.

24. Ms. Mich. 465, f. 257v.

25. Eybeschütz, *Kreti u-fleti,* introduction. Samet, "Eybeschütz, Yonatan."

26. Eybeschütz, "Approbation," in Hillel b. Mordekhai of Tismenitz, *Beit Hillel* (Frankfurt/Oder, 1744). See the collection assembled in Leiman, "Haskamot Rabi Yehonatan Eybeschutz ve-Rabi Yaakov Emden."

27. *Sefer hiddushei ha-Gershuni* (Frankfurt am Main, 1710): "Introduction of the composer's grandson." The text reads as follows: "A haskamah on the instructions of the great and famous sage, our teacher Abraham Broda . . . given that for some time our master, teacher, and rabbi, the great and famous sage, chief judge and chief rabbi of our community, may God protect it, has withheld his hand as signatory to give any approbation to any man in the world to print books" (n.p.). Yet given those circumstances, Broda's amanuenses accounted for his acquiescence on account of the great honor deserved by the author, the authenticity of the text being published, and the appeals by colleagues to support the publication and economic protection. Broda also issued an "instruction" to approbate, rather than a direct approbation in his *haskamah* to the Haggadah *Be'er Avraham* (Sulzbach, 1708) and betrayed the same reluctance in an approbation to the responsa of Mordechai Ziskind Rotenberg, when he explicitly stated his discomfort with the excessive praise of approbata, yet produced one all the same.

28. On protest as a trope in modern approbata as well, which often begin with an assertion that the present text is an exception to one's principled practice, see Ahrend, "Haskamot le-sifrei kodesh be-doreinu," 162.

29. *Rabbeinu Asher* (Furth, 1745).

30. *Meginei Eretz* (Dyhernfurth, 1692).

31. Other contemporaneous books, on the other hand, accorded only one or the other the title of chief rabbi, for example, *'Ale de-Yonah* (Furth, 1693).

32. Of the range of Yiddish books in Oppenheim's collection, only the smallest portion carry approbata. On paratextual material in Yiddish writing, see Berger, *Producing Redemption in Amsterdam.* Berger's study rightly explores the range of paratextual material, not approbata alone. Yiddish books were

not the only works that did not carry approbata. For example, none of the Hebrew versions of the *Shevet Yehuda* carry approbata (Adrianople, ca. 1560–1567; Prague, 1608; Amsterdam, 1655; Amsterdam, 1709), nor do all the Yiddish ones (Krakow, 1591; Amsterdam, 1648; Amsterdam, 1700), although the one from Sulzbach (1700) does.

33. This is not to suggest that paratextual material was not present in Yiddish works, nor is it to say that copyright and advertising were unimportant matters. It is simply that rabbis were not deemed essential to that process in Yiddish texts, which raises questions about their efficacy in the domain of Hebrew printing.

34. The alleged power of the approbation found both supporters and detractors in the nineteenth century and beyond. Some rabbinic figures still prided themselves on their rigorous oversight of the production of books, such as the rabbi of Lemberg, Joseph Saul Nathanson, called "Sar ha-Maskim" (a play on the biblical cup-bearer who shared a prison cell with Joseph), on account of his prolific pen. Others, like the maskil Abraham Jacob Papirna (1840–1919) tacitly and grudgingly acknowledged the stranglehold held by the rabbinic elite as he railed against the efficacy of the *haskamah*. In support or dissent, both acknowledged and confirmed an understanding of the approbation in its regulatory role, albeit one that was different from what it purported to be. Gries, *The Book in the Jewish World*, 117–118. Parush, *Reading Jewish Women*, 21.

35. Wetzlar and Faierstein, *The Libes Briv of Isaac Wetzlar*, 32a.

36. For a full treatment of the affair, see Carlebach, *The Pursuit of Heresy*, 75–159. On Teomim Fränkel, see Kaufmann, "R. Chajjim Jona Theonim-Fränkel." While Hayon was a guest in his home, Oppenheim was apparently out of the city. This was the year of his wife's death, so perhaps he was attending to matters on behalf of her estate, or, perhaps as on other occasions, he was traveling in the service of his library. Jacob Emden credited Oppenheim with an excommunication of a previous Sabbatean traveler through Moravia and Bohemia, Judah Leib "Leibele" of Prossnitz, who claimed to be the Messiah, son of Joseph, a forerunner of the messianic redeemer. See Jacob Emden, *Torat ha-kenaot* (Altona, 1752), 39b.

37. Kaufmann, "La Lutte de R. Naftali Cohen contre Hayyoun." On the controversy, see Carlebach, *The Pursuit of Heresy*, 89, 95. On Kohen (Katz), see Liebes, "A Profile of R. Naphtali Katz."

38. "Haskamah of David Oppenheim," in front matter of Hayon's works. Two copies of Hayon's *Divrei Nehemiah* (Opp. 4° 277 and Opp. 4° 278 [blue paper copy]) and one copy of his *Oz le-Elohim* (Opp. 4° 805) joined Oppenheim's

collection (all Berlin, 1713). See also Ms. Opp. 764, a manuscript containing biographical information about various kabbalists, including Nehemiah Hayon. On this text, see Scholem, "Teudah le-toldot Nehemiah Hayon ve-ha-Shabta'ut"; and Benayahu, *Sefer toldot ha-Ari.*

39. Carlebach, *The Pursuit of Heresy,* 123–124.

40. NLI Ms. Heb. 4° 966, published in Feld, "Mikhtav shalom me-kavod ha-gaon rabenu David Oppenheim Zt"L."

41. See Feld, "Mikhtav shalom," 184–185.

42. Emden, *Megilat sefer,* 37.

43. "Approbation of David Oppenheim," in Rovigo and Ashkenazi, *Sefer eshel Avraham.* See also the approbata of Wolf Wedeles and Abraham Broda, both rabbis in Prague. See also Doktór, "Erster Missionar Neuen Stils und Verleger," 276.

44. Lipschitz, *Sefer derekh Hayyim.* See the comments on Lipschitz in Tishby, *Netivei emunah ve-minut,* 43–44, 206–207. Oppenheim's associates similarly straddled the frontiers of licit and illicit Jewish texts. Likewise, Joseph Darshan, the preacher who was so instrumental in shepherding the Rashbam manuscript through Jablonski's workshop, was also later tarred with the smear of Sabbateanism. His kabbalistic prayer book, *Keter Yosef* (Berlin, 1700), was subsequently condemned as heretical by Moses Hagiz. In this case, however, even Jacob Emden defended the work, claiming that Sabbatean material had been added unbeknownst to its author by others involved with the publication. Maciejko, *The Mixed Multitude,* 77–78.

45. Ms. Opp. 410: Nathan of Gaza, *Sefer ha-beriah.*

46. Opp. 12° 364.

47. Ms. Opp. 773.

48. See "Sermons of Solomon Molkho," Ms. Opp. 422, 423 (copied in Prague on January 5, 1712), 424; and Molkho, *Sefer ha-mefo'ar,* Ms. Opp. 568.

49. Opp. 8° 654: Jacob Taussig of Prague, *Ayn shayn naye lid fun mashiah* (Prague?, 1666). The library also included the works of the anti-Sabbatean movement as well, for example, Joseph Ergas's 1715 tract against Hayon, listed in a late catalogue of the Oppenheim collection, Universitätsbibliothek JCS, Frankfurt am Main, Ms. hebr. oct. 231, 18.

50. Elisheva Carlebach (*The Pursuit of Heresy,* 76–80) has argued that before 1713 a "conspiracy of silence" prevailed, in which rabbis elected to stifle all mention of Sabbateanism rather than run the risk of publicizing its spread, fearing its impact either on other Jews or on the Jewish image in the eyes of Christian observers. For the tension between ownership of these books and recognition of their illicit pedigree in the writings of Pinhas Katzenellinbogen

of Boskowice (a former student of Oppenheim's), see Kahana, "The Allure of Forbidden Knowledge."

51. Benayahu, "He-'hevra kedosha' shel rabi Yehuda Hasid," 133–134. On Oppenheim's relationship to this movement, see Teplitsky, "A 'Prince of the Land of Israel' in Prague."

52. See Prokeš, "Der Antisemitismus der Behörden," 58–61; Putík, "The Prague Jewish Community," 37–42; Matušíková, "Licences for the Baptism of Jews"; Carlebach, *The Death of Simon Abeles;* and Shore, *The Eagle and the Cross,* 74–75.

53. Evans, *The Making of the Habsburg Monarchy,* 311; Louthan, *Converting Bohemia,* 81. On "composite monarchies" as a routine feature of dynastic political life, see Elliott, "A Europe of Composite Monarchies."

54. For seventeenth-century confessional absolutism, see Bireley, "Confessional Absolutism in the Habsburg Lands." For evidence of Joseph's partial curbing of Jesuit influence, see Ingrao, *In Quest and Crisis,* 11, 15–16. See also Catalano, "'Das Temporale Wird Schon So Weith Extendiret.'"

55. In 1627 the Habsburg monarchy issued a far-reaching "renewed constitution" (*Obnovené zřízení zemské; Veneuerte Landesordnung*) that abolished elective monarchy in Bohemia (making the Bohemian crown the hereditary property of the Habsburgs), raised German to official state usage alongside Czech, and subordinated state functionaries exclusively to the king, rather, as previously, to the commonwealth of Bohemia. Evans, *The Making of the Habsburg Monarchy,* 198–200; Evans, "The Habsburg Monarchy and Bohemia," 86–87; Bergerhausen, "Die 'Verneuerte Landesordnung' in Böhmen 1627." It also made all non-Catholic religions illegal except for Judaism, which was permitted on account of the economic utility of Jews to the state, but not without efforts to mitigate and minimize the Jewish presence in the city. See Prokeš, "Der Antisemitismus der Behörden"; and Lipscher, "Jüdische Gemeinden in Böhmen."

56. NA Ms. J4/16, f. 2–4; Prokeš, "Der Antisemitismus der Behörden," 80–82. The tug-of-war over censorship of Jewish books had begun more than a century earlier. See Lieben, "Beiträge zur Geschichte der Zensur Hebräischer Drucke in Präg"; Kisch, "Die Zensur Judischer Bücher in Böhmen"; and Putík, "The Censorship of Hebrew Books in Prague."

57. NA Ms. J4/16, f. 5; Putík, "The Prague Jewish Community," 28–30.

58. Popper, *The Censorship of Hebrew Books,* 104–117.

59. Katzenellinbogen, *Sefer yesh manhilin,* 188.

60. JMP Ms. 120064 ("Kopialbuch of David Oppenheim"): §65 (pp. 224–226). As Jeffrey Freedman (*Books Without Borders, 69–70*) has noted, it was in the

interests of customs officers not to be too scrupulous in halting the movement of suspect literature, lest they forfeit the duties they might collect for the objects to travel through their ports and beyond into other lands, where the offensive material would be someone else's problem.

61. Wolf, "Auto da Fé Jüdischer Bücher in Prag 1714."

62. JMP Ms. 120064 ("Kopialbuch of David Oppenheim"): §95 (pp. 319–321).

63. Ducreux, "Reading unto Death." The Prague Jesuit Antonín Koniáš (1691–1760) created both an index of prohibited Protestant Bohemian books and pamphlets approved for distribution. Svatoš, "Les Usages du livre religieux"; Clossey, *Salvation and Globalization in the Early Jesuit Missions,* 247. For a discussion of the Janus-face of censorship, see Raz-Krakotzkin, *The Censor, the Editor, and the Text.* On the role of Hebraists in Jewish book regulation, see Burnett, "The Regulation of Hebrew Printing in Germany." On Hebraism in the service of conversion, see Boxel, *Jewish Books in Christian Hands.*

64. Haselbauer, *Des gründlichen Berichts,* vol. 1, A. The Yiddish translation is only slightly different. This literary strategy was also born of Haselbauer's personal experience with proselytizing. The Jesuit recounted his interactions with two Jewish youths, one age seven, the other age nine, who were both better versed in the *Toledot Yeshu* and the curses against Edom than they were in the Pentateuch. Haselbauer, ibid., 4–5.

65. Haselbauer, *Des gründlichen Berichts,* A–A2.

66. Haselbauer, *Kurtzer Inhalt deß Christl.*

67. For examples of Christian Hebraism in this more classic understanding, see Manuel, *The Broken Staff;* and Deutsch, "Polemical Ethnographies." Grafton and Weinberg, *"I Have Always Loved the Holy Tongue."*

68. Wolf, "Zur Geschichte des Jüdischen Gemeinwesens in Prag." On the contract agreement between the monarchy and the tax consortium of Samuel Taussig, see CAHJP Ms. CS263: "Kontrakt Zwischen der Hofkamer in Wien und der Pragerischen Judengemeinde Primatorn Samuel Isaac Sachssel und seiner Konsorten, die haupt Perdonskassa betr" (1702).

69. NA Ms. J4/16, f. 194–201. This matter has been recently treated more fully in Maciejko, "The Rabbi and the Jesuit," esp. 157–161. See also Putík, "The Prague Jewish Community," 30–37.

70. It remains unclear whether Oppenheim fulfilled these duties at any point. A letter to the imperial offices by the Prague printers Loebel Jeiteles and Berl Back (also spelled Pack) of April 1714 acknowledged the work of the censor "and the corrections of the chief rabbi of Prague." NA Ms. J4/16, f. 117r.

71. Rabinowitz and Haberman, *Ma'amar 'al hadpasat ha-Talmud,* 112–114. See the more recent careful reconstruction of this episode in Maciejko, "The

Rabbi and the Jesuit." In his Introduction to *Kreti u-fleti,* Eybeschütz explained that anti-Christian sentiment in Jewish books was a holdover from ancient texts and was largely misplaced with regard to the Christians of his time, who "observe law and justice, believe in creation, and the existence of God, and his providence, and the Torah of Moses and the prophets."

72. For Eybeschütz's financing, see *Rabbeinu Asher* (Furth, 1745), printed in Leiman, "Haskamot rabi Yehonatan Eybeschutz ve-rabi Yaakov Emden," 175. See also Leiman, "Perush ha-gaon Rabi Yehonatan Eybeschuz." On his claims regarding his role as a disputant, see the Introduction, in Eybeschütz, *Kreti u-fleti.*

73. Emden, *Hitabkut,* 3b.

74. Samet, "Eybeschütz, Yonatan."

75. The only surviving document from this apologetic was published a century and a half later in the Hebrew newspaper *Ha-magid.* Some have expressed doubts as to its authenticity. R"K, "Ktav hitnazlut ve-teshuvah me-hokhmei Prag al hadpasat ha-Talmud 'im hashmatot bi-shnat 487 le-P"K."

76. Opp. Fol. 591.

77. On this sensational affair, see also Lieben, "David Oppenheim"; Nosek and Sadek, "Georgio Diodato und David Oppenheim"; Putík, "Prague Jews and Judah Hasid"; Teplitsky, "Jewish Money, Jesuit Censors, and the Habsburg Monarchy"; and Miller, "Rabbi David Oppenheim on Trial."

78. For the coffeehouse as a site of interaction, see Ellis, *The Coffee-House.* See also Cowan, *The Social Life of Coffee.* On the place of the coffeehouse in the world of the book, see Johns, "Coffeehouses and Print Shops."

79. Rabbis actually saw little problem with coffeehouse interaction during its early decades, and Christian concern with Jews in the coffeehouse was explicitly linked with the visit of the imperial retinue in 1723, perhaps offering the exception to a more congenial rule. For the incorporation of coffee into Jewish rites and routines, see Horowitz, "Coffee, Coffeehouses." On rabbis and coffee, see Liberles, *Jews Welcome Coffee,* 55–57. For the imperial visit of 1723, see Weber, "Eine Kaiserreise nach Böhmen I.J. 1723," 164–165. On Jews and coffee in Prague, see Kahana, "Shabbat be-veit ha-kafe shel kehillat kodesh Prag." On coffee in the German lands, see Hochmuth, *Globale Güter.*

80. Jesuits established outposts across the Ottoman lands, alongside Dominicans, Capuchins, Franciscans, Carmelites, and others in Damascus, Constantinople, Sidon, Acre, Tripoli, and Aleppo. Diodato, *Wehe-Klag oder Lamentation,* A(r), C2(r). Missionary activity and educational work were the hallmarks of early modern Jesuit activity (and success). On the educational thrust of the traditional religious orders during the Counter-Reformation, see Hsia, *The*

World of Catholic Renewal, 27–31. On mobility, even across imperial frontiers, as a feature of early modern life, see Subrahmanyam, "Connected Histories."

81. Diodato, *Anfang der Weißheit,* A(v). Demetz, *Prague in Black and Gold,* 239; Shore, *The Eagle and the Cross,* 15–16. On the role of Armenians in Vienna's coffee culture, especially the founding role of one Johannes Diodato, whose name and prominence in Vienna at the time of Georgio Diodato's six-month sojourn are too coincidental to ignore, see Teply, "Johannes Diodato"; and Teply, "Kundschafter, Kuriere, Kaufleute, Kaffeesieder."

82. Diodato, *Wehe-Klag oder Lamentation.* Jesuit missionaries from Mexico to China would literally use maps to demonstrate the expansiveness, and thus supremacy, of this world religion. Clossey, *Salvation and Globalization,* 102–104.

83. Jerusalem was home to both Ashkenazic and Sephardic communities that operated distinctly from each other, both in their internal constitution and in their relations with Jewish diasporas. See Teplitsky, "A 'Prince of the Land of Israel,'" 255–263.

84. NA, Ms. CK 1718, VII c (KK) 324, 10r; Diodato, *Anfang der Weißheit,* A(v). The pasha had become the Jews' creditor by acquiring a promissory note from one Tasthan (or Taschtan), to whom the Jews owed a significant amount of money and who was no friend of the community. In the hyperbole of the Jerusalem elders, "he sharpened his teeth and decreed that the entire Jewish population, from great to small . . . should be arrested." NA, ČDK, sign. 2065, karton 912, 18v. See the letters to Breslau and to Samson Wertheimer in Vienna and Frankfurt published in Rivkind, "Tseror Ketavim Le-Korot Ha-Yehudim Be-Erets Yisrael," 318.

85. Diodato, *Anfang der Weißheit,* A(r). Also cited in Lieben, "David Oppenheim," 31. The name "Siman Toff" is recorded in the most complete extant contemporary document relating to this affair. It was likely "Siman-Tov." The monies were not necessarily Toff's alone to dispose of; they technically belonged to his underage and orphaned niece. NA, ČDK, sign. 2065, karton 912, 2r.

86. NA, ČDK, sign. 2065, karton 912, 2v.

87. Diodato, *Anfang der Weißheit,* A2r.

88. Putík, "Prague Jews and Judah Hasid," 51.

89. Diodato, *Anfang der Weißheit,* A2r. For an early study tracing Diodato's biography through his two published works, see Zíbrt, "Giorgio Diodato."

90. Diodato, *Anfang der Weißheit,* A2r.

91. Ibid., A2r.

92. Ibid., A2v.

93. NA, CK 1718, VII c (KK) 324, 3v.

94. Diodato, *Anfang der Weißheit,* A2(r).

95. NA, CK 1718, VII c (KK) 324, 7r.

96. Diodato, *Anfang der Weißheit,* D(v).

97. NA, CK 1718, VII c (KK) 324, 6r.

98. Imperial Order, January 30, 1723, published in Diodato, *Anfang der Weiß-heit,* A2v–Br. The commission was ordered into existence by Charles VI on January 1, 1714, to offer suggestions for reducing the Jewish population of the city. Its establishment was part of a more vigorous Habsburg effort at domestic reform afforded by the peacetime in the wake of the War of Spanish Succession (1701–1714) that included changes in diplomacy and finance. The commission's instructions included a comprehensive collection of historical documents pertaining to the Jewish question in Prague. JMP Ms. 120064 ("Kopialbuch of David Oppenheim"): §120 (pp. 390–395). See also Prokeš, "Der Antisemitismus der Behörden," 199–218. For the administrative reforms of the second decade of the eighteenth century, see Stoye, "Emperor Charles VI." In Prussia a similar body was established in 1708 and again in 1720, only to be abolished in 1769. On "Jewry commissions" as a feature of absolutist states across the German lands, see Breuer, "Part 1," 145–146. See also Hsia, "The Jews and the Emperors," 79.

99. Before 1718 the trial records mention Hebrew books only once, and in a perfunctory way. Only with Jesuit involvement did the focus shift. See NA, CK 1718, VII c (KK) 324, 19r.

100. Listing case after case, Diodato marshaled the testimony of travelers and citizens to speak to the movement of people, and their money, out of Prague. NA, ČDK, sign. 2065, karton 912, 37v–43r.

101. Lieben, "David Oppenheim," 34–35.

102. Diodato, *Anfang der Weißheit,* A2v. Much of Diodato's knowledge of Jews and Judaism, and therefore his animosity toward them, may have come from Haselbauer's teaching. Nosek and Sadek, "Georgio Diodato und David Oppenheim," 18–19. On the motif of secrecy in anti-Jewish accusations, see Carlebach, "Attribution of Secrecy and Perceptions of Jewry"; and Jütte, *The Age of Secrecy.*

103. NA, ČDK, sign. 2065, karton 912, 35v–36v; NM VII_C_6, 20r–22r.

104. NA, ČDK, sign. 2065, karton 912, 54r.

105. Some of the books assembled by Haselbauer actually bore the imprimatur of local censors, such as Lipschitz, *Sefer derekh Hayyim,* and Joel b. Gad of Shebrshin, *Sefer meginei zahav.*

106. On the imperial and territorial conflicts over censorship, see Eisenhardt, *Die Kaiserliche Aufsicht über Buchdruck,* esp. 10–15. For Bohemia, see Putík,

"The Prague Jewish Community," 31. For the porous boundaries on account of the fragmented political state of the Reich, see Freedman, *Books Without Borders,* 115–118.

107. Samet, "Eybeschütz, Yonatan." See Eybeschütz, Introduction to *Kreti u-fleti,* where he explains that approbata serve little purpose other than to heap praise upon the author and create haughtiness.

108. Diodato, *Anfang der Weißheit,* D2v; NA, ČDK, sign. 2065, karton 912, 101–103.

109. NA, ČDK, sign. 2065, karton 912, 59v; JMP, Ms. 120064, 641-644. See also Brilling, "Ha-gezerah al maot a"y be-ostryah be-shnat 1723"; and Abraham Yaari, "Mi hayu shnei shlihei a"y."

110. NA, ČDK, sign. 2065, karton 912, 64r–65v.

111. Oppenheim did not entirely fall from imperial grace. This ruling only further incorporated him within the apparatus of the Habsburg absolutist state, bringing his jurisdiction more tightly into line with imperial policy and philosophy. His chief rabbinic functions remained fully intact, as did his imperial patronage. In 1723 Oppenheim greeted Emperor Charles VI and his wife on their first imperial visit to Prague and blessed the royal couple on behalf of the city's Jews. See JMP Ms. 120064 ("*Kopialbuch* of David Oppenheim"), pp. 628–631.

112. Diodato, *Anfang der Weißheit,* Bv.

113. See *Hiddushei ha-Rashba* on Talmud Tractate Bava Kama (Prague, 1734); and *Sefer hiddushei hulin le-ha-Ritva zlh"h* (Prague: Grandsons of Moses Katz, 1735).

Epilogue and Conclusion

1. Findlen, *Possessing Nature,* 391.

2. Graetz, "Court Jews in Economics and Politics," 34.

3. Lieben, "David Oppenheim," 20–21; Duschinsky, *Toldot Ha-Ga'on Rav David Openhaymer,* 80–84.

4. For a contemporary account, see Jost, "Eine Familien-Megillah." On Behrens and his family, see Schedlitz, *Leffmann Behrens.*

5. Michaelis (*Orientalische und exegetische Bibliothek,* 14) explicitly tells us that he viewed the library in Hildesheim: "Dies Bibliothek kam nun mit Hirschel Isaac Oppenheimer, ich weiß nicht in welchem Jahr, nach Hildesheim."

6. "Verzeichniz von Büchern und Handschriften der Sammlung des David Oppenheimer," Universitätsbibliothek JCS, Frankfurt am Main, Ms. hebr oct 231. It is not quite clear when this visit occurred. Some of the books

listed were published in the last year of Oppenheim's life, perhaps even after his death, for example, *Sefer minhat Yehudah* (Hamburg, 1736) and *Be'er tov* (Altona, 1737).

7. The dating of this text's composition is not known, and it may be that this is the catalogue that Oppenheim kept with him during his travels (as attested to by the library's visitors), although the absence of his handwriting anywhere in the text makes this unlikely.

8. Marx, "The History of David Oppenheimer's Library," 245.

9. McKitterick, *Print, Manuscript, and the Search for Order,* 14–15.

10. Ms. Mich. 630. Marx, "Some Jewish Book Collectors," 221–224.

11. These included manuscript editions of *Nish'al David,* Ms. Mich. 430, 431, 438. Oppenheim letters, Ms. Mich. 465, 466, 479. *Metziat David* on Bava Metzia, Ms. Mich. 566–567; *Mei shiloah* on Gittin, Ms. Mich. 591; Hiddushim on Hullin, Ms. Mich. 590; Hiddushim on Bava Batra, Ms. Mich. 598; Ir David on aggadah, Ms. Mich. 601, 452, 578, 90–92, 593; *Tehilla le-David,* Ms. Mich. 447; Notes on Bible and Midrash and Perek Shira, Ms. Mich. 453–454. For Michael's description of Oppenheim's books and manuscripts, many of which were in his own possession, see Michael, Loeb, and Berliner, *Or ha-hayyim,* §696. For a catalogue of Michael's library, see Steinschneider Zunz, *Ozerot Hayyim.*

12. One such book, Ms. Mich. 385, which combines three titles in a single binding, identifies the first *Sefer he-hayyim* as copied for David Oppenheim, and the latter two titles, *Sefer ha-shem* and *Sodot ha-tefillah,* as copied for his son-in-law Michael Beer in Friedberg.

13. Marx, "The History of David Oppenheimer's Library," 245.

14. Ms. Rosenthaliana H. Ros. 24, 2r.

15. Ibid., 3r.

16. Ibid., 6r–v.

17. Ibid., 8r.

18. Ibid., 15r. Marx, "The History of David Oppenheimer's Library," 248–249; Pelger, "Die Bibliothek des David Oppenheimer," 76–77. See also Pelger, *Wissenschaft des Judentums.*

19. The interest of Daniel Itzig in Berlin was reported by Jakob Jonas Björnståhl. See Hartman, "Ueber die Berühmte," 121; Marx, "The History of David Oppenheimer's Library," 250; and Pelger, "Die Bibliothek des David Oppenheimer," 78.

20. Marx, "The History of David Oppenheimer's Library," 249–250; Pelger, "Die Bibliothek des David Oppenheimer," 77.

21. Johann Michael Brauer, *Catalogus . . . hebraischen Bibliothek . . . David*

Oppenheimers (Hamburg, 1782). Michaelis still found the catalogue to be lacking and criticized its shortcomings in print the following year (*Orientalische und exegetische Bibliothek*). Marx, "The History of David Oppenheimer's Library," 250–251; Pelger, "Die Bibliothek des David Oppenheimer," 77.

22. Findlen, *Possessing Nature*, 393–407.

23. Michaelis, *Orientalische und exegetische Bibliothek*, 17–19; Pelger, "Die Bibliothek des David Oppenheimer," 82.

24. Marx, "The History of David Oppenheimer's Library," 251–252; Pelger, "Die Bibliothek des David Oppenheimer," 77–78.

25. On the demands of the emancipating state upon the reform of Jewish identity and practice, see Berkovitz, *The Shaping of Jewish Identity;* and Sorkin, *The Transformation of German Jewry*. On Jacobson, see Jacob Rader Marcus, *Israel Jacobson.*

26. Heinemann, "An den Geehrten Verfasser des Aufsatzes im Orient."

27. Meyer, "Materialien zur Geschichte der Bibliothek David Oppenheims"; Marx, "The History of David Oppenheimer's Library," 252–253; Pelger, *Wissenschaft des Judentums,* 114.

28. Hartman, "Ueber die Berühmte," 134.

29. Pelger, "Die Bibliothek des David Oppenheimer," 79–80.

30. Yitzhak Ayzik ben Asher Metz, *Kohelet David/Collectio Davidis* (Hamburg: Samuel and Judah Bonn, 1826), introduction. See also Lebrecht, "Die Oppenheimer'sche Bibliothek," 277–278.

31. Marx, "The History of David Oppenheimer's Library," 254; Pelger, *Wissenschaft des Judentums,* 115–116.

32. See JMP Ms. 93 (NLI Film F46568), "Collection of notebooks that were copied for me . . ." (May 24, 1829).

33. Nicoll (1793–1828), originally of Balliol College, was a young enthusiast of Judaica. He was appointed sub-librarian at the Bodleian in 1814 and was promoted to the Regius Professorship of Hebrew and Canonry at Christ Church College, Oxford, in 1822 at the age of only twenty-nine. Nicoll, *Sermons;* Macray, *Annals of the Bodleian Library,* 296.

34. Bodleian Ms. Add. C. 166, 2r.

35. Ibid., 2r.

36. Ibid., 4r.

37. Ibid., 6r.

38. Ibid., 8r; Nicoll, *Sermons,* xl. This sum was a pittance: in 1848 the library bought 862 manuscripts of the H. J. Michael collection (which included most of Oppenheim's personal correspondence and manuscript commentaries on the Talmud and Midrash) for 1,030 pounds, nearly half the price of the Oppenheim collection for a fraction of the material.

39. Their importance for the holdings at the Bodleian cannot be exaggerated. The university's previous major acquisition of Hebraica was in 1659 with the library of John Selden (1584–1654). Some 225 volumes were added with the combined collections of Pococke and Huntington in 1693. Another 2,100 volumes were added to the collections between 1844 and 1857. Macray, *Annals of the Bodleian Library*, 319–320; Craster, *History of the Bodleian Library*, 105–107. For the few books that were separated from the collection but made their way back, see Fürst, *Bibliotheca Judaica:* 42–51.

40. Quoted in Trautmann-Waller, "Leopold Zunz and Moritz Steinschneider," 94.

41. Zunz, *Zur Geschichte und Literatur*, 235.

42. Duschinsky, "Rabbi David Oppenheimer," 219.

Bibliography

Manuscripts

MICHAEL COLLECTION, BODLEIAN LIBRARIES,
OXFORD UNIVERSITY

Ms. Mich. 90

Ms. Mich. 181

Ms. Mich. 194

Ms. Mich. 325

Ms. Mich. 385

Ms. Mich. 430

Ms. Mich. 431

Ms. Mich. 438

Ms. Mich. 447

Ms. Mich. 453

Ms. Mich. 465

Ms. Mich. 466

Ms. Mich. 479

Ms. Mich. 541

Ms. Mich. 544

Ms. Mich. 566

Ms. Mich. 567

Ms. Mich. 591

OPPENHEIM COLLECTION, BODLEIAN LIBRARIES,
OXFORD UNIVERSITY

Ms. Opp. 1 (Neu. 75)

Ms. Opp. 2 (Neu. 74)

Ms. Opp. 11 (Neu. 1669)

Ms. Opp. 19 (Neu. 170)

Ms. Opp. 42 (Neu. 678)

Ms. Opp. 71 (Neu. 810)

Ms. Opp. 75 (Neu. 833)

Ms. Opp. 78 (Neu. 881)

Ms. Opp. 94 (Neu. 800)

Ms. Opp. 96 (Neu. 445)

Ms. Opp. 98 (Neu 433)

Ms. Opp. 99 (Neu 446)

Ms. Opp. 103 (Neu. 1563)

Ms. Opp. 111 (Neu. 1566)

Ms. Opp. 134 (Neu. 1958)

Ms. Opp. 139 (Neu. 924)

Ms. Opp. 149 (Neu. 2217)

Ms. Opp. 156 (Neu. 1114)

Ms. Opp. 175 (Neu. 1154)

Ms. Opp. 184 (Neu. 2060)

Ms. Opp. 186 (Neu. 37)

Ms. Opp. 197 (Neu. 212)

Ms. Opp. 199 (Neu. 149)

Ms. Opp. 200 (Neu. 210)

Ms. Opp. 214 (Neu. 2272)

Ms. Opp. 231 (Neu. 980)

Ms. Opp. 234 (Neu. 265)

Ms. Opp. 238 (Neu. 987)

Ms. Opp. 242 (Neu. 941)

Ms. Opp. 243 (Neu. 387)

Ms. Opp. 246 (Neu. 388)

Ms. Opp. 258 (Neu. 727)

Ms. Opp. 259 (Neu. 922)

Ms. Opp. 279 (Neu. 920)

Ms. Opp. 289 (Neu. 686)

Ms. Opp. 302 (Neu. 802)

Ms. Opp. 304 (Neu. 803)

Ms. Opp. 305 (Neu. 808)

Ms. Opp. 316 (Neu. 809)

Ms. Opp. 329 (Neu. 817)

Ms. Opp. 334 (Neu. 863)

Ms. Opp. 337 (Neu. 884)

Ms. Opp. 338 (Neu. 874)

Ms. Opp. 340 (Neu. 875)

Ms. Opp. 353 (Neu. 503)

Ms. Opp. 355 (Neu. 480)

Ms. Opp. 358 (Neu. 536)

Ms. Opp. 361 (Neu. 440)

Ms. Opp. 369 (Neu. 454)

Ms. Opp. 380 (Neu. 437)

Ms. Opp. 381 (Neu. 436)

Ms. Opp. 383 (Neu. 411)

Ms. Opp. 392 (Neu. 2199)

Ms. Opp. 395 (Neu. 1829)

Ms. Opp. 410 (Neu. 1963)

Ms. Opp. 422 (Neu. 1661)

Ms. Opp. 423 (Neu. 1659)

Ms. Opp. 424 (Neu. 1660)

Ms. Opp. 429 (Neu. 1786)

Ms. Opp. 463 (Neu. 1954)

Ms. Opp. 467 (Neu. 1791)

Ms. Opp. 469 (Neu. 1782)

Ms. Opp. 485 (Neu. 1965)

Ms. Opp. 506 (Neu. 1812)

Ms. Opp. 508 (Neu. 1778)

Ms. Opp. 511 (Neu. 1882)

Ms. Opp. 512 (Neu. 1882)

Ms. Opp. 513 (Neu. 1882)

Ms. Opp. 514 (Neu. 1887)

Ms. Opp. 515 (Neu. 1883)

Ms. Opp. 516 (Neu. 1883)

Ms. Opp. 517 (Neu. 1883)

Ms. Opp. 540 (Neu. 1567)

Ms. Opp. 545 (Neu. 1872)

Ms. Opp. 568 (Neu. 1551)

Ms. Opp. 614 (Neu. 2275)

Ms. Opp. 615 (Neu. 2230)

Ms. Opp. 616 (Neu. 2216)

Ms. Opp. 618 (Neu. 1800)

Ms. Opp. 643 (Neu. 1109)

Ms. Opp. 648 (Neu. 1127)

Ms. Opp. 650 (Neu. 1128)

Ms. Opp. 652 (Neu. 1770)

Ms. Opp. 665 (Neu. 1185)

Ms. Opp. 667 (Neu. 1167)

Ms. Opp. 674 (Neu. 1152)

Ms. Opp. 680 (Neu. 2376)

Ms. Opp. 685 (Neu. 2084)

Ms. Opp. 688 (Neu. 2123)

Ms. Opp. 699 (Neu. 2075)

Ms. Opp. 700 (Neu. 2058)

Ms. Opp. 702 (Neu. 2057)

Ms. Opp. 708 (Neu. 2059)

Ms. Opp. 711 (Neu. 2209)

Ms. Opp. 715 (Neu. 2206)

Ms. Opp. 716 (Neu. 2205)

Ms. Opp. 721 (Neu. 951)

Ms. Opp. 730 (Neu. 806)

Ms. Opp. 741 (Neu. 1538)

Ms. Opp. 750 (Neu. 910)

Ms. Opp. 751 (Neu. 909)

Ms. Opp. 764 (Neu. 2211)

Ms. Opp. 773 (Neu. 1175)

Ms. Opp. 775 (Neu. 1518)

Ms. Add. C. 166

Ms. Opp. Add. 4° 43

Ms. Opp. Add. 4° 68 (Neu. 2015)

Ms. Opp. Add. 4° 135

Ms. Opp. Add. Fol. 6-7

Printed Books, Oppenheim Collection, Bodleian Libraries, Oxford University

Opp. 4° 49: *Hamisha Humshe Torah.* Amsterdam, 1680.

Opp. 4° 215: *Beit avot.* Wilhermsdorf, 1712.

Opp. 4° 219: *Devek tov.* Venice, 1588.

Opp. 4° 277: Nehemiah Hayon, *Divrei Nehemiah.* Berlin, 1713.

Opp. 4° 278: Nehemiah Hayon, *Divrei Nehemiah.* Berlin, 1713.

Opp. 4° 320: *Sermoes Que Pragaraõ os doctos ingenious. . . .* Amsterdam, 1675.

Opp. 4° 468: *Biur al sha'arei dura.* Prague, 1629; *Kiryat Hannah.* Prague, 1612; *Sha'arei teshuva.* Krakow, 1581; *Tola'at Yaakov.* Krakow, 1581; *Kitzur amudei golah.* Krakow, 1579; *Birkat ha-mazon.* Amsterdam, 1694.

Opp. 4° 517: Benjamin Slonik, *Seder mitzvot nashim.* Basel, 1602.

Opp. 4° 518: Benjamin Slonik, *Seder mitzvot nashim.* Krakow, 1577.

Opp. 4° 519: Benjamin Slonik, *Seder mitzvot nashim.* Hanau, 1627.

Opp. 4° 541: Jacob Weil, *Shehitot u-vedikot.* Krakow, 1577.

Opp. 4° 544: Jacob Weil, *Shehitot u-vedikot.* Basel, 1602.

Opp. 4° 557: "Takkanot of the Perdons Contract." Prague, 1702.

Opp. 4° 605 (1): *Sefer tikkunei zevah.* Prague, 1604.

Opp. 4° 612: Johanan b. Isaac, *Ma'ase rav po K"K London.* Amsterdam, 1707.

Opp. 4° 643: *She'elot ve-teshuvot.* Venice, 1663; Yedaya b. Abraham Bedarshi, *Leshon ha-zahav.* Venice, 1599.

Opp. 4° 758: Shabbetai Bass, *Sefer siftei yeshenim.* Amsterdam, 1680.

Opp. 4° 759: Shabbetai Bass, *Sefer siftei yeshenim.* Amsterdam, 1680.

Opp. 4° 792: *Hesed le-Avraham.* Sulzbach, 1685; *Sefer Hasidim.* Sulzbach, 1685; *Ta'anugei Shabbat.* Sulzbach, 1685; *Davar she-bi-kedusha.* Sulzbach, 1685; *Zera Avraham* Sulzbach, 1685.

Opp. 4° 805: Nehemiah Hayon, *Oz le-Elohim.* Berlin, 1713.

Opp. 4° 868: *Judscher Tiryak.* Altdorf, 1680.

Opp. 4° 886: *Judscher Tiryak.* Hanau, 1615.

Opp. 4° 903 (1): Don Isaac Abarbanel, *Sefer rosh amanah.* Venice, 1545.

Opp. 4° 959: Eliezer Lieberman b. Juspe Schammes, Broadside. Amsterdam, 1692.

Opp. 4° 1018: *Ot emet.* Salonika, 1565.

Opp. 4° 1064: Elyakim b. Jacob Melammed, *Leshon limmudim.* Amsterdam, 1686.

Opp. 4° 1102 (1): Saul Levi Mortara, *Sermaô funeral.* Amsterdam, 1652.

Opp. 4° 1239: *Tefillah le-omram be-khol yom erev va-voker.* Prague, 1713.

Opp. 4° 1240: *Selihot.* Prague, 1713.

Opp. 4° 1241: *Tefillah le-omram be-khol yom erev va-voker.* Prague, 1713.

Opp. 4° 1342: *Midrash be-hidush perush le-Hagadat Pesah.* Venice, 1641.

Opp. 4° 1401: *Yosippon.*

Opp. 4° 1422 (1): *Kenig Artur's hof.* Prague, ca. 1652–1659?

Opp. 8° 49: *Hamishah Humshe Torah.* Berlin, 1705.

Opp. 8° 53: *Hamishah Humshe Torah.* Berlin, 1705.

Opp. 8° 292: Benjamin Slonik, *Seder mitzvot nashim.* Dessau, 1699.

Opp. 8° 293: Benjamin Slonik, *Seder mitzvot nashim.* Frankfurt am Main, 1714.

Opp. 8° 324 (4): *Ilan she-anafav Merubin . . . Vocabulario da lingua Portuguesa, explicado em Hebraico.* Amsterdam, 1665.

Opp. 8° 406: *Judscher Tiryak.* Amsterdam, 1737.

Opp. 8° 473: Moses b. Yakar Ashkenazi, *Sefer petah einayim.* Amsterdam, 1664.

Opp. 8° 545: Joseph Maarsen, *Hanokh le-na'ar.* Amsterdam, 1713.

Opp. 8° 557^A: Solomon Altschul B. Joshua, *Megillat sefer.* Cremona, 1566.

Opp. 8° 557^B: Solomon Altschul B. Joshua, *Megillat sefer.* Basel, 1611.

Opp. 8° 563 (12): *Yefe nof.* Prague, ca. 1605–1615.

Opp. 8° 565: Joseph Maarsen, *Hanokh le-na'ar.* Amsterdam, 1713.

Opp. 8° 568: Joseph Maarsen, *Leshon zahav.* Amsterdam, 1715.

Opp. 8° 592: Solomon Altschul B. Joshua, *Megillat sefer.* Frankfurt am Main, 1736.

Opp. 8° 593: Joseph Maarsen, *Tikun sohrim ve-tikun hilufin.* Amsterdam, 1714.

Opp. 8° 603 (2): Solomon Altschul B. Joshua, *Megillat sefer.* Venice, 1552.

Opp. 8° 619: Berahya ha-Naqdan, *Mishlei shualim.* Prague, 1661.

Opp. 8° 627 (8): Solomon Altschul B. Joshua, *Megillat sefer.* Venice, 1552.

Opp. 8° 632: *Ayn naye klog lid.* Amsterdam, 1714.

Opp. 8° 634 (2): *Dinim ve-seder.* Venice, 1601–1602.

Opp. 8° 643 (4): *Ipesh lid fun Prague.* Prague, ca. 1714.

Opp. 8° 644 (3): *Ipesh lid fun Prague.* Prague, ca. 1714.

Opp. 8° 645 (4): *Far loyf den ipesh.* Prague, ca. 1714.

Opp. 8° 652: Hirsch Taussig b. Judah, *Ayn hipesh lid fun R. Lipmann Hazzan.* Prague, ca. 1670.

Opp. 8° 654: Jacob Taussig of Prague, *Ayn shayn naye lid fun mashiah.* Prague, 1666.

Opp. 8° 930: *Iggeret ha-Ramban.* Amsterdam, 1652.

Opp. 8° 969 (1): Judah b. Samuel ha-Levi, *Mi kamoha.* Mantua, 1557.

Opp. 8° 969 (2): *Shir naeh le-simhat Purim.* Mantua, 1619.

Opp. 8° 1023: Akiva b. Jacob Ginzburg, *Elu ha-zemirot.* Berlin, 1713.

Opp. 8° 1025: Isaac b. Eleazar Perles, *Tikkun motzaei Shabbat.* Amsterdam, 1660.

Opp. 8° 1025 (4): *Yezamru be-se'udat Purim.* Mantua, 1700.

Opp. 8° 1035: *Dimyon ha-refuot/Harmonia Wallachia Medica.* Frankfurt am Main, 1700.

Opp. 8° 1036: Moses b. Benjamin Wolf Meseritz, *Yerushat Moshe*. Wilmersdorf?, 1677.

Opp. 8° 1037: *Sefer segulot ve-refuot*. Prague, 1694.

Opp. 8° 1038: *Segulot ve-refuot*, n.d.

Opp. 8° 1122: *Mayse shel ha-ru'ah de-k"k N"Sh.*

Opp. 8° 1137: Solomon ibn Verga, *Shevet Yehuda*. Amsterdam, 1655.

Opp. 8° 1159: *Vara de Iuda*. Amsterdam, 1640.

Opp. 12° 364: Nathan of Gaza, *Tikun ha-yom*. Constantinople, 1666.

Opp. Fol. 265: Moses b. Nahman Gerondi, *Biur al ha-Torah*. Venice, 1580.

Opp. Fol. 283: Aaron Teomim, *Sefer bigdei Aharon*. Frankfurt, 1710.

Opp. Fol. 322: Edmundo Castello, *Lexicon Heptaglotton*. London, 1669.

Opp. Fol. 390–396: *Babylonian Talmud*. Basel, 1578–1581.

Opp. Fol. 583: *Talmud. Tractate Berakhot*. Soncino, 1484.

Opp. Fol. 591: *Hilkhot Berakhot*. Prague, 1728.

Opp. Fol. 833: Mordekhai b. Hillel, *Sefer rav Mordekhai*. Riva di Trento, 1558.

Opp. Fol. 834: *Mordecai*. Riva di Trento, 1558.

Opp. Fol. 858: *Alfasi*. Krakow, 1597.

Opp. Fol. 1066: Bezalel b. Abraham Ashkenazi, *Sefer asefat zekenim ve-hu hiddushei bava metziah*. Amsterdam, 1721.

Opp. Fol. 1067: Bezalel b. Abraham Ashkenazi, *Sefer asefat zekenim ve-hu hiddushei bava metziah*. Amsterdam, 1721.

Opp. Fol. 1299: Haggadah "Mah nishtanah." Prague, 1713.

Opp. Fol. 1305: Avicenna, *Canon*. 1491.

Opp. Fol. 1347: Johanni Buxtorfi, *Concordantiae Bibliorum Hebraicae*. Basel, 1632.

Opp. Fol. 1159: Philippus Aquinas, *Ma'arikh ha-ma'arakhot*. Paris, 1629.

Opp. Fol. 1174 (2): Elijah Levita, *Meturgeman*. Isny, 1541.

Other Manuscripts, Marginalia, and Unique Copies

ARCHIV DER FRANCKESCHEN STIFTUNG/
HAUPTARCHIV, HALLE

Ms. (AFSt/H) K 55

BIBLIOTHECA ROSENTHALIANA, AMSTERDAM

Ms. Rosenthaliana H. Ros. 24

CENTRAL ARCHIVES FOR THE HISTORY OF THE JEWISH PEOPLE, JERUSALEM

Ms. HM2/8202
Ms. FME264
CS 263

JEWISH MUSEUM IN PRAGUE

Ms. Hsg. 060786
Ms. 93 (NLI Film F46568)
Ms. 47284
Ms. 47380
Ms. 109142
Ms. 109145
Ms. 109493
Ms. 120064 ("Kopialbuch of David Oppenheim")

JEWISH THEOLOGICAL SEMINARY OF AMERICA, NEW YORK

JTSA 1870:2 *Sefer asifat zekenim ve-hu hiddushei bava metziah.* Amsterdam, 1721.

NÁRODNI ARCHIV (NATIONAL ARCHIVES, CZECH REPUBLIC), PRAGUE

Ms. SM 1505 J4/23
Ms. SM 1505 J4/27
Ms. SM 1505 J4/28
Ms. SM 1505 J4/33
Ms. CK 1718, VII c (KK) 324
Ms. ČDK, sign. 2065, karton 912
Národni Muzeum (National Museum, Czech Republic), Prague
VII_C_6.

NATIONAL LIBRARY OF ISRAEL, JERUSALEM

Ms. Heb. 4° 966
Ms. Sassoon 981

SPERTUS INSTITUTE FOR JEWISH LEARNING AND LEADERSHIP, ASHER LIBRARY, CHICAGO

Inscription to Moses ben Mordecai Galante, *She'elot u-teshuvot.* Venice, 1608. Held by Spertus Library (BM522 G146 1608) and deciphered by Tali Winkler. https://footprints.ccnmtl.columbia.edu/footprint/249/.

Universitätsbibliothek JCS, Frankfurt am Main

Ms. hebr. oct. 231

Printed Primary Sources

Acta Ester mit Ahashverosh. Prague, 1720.

Asevilli, Yom Tov b. Abraham. *Hidushei ha-Ritva.* Amsterdam, 1729.

———. *Hidushei Hulin le-ha-Ritva.* Prague, 1735.

Asher b. Yehiel. *Pi shnayim.* Altona: Aaron b. Elijah Katz, 1735.

———. *Rabbeinu Asher.* Furth: Zvi Hirsch, 1745.

Ashkenazi, Bezalel b. Abraham. *Sefer asefat zekenim ve-hu hiddushei bava metziah.* Amsterdam, 1721.

Ashkenazi, Gerson Ulif. *Avodat ha-Gershuni.* Frankfurt am Main, 1699.

———. *Sefer hiddushei ha-Gershuni.* Frankfurt am Main, 1710.

———. *Tifferet ha-Gershuni.* Frankfurt am Main, 1699.

Ashkenazi, Samuel Jaffee. *Yefe anaf.* Frankfurt (Oder), 1696.

Ashkenazi, Zevi Hirsch b. Jacob. *She'elot ve-teshuvot Hakham Zevi.* Amsterdam, 1712.

Austerlist, Barukh b. Zalman. *Derush.* Prague, 1713.

Ayn naye klog lid. Amsterdam, 1714.

Azulai, Hayyim Yosef David. *Ma'agal tov.* Edited by Aron Freimann. Berlin, 1921.

———. *Shem ha-Gedolim.* 2 vols. Livorno, 1774.

Bachrach, Abraham. *Sefer hut ha-shani.* Frankfurt, 1679.

Bachrach, Yair Hayyim. *She'elot ve-teshuvot havot Yair.* Frankfurt am Main, 1699.

Baer, Aaron (of Frankfurt). *Seder ve-hanhaga shel nisuin ha-hatunah breileft ke-minhag shel k"k vrankfurt de-main.* Frankfurt, 1701.

Bass, Shabbetai. *Sefer siftei yeshenim.* Amsterdam, 1680.

Be'er Avraham. Sulzbach, 1708.

Berliner, Abraham, ed. "Sefer hazakarat neshamot kehillat Vermaiza." *Kovetz al Yad* 3 (1886): 1–62.

Brauer, Johann Michael. *Catalogus . . . hebraischen Bibliothek . . . David Oppenheimers.* Hamburg, 1782.

Cuenque, Abraham b. Levi. *Avak sofrim*. Amsterdam, 1704.

David b. Solomon Avi Zimra. *Magen David*. Amsterdam, 1713.

Delmedigo, Joseph Solomon. *Sefer novelot hokhmah*. Basel, 1631.

Diodato, Georgio. *Anfang der Weißheit ist die Furcht Gottes*. Leipzig, 1724.

——. *Wehe-Klag oder Lamentation: Der Asiatischen Christen zu den Christglau-bigen Evropaeischen gesalbten Häuptern Absonderlich*. Prague, 1716.

Eisenstadt, Meir. *She'elot ve-teshuvot panim me'irot*. Amsterdam, 1715-1738.

Emden, Jacob b. Zevi. *Akizat akrav*. Altona, 1752.

——. *Bet Yehonatan ha-sofer*. Altona, 1762.

——. *Edut be-Ya'akov*. Altona, 1756.

——. *Hit'abkut*. Altona, 1762.

——. *Megilat sefer*. Warsaw, 1897.

——. *She'elat Yavez*, Vol. 1. Altona, 1739.

——. *Shevirat luhot ha-aven*. Altona, 1756.

——. *Torat ha-kenaot*. Altona, 1752.

Eybeschütz, Jonathan. *Bene ahuva*. Prague, 1819.

——. *Kreti u-fleti*. Altona, 1763.

Fano, Menahem Azaria da. *Maamar ha-itim*. Dyhernfurth, 1694.

Far loyf den ipesh. Prague, ca. 1714.

Fleckeles, Eleazar. *Teshuva me-ahava*. Prague, 1809-1820.

Frankfurter, Joseph Isaachar Ber b. Elhanan. *Shelosha serigim*. Venice, 1701.

Fürst, Julius. *Bibliotheca judaica: Bibliographisches Handbuch der gesammten jüdischen Literatur*. Leipzig, 1863.

Getz, Elyakim. *Even ha-shoham u-meirat inayim*. Dyhernfurth, 1733.

Graf, Moses b. Menahem. *Zera kodesh matzevata*. Fürth, 1696.

Grünhut, David b. Nathan. *Tov roi*. Frankfurt, 1702.

Hagiz, Israel Jacob b. Samuel, *Halakhot ketanot*. Venice, 1704.

Hagiz, Moses. *Leket ha-kemah*. Amsterdam, 1707.

Halpern, Israel. *Takkanot medinat Mehrin (410–508)*. Jerusalem: Mekize Nirda-mim, 1992.

Halpern, Israel, and Yisrael Bartal. *Pinkas Va'ad Arba Aratsot: Likute takkanot, ketavim u-reshumot*. Jerusalem: Mosad Bialik, 1989.

Haselbauer, Franciscus. *Des gründlichen Berichts von dem Christenthum*. 2 vols. Prague, 1719-1722.

——. *Kurtzer Inhalt Deß Christl. Gesatzes, In 100 Unterweisungen, Allen Kin-dern Israel, welche von Gott erleuchtet, an Jesum Christum den wahren Mes-siam glauben wollen*. Prague, 1729.

Heller, Yom Tov Lipmann. *Megilat evah*. Lemberg, 1837.

Hillel b. Mordekhai, of Tismenitz. *Beit Hillel*. Frankfurt/Oder, 1744.

Israel b. Abraham of Jessnitz. *Divrei hakhamim.* Jessnitz, 1726.

Jacob b. Asher. *Arba turim.* Berlin, 1702–1703.

Jaffee, Israel b. Aaron. *Sefer or Yisrael.* Frankfurt, 1702.

Joel b. Gad of Shebrshin. *Sefer meginei zahav.* Prague, 1720.

Jonathan b. Jacob of Budapest. *Keset Yehonatan.* Dyhernfurth, 1691 (reprinted 1697, Prague).

Joshua b. Joseph of Krakow. *Sefer meginei Shlomo.* Amsterdam, 1715.

Joshua (Raphael) Benveniste b. Israel. *Sefer sdeh Yehoshua.* Constantinople, 1662.

Judah Leow b. Bezalel. *Sefer gevurot Hashem.* Krakow, 1582.

Judah b. Nisan. *Beit Yehudah.* Dessau, 1698.

Juspe Schammes (Yiftah Yosef ben Naftali Hirts Segal Manzpach). *Mayse nissim.* Amsterdam, 1696.

———. *Minhagim De-K"K Virmaiza.* Jerusalem: Mifal Torat Hakhmei Ashkenaz, 1992.

Katzenellinbogen, Ezekiel b. Abraham. *Shu"t knesset Yehezkel.* Altona, 1732.

Katzenellinbogen, Pinhas. *Sefer yesh Manhilin.* Edited by Isaac Dov Feld. Jerusalem: Mekhon Hatam Sofer, 1986.

Kozuchowski, David Todros. "The Will of David Theodore [Todros] Kozuchowski Zava'ato shel David Teodor [Todros] Kozuchowski." Translated by Moshe Rosman. Early Modern Workshop: Jewish History Resources. Volume 3: Gender, Family, and Social Structures. Middletown, CT: Wesleyan University Press, 2006, 57–63.

Krochmal, Menahem Mendel. *She'elot ve-teshuvot tsemah tsedek.* Amsterdam, 1675.

Liberles, Hirsch. *Arukh ha-katsar.* Prague, 1707.

Lipschitz, Hayyim b. Moses. *Sefer derekh Hayyim.* Sulzbach, 1702.

Luntschitz, Shlomo Ephraim ben Aaron. *Olelot Ephraim.* Lublin, 1590.

Mahadurah batrah shel avodat bore. Sulzbach, 1707.

Megillat Shmuel. Vol. 15, *Kobez Al Jad.* Edited by Aron Freimann. Berlin: Mekize Nirdamim, 1899.

Meginei eretz. Dyhernfurth: Shabbetai Bass, 1692.

Meir of Eistenstadt b. Hayyim. *Mishte yayin.* Furth, 1737.

Meoznei zedek. Dyhernfurth: Shabbetai Bass, 1707.

Metz, Yitzhak Ayzik ben Asher. *Kohelet David/Collectio Davidis.* Hamburg: Samuel and Judah Bonn, 1826.

Michaelis, Johann David. *Orientalische und exegetische Bibliothek,* Vol. 21. Frankfurt am Main, 1783.

Midrash rabbot. Amsterdam, 1725.

Modena, Judah Arye b. Isaac. *Sefer beit lehem Yehuda.* Prague, 1705.

Neumark, Judah Leib. *Shoresh David.* Frankfurt am Main, 1692.

Nicoll, Alexander. *Sermons.* Edited by James Parsons. Oxford: C & J Rivington, 1830.

Oppenheim, David. "Drush al Hagadah shel Pesah." *Kovetz bet aharon ve-yisrael* 70 (1997): 5–7.

———. "Iggeret le-hokhmei Brisk." Broadside letter by David Oppenheim to the Jewish community of Brisk (written March 25, 1698).

———. *She'elot ve-teshuvot Nish'al David.* Edited by Isaac Dov Feld. 3 vols. Jerusalem: Mekhon Hatam Sofer, 1971.

Oppenheim, Judah Leib b. Isaachar Dov Ber. *Sefer minhat Yehudah.* Hamburg, 1736.

Oppenheim, Judah Liva b. Samuel Zanwill. *Sefer mateh Yehudah.* Offenbach, 1721.

Peiser, Simeon b. Judah Leob. *Nahalat Shimoni.* Wandsbeck, 1728.

Perles, Moses Meir. *Megillat sefer.* Prague, 1710.

Poppers, Jacob b. Benjamin Katz. *Shev Yaakov.* Frankfurt am Main, 1742.

Poriyat (Porges), Moses (Prager) b. Israel Naphtali Hirsch. *Darkhei Ziyyon.* Amsterdam or Prague, 1650.

Prager, Moses b. Menahem. *Zera kodesh matzevata.* Munkacs, 1893.

R"K. "Ktav hitnazlut ve-teshuvah me-hokhmei Prag al hadpasat ha-Talmud im hashmatot bi-shnat 487 le-P"K." *Ha-magid,* May 9, 1877.

Rohden, Frauke von, ed. *Meneket Rivkah: A Manual of Wisdom and Piety for Jewish Women by Rivkah Bat Meir (of Tikotin).* Philadelphia: Jewish Publication Society, 2008.

Rotenberg, Mordecai Ziskind b. Moshe. *She'elot ve-teshuvot.* Hamburg, 1716.

Rotenberg, Mordekhai Zusskind. *She'elot teshuvot.* Amsterdam, 1746.

Rovigo, Abraham, and Mordecai b. Judah Leib Ashkenazi. *Sefer eshel Avraham.* Fürth, 1701.

Rzeszów (Reischer), Jacob b. Josef. *She'elot ve-teshuvot shvut Yaakov,* Vol. 1. Halle, 1707.

———. *She'elot ve-teshuvot shvut Yaakov,* Vol. 2. Halle, 1719.

———. *She'elot ve-teshuvot shvut Yaakov,* Vol. 3. Metz, 1789.

Samuel b. Elkana of Altona. *Mekom Shmuel.* Altona, 1738.

Samuel b. Joseph b. Joshua. *Leket Shmuel.* Venice, 1694.

Schudt, Johann Jakob. *Jüdisches Merwürdigkeiten.* Frankfurt, 1715.

Solomon b. Isaiah Nizza. "Poem on Death of Samuel Oppenheim." Venice, ca. 1703.

Stadthagen, Joseph. *Divrei zikaron.* Amsterdam, 1705.

Stadthagen, Joseph, and Abraham Berliner. *Religionsgespräch Gehalten am Kurfürstlichen Hofe zu Hannover 1704, nach einer Hebräischen Handschrift.* Berlin: L. Lamm, 1914.

Steinschneider, Moritz, and Leopold Zunz, eds. *Ozerot Hayyim, Katalog der Michael'schen Bibliothek.* Hamburg, 1848.

Strata, Filippo de. "Polemic Against Printing." Edited by Shelagh Grier and Martin Lowry. Birmingham: Hayloft, 1986.

Talmud. Tractate Berakhot. Frankfurt an der Oder, 1697.

Talmud. Tractate Shabbat. Amsterdam, 1714.

Talmud Yerushalmi. Amsterdam, 1710.

Tefilah derekh siah ha-sadeh. Berlin, 1713.

Turniansky, Chava, ed. *Glikl: Zikhronot, 1691–1719.* Jerusalem: Merkaz Zalman Shazar le-toldot Yisrael, 2006.

Unger, Christian Theophilo. "Schreiben des Pastor Unger an Dr. Cantarini." In *Ozar Nechmad. Brief und Abhandlungen jüdische Literatur betreffend.* Vol. 3. Edited by Ignaz Blumenfeld, 141–143. Vienna: J. Knöpflmacher & Söhne, 1860.

Wagenseil, Johann Christoph. *Belehrung der jüdisch-teutschen Red- und Schreibart.* Königsberg, 1699.

Wedeles, Elia. *Sefer Elia rabbah.* Sulzbach, 1705.

Wetzlar, Isaac, and Morris M. Faierstein. *The Libes Briv of Isaac Wetzlar.* Brown Judaic Studies. Atlanta: Scholars Press, 1996.

Wolff, Isaac Benjamin. *Sefer nahalat Binyamin.* Amsterdam, 1682.

Wolff, Johann Christoff. *Bibliotheca Hebrea.* 4 vols. Hamburg, 1715–1727.

Yehiel Michael b. Abraham Zalman. *Sreyfe leid fun Prag.* Prague, 1689.

Zacut, Moses b. Mordecai. *Sefer kol ha-Ramaz.* Amsterdam, 1719.

Zot Torah asher sam Moshe. Amsterdam, 1698.

Zunz, Leopold. *Zur Geschichte und Literatur.* Berlin: Veit und Comp., 1845.

Secondary Sources

Adams, Julia. *The Familial State: Ruling Families and Merchant Capitalism in Early Modern Europe.* Ithaca, NY: Cornell University Press, 2005.

Aebbtlin, Georg. *Anfürung zu der Registratur-Kunst Vorderist denen Hoch-Löblichen Herrschafften und Obrigkeiten zu . . . Bericht und Erinnerung, wie auch Deroselben Registratorn, Secretariis, Cancellisten, Verwaltern . . . zu Dienst.* Ulm, 1669.

Ahrend, Aaron. "Haskamot Le-Sifrei Kodesh Be-Doreinu." *Alei Sefer* 18 (1996): 157–170.

Algazi, Gadi Valentin Groebner, and Bernhard Jussen. *Negotiating the Gift: Premodern Figurations of Exchange.* Veröffentlichungen des Max-Planck-Instituts für Geschichte, vol. 188. Göttingen: Vandenhoeck & Ruprecht, 2003.

Appadurai, Arjun. "Commodities and the Politics of Value." In *The Social Life of Things: Commodities in Cultural Perspective,* edited by Arjun Appadurai, 3–63. Cambridge: Cambridge University Press, 1986.

Arendt, Hannah. *On Violence.* New York: Harcourt, 1970.

Armstrong, Elizabeth. *Before Copyright: The French Book-Privilege System 1498–1526.* Cambridge Studies in Publishing and Printing History. Cambridge: Cambridge University Press, 1990.

Avivi, Yosef. *Kabalat ha-Ari.* 3 vols. Vol. 2. Jerusalem: Kerem Eliyahu Mekhon Ben Tsevi le-heker kehilot Yisrael ba-Mizrah, 2007.

———. "Kitvei ha-Rm"a mi-Fano be-hokhmat ha-Kabbalah." *Sefunot* 19 (n.s. 4) (1989): 347–376.

Baer, Yitzhak. *A History of the Jews in Christian Spain.* 2 vols. Philadelphia: Jewish Publication Society of America, 1961.

Baker, Keith Michael. *The French Revolution and the Creation of Modern Political Culture.* Oxford: Pergamon, 1987.

Baldwin, Peter. *The Copyright Wars: Three Centuries of Trans-Atlantic Battle.* Princeton, NJ: Princeton University Press, 2014.

Bar-Levav, Avriel. "Bein toda'at ha-sifriyah le-republika ha-sifrutit ha-Yehudit." In *Sifriyot ve-osfe sefarim,* edited by Moshe Sluhovsky and Yosef Kaplan, 201–224. Jerusalem: Merkaz Zalman Shazar le-toldot Yisrael, 2006.

———. "Ha-merhav ha-kadosh shel moledet ha-mitaltelet: Archeologiyah shel ha-sifriyot ha-smuyot min ha-ayin be-tarbut ha-Yehudit mi-yeme ha-beinayim ve-ad le-yamenu." In *Liot ve-laga'at: Aliyah la-regel u-mekomot kedoshim be-Yahadut, be-Natsrut u-va-Islam; Mehkarim li-khvod Orah Limor,* edited by Yitzhak Hen and Iris Shagrir, 297–320. Ra'anana: Ha-Universitah ha-petuhah, 2011.

———. "The Religious Order of Jewish Books: Structuring Hebrew Knowledge in Amsterdam." *Studia Rosenthaliana* 44 (2012): 1–27.

Baron, Salo Wittmayer. *The Jewish Community: Its History and Structure to the American Revolution.* Philadelphia: Jewish Publication Society of America, 1942.

Baruchson-Arbib, Shifra. "Hamesh iggerot me-hakhmei Ashkenaz be-me'ah ha-16 (R. Yaakov Margaliot, R. Yuzman Katz, R. Aharon Yonah Me-Regensburg, R. Zeligman Ha-Levi Ziyyon)." *Ale Sefer* 6–7 (1979): 85–101.

Battenberg, Friedrich. "Die Jüdische Wirtschaftselite der Hoffaktoren und Residenten im Zeitalter des Merkantilismus—Ein Europaweites System?" *Aschkenas* 9, no. 1 (2009): 31–66.

Baumgarten, Elisheva. "Charitable like Abigail: The History of an Epitaph." *Jewish Quarterly Review* 105, no. 3 (2015): 312–339.

———. *Mothers and Children: Jewish Family Life in Medieval Europe.* Princeton, NJ: Princeton University Press, 2004.

———. *Practicing Piety in Medieval Ashkenaz: Men, Women, and Everyday Religious Observance.* Jewish Culture and Contexts. Philadelphia: University of Pennsylvania Press, 2014.

Baumgarten, Jean, and Jerold C. Frakes. *Introduction to Old Yiddish Literature.* Oxford: Oxford University Press, 2005.

Beit-Arié, Malachi. *Catalogue of the Hebrew Manuscripts in the Bodleian Library: Supplement of Addenda and Corrigenda to Volume I.* Oxford: Oxford University Press, 1995.

Bell, Dean Phillip. *Jewish Identity in Early Modern Germany: Memory, Power and Community.* Aldershot: Ashgate, 2007.

———. *Jews in the Early Modern World.* Lanham, MD: Rowman & Littlefield, 2008.

Ben-Amos, Ilana Krausman. *The Culture of Giving: Informal Support and Gift-Exchange in Early Modern England.* Cambridge Social and Cultural Histories. Cambridge: Cambridge University Press, 2008.

Benayahu, Meir. "Halifat iggerot bein ha-kehillah he-Ashkenazit bi-Yerushalayim ve-R David Oppenheim." *Yerushalayim* 3 (1950): 108-129.

———. "Ha-takkanah she-lo le-hotsi sefarim mi-Yerushalayim ve-hishtalshelutah." In *Minha Le-Yehuda: Mugash le-ha-rav Yehudah Leib Zlotnik le-yovlo ha-shishim me-et haverav ve-yedidav*, 226-234. Jerusalem: Mosad ha-rav Kook, 1950.

———. "Ha-'Hevra Kedosha' shel rabi Yehuda Hasid ve-aliyata le-Erets Yisrael." *Sefunot* 3-4 (1959-1960): 131-182.

———. *Sefer toldot ha-Ari: gilgule nusha'otav ve-erkho mi-behinah historit: Nosfu alav hanhagot ha-ARI ve-azkarot rishonot.* Jerusalem: Makhon Ben-Tsvi be-Universitah ha-Ivrit, 1967.

———. "Sfarim she-hibram rabi Moshe Hagiz ve-sfarim she-hotziam le-or." *Ale Sefer* 2 (1986): 121-162.

———. "Shemu'ot Shabtai'iyot — mi-pinkasehem shel R. Benyamin Ha-Kohen ve-R. Avraham Rovigo." *Michael: On the History of the Jews in the Diaspora* 3, no. 1 (1973): 9-87.

Benedict, Barbara M. *Curiosity: A Cultural History of Early Modern Inquiry.* Chicago: University of Chicago Press, 2001.

Benjamin, Walter. "Unpacking My Library: A Talk About Book Collecting." In *Illuminations: Essays and Reflections*, 56-67. New York: Schocken, 2007.

Ben-Naeh, Yaron. "'Ve-khi lo aheihem anahnu?' Yahasei Ashkenazim ve-Sepharadim bi-Yerushalayim be-sof ha-me'ah ha-shva-esreh." *Cathedra* 103 (2002): 33-52.

Bepler, Jill. "Vicissitudo Temporum: Some Sidelights on Book Collecting in the Thirty Years' War." *Sixteenth Century Journal* 32, no. 4 (2001): 953–968.

Berger, Shlomo. "An Invitation to Buy and Read: Paratexts of Yiddish Books in Amsterdam, 1650–1800." *Book History* 7 (2004): 31–61.

———. "The Oppenheim Collection and Early Modern Yiddish Books: Prague Yiddish 1550–1750." *Bodleian Library Record* 25, no. 1 (2012): 37–51.

———. *Producing Redemption in Amsterdam: Early Modern Yiddish Books in Paratextual Perspective.* Studies in Jewish History and Culture. Leiden: Brill, 2013.

Berger, Shlomo Z. "Yiddish Books in Early Modern Prague." In *Hebrew Printing in Bohemia and Moravia,* edited by Olga Sixtová, 177–185. Prague: Academia: Jewish Museum in Prague, 2012.

Bergerhausen, Hans-Wolfgang. "Die 'Verneuerte Landesordnung' in Böhmen 1627: Ein Grunddokument des Habsburgischen Absolutismus." *Historische Zeitschrift* 272, no. 2 (2001): 327–351.

Berkovitz, Jay R. "Crisis and Authority in Early Modern Ashkenaz." *Jewish History* 26, nos. 1–2 (2012): 179–199.

———. "Dyukono he-azmi shel posek halakha be-me'ah ha-17: Bein biyographyah le-autobiographyah." In *Yosef Da'at: Mehkarim be-historyah Yehudit Modernit mugashim le-Prof Yosef Salmon le-hag yovlo,* edited by Yossi Goldstein, 33–66. Beersheba: Ben Gurion University of the Negev Press, 2010.

———. "The Persona of a 'Poseq': Law and Self-Fashioning in Seventeenth-Century Ashkenaz." *Modern Judaism* 32, no. 3 (2012): 251–269.

———. *Protocols of Justice: The Pinkas of the Metz Rabbinic Court, 1771–1789.* 2 vols. Leiden: Brill, 2014.

———. *The Shaping of Jewish Identity in Nineteenth-Century France.* Detroit: Wayne State University Press, 1989.

Biagioli, Mario. *Galileo, Courtier: The Practice of Science in the Culture of Absolutism.* Chicago: University of Chicago Press, 1993.

———. "Galileo's System of Patronage." *History of Science* 28, no. 1 (1990): 1–62.

Biale, David. *Power and Powerlessness in Jewish History.* New York: Schocken, 1986.

Bireley, Robert. "Confessional Absolutism in the Habsburg Lands in the Seventeenth Century." In *State and Society in Early Modern Austria,* edited by Charles W. Ingrao, 36–53. West Lafayette, IN: Purdue University Press, 1994.

Black, Jeremy. *Beyond the Military Revolution: War in the Seventeenth-Century World.* Houndmills: Palgrave Macmillan, 2011.

Blair, Ann. "Reading Strategies for Coping with Information Overload ca. 1550–1700." *Journal of the History of Ideas* 64, no. 1 (2003): 11–28.

————. *Too Much to Know: Managing Scholarly Information Before the Modern Age*. New Haven, CT: Yale University Press, 2010.

Bonfil, Robert. "Sifriyotehem shel Yehudei Italiah bein yemei ha-beinayim le-Et He-Hadashah." *Peamim* 53 (1992): 4-15.

Boruchoff, David A. "The Three Greatest Inventions of Modern Times: An Idea and Its Public." In *Entangled Knowledge: Scientific Discourses and Cultural Difference*, edited by Klaus Hock and Gesa Mackenthum, 133-163. Münster: Waxmann, 2012.

Bourdieu, Pierre. *Distinction: A Social Critique of the Judgement of Taste*. Cambridge, MA: Harvard University Press, 1984.

————. "Intellectual Field and Creative Project." *Social Science Information* 8, no. 2 (1969): 89-119.

————. *The Logic of Practice*. Stanford, CA: Stanford University Press, 1990.

————. *Outline of a Theory of Practice*. Cambridge: Cambridge University Press, 1977.

Boxel, Piet van. *Jewish Books in Christian Hands: Theology, Exegesis and Conversion Under Gregory XIII (1572–1585)*. Vatican City: Biblioteca Apostolica Vaticana, 2016.

Boyarin, Daniel. *Unheroic Conduct: The Rise of Heterosexuality and the Invention of the Jewish Man*. Contraversions. Berkeley: University of California Press, 1997.

Brady, Thomas A. *German Histories in the Age of Reformations, 1400–1650*. Cambridge: Cambridge University Press, 2009.

Bregoli, Francesca. *Mediterranean Enlightenment: Livornese Jews, Tuscan Culture, and Eighteenth-Century Reform*. Stanford, CA: Stanford University Press, 2014.

Breuer, Mordechai. "Makom ha-Yeshiva be-ma'arakh he-irgun ha-atzmi ha-Yehudi." In *Kehal Yisrael: ha-Shilton ha-atsmi ha-Yehudi le-dorotav*, edited by Yosef Kaplan, Israel Halpern, Avraham Grossman, and Yisrael Bartal, 243-259. Jerusalem: Merkaz Zalman Shazar le-toldot Yisrael, 2001.

————. "Part 1: The Early Modern Period." In *German-Jewish History in Modern Times, Vol. 1: Tradition and Enlightenment, 1600–1780*, edited by Michael A. Meyer, Michael Brenner, Mordechai Breuer, and Michael Graetz, 79-260. New York: Columbia University Press, 1996.

Brilling, Dov (Bernhard). "Ha-gezerah al maot a"y be-ostryah be-shnat 1723." *Zion* 12, nos. 1-2 (1947/1948): 89-96.

Brown, Bill. "Thing Theory." *Critical Inquiry* 28, no. 1 (2001): 1-22.

Buchanan, Mark. *Nexus: Small Worlds and the Groundbreaking Science of Networks*. New York: W. W. Norton, 2003.

Burke, Peter. *The Art of Conversation*. Cambridge: Polity, 1993.

——. *A Social History of Knowledge: From Gutenberg to Diderot.* Cambridge: Polity, 2000.

Burnett, Stephen G. *From Christian Hebraism to Jewish Studies: Johannes Buxtorf (1564–1629) and Hebrew Learning in the Seventeenth Century.* Leiden: Brill, 1996.

——. "Hebrew Censorship in Hanau: A Mirror of Jewish-Christian Coexistence in Seventeenth-Century Germany." In *The Expulsion of the Jews: 1492 and After,* edited by Raymond B. Waddington and Arthur H. Williamson, 199–222. New York: Garland, 1994.

——. "The Regulation of Hebrew Printing in Germany, 1555–1630." In *Infinite Boundaries: Order, Disorder, and Reorder in Early Modern German Culture,* edited by Max Reinhart and Thomas Robisheaux, 329–348. Kirksville, MO: Sixteenth Century Journal Publishers, 1998.

Cahen, Abraham. "Le Rabbinat de Metz pendant la période Française (1567–1871)." *Revue des Études Juives* 7 (1883): 1103–1116, 1204–1226; 8 (1884): 1255–1258; 12 (1886): 1283–1297; 13 (1886): 1105–1126.

Carlebach, Elisheva. "Attribution of Secrecy and Perceptions of Jewry." *Jewish Social Studies* 2, no. 3 (1996): 115–136.

——. "Community, Authority, and Jewish Midwives in Early Modern Europe." *Jewish Social Studies* 20, no. 2 (2014): 5–33.

——. *The Death of Simon Abeles: Jewish-Christian Tension in Seventeenth-Century Prague.* Third Annual Herbert Berman Memorial Lecture. New York: Center for Jewish Studies, Queens College, CUNY, 2001.

——. *Divided Souls: Converts from Judaism in Germany, 1500–1750.* New Haven, CT: Yale University Press, 2001.

——. "Letter into Text: Epistolarity, History, and Literature." In *Jewish Literature and History,* edited by Eliyana R. Adler and Sheila E. Jelen, 113–133. Bethesda: University Press of Maryland, 2008.

——. *Palaces of Time: Jewish Calendar and Culture in Early Modern Europe.* Cambridge, MA: Belknap, 2011.

——. *The Pursuit of Heresy: Rabbi Moses Hagiz and the Sabbatian Controversies.* New York: Columbia University Press, 1990.

——. "The Status of the Talmud in Early Modern Europe." In *Printing the Talmud: From Bomberg to Schottenstein,* edited by Sharon Liberman Mintz and Gabriel M. Goldstein, 79–88. New York: Yeshiva University Museum, 2005.

Catalano, Alessandro. "'Das Temporale Wird Schon so Weith Extendiret, daß der Spritualität Nichts als eie Arme Seel Überbleibet.' Kirche und Staat in Böhmen (1620–1740)." In *Die Habsburgermonarchie 1620 bis 1740: Leistungen und Grenzen des Absolutismusparadigmas,* edited by Petr Maťa and Thomas Winkelbauer, 317–343. Stuttgart: Steiner, 2006.

Cavallo, Sandra. *Charity and Power in Early Modern Italy: Benefactors and Their Motives in Turin, 1541–1789.* Cambridge History of Medicine. Cambridge: Cambridge University Press, 1995.

Cerman, Ivo. "Anti-Jewish Superstitions and the Expulsion of the Jews from Vienna in 1670." *Judaica Bohemiae* 36, no. 1 (2000): 5–34.

Certeau, Michel de. *The Practice of Everyday Life.* Berkeley: University of California Press, 1984.

Chartier, Roger. *The Order of Books: Readers, Authors and Libraries in Europe Between the Fourteenth and Eighteenth Centuries.* Cambridge: Polity, 1994.

Chartier, Roger, and Peter Stallybrass. "What Is a Book?" In *The Cambridge Companion to Textual Scholarship,* edited by Neil Fraistat and Julia Flanders, 188–204. Cambridge: Cambridge University Press, 2013.

Chazan, Robert. "Christian Condemnation, Censorship, and Exploitation of the Talmud." In *Printing the Talmud: From Bomberg to Schottenstein,* edited by Sharon Liberman Mintz and Gabriel M. Goldstein, 53–59. New York: Yeshiva University Museum, 2005.

———. *The Jews of Medieval Western Christendom, 1000–1500.* Cambridge: Cambridge University Press, 2006.

Clanchy, M. T. *From Memory to Written Record in England, 1066–1307.* London: E. Arnold, 1979.

Clark, William. "On the Bureaucratic Plots of the Research Library." In *Books and the Sciences in History,* edited by Marina Frasca-Spada and Nicholas Jardine, 190–206. Cambridge: Cambridge University Press, 2000.

Clossey, Luke. *Salvation and Globalization in the Early Jesuit Missions.* New York: Cambridge University Press, 2008.

Cohen, Jeremy. *The Friars and the Jews: The Evolution of Medieval Anti-Judaism.* Ithaca, NY: Cornell University Press, 1982.

Cohen, Richard I. "Creating an Elite Norm of Behaviour—Court Jews as Patrons and Collectors of Art." In *Hofjuden: Ökonomie und Interkulturalität: Die Jüdische Wirtschaftselite im 18. Jahrhundert,* edited by J. Friedrich Battenberg and Rotraud Ries, 143–153. Hamburg: Christians Verlag, 2002.

———. *Jewish Icons: Art and Society in Modern Europe.* Berkeley: University of California Press, 1998.

Cook, Harold John. *Matters of Exchange: Commerce, Medicine, and Science in the Dutch Golden Age.* New Haven, CT: Yale University Press, 2007.

Cooper, Alix. *Inventing the Indigenous: Local Knowledge and Natural History in Early Modern Europe.* Cambridge: Cambridge University Press, 2007.

Coudert, Allison, and Jeffrey S. Shoulson. *Hebraica Veritas?: Christian Hebraists and the Study of Judaism in Early Modern Europe.* Philadelphia: University of Pennsylvania Press, 2004.

Cover, Robert M. "Nomos and Narrative (Forward to the Supreme Court, 1982 Term)." *Harvard Law Review* 97, no. 1 (1983): 1–306.

Cowan, Brian William. *The Social Life of Coffee: The Emergence of the British Coffeehouse.* New Haven, CT: Yale University Press, 2005.

Craster, H. H. E. *History of the Bodleian Library, 1845–1945.* Oxford: Clarendon, 1952.

Crawford, Alice, ed. *The Meaning of the Library: A Cultural History.* Princeton, NJ: Princeton University Press, 2015.

Crowston, Clare Haru. *Credit, Fashion, Sex: Economies of Regard in Old Regime France.* Durham, NC: Duke University Press, 2013.

Cser, Andreas. "Zwischen Stadtverfassung und Absolutistischen Herrschaftanspruch (1650 bis zum Ende der Kurpfalz 1802)." In *Geschichte der Juden in Heidelberg,* edited by Peter Blum, 46–153. Heidelberg: B. Guderjahn, 1996.

Dan, Joseph. *Iyunim be-sifrut Hasidei Ashkenaz.* Ramat Gan: Masada, 1975.

Darnton, Robert. *The Forbidden Best-Sellers of Pre-Revolutionary France.* New York: W. W. Norton, 1995.

Dauber, Jeremy Asher. *In the Demon's Bedroom: Yiddish Literature and the Early Modern.* New Haven, CT: Yale University Press, 2010.

Davis, Joseph M. "Concepts of Family and Friendship in the 1619 Yiddish Letters of Prague Jews." *Judaica Bohemiae* 49, no. 1 (2014): 27–58.

Davis, Natalie Zemon. "Beyond the Market: Books as Gifts in Sixteenth-Century France (the Prothero Lecture)." *Transactions of the Royal Historical Society (Fifth Series)* 33 (1983): 69–88.

———. *The Gift in Sixteenth-Century France.* Madison: University of Wisconsin Press, 2000.

———. *The Return of Martin Guerre.* Cambridge, MA: Harvard University Press, 1983.

———. "Riches and Dangers: Glikl Bas Judah Leib on Court Jews." In *From Court Jews to the Rothschilds: Art, Patronage, and Power 1600–1800,* edited by Vivian B. Mann, Richard I. Cohen, and Fritz Backhaus, 45–57. Munich: Prestel, 1996.

Demetz, Peter. *Prague in Black and Gold: Scenes from the Life of a European City.* New York: Hill and Wang, 1997.

Deutsch, Yaacov. "Polemical Ethnographies: Descriptions of Yom Kippur in the Writings of Christian Hebraists and Jewish Converts to Christianity in Early Modern Europe." In *Hebraica Veritas?: Christian Hebraists and the Study of Judaism in Early Modern Europe,* edited by Allison Coudert and Jeffrey S. Shoulson, 202–233. Philadelphia: University of Pennsylvania Press, 2004.

Dimitrovsky, Haim Z. "Al derekh ha-pilpul." In *Salo Wittmayer Baron, Jubilee Volume on the Occasion of His Eightieth Birthday,* edited by Saul Lieberman and Arthur Hyman, 111–181. Jerusalem: American Academy for Jewish Research, 1974.

Doktór, Jan. "Erster Missionar Neuen Stils und Verleger. Mordechaj Ben Mosche Schemaja—Philipp Ernst Christfels (1671-1759)." *Kwartalnik Historii Żydów* 2009, no. 3 (2009): 269-289.

———. "Georg Widmann und die Anfänge Der Pietistischen Judenmission." *Kwartalnik Historii Żydów* 2009, no. 232 (2009): 449-490.

Ducreux, Marie-Elizabeth. "Reading unto Death: Books and Readers in Eighteenth-Century Bohemia." In *The Culture of Print: Power and the Uses of Print in Early Modern Europe,* edited by Alain Boureau and Roger Chartier, 191-229. Princeton, NJ: Princeton University Press, 1989.

Duhamelle, Christophe. "The Making of Stability: Kinship, Church, and Power Among the Rhenish Imperial Knighthood, Seventeenth and Eighteenth Centuries." In *Kinship in Europe: Approaches to Long-Term Developments (1300–1900),* edited by David Warren Sabean, Simon Teuscher, and Jon Mathieu, 125-144. New York: Berghahn, 2007.

Duindam, Jeroen. "The Courts of the Austrian Habsburgs, c. 1500-1750." In *The Princely Courts of Europe: Ritual, Politics and Culture Under the Ancien Régime, 1500-1750,* edited by John Adamson, 165-187. London: Weidenfeld & Nicolson, 1999.

———. "Versailles, Vienna and Beyond: Changing Views of Household and Government in Early Modern Europe." In *Royal Courts in Dynastic States and Empires: A Global Perspective,* edited by Jeroen Duindam, Tülay Artan, and Metin Kunt, 401-431. Boston: Brill, 2011.

———. *Vienna and Versailles: The Courts of Europe's Dynastic Rivals, 1550-1780.* Cambridge: Cambridge University Press, 2003.

Dunkelgrün, Theodor. "The Humanist Discovery of Hebrew Epistolography." In *Jewish Books and Their Readers: Aspects of the Intellectual Life of Christians and Jews in Early Modern Europe,* edited by Scott Mandelbrote and Joanna Weinberg, 211-259. Leiden: Brill, 2016.

Duschinsky, C. "Rabbi David Oppenheimer. Glimpses of His Life and Activity, Derived from His Manuscripts in the Bodleian Library." *Jewish Quarterly Review* 20, no. 3 (1930): 217-247.

———. *Toldot ha-ga'on rav David Openhaymer.* Budapest: Defus shel ha-ahim Kattsburg, 1921.

Dweck, Yaacob. *The Scandal of Kabbalah: Leon Modena, Jewish Mysticism, Early Modern Venice.* Princeton, NJ: Princeton University Press, 2011.

———. "What Is a Jewish Book?" *AJS Review* 34, no. 2 (2010): 367–375.

Eidelberg, Shlomo, ed. *R. Yuzpa Shamash di-kehilat Vermaisa: olam Yehudeha ba-me'ah ha-17.* Jerusalem: Hotsaat sefarim a. sh. Y. L. Magnes, ha-Universitah ha-Ivrit, 1991.

Eisenhardt, Ulrich. *Die Kaiserliche Aufsicht über Buchdruck, Buchhandel und Presse im Heiligen Römischen Reich Deutscher Nation, 1496–1806. Ein Bei-trag zur Geschichte der Bücher- und Pressezensur.* Karlsruhe: Verlag C. F. Müller, 1970.

Eisenstein, Elizabeth L. *The Printing Revolution in Early Modern Europe.* Cambridge: Cambridge University Press, 1983.

———. "Reply." *American Historical Review* 107, no. 1 (2002): 126–128.

———. "An Unacknowledged Revolution Revisited." *American Historical Review* 107, no. 1 (2002): 87–105.

Elbaum, Avishai, and Aryeh Elbaum. "Mahadurah genuzah shel shut nish'al David." *Ha-Ma'ayan* 77, no. 2 (1995): 11–16.

Elbaum, Jacob. *Petihut ve-histagrut: ha-yetsirah ha-ruhanit-ha-sifrutit be-Folin u-ve-artsot Ashkenaz be-shilhe ha-me'ah ha-shesh-esreh.* Jerusalem: Machon Shazar, 1990.

Elliott, J. H. "A Europe of Composite Monarchies." *Past and Present,* no. 137 (1992): 48–71.

Ellis, Markman. *The Coffee-House: A Cultural History.* London: Weidenfeld & Nicolson, 2004.

Elyada, Aya. *A Goy Who Speaks Yiddish: Christians and the Jewish Language in Early Modern Germany.* Stanford, CA: Stanford University Press, 2012.

Engel, Alfred. "Die Ausweisung der Juden aus der Königlichen Städten Mährens und ihre Folgen." *Jahrbuch der Gesellschaft für Geschichte der Juden in der Čechoslovakischen Republik* 2 (1930): 50–96.

Evans, R. J. W. "The Court: A Protean Institution and an Elusive Subject." In *Princes, Patronage, and the Nobility: The Court at the Beginning of the Modern Age, c. 1450–1650,* edited by Ronald G. Asch and Adolf M. Birke, 481–491. London: German Historical Institute London, 1991.

———. "The Habsburg Monarchy and Bohemia, 1526–1848." In *Austria, Hungary, and the Habsburgs: Essays on Central Europe, c. 1683–1867,* 75–98. Oxford: Oxford University Press, 2006.

———. *The Making of the Habsburg Monarchy, 1550–1700: An Interpretation.* Oxford: Clarendon, 1979.

Febvre, Lucien, and Henri-Jean Martin. *The Coming of the Book: The Impact of Printing 1450–1800.* London: Verso, 1976.

Febvre, Lucien Paul Victor, Henri-Jean Martin, Geoffrey Nowell-Smith, and David

Wootton. *The Coming of the Book: The Impact of Printing, 1450–1800.* London: Verso, 2010.

Feiner, Shmuel. *The Jewish Enlightenment.* Philadelphia: University of Pennsylvania Press, 2004.

———. *Moses Mendelssohn: Sage of Modernity.* Jewish Lives. New Haven, CT: Yale University Press, 2010.

Feld, Isaac Dov. "Mikhtav shalom me-kvod ha-gaon rabeinu David Oppenheim Zt"L." *HaDarom* 42 (1975): 173–187.

Findlen, Paula. *Possessing Nature: Museums, Collecting, and Scientific Culture in Early Modern Italy.* Berkeley: University of California Press, 1994.

Finkelstein, Louis. *Jewish Self-Government in the Middle Ages.* Westport, CT: Greenwood, 1972.

Fishman, Talya. *Becoming the People of the Talmud: Oral Torah as Written Tradition in Medieval Jewish Cultures.* Philadelphia: University of Pennsylvania Press, 2011.

Flood, John L. *"Omnium Totius Orbis Emporiorum Compendium": The Frankfurt Fair in the Early Modern Period.* In *Fairs, Markets and the Itinerant Book Trade,* edited by Robin Myers, Michael Harris, and Giles Mandelbrote, 1–40. New Castle, DE: Oak Knoll, 2007.

Foucault, Michel. "Governmentality." In *The Foucault Effect: Studies in Governmentality: With Two Lectures by and an Interview with Michel Foucault,* edited by Graham Burchell, Colin Gordon, and Peter Miller, 87–104. Chicago: University of Chicago Press, 1991.

Fraenkel-Goldschmidt, Chava. *R. Yosef Me-Rosheim: ketavim historiyim.* Mekorot U-Mehkarim. Jerusalem: Hotsaat sefarim a. sh. Y. L. Magnes, ha-Universitah ha-Ivrit, 1996.

Fram, Edward. "Bein ma'arav le-mizrah u-mizrah le-ma'arav: keta mi-pinkasei Krakow mi-tehilat ha-me'ah ha-18." *Gal-Ed* 23 (2013): 157–170.

———. *Ideals Face Reality: Jewish Law and Life in Poland, 1550–1655.* Cincinnati, OH: Hebrew Union College Press, 1997.

———. *My Dear Daughter: Rabbi Benjamin Slonik and the Education of Jewish Women in Sixteenth-Century Poland.* Cincinnati, OH: Hebrew Union College Press, 2007.

———. *A Window on Their World: The Court Diary of Rabbi Hayyim Gundersheim, Frankfurt Am Main 1773–1794.* Cincinnati, OH: Hebrew Union College Press, 2012.

Freedman, Jeffrey. *Books Without Borders in Enlightenment Europe: French Cosmopolitanism and German Literary Markets.* Philadelphia: University of Pennsylvania Press, 2012.

Freehof, Solomon B. "Some Autographs on Title Pages of Hebrew Books." *Studies in Bibliography and Booklore* 9, no. 2/3 (1970): 106–112.

Freudenthal, Max. "David Oppenheim als Mährischer Landrabbiner." *Monatschrift für Geschichte und Wissenschaft des Judentums* 10 (n.s.), nos. 5–6 (1902): 262–274.

———. *Leipziger Messegäste: Die Jüdischen Besucher D. Leipziger Messen in D. Jahren 1675 bis 1764.* Frankfurt am Main: Kauffmann, 1928.

———. "Zum Jubiläum des Ersten Talmuddrucks in Deutschland." *Monatschrift für Geschichte und Wissenschaft des Judentums* 42 (1898): 80–89, 134–143, 180–185, 229–236, 278–285.

Friedrich, Martin. *Zwischen Abwehr und Bekehrung: Die Stellung der Deutschen Evangelischen Theologie Zum Judentum im 17. Jahrhundert.* Tübingen: J. C. B. Mohr (P. Siebeck), 1988.

Funkenstein, Amos. *Perceptions of Jewish History.* Berkeley: University of California Press, 1993.

Furst, Rachel. "Striving for Justice: A History of Women and Litigation in the Jewish Courts of Medieval Ashkenaz." PhD diss., Hebrew University, 2014.

Füssel, Marian. "Die Materialität der Frühen Neuzeit. Neuere Forschungen Zur Geschichte der Materiellen Kultur." *Zeitschrift für Historische Forschung* 42, no. 3 (2015): 433–463.

Garberson, Eric. "Libraries, Memory and the Space of Knowledge." *Journal of the History of Collections* 18, no. 2 (2006): 105–136.

Genette, Gérard. *Paratexts: Thresholds of Interpretation.* Cambridge: Cambridge University Press, 1997.

Ghobrial, John-Paul. "The Secret Life of Elias of Babylon and the Uses of Global Microhistory." *Past and Present* 222, no. 1 (2014): 51–93.

Godelier, Maurice. *The Enigma of the Gift.* Chicago: University of Chicago Press, 1999.

Goldgar, Anne. *Impolite Learning: Conduct and Community in the Republic of Letters, 1680–1750.* New Haven, CT: Yale University Press, 1995.

Gömmel, Rainer. "Hofjuden und Wirtschaft im Merkantilismus." In *Hofjuden: Ökonomie und Interkulturalität: Die Jüdische Wirtschaftselite im 18. Jahrhundert,* edited by J. Friedrich Battenberg and Rotraud Ries, 59–65. Hamburg: Christians Verlag, 2002.

Goodman, Dena. *The Republic of Letters: A Cultural History of the French Enlightenment.* Ithaca, NY: Cornell University Press, 1994.

Gordan, Phyllis Walter Goodhart. *Two Renaissance Book Hunters: The Letters of Poggius Bracciolini to Nicolaus de Niccolis.* New York: Columbia University Press, 1991.

Graeber, David. *Debt: The First 5,000 Years.* Brooklyn: Melville House, 2011.

Graetz, Michael. "Court Jews in Economics and Politics." In *From Court Jews to the Rothschilds: Art, Patronage, and Power: 1600–1800,* edited by Vivian B. Mann, Richard I. Cohen, and Fritz Backhaus, 27–43. Munich: Prestel, 1996.

Grafton, Anthony. "A Sketch Map of a Lost Continent: The Republic of Letters." *Republics of Letters: A Journal for the Study of Knowledge, Politics, and the Arts* 1, no. 1 (2009): 1–18.

Grafton, Anthony, and Joanna Weinberg. *"I Have Always Loved the Holy Tongue": Isaac Casaubon, the Jews, and a Forgotten Chapter in Renaissance Scholarship.* Cambridge, MA: Belknap, 2011.

Greenblatt, Rachel L. "'Asot sfarim ad eyn ketz': defus, zikaron, ktivah autobiografit u-Maharal mi-Prag." In *Maharal: Akdamot,* edited by Elchanan Reiner, 75–99. Jerusalem: Mercaz Zalman Shazar, 2015.

———. *To Tell Their Children: Jewish Communal Memory in Early Modern Prague.* Stanford, CA: Stanford University Press, 2014.

Greenblatt, Stephen. *Renaissance Self-Fashioning: From More to Shakespeare.* Chicago: University of Chicago Press, 2005.

Greengrass, Mark. *Christendom Destroyed: Europe 1517–1648.* New York: Viking, 2014.

Gries, Zeev. *The Book in the Jewish World: 1700–1900.* Oxford: Littman Library of Jewish Civilization, 2007.

———. "Le-demuto shel ha-mevi le-defus ha-Yehudi be-shilhei yeme ha-beinayim." *Iggeret ha-Akademiah ha-Le'umit ha-Yisra'elit le-Mada'im* 11 (1992): 7–11.

Groebner, Valentin. *Who Are You?: Identification, Deception, and Surveillance in Early Modern Europe.* Brooklyn: Zone Books, 2007.

Grunwald, Max. "Handschriftliches aus der Hamburger Stadtbibliothek." *Monatschrift für Geschichte und Wissenschaft des Judentums* 40–41 (1895/1896): no. 6, 280–283; no. 9, 422–429; no. 10, 457–461; (1896/1897): no. 8, 356–362; no. 9, 410–423; no. 12 571–574.

———. *Samuel Oppenheimer und Sein Kreis (Ein Kapitel aus der Finanzgeschichte Österreichs).* Vienna: W. Braunmüller, 1913.

Gullick, Michael. "How Fast Did Scribes Write? Evidence from Romanesque Manuscripts." In *Making the Medieval Book: Techniques of Production: Proceedings of the Fourth Conference of the Seminar in the History of the Book to 1500, Oxford, July 1992,* edited by Linda L. Brownrigg, 39–53. Los Altos Hills, CA: Anderson-Lovelace, 1995.

Hacker, Joseph. "The Sephardim in the Ottoman Empire in the Sixteenth Century." In *Moreshet Sepharad = The Sephardi Legacy,* edited by Haim Beinart, 109–133. Jerusalem: Magnes, 1992.

Hailwood, Mark. *Alehouses and Good Fellowship in Early Modern England.* Studies in Early Modern Cultural, Political, and Social History. Woodbridge: Boydell & Brewer, 2014.

Halpern, Israel. "Haskamot Va'ad Arba Arazot." *Kiryat Sefer* 11, no. 1 (1934): 105–110; no. 2 (1934): 252–264.

———. "Mahloket 'al breirat he-Kahal be-Frankfurt de-Main ve-hedeha be-Folin u-be-Vihem." In *Yehudim ve-Yahadut be-Mizrah-Europah,* 108–135. Jerusalem: Magnes, 1969.

Hartman, D. "Ueber die Berühmte in ihrer Art Einzige Sammlung Von Hebräischen, Chaldäischen, Talmudischen, Rabbinischen und Andern Büchern un Handschriften, die der Ehemalige Oberrabbiner zu Prag, David Oppenheimer, Hinterlassen Hat." *Jedidja* 6 (1820–1821): 118–134.

Ha-yisraeli, Reuven. "Toldot kehilat Prag be-shanim 1680–1730 le-or ha-'Kopiar' shel R' David Oppenheim." Master's thesis, Tel-Aviv University, 1965.

Head, Randolph. "Knowing Like a State: The Transformation of Political Knowledge in Swiss Archives, 1450–1770." *Journal of Modern History* 75, no. 4 (2003): 745–782.

Head, Randolph C. "Configuring European Archives: Spaces, Materials and Practices in the Differentiation of Repositories from the Late Middle Ages to 1700." *European History Quarterly* 46, no. 3 (2016): 498–518.

Heal, Felicity. *The Power of Gifts: Gift Exchange in Early Modern England.* Oxford: Oxford University Press, 2014.

Heinemann, Jeremiah. "An den Geehrten Verfasser des Aufsatzes im Orient (Monat April 1844) über die Oppenheimer'ssche Bibliothek." In *Der Orient (Literaturblatt des Orients),* 474–473. Leipzig, 1844.

Heller, Marvin J. "Earliest Printings of the Talmud." In *Printing the Talmud: From Bomberg to Schottenstein,* edited by Sharon Liberman Mintz and Gabriel M. Goldstein, 61–79. New York: Yeshiva University Museum, 2005.

———. "Moses Benjamin Wulff—Court Jew." In *Studies in the Making of the Early Hebrew Book.* Studies in Jewish History and Culture, 206–217. Leiden: Brill, 2008.

———. "Often Overlooked: Hebrew Printing in Prostejov (Prossnitz)." In *Further Studies in the Making of the Early Hebrew Book,* 117–127. Leiden: Brill, 2013.

———. *Printing the Talmud: A History of the Earliest Printed Editions of the Talmud.* Brooklyn: Im Hasefer, 1992.

———. *Printing the Talmud: A History of the Individual Treatises Printed from 1700 to 1750.* Brill's Series in Jewish Studies. Leiden: Brill, 1999.

Hill, Brad Sabin. "Hebrew Printing on Blue and Other Coloured Papers." In *Treasures of the Valmadonna Trust Library: A Catalogue of 15th-Century Books and Five Centuries of Deluxe Hebrew Printing*, edited by David Sclar, Brad Sabin Hill, Adri K. Offenberg, and Yitshak Yudlov, 84–111. London: Valmadonna Trust Library, 2011.

Höbelt, Lothar. "The Westphalian Peace: Augsburg Mark II or Celebrated Armistice?" In *The Holy Roman Empire, 1495–1806: A European Perspective*, edited by Robert John Weston Evans and Peter H. Wilson, 19–34. Leiden: Brill, 2012.

Hochmuth, Christian. *Globale Güter—Lokale Aneignung. Kaffee, Tee, Schokolade und Tabak im Frühneuzeitlichen Dresden.* Konstanz: UVK Verlag, 2008.

Hochner, Nicole. "Reshitah shel ha-sifriyah ha-malkhutit be-Tsarfat: Meni'im ta'amulti'im u-foliti'im be-idan ha-defus." In *Sifriyot ve-osfe sefarim*, edited by Moshe Sluhovsky and Yosef Kaplan, 127–140. Jerusalem: Merkaz Zalman Shazar le-toldot Yisrael, 2006.

Hoffman, Adina, and Peter Cole. *Sacred Trash: The Lost and Found World of the Cairo Geniza.* Jewish Encounters. New York: Nextbook: Schocken, 2011.

Holenstein, André. "'Gute Policey' und Lokale Gesellschaft: Erfahrung als Katergorie im Verwaltungshandeln des 18. Jahrhuderts." In *"Erfahrung" als Katergorie der Frühneuzeitgeschichte,* edited by Paul Münch, 433–450. Munich: R. Oldenburg, 2001.

Horowitz, Elliott. "Coffee, Coffeehouses, and the Nocturnal Rituals of Early Modern Jewry." *AJS Review* 14, no. 1 (1989): 17–46.

Horowski, Leonhard. "'Such a Great Advantage for My Son': Office-Holding and Career Mechanisms at the Court of France, 1661–1789." *Court Historian* 8, no. 2 (2003): 125–175.

Hsia, R. Po-chia. "The Jews and the Emperors." In *State and Society in Early Modern Austria,* edited by Charles W. Ingrao, 71–80. West Lafayette, IN: Purdue University Press, 1994.

———. *The World of Catholic Renewal, 1540–1770.* New Approaches to European History. 2nd ed. New York: Cambridge University Press, 2005.

Hundert, Gershon David. "Was There an East European Analogue to Court Jews?" In *The Jews in Poland,* edited by Andrzej K. Paluch and Sławomir Kapralski, 67–75. Cracow: Jagiellonian University, Research Center on Jewish History and Culture in Poland, 1992.

Hunt, Lynn. *Politics, Culture, and Class in the French Revolution.* Berkeley: University of California Press, 1984.

Hurvitz, Mark. "The Rabbinic Perception of Printing as Depicted in Haskamot and Responsa." Master's thesis, Hebrew Union College, Jewish Institute of Religion, 1978.

Idel, Moshe. "Italy in Safed, Safed in Italy: Toward an Interactive History of Sixteenth-Century Kabbalah." In *Cultural Intermediaries: Jewish Intellec-*

tuals in Early Modern Italy, edited by David B. Ruderman and Giuseppe Veltri, 239-269. Philadelphia: University of Pennsylvania Press, 2004.

Ingrao, Charles W. *In Quest and Crisis: Emperor Joseph I and the Habsburg Monarchy.* West Lafayette, IN: Purdue University Press, 1979.

Israel, Jonathan I. *European Jewry in the Age of Mercantilism, 1550–1750.* The Littman Library of Jewish Civilization. 3rd ed. London: Littman Library of Jewish Civilization, 1998.

———. *Radical Enlightenment: Philosophy and the Making of Modernity, 1650–1750.* Oxford: Oxford University Press, 2001.

Jackson, H. J. *Marginalia: Readers Writing in Books.* New Haven, CT: Yale University Press, 2001.

Jakobovits, Tobias. "Das Prager und Böhmische Landesrabbinat ende des Siebzehnten und Anfang des Achtzehnten Jahrhunderts." *Jahrbuch der Gesellschaft für Geschichte der Juden in der Čechoslovakischen Republik* 5 (1933): 79-136.

———. "Wer ist Abraham Aron Lichtenstadt." *Monatschrift für Geschichte und Wissenschaft des Judentums* 74 (1930): 35-41.

Jardine, Lisa. *Worldly Goods: A New History of the Renaissance.* New York: W. W. Norton, 1998.

Jelinková, Andrea. "Hebrew Printing in Moravia at the Beginning of the 17th Century." In *Hebrew Printing in Bohemia and Moravia,* edited by Olga Sixtová, 153-163. Prague: Academia: Jewish Museum in Prague, 2012.

Johns, Adrian. "Coffeehouses and Print Shops." In *The Cambridge History of Science,* edited by Katharine Park and Lorraine Daston, 320-340. Cambridge: Cambridge University Press, 2006.

———. "The Coming of Print to Europe." In *The Cambridge Companion to the History of the Book,* edited by Leslie Howsam, 107-124. Cambridge: Cambridge University Press, 2014.

———. "How to Acknowledge a Revolution." *American Historical Review* 107, no. 1 (2002): 106-125.

———. *The Nature of the Book: Print and Knowledge in the Making.* Chicago: University of Chicago Press, 1998.

———. *Piracy: The Intellectual Property Wars from Gutenberg to Gates.* Chicago: University of Chicago Press, 2009.

Joskowicz, Ari. "Toleration in the Age of Projects: Cameralism, German Police Science, and the Jews." *Jewish Social Studies* 22, no. 2 (2017): 1-37.

Jost, Isaak Marcus. "Eine Familien-Megillah, aus der Ersten Hälfte des 18. Jarhhunderts." *Jahrbuch für die Geschichte der Juden und des Judenthums* 6, no. 1 (1861): 40-82.

Justice, Steven. *Writing and Rebellion: England in 1381.* The New Historicism. Berkeley: University of California Press, 1994.

Jütte, Daniel. *The Age of Secrecy: Jews, Christians, and the Economy of Secrets, 1400–1800.* New Haven, CT: Yale University Press, 2015.

Kahana, Maoz. "The Allure of Forbidden Knowledge: The Temptation of Sabbatean Literature for Mainstream Rabbis in the Frankist Moment, 1756–1761." *Jewish Quarterly Review* 102, no. 4 (2012): 589–616.

———. "Shabbat be-veit ha-kafe shel kehillat kodesh Prag." *Zion* 78, no. 1 (2013): 5–50.

Kanarfogel, Ephraim. "Unanimity, Majority, and Communal Government in Ashkenaz During the High Middle Ages: A Reassessment." *Proceedings of the American Academy for Jewish Research* 58 (1992): 79–106.

Kaplan, Benjamin J. *Divided by Faith: Religious Conflict and the Practice of Toleration in Early Modern Europe.* Cambridge, MA: Belknap, 2007.

Kaplan, Debra. *Beyond Expulsion: Jews, Christians, and Reformation Strasbourg.* Stanford, CA: Stanford University Press, 2011.

———. "Rituals of Marriage and Communal Prestige: The 'Breileft' in Medieval and Early Modern Germany." *Jewish History* 29, no. 3 (2015): 273–300.

Katz, Jacob. "Le-Toldot ha-rabanut be-motzaei yeme ha-beinayim." In *Sefer zikaron le-Binyamin De-Vries,* edited by B. Z. Melamed, 281–294. Tel Aviv: Tel Aviv University Press, 1969.

———. "Post-Zoharic Relations Between Halakhah and Kabbbalah." In *Divine Law in Human Hands: Case Studies in Halakhic Flexibility,* 31–55. Jerusalem: Magnes, 1998.

———. *Tradition and Crisis: Jewish Society at the End of the Middle Ages.* Translated by Bernard Dov Cooperman. Syracuse, NY: Syracuse University Press, 2000.

Kaufmann, David. *Die Letzte Vertreibung der Juden aus Wien und Niederösterreich ihre Vorgeschichte (1625–1670) und ihre Opfer.* Vienna: Bei C. Konegen, 1889.

———. "Jair Chayim Bacharach: A Biographical Sketch." *Jewish Quarterly Review* 3, nos. 2–3 (1891): 292–313, 485–536.

———. "La Lutte de R. Naftali Cohen contre Hayyoun." *Revue des Études Juives* 36 (1897): 236–286; 37 (1898): 274–283.

———. "R. Chajjim Jona Theonim-Fränkel." *Monatschrift für Geschichte und Wissenschaft des Judentums* 42, no. 7 (1898): 322–328.

———. *Urkundliches aus dem Leben Samson Wertheimers.* Vienna: C. Konegen, 1892.

Kieval, Hillel J. *Languages of Community: The Jewish Experience in the Czech Lands.* Berkeley: University of California Press, 2000.

Kinarti, Amihai, ed. *Yosef Ometz of Yuspe Hahn Norlingen.* Shaalvim: Machon Shlomo Omen, 2016.

Kisch, Guido. "Die Zensur Judischer Bücher in Böhmen." *Jahrbuch der Gesellschaft für Geschichte der Juden in der Čechoslovakischen Republik* 2 (1930): 456–490.

Klein, Birgit E. "The 1603 Assembly in Frankfurt: Prehistory, Ordinances, Effects." *Jewish Culture and History* 10, nos. 2–3 (2008): 111–124.

Klemperer, Gutmann. "The Rabbis of Prague." *Historia Judaica* 12 (1950): 33–66, 143–152; 13 (1951): 55–82.

Knight, Jeffrey Todd. *Bound to Read: Compilations, Collections, and the Making of Renaissance Literature.* Philadelphia: University of Pennsylvania Press, 2013.

———. "Fast Bind, Fast Find: The History of the Book and the Modern Collection." *Criticism* 51, no. 1 (2009): 79–104.

———. "'Furnished' for Action: Renaissance Books as Furniture." *Book History* 12 (2009): 37–73.

Lebrecht, Fürchtegott. "Die Oppenheimer'sche Bibliothek." *Der Orient Leipzig: Berichte, Studien und Kritiken für jüdische Geschichte und Literatur* 5 (1844): no. 16: 247–250; no. 18: 273–278.

Lehmann, Matthias B. *Emissaries from the Holy Land: The Sephardic Diaspora and the Practice of Pan-Judaism in the Eighteenth Century.* Stanford Studies in Jewish History and Culture. Stanford, CA: Stanford University Press, 2014.

———. "Rabbinic Emissaries from Palestine and the Making of a Modern Jewish Diaspora: A Philanthropic Network in the Eighteenth Century." In *Envisioning Judaism: Studies in Honor of Peter Schäfer on the Occasion of His Seventieth Birthday,* edited by Ra'anan S. Boustan, Klaus Herrmann, Reimund Leicht, Annette Yoshiko Reed, and Giuseppe Veltri, 1229–1246. Tübingen: Mohr Siebeck, 2013.

Lehmstedt, Mark. "'Ein Notwendiges Übel': Die Leipziger Buchhändlermesse im 18. Jahrhundert." In *Leipzig, Stadt der Wa(h)ren Wunder: 500 Jahre Reichsmesseprivileg,* edited by Volker Rodekamp, 65–76. Leipzig: Leipziger Messe, 1997.

Lehnardt, Andreas. "Genisa—Die Materielle Kultur des Deutschen Judentums im Spiegel Neu Entdeckter Synagogaler Ablageräume." In *Einführungen in die Materiellen Kulturen des Judentums,* edited by Nathanael Riemer, 173–202. Wiesbaden: Harrassowitz, 2016.

Leibetseder, Mathis. "Across Europe: Educational Travelling of German Noblemen in a Comparative Perspective." *Journal of Early Modern History* 14 (2010): 417–449.

Leiman, Shnayer Z. "Haskamot rabi Yehonatan Eybeschutz ve-rabi Yaakov Emden." *Or ha-Mizrah* 51, nos. 1-2 (2005): 169-203.

———. "Perush ha-gaon Rabi Yehonatan Eybeschuz Zt"L le-kezat agadot mi-masekhet Berakhot." *Or ha-Mizrah* 29, nos. 3-4 (1981): 418-428.

Lewinsky. "Ein Brief der Pfälzischen Gemeinde-Vorsteher an David Oppenheim." *Blaetter für Jüdische Geschichte und Litterature* 2, no. 7 (1901): 62-63.

Liberles, Robert. *Jews Welcome Coffee: Tradition and Innovation in Early Modern Germany*. Waltham, MA: Brandeis University Press, 2012.

Lieben, S. H. "Beiträge zur Geschichte der Zensur Hebräischer Drucke in Präg." *Soncino-Blätter* 3, no. 1 (1929): 51-55.

———. "David Oppenheim." *Jahrbuch der Jüdisch-Literarischen Gesellschaft* 19 (1928): 1-38.

———. "Oppenheimiana." *Jahrbuch der Gesellschaft für Geschichte der Juden in der Čechoslovakischen Republik* 7 (1935): 437-485.

Liebersohn, Harry. *The Return of the Gift: European History of a Global Idea*. New York: Cambridge University Press, 2011.

Liebes, Yehuda. "A Profile of R. Naphtali Katz from Frankfurt and His Attitude Towards Sabbateanism." In *Mysticism, Magic, and Kabbalah in Ashkenazi Judaism: International Symposium Held in Frankfurt A.M. 1991,* edited by Karl-Erich Grözinger and Joseph Dan, 208-222. Berlin: Walter de Gruyter, 1995.

Lipscher, Vladimir. "Jüdische Gemeinden in Böhmen und Mähren im 17. und 18. Jahrhundert." In *Die Juden in den Böhmischen Ländern,* edited by Ferdinand Seibt, 73-86. Munich: R. Oldenburg, 1983.

Litt, Stefan, ed. *Jüdische Gemeindestatuten aus dem Aschkenasischen Kulturraum 1650-1850,* vol. 1. Göttingen: Vandenhoeck & Ruprecht, 2014.

———. *Pinkas, Kahal, and the Mediene: The Records of Dutch Ashkenazi Communities in the Eighteenth Century as Historical Sources.* Leiden: Brill, 2008.

Louthan, Howard. *Converting Bohemia: Force and Persuasion in the Catholic Reformation.* Cambridge: Cambridge University Press, 2009.

Löwenstein, Leopold. "David Oppenheim." In *Gedenkbuch zur Erinnerung an David Kaufmann,* edited by M. Brann and F. Rosenthal, 538-559. Breslau: V. S. Schottlaender, 1900.

———. *Index Approbationum.* Berlin: Marx, 1923.

Maciejko, Paweł. *The Mixed Multitude: Jacob Frank and the Frankist Movement, 1755-1816.* Philadelphia: University of Pennsylvania Press, 2011.

———. "The Rabbi and the Jesuit: On Rabbi Jonathan Eibeschütz and Father Franciscus Haselbauer Editing the Talmud." *Jewish Social Studies* 20, no. 2 (2014): 147-184.

Macray, William Dunn. *Annals of the Bodleian Library, Oxford.* 2nd ed. Oxford: Clarendon, 1984.

Malkiel, David. "The Ghetto Republic." In *The Jews of Early Modern Venice,* edited by Robert C. Davis and Benjamin C. I. Ravid, 117-142. Baltimore: Johns Hopkins University Press, 2001.

Mann, Vivian B., Richard I. Cohen, and Fritz Backhaus, eds. *From Court Jews to the Rothschilds: Art, Patronage, and Power 1600–1800.* Munich: Prestel, 1996.

Manuel, Frank Edward. *The Broken Staff: Judaism Through Christian Eyes.* Cambridge, MA: Harvard University Press, 1992.

Marcus, Ivan G. "The Recensions and Structure of 'Sefer Hasidim.'" *Proceedings of the American Academy for Jewish Research* 45 (1978): 131-153.

———. *Rituals of Childhood: Jewish Acculturation in Medieval Europe.* New Haven, CT: Yale University Press, 1996.

Marcus, Jacob Rader. *Israel Jacobson, the Founder of the Reform Movement in Judaism.* 2nd ed. Cincinnati, OH: Hebrew Union College Press, 1972.

Margaliot, Reuven. "Le-Toldot 'Anshe Shem' be-Lvov." *Sinai* 29 (1951): 215-223, 378-388.

Marx, Alexander. "The History of David Oppenheimer's Library." Chap. 14 In *Studies in Jewish History and Booklore,* 238-255. New York: Jewish Theological Seminary of America, 1944.

———. "Some Jewish Book Collectors." Chap. 13 In *Studies in Jewish History and Booklore,* 198-237. New York: Jewish Theological Seminary of America, 1944.

Matušíková, Lenka. "Licences for the Baptism of Jews Granted by the Archbishopric Consistory to the Jesuit College in Prague's Old Town, 1664-1755." *Judaica Bohemiae* 41 (2005): 261-322.

Mauss, Marcel, and W. D. Halls. *The Gift: The Form and Reason for Exchange in Archaic Societies.* New York: W. W. Norton, 1990.

McKenzie, D. F. *Bibliography and the Sociology of Texts.* The Panizzi Lectures. London: British Library, 1986.

McKitterick, David. *Print, Manuscript, and the Search for Order, 1450–1830.* Cambridge: Cambridge University Press, 2003.

McLuhan, Marshall. *Understanding Media: The Extensions of Man.* New York: McGraw-Hill, 1964.

Melvin, Karen. "Charity Without Borders: Alms-Giving in New Spain for Captives in North Africa." *Colonial Latin American Review* 18, no. 1 (2009): 75-97.

Meyer, Hermann. "Materialien zur Geschichte der Bibliothek David Oppenheims." *Soncino-Blätter* 2 (1927): 59-80.

Michael, Heimann Joseph, Elieser Loeb, and Abraham Berliner. *Or ha-hayyim.* Frankfurt am Main: J. Kauffmann, 1891.

Miller, Michael Laurence. "Rabbi David Oppenheim on Trial: Turks, Titles, and Tribute in Counter-Reformation Prague." *Jewish Quarterly Review* 106, no. 1 (2016): 42–75.

———. *Rabbis and Revolution: The Jews of Moravia in the Age of Emancipation.* Stanford Studies in Jewish History and Culture. Stanford, CA: Stanford University Press, 2011.

Miller, Peter N. *Peiresc's Europe: Learning and Virtue in the Seventeenth Century.* New Haven, CT: Yale University Press, 2000.

Moran, Bruce T. *Patronage and Institutions: Science, Technology, and Medicine at the European Court, 1500–1750.* Rochester, NY: Boydell, 1991.

Moraw, Peter. "Soziale Verflechtungen im Reich Unter Den Gesichtspunken Recht, Konfession un Politik: Einleitung zur Diskussion." In *Klientelsysteme im Europa der Frühen Neuzeit,* edited by Antoni Mączak and Elisabeth Müller-Luckner, 1–18. Munich: R. Oldenbourg, 1988.

Naudé, Gabriel. *Advice on Establishing a Library.* Berkeley: University of California Press, 1950.

Nelles, Paul. "The Library as an Agent of Discovery: Gabriel Naudé and the Uses of History." In *History and the Disciplines: The Reclassification of Knowledge in Early Modern Europe,* edited by Donald R. Kelley, 41–60. Rochester, NY: University of Rochester Press, 1997.

———. "Stocking a Library: Montaigne, the Market, and the Diffusion of Print." In *La Librairie de Montaigne: Proceedings of the Tenth Cambridge French Renaissance Colloquium, 2–4 September 2008,* edited by Philip Ford and Neil Kenny, 1–24. Cambridge: Cambridge French Colloquia, 2012.

Netanel, Neil. *From Maimonides to Microsoft: The Jewish Law of Copyright Since the Birth of Print.* New York: Oxford University Press, 2016.

Nosek, Bedřich, and Vladimír Sadek. "Georgio Diodato und David Oppenheim." *Judaica Bohemiae* 6, no. 1 (1970): 5–27.

Offer, Avner. "Between the Gift and the Market: The Economy of Regard." *Economic History Review* 50, no. 3 (1997): 450–476.

Outram, Dorinda. *The Enlightenment.* 2nd ed. Cambridge: Cambridge University Press, 2005.

Parker, Geoffrey. *The Military Revolution: Military Innovation and the Rise of the West, 1500–1800.* Cambridge: Cambridge University Press, 1988.

Parkin, D. J. "Mementoes as Transitional Objects in Human Displacement." *Journal of Material Culture* 4, no. 3 (1999): 303–320.

Parrott, David. *The Business of War: Military Enterprise and Military Revolution in Early Modern Europe.* Cambridge: Cambridge University Press, 2012.

Parush, Iris. *Reading Jewish Women: Marginality and Modernization in Nineteenth-Century Eastern European Jewish Society.* Waltham, MA: Brandeis University Press, 2004.

Pearce, Susan M. *On Collecting: An Investigation into Collecting in the European Tradition.* London: Routledge, 1994.

Pelger, Gregor. "Die Bibliothek des David Oppenheimer als 'Jewish Space' zwischen Christlichen und Jüdischen Interessen: Historische Konstellationsforschung im Jüdischen Kontext." *Transversal* 8, no. 2 (2008): 71–94.

———. *Wissenschaft des Judentums und Englische Bibliotheken: Zur Geschichte Historischer Philologie im 19. Jahrhundert.* Berlin: Metropol, 2010.

Pettegree, Andrew. *The Book in the Renaissance.* New Haven, CT: Yale University Press, 2010.

Pollmann, Judith. "Archiving the Present and Chronicling for the Future in Early Modern Europe." *Past and Present* 230, suppl 11 (2016): 231–252.

Pomian, Krzysztof. *Collectors and Curiosities: Paris and Venice, 1500–1800.* Cambridge: Polity, 1990.

Popper, William. *The Censorship of Hebrew Books.* New York: Ktav, 1969.

Press, Volker. "The Habsburg Court as Center of the Imperial Government." *Journal of Modern History* 58 (1986): S23–S45.

Prokeš, Jaroslav. "Der Antisemitismus der Behörden und das Prager Ghetto in Nachweißenbergischer Zeit." *Jahrbuch der Gesellschaft für Geschichte der Juden in der Čechoslovakischen Republik* 1 (1929): 41–262.

Putík, Alexandr. "The Censorship of Hebrew Books in Prague, 1512–1670 (1672)." In *Hebrew Printing in Bohemia and Moravia,* edited by Olga Sixtová, 187–214. Prague: Academia: Jewish Museum in Prague, 2012.

———. "The Origin of the Symbols of the Prague Jewish Town: The Banner of the Old-New Synagogue—David's Shield and the 'Swedish' Hat." *Judaica Bohemiae* 29, nos. 1–2 (1993): 4–37.

———. "The Prague Jewish Community in the Late 17th and Early 18th Centuries." *Judaica Bohemiae* 35 (2000): 4–140.

———. "Prague Jews and Judah Hasid: A Study on the Social, Political and Religious History of the Late Seventeenth and Early Eighteenth Centuries, Part 1." *Judaica Bohemiae* 38 (2002): 72–105.

———. "Prague Jews and Judah Hasid: A Study on the Social, Political and Religious History of the Late Seventeenth and Early Eighteenth Centuries, Part 3." *Judaica Bohemiae* 41, no. 1 (2011): 33–72.

Rabinowitz, Raphael Nathan, and A. M. Haberman. *Ma'Amar ʿal hadpasat ha-Talmud.* Jerusalem: Mossad Harav Kook, 1965.

Raines, Dorit. "Tafkidam shel ha-sifriyot ve-ha-archiyonim ha-pratiyim be-hinukham ha-foliti shel ha-patrikim ha-Venezianim." *Sifriyot ve-osfe sefarim.* Edited by Moshe Sluhovsky and Yosef Kaplan Jerusalem: Merkaz Zalman Shazar le-toldot Yisrael, 2006.

Rakower, Nahum. "Ha-yesod ha-mishpati shel isur ha-hadpasah be-'haskamot' le-sfarim." *Divrei ha-Congress ha-olami le-mada'ei ha-Yahadut* 5, no. 3 (1972): 333–343.

———. *Zekhut ha-yozrim be-mekorot ha-Yehudiim.* Jerusalem: Sifriyat ha-Mishpat ha-Ivri, 1991.

Raspe, Lucia. "Die Lebensbedingungen des Ghettos in der Jüdischen Braucht-umsliteratur der Frühen Neuzeit." In *Frühneuzeitliche Ghettos in Europa im Vergleich,* edited by Fritz Backhaus, Gisela Engel, Gundula Grebner, and Robert Liberles, 303–331. Berlin: Trafo, 2012.

———. "Die Schum-Gemeinden in der Narrativen Überlieferung aus Mittelalter und Früher Neuzeit." In *Die Schum-Gemeinden Speyer—Worms—Mainz; auf dem Weg zum Welterbe,* edited by Pia Heberer and Ursula Reuter, 313–326. Regensburg: Schnell & Steiner, 2013.

———. "Individueller Ruhm und Kollektiver Nutzen—Berend Lehmann Als Mäzen." In *Hofjuden: Ökonomie und Interkulturalität: Die Jüdische Wirt-schaftselite im 18. Jahrhundert,* edited by J. Friedrich Battenberg and Ro-traud Ries, 191–208. Hamburg: Christians Verlag, 2002.

Ray, Jonathan. *After Expulsion: 1492 and the Making of the Sephardic Jewry.* New York: New York University Press, 2012.

Raz-Krakotzkin, Amnon. *The Censor, the Editor, and the Text: The Catholic Church and the Shaping of the Jewish Canon in the Sixteenth Century.* Philadelphia: University of Pennsylvania Press, 2007.

Reiner, Elchanan. "Aliyat 'Ha-Kehilla Ha-Gedola'—al shorshei ha-kehillah ha-Yehudit he-ironit be-Folin be-et ha-hadasha." *Gal-Ed* 20 (2006): 13–37.

———. "A Biography of an Agent of Culture: Eleazar Altschul of Prague and His Literary Activity." In *Schöpferische Momente des Europäischen Judentums in der Frühen Neuzeit,* edited by Michael Graetz, 229–247. Heidelberg: C. Win-ter, 2000.

———. "Darshan noded madpis et sfarav: Perek alum be-toldot ha-tarbut ha-Ivrit be-Europah be-me'ah ha-shva esreh." In *Hut shel hen: Shai le-Hava Tur-niansky,* edited by Israel Bartal, Galit Hasan-Rokem, Ada Rapoport-Albert, Claudia Rosenzweig, Vicky Shifriss, and Erika Timm, 123–156. Jerusalem: Zalman Shazar Center for Jewish History, 2013.

———. " 'Ein tsarikh shum Yehudi lilmod davar rak ha-Talmud levado': Al kimud ve-tokhnei limud be-Ashkenaz bi-yeme ha-sefer ha-rishonim." In *Ta Shma: Mehkarim be-mada'ei ha-Yahadut le-zikhro shel Yisrael M. Ta-Shma,* edited by Avraham Reiner, 705–746. Alon Shvut: Herzog College, 2011.

————. "Hon, ma'amad hevrati ve-talmud Torah: Ha-kloyz be-hevrah ha-Yehudit ba-Mizrah Europa be-meot ha-17-18." *Zion* 58, no. 3 (1993): 287–328.

————. "Temurot be-yeshivot Polin ve-Ashkenaz be-meot ha-16-ha-17 ve-ha-vikuah al ha-pilpul." In *Ke-Minhag Ashkenaz U-Folin: Sefer yovel le-Hana Shmeruk: Kovets mehkarim be-tarbut Yehudit,* edited by Israel Bartal, Chava Turniansky, and Ezra Mendelsohn, 9–80. Jerusalem: Merkaz Zalman Shazar le-toldot Yisrael, 1993.

————. "Yashan mipnei hadash: Al temurot be-tokhnei limud be-yeshivot Polin be-me'ah ha-16 ve-yeshivato shel Rema be-Krakov." In *Zekher davar le-avdekha: Asufat ma'amarim le-zekher Dov Rafel,* edited by Shmuel Glick, 183–206. Jerusalem: Bet ha-Sefer le-Hinukh al shem Prof P. Churgin, 2007.

Reuter, Fritz. "Mehrkonfessionalität in der Freien Stadt Worms im 16.–18. Jahrhundert." In *Städtische Randgruppen und Minderheiten,* edited by Bernhard Kirchgässner and Fritz Reuter, 9–48. Stuttgart: Jan Thorbecke Verlag, 1986.

————. *Warmaisa: 1000 Jahre Juden in Worms.* Frankfurt am Main: Jüdischer Verlag bei Athenäum, 1987.

Reuter, Ursula. "Die Wormser Judengasse in der Frühen Neuzeit." In *Frühneuzeitliche Ghettos in Europa im Vergleich,* edited by Fritz Backhaus, Gisela Engel, Gundula Grebner, and Robert Liberles, 205–240. Berlin: Trafo Wissenschaftsverlag, 2012.

Rivkind, Yitshak. "Tseror ketavim le-korot ha-Yehudim be-Erets Yisrael." *Reshumot* 4 (1925): 301–344.

Roemer, Nils H. *German City, Jewish Memory: The Story of Worms.* Waltham, MA: Brandeis University Press, 2010.

Rose, Mark. *Authors and Owners: The Invention of Copyright.* Cambridge, MA: Harvard University Press, 1993.

Rosenzweig, Claudia. "Kitve Hava Turniansky." In *Hut shel sen: Shai le-Havah Turniansky,* edited by Israel Bartal, Galit Hasan-Rokem, Ada Rapoport-Albert, Claudia Rosenzweig, Vicky Shifriss, and Erika Timm, 551–559. Jerusalem: Zalman Shazar, 2013.

Rosman, Moshe (Murray) J. "Dimuyav shel beit Yisrael be-Folin ke-merkaz Torah aharei gezerot 408-409." *Zion* 51, no. 4 (1986): 435–448.

Ruderman, David B. *Jewish Thought and Scientific Discovery in Early Modern Europe.* New Haven, CT: Yale University Press, 1995.

Rustow, Marina. *Heresy and the Politics of Community: The Jews of the Fatimid Caliphate.* Ithaca, NY: Cornell University Press, 2008.

Sabean, David Warren. "Kinship and Prohibited Marriages in Baroque Germany: Divergent Strategies Among Jewish and Christian Populations." *Leo Baeck Institute Yearbook* 47, no. 1 (2002): 91–103.

Samet, Moshe. "Eybeschütz, Yonatan." In *YIVO Encyclopedia of Jews in Eastern Europe,* edited by Gershon David Hundert, 486–488. New Haven, CT: Yale University Press, 2008.

Schacter, Jacob Joseph. "Rabbi Jacob Emden: Life and Major Works." PhD diss., Harvard University, 1988.

Schedlitz, Bernd. *Leffmann Behrens: Untersuchungen zum Hofjudentum Im Zeitalter des Absolutismus.* Hildesheim: A. Lax, 1984.

Schmelzer, Menahem. "Hebrew Printing and Publishing in Germany, 1650–1750: On Jewish Book Culture and the Emergence of Modern Jewry." *Leo Baeck Institute Year Book* 33 (1988): 369–383.

Schmidt, Frieder. "Die Internationale Papierversorgung der Buchproduktion im Deutschsprachigen Gebiet Vornehmlich Während des 18. Jahrhunderts." *Paper History* 10 (2000): 2–24.

Scholem, Gershom. *Halomotav shel ha-shabtai'i R. Mordekhai Ashkenazi: Al devar pinkas ha-halomot shel R. Mordekhai Ashkenazi talmido Shel R. Avraham Rovigo.* Jerusalem: Schocken, 1937.

———. *Sabbatai Sevi: The Mystical Messiah, 1626–1676.* Bollingen Series. Princeton, NJ: Princeton University Press, 1973.

———. "Teudah le-toldot Nehemiah Hayon ve-ha-Shabta'ut." *Zion: Me'asef ha-Hevra ha-erets-yisre'elit le-Historyah ve-Etnografyah* 3 (1928): 172–179.

Schorsch, Ismar. "On the Political Judgement of the Jew." In *From Text to Context: The Turn to History in Modern Judaism,* 118–132. Waltham, MA: Brandeis University Press, 1994.

Schotte, Margaret. " 'Books for the Use of the Learned and Studious': William London's Catalogue of Most Vendible Books." *Book History* 11 (2008): 33–57.

Shapin, Steven. *The Scientific Life: A Moral History of a Late Modern Vocation.* Chicago: University of Chicago Press, 2008.

———. *A Social History of Truth: Civility and Science in Seventeenth-Century England.* Science and Its Conceptual Foundations. Chicago: University of Chicago Press, 1994.

Shear, Adam. *The Kuzari and the Shaping of Jewish Identity, 1167–1900.* Cambridge: Cambridge University Press, 2008.

Sherman, William H. "On the Threshold: Architecture, Paratext, and Early Print Culture." In *Agent of Change: Print Culture Studies After Elizabeth L. Eisenstein,* edited by Sabrina A. Baron, Eric N. Lindquist, and Eleanor F. Shevlin, 67–81. Amherst: University of Massachusetts Press, 2007.

Shilo, Shmuel. "Ha-Rav Ya'akov Raischer ba'al ha-sefer *Shevut Ya'akov:* Ha-ish bizemano le-zemano ve-le-zemanenu?" *Asufot* 11 (1998): 65–86.

Shmeruk, Chone. "Bahurim mi-Ashkenaz be-yeshivot Polin." In *Sefer Yovel Le-*

Yitzhak Baer, edited by Salo W. Baron, Ben Zion Dinur, Shmuel Ettinger, and Israel Halpern, 304–317. Jerusalem: Historical Society of Israel, 1960.

———. *Mahazot Mikra'iyim be-Yidish, 1697–1750.* Kitve Ha-Akademyah Ha-Le'umit Ha-Yisra'elit Le-Mada'im, Ha-Hativah Le-Mada'e-Ha-Ruah. Jerusalem: Ha-Akademyah ha-le'umit ha-Yisra'elit le-mada'im, 1979.

Shore, Paul J. *The Eagle and the Cross: Jesuits in Late Baroque Prague.* St. Louis, MO: Institute of Jesuit Sources, 2002.

Siebenhüner, Kim. "Things That Matter. Zur Geschichte der Materiellen Kultur in der Frühneuzeitforschung." *Zeitschrift für Historische Forschung* 42, no. 3 (2015): 373–409.

Sixtová, Olga. "The Beginnings of Prague Hebrew Typography 1512–1569." In *Hebrew Printing in Bohemia and Moravia,* edited by Olga Sixtová, 75–121. Prague: Academia: Jewish Museum in Prague, 2012.

———. "Jewish Printers and Printing Presses in Prague, 1512–1670 (1672)." In *Hebrew Printing in Bohemia and Moravia,* edited by Olga Sixtová, 33–74. Prague: Academia: Jewish Museum in Prague, 2012.

Sluhovsky, Moshe, and Yosef Kaplan. *Sifriyot ve-osfe sefarim.* Jerusalem: Merkaz Zalman Shazar le-toldot Yisrael, 2006.

Smith, Pamela H. *The Business of Alchemy: Science and Culture in the Holy Roman Empire.* Princeton, NJ: Princeton University Press, 1994.

Soll, Jacob. *The Information Master: Jean-Baptiste Colbert's Secret State Intelligence System.* Cultures of Knowledge in the Early Modern World. Ann Arbor: University of Michigan Press, 2009.

Soloveitchik, Haym. "Piety, Pietism and German Pietism: 'Sefer Hasidim I' and the Influence of Hasidei Ashkenaz." *Jewish Quarterly Review* 92, no. 3/4 (2002): 455–493.

———. "Religious Law and Change: The Medieval Ashkenazic Example." *AJS Review* 12, no. 2 (1987): 205–221.

———. *Shut ke-mekor histori.* Jerusalem: Merkaz Zalman Shazar le-toldot Yisrael, 1990.

Sorkin, David. "The Early Haskalah." In *New Perspectives on the Haskalah,* edited by Shmuel Feiner and David Sorkin, 9–26. London: Littman Library of Jewish Civilization, 2001.

Sorkin, David Jan. *The Transformation of German Jewry, 1780–1840.* Detroit: Wayne State University Press, 1999.

Spicer, Joaneath. "The Star of David and Jewish Culture in Prague Around 1600, Reflected in Drawings of Roelandt Savery and Paulus Van Vianen." *Journal of the Walters Art Gallery* 54 (1996): 203–224.

Spiegel, Gabrielle M. *The Past as Text: The Theory and Practice of Medieval Historiography.* Baltimore: Johns Hopkins University Press, 1997.

Spielman, John P. *The City and the Crown: Vienna and the Imperial Court, 1600–1740.* West Lafayette, IN: Purdue University Press, 1993.

Stallybrass, Peter. "'Little Jobs': Broadsides and the Printing Revolution." In *Agent of Change: Print Culture Studies After Elizabeth L. Eisenstein,* edited by Sabrina A. Baron, Eric N. Lindquist, and Eleanor F. Shevlin, 315–341. Amherst: University of Massachusetts Press, 2007.

———. "Printing and the Manuscript Revolution." In *Explorations in Communication and History,* edited by Barbie Zelizer, 93–101. London: Routledge, 2009.

Steinschneider, Moritz. "Mathematik bei den Juden (1551–1840)." *Monatschrift für Geschichte und Wissenschaft des Judentums* (1905): 78–95, 193–204, 300–314, 490–498, 581–605, 722–743.

Stern, David. "The Rabbinic Bible in Its Sixteenth-Century Context." In *The Hebrew Book in Early Modern Italy,* edited by Joseph Hacker and Adam Shear, 76–108. Philadelphia: University of Pennsylvania Press, 2011.

Stern, Eliyahu. *The Genius: Elijah of Vilna and the Making of Modern Judaism.* New Haven, CT: Yale University Press, 2013.

Stern, Selma. *The Court Jew: A Contribution to the History of the Period of Absolutism in Central Europe.* Philadelphia: Jewish Publication Society of America, 1950.

———. *Josel of Rosheim, Commander of Jewry in the Holy Roman Empire of the German Nation.* Philadelphia: Jewish Publication Society of America, 1965.

Sternberg, Giora. "Epistolary Ceremonial: Corresponding Status at the Time of Louis XIV." *Past and Present* 204, no. 1 (2009): 33–88.

Stollberg-Rilinger, Barbara. *The Emperor's Old Clothes: Constitutional History and the Symbolic Language of the Holy Roman Empire.* Translated by Thomas Dunlap. New York: Berghahn, 2015.

Stoye, J. W. "Emperor Charles VI: The Early Years of the Reign." *Transactions of the Royal Historical Society* 12 (1962): 63–84.

Subrahmanyam, Sanjay. "Connected Histories: Notes Towards a Reconfiguration of Early Modern Eurasia." *Modern Asian Studies* 31, no. 3 (1997): 735–762.

Svatoš, Martin. "Les usages du livre religieux chez le missionnaire Jésuite Antonín Koniáš. Theorie et pratique." In *Libri prohibiti: La censure dans l'espace Habsbourgeois, 1650–1850,* edited by Marie-Elizabeth Ducreux and Martin Svatoš, 181–202. Leipzig: Leipziger Universitätsverlag, 2005.

Swann, Marjorie. *Curiosities and Texts: The Culture of Collecting in Early Modern England.* Philadelphia: University of Pennsylvania Press, 2001.

Sykes, Karen Margaret. *Arguing with Anthropology: An Introduction to Critical Theories of the Gift.* London: Routledge, 2005.

Talabardon, Susanna. "Die Biblia Hebraica des Daniel Ernst Jablonski." In *Daniel*

Ernst Jablonski: Religion, Wissenschaft und Politik um 1700, edited by Joachim Bahlcke and Werner Korthaase, 463–489. Wiesbaden: Harrassowitz, 2008.

Ta-Shma, Israel M. "Al kama inyanei Mahzor Vitry." In *Kneset mehkarim: Iyunim be-sifrut ha-rabanit bi-yeme ha-beinayim,* 62–76. Jerusalem: Mosad Bialik, 2004.

———. "Le-Toldot ha-Yehudim be-Folin be-me'ot ha-12-13. *Zion* 53, no. 4 (1988): 347–369.

———. "Mevo se-sifrut ha-Shu"T shel Rishoni Ashkenaz Ve-Tzarfat." In *Kneset mehkarim: Iyunim be-sifrut ha-rabanit bi-yeme ha-beinayim,* 117–125. Jerusalem: Mosad Bialik, 2004.

———. "Seder hadpasatam shel hiddushei ha-rishonim le-Talmud." In *Kneset mehkarim: Iyunim be-sifrut ha-rabanit bi-yeme ha-beinayim,* 219–236. Jerusalem: Mosad Bialik, 2004.

Teller, Adam. "The Laicization of Early Modern Jewish Society: The Development of the Polish Communal Rabbinate in the 16th Century." In *Schöpferische Momente des Europäischen Judentums: In der Frühen Neuzeit,* edited by Michael Graetz, 333–349. Heidelberg: Winter, 2000.

———. "Telling the Difference: Some Comparative Perspectives on the Jews' Legal Status in Poland and in the Holy Roman Empire." *Polin* 22 (2010): 109–141.

Teplitsky, Joshua. "Between Court Jew and Jewish Court: David Oppenheim, the Prague Rabbinate, and Eighteenth-Century Jewish Politics." PhD diss., New York University, 2012.

———. "Jewish Money, Jesuit Censors, and the Habsburg Monarchy: Politics and Polemics in Early Modern Prague." *Jewish Social Studies* 19, no. 3 (2014): 109–138.

———. "A 'Prince of the Land of Israel' in Prague: Jewish Philanthropy, Patronage, and Power in Early Modern Europe and Beyond." *Jewish History* 29 (2015): 245–271.

Teply, Karl. "Johannes Diodato: Der Patriarch der Ersten Armenier in Wien." *Jahrbuch des Vereins für Geschichte der Stadt Wien* 28 (1972): 31–61.

———. "Kundschafter, Kuriere, Kaufleute, Kaffeesieder: Die Legende des Wiener Kaffeehauses auf dem Röntgenschirm der Geschichte und der Volkskunde." *Österreich in Geschichte und Literatur mit Geographie* 22, no. 1 (1978): 1–17.

Tishby, Isaiah. *Netivei emunah ve-minut* Jerusalem: Magnes, 1982.

Transier, Werner. "Die Schum-Gemeinden: Wiegen und Zentren des Judentums am Rhein im Mittelalter." In *Europas Juden im Mittelalter,* edited by Alfred Haverkamp, 59–67. Speyer: Hatje Cantz, 2005.

Trautmann-Waller, Céline. "Leopold Zunz and Moritz Steinschneider: *Wissenschaft des Judentums* as a Struggle Against Ghettoization in Science." In *Studies on Steinschneider: Moritz Steinschneider and the Emergence of the Science of Judaism in Nineteenth-Century Germany,* edited by Reimund Leicht and Gad Freudenthal, 81–107. Leiden: Brill, 2012.

Tribe, Keith. "Cameralism and the Science of Government." *Journal of Modern History* 56, no. 2 (1984): 263–284.

Trivellato, Francesca. *The Familiarity of Strangers: The Sephardic Diaspora, Livorno, and Cross-Cultural Trade in the Early Modern Period.* New Haven, CT: Yale University Press, 2009.

Turniansky, Chava. "Yiddish Song as Historical Source Material: Plague in the Judenstadt of Prague in 1713." In *Jewish History: Essays in Honour of Chimen Abramsky,* edited by Chimen Abramsky, Ada Rapoport-Albert, and Steven J. Zipperstein, 189–198. London: P. Halban, 1988.

Twersky, Isadore. "Law and Spirituality in the Seventeenth Century: A Case Study in Yair Hayyim Bachrach." In *Jewish Thought in the Seventeenth Century,* edited by Isadore Twersky and Bernard Septimus, 447–467. Cambridge, MA: Harvard University Center for Jewish Studies, 1987.

Ulbrich, Claudia. *Shulamit and Margarete: Power, Gender, and Religion in a Rural Society in Eighteenth-Century Europe.* Boston: Brill Academic Publishers, 2004.

Ury, Scott. "The 'Shtadlan' of the Polish-Lithuanian Commonwealth: Noble Advocate or Unbridled Opportunist?" *Polin* 15 (2002): 267–299.

Vehlow, Katja. *Abraham Ibn Daud's Dorot 'Olam (Generations of the Ages): A Critical Edition and Translation of Zikhron Divrey Romi, Divrey Malkhey 'Israel, and the Midrash on Zechariah.* Leiden: Brill, 2013.

Veselá, Lenka. "Hebrew Typography at Non-Jewish Bohemian Printing Houses During the 16th and 17th Centuries." In *Hebrew Printing in Bohemia and Moravia,* edited by Olga Sixtová, 165–176. Prague: Academia: Jewish Museum in Prague, 2012.

Voit, Petr. "Ornamentation of Prague Hebrew Books During the First Half of the 16th Century as Part of Bohemian Book Design." In *Hebrew Printing in Bohemia and Moravia,* edited by Olga Sixtová, 123–152. Prague: Academia: Jewish Museum in Prague, 2012.

Walker, Mack. *German Home Towns: Community, State and General Estate, 1648–1871.* Ithaca, NY: Cornell University Press, 1971.

Watanabe-O'Kelly, Helen. "Literature and the Court 1450–1720." In *Early Modern German Literature, 1350–1700,* edited by Max Reinhart, 621–651. Camden House History of German Literature. Rochester, NY: Camden House, 2007.

Weber, Ottocar. "Eine Kaiserreise nach Böhmen I.J. 1723." *Geschichte der Deutchen in Böhmen* 36, no. 2 (1897): 137–204.

Weinstein, Roni. *Shivru et ha-kelim: Ha-Kabbalah ve-ha-moderniyut he-Yehudit.* Tel Aviv: Tel Aviv University Press, 2011.

Weissler, Chava. "'For Women and for Men Who Are Like Women': The Construction of Gender in Yiddish Devotional Literature." *Journal of Feminist Studies in Religion* 5, no. 2 (1989): 7–24.

———. *Voices of the Matriarchs: Listening to the Prayers of Early Modern Jewish Women.* Boston: Beacon, 1998.

Whaley, Joachim. *Germany and the Holy Roman Empire, Vol. 2: The Peace of Westphalia to the Dissolution of the Reich, 1648–1806.* Oxford: Oxford University Press, 2012.

Wilson, Peter H. *Europe's Tragedy: A History of the Thirty Years War.* London: Penguin, 2009.

———. "Still a Monstrosity? Some Reflections on Early Modern German Statehood." *Historical Journal* 49, no. 2 (2006): 565–576.

Wolf, Gerson. "Auto da Fé jüdischer Bücher in Prag 1714." *Zeitschrift für Hebraeische Bibliographie* 4 (1863): 35–44.

———. "Der Prozeß Eisenmenger." *Monatsschrift für Geschichte und Wissenschaft des Judentums* 18 (n.s. 1) (1869): 378–384, 425–432, 465–473.

———. "Zur Geschichte des Jüdischen Gemeinwesens in Prag." *Allgemeine Zeitung des Judenthums* (1863): 255–257.

Yaari, Abraham. "Mi hayu shnei shlihei a"y she-nitfasu be-nikolsburg be-shnat 1722?" *Zion* 12, nos. 3–4 (1947): 190–192.

———. *Sheluhe Erets Yisrael: Toldot ha-shelihut me-ha-Arets la-Golah me-hurban Bayit Sheni ad ha-me'ah ha-tsha'esreh.* Jerusalem: Mosad ha-Rav Kook, 1977.

Yerushalmi, Yosef Hayim. *The Lisbon Massacre of 1506 and the Royal Image in the Shebet Yehudah.* Cincinnati, OH: Hebrew Union College, Jewish Institute of Religion, 1976.

———. *"Servants of Kings and Not Servants of Servants": Some Aspects of the Political History of the Jews.* Tenenbaum Family Lecture Series in Judaic Studies. Atlanta: Tam Institute for Jewish Studies, Emory University, 2005.

———. *Zakhor, Jewish History and Jewish Memory.* The Samuel and Althea Stroum Lectures in Jewish Studies. Seattle: University of Washington Press, 1982.

Yudlov, Yitshak. "Hebrew Books Printed on Vellum in the Valmadonna Trust Library." In *Treasures of the Valmadonna Trust Library: A Catalogue of 15th-Century Books and Five Centuries of Deluxe Hebrew Printing*, edited by David Sclar, Brad Sabin Hill, Adri K. Offenberg, and Yitshak Yudlov, 52–61. London: Valmadonna Trust Library, 2011.

Zfatman, Sara. *Ze tmeh: Gerush ruhot be-Yahadut Ashkenaz be-reishit ha-et ha-hadashah.* Jerusalem: Magnes, 2015.

Zíbrt, Čeněk. "Giorgio Diodato, Damascenus, První Kavárník Pražský." *Český Lid* 17 (1908): 47–55.

Zimmer, Eric. *Jewish Synods in Germany During the Late Middle Ages, 1286–1603.* New York: Yeshiva University Press, 1978.

Zimmer, Yitshak (Eric). "Hanhaga u-manhigut be-kehillot Germanyah be-me'ot ha-16 ve-ha-17." In *Kehal Yisrael: Ha-shilton ha-atsmi ha-Yehudi le-dorotav,* edited by Yosef Kaplan, Israel Halpern, Avraham Grossman, and Yisrael Bartal, 261–286. Jerusalem: Merkaz Zalman Shazar le-toldot Yisrael, 2001.

Zwick, Judith Halevi. *Toldot sifrut ha-igronim: Ha-brivenshtellers ha-Ivri'im (me'ah 16-me'ah 20).* Tel Aviv: Papyrus–Tel Aviv University, 1990.

Index